Prozak Diaries

Orkideh Behrouzan

Prozak Diaries

Psychiatry and Generational Memory in Iran

Stanford University Press
Stanford, California

Stanford University Press
Stanford, California

Printed in the United States of America on acid-free, archival-quality paper

Library of Congress Cataloging-in-Publication Data

Names: Behrouzan, Orkideh, 1977- author.
Title: Prozak diaries : psychiatry and generational memory in Iran / Orkideh Behrouzan.
Description: Stanford, California : Stanford University Press, 2016. | Includes bibliographical references and index.
Identifiers: LCCN 2016027702 (print) | LCCN 2016028655 (ebook) | ISBN 9780804797429 (cloth : alk. paper) | ISBN 9780804799416 (pbk. : alk. paper) | ISBN 9780804799591 (ebook)
Subjects: LCSH: Psychiatry--Iran. | Depression, Mental--Iran. | Youth--Iran--Psychology. | Medical anthropology--Iran.
Classification: LCC RC451.I7 B44 2016 (print) | LCC RC451.I7 (ebook) | DDC 362.1968900955--dc23
LC record available at https://lccn.loc.gov/2016027702

Typeset by Bruce Lundquist in 10/14 Minion Pro

Contents

Note on Transliteration

I use a modified form of the *Iranian Studies* transliteration scheme for Persian as outlined by the International Society of Iranian Studies. Consonants are consistent with this system, but I use only one diacritic to distinguish pronunciation in Persian. I mark the long vowel *aleph* with the diacritic *ā* (similar to the English *a* in *all*) as contrasted with *a*, the short vowel, which is very close to the English *a* in *ask*. The short vowels are rendered with the closest English equivalent to the way they are spoken in standard contemporary Iranian Persian; thus I use *e* (e.g., *ejtemā'i*, or *hejāb*) and *o* (e.g., *gol*) rather than *i* and *u*. I use *i* for long ی (e.g., *pezeshki*) rhyming with English *me*, and *u* for long و (e.g., *sukhteh*) rhyming with English *soon*. I double letters to indicate *tashdid* (e.g., *takhassos*). The silent final *h* is written and indicated by *eh* (e.g., *khātereh*); and 'ayn and hamza are indicated by '. I write the *ezafeh* as *-e* after consonants (e.g., *nasl-e*) and as *-ye* after vowels and silent final *h* (e.g., *daheh-ye*). Similarly, I add the plural *hā* to singular words as in *daheh-ye shasti-hā*. All dates are AD (Anno Domini) except those in Persian-language references, which follow the format Anno Persico–Anno Domini. "Anno Persico" refers to the Iranian solar Hejri calendar. The year 1981 AD, for instance, equals 1360 AP. All date formats are day/month/year.

Abbreviations

ADHD	attention deficit hyperactivity disorder
CBT	cognitive behavioral therapy
CIDI	Composite International Diagnostic Interview
CNS	central nervous system
DALY	disability-adjusted life year
DIS	Diagnostic Interview Schedule
DSM	*Diagnostic and Statistical Manual of Mental Disorders*
EBM	evidence-based medicine
ECT	electroconvulsive therapy
EEG	electroencephalography
EMR	Eastern Mediterranean Region
IACAP	Iranian Association for Child and Adolescent Psychiatry
IBS	irritable bowel syndrome
ICD	*International Classification of Diseases*
IPA	Iranian Psychiatric Association
IPM	Iranian Institute for Theoretical Physics and Mathematics
IRIB	Islamic Republic of Iran Broadcasting
NIMH	National Institute of Mental Health
NMHP	National Mental Health Program
PANA	*Parvaresh-e Niruhā-ye Ensāni* ("Developing Human Skills")
PHC	primary health care
PTSD	post-traumatic stress disorder
SSRI	selective serotonin reuptake inhibitor
WHO	World Heath Organization
WPA	World Psychiatric Association

Prozak Diaries

The Anthropologist

It all began with *depreshen*: how people were talking about it, online or offline, discussing it in casual daily talk along with other psychiatric metaphor and diagnostic or therapeutic terminology. What to think—I started asking ten years ago—of the growing circulation of varying epidemiological and clinical data and the seemingly casual usage of psychiatric vernacular in everyday life? Surely, not everyone related to psychiatric diagnoses nor to medication. But what was striking during the 1990s was how a clinical discourse was inserting itself in the way people spoke about life, how psychiatry had entered the common langauge and *zeitgeist*, and how life was at times expressed in new psychological and psychiatric terms. What was once articulated in the richly layered poetics of the Persian langauge was now becoming part of a clinical discourse on mood and affect.

At first glance, it would be too easy to take such clinical articulations at face value and to interpret the spread of psychiatric talk simply as an indication of a surge in (psychiatric) illness or other such generalizing conclusions about Iranian society. But a nuanced analysis of an emerging discourse should explore it, foremost, as a signifier of changing cultural interpretations. How and when did this change come about? What was happening in the language? How do clinical terms inject themselves in our daily lives? What cultural work do they perform? How would doctors explain this shift in articulation and interpretation? And how had psychiatry as a discipline emerged and evolved in its Iranian context in the first place?

Indeed, since the 1990s, depression has become less stigmatized; the use of antidepressants, Prozac included, has surged globally, with distinctive variations in different parts of the world in prescribing, in consumption, and in how patients talk about their medicalized reliance on psychopharmacological solutions. But each context has its own story, each language its own psychological grammar. How could this happen, one might ask, in a society where lively youth have made strides in realms from the sciences to sports and the arts? I thus turned to the narratives of psychiatrists and patients alike: How did Iranian psychiatry operate? And what were the stories behind terms such as *depreshen*?

Stories choose and change us by the ways in which they compel us to listen and the energy with which they keep returning. The stories that have been entrusted to me (of what psychiatry would call depression, ADHD, or PTSD) have, at different points, transformed, overwhelmed, and perplexed me. Above all, they have humbled me. Their narrators taught me much about storytelling. I set out to communicate and interpret (if such a task is even possible) the experience of young people who were diagnosed with depression or identified themselves as *depress*. I learned instead the languages and modes of thinking that *they* used to interpret and make life and its complexities intelligible. Psychiatry is now one of those languages, pathology one of those modes of thinking.

But what about hope? These were as much stories of hope as they were of *depreshen*, cycles of hope and despair merging with performative claims to dysphoria. How is one to write about depression in a way that would convey the compelling presence of dysphoria infused into the simple pleasures of daily life? How is one to talk about the desires and hopes behind clinical decisions and still walk the fine line between the white and the black? It is never easy to write about the gray.

Inevitably, these narratives of illness come from interviews with psychiatrists and individuals who performatively identify with psychiatric categories or medication; they are not meant to represent everyone. The accounts presented throughout the book also belong to a range of diverse ideological persuasions; my analysis specifically aims to look beyond them to discover what they share and reveal, psychologically, clinically, and culturally. Understanding medical subjectivities in their own cultural frames has for long been an urgent call in anthropology; but it is even more so today, not least because we have become habituated to partial and black-and-white representations of (Iranian) youth in the Western media that swing between extremes, from sensational accounts to sweeping generalizations, from tales of rebellion to narratives of subjugation. But there are many stories in between, where ordinary life happens. They are scattered in a multitude of fragmented scenes and ought to be investigated as such. I try to write of such fragments that are pieces of a larger puzzle other scholars' work will complete. I turn to stories of the everyday, of illness and ordinary life, of doctors and patients, of the life of psychiatry itself, and of varied moments of joy and sorrow that compose most lives. I write in the belief that to write about psychological conditions does not take away the hope that still persists in likely and unlikely corners of life.

It all began with *words*, why we choose them, how we use them, and what cultural forms they generate. This book is an exploration of language as experience; in other words, an exploration of how clinical interpretations become part of ordinary life and discourses of affect. Since the time this research was conducted much has changed and much has evolved, both internally and externally, this brief note included: I started writing it during early fieldwork and ended it during the final revisions of the manuscript. It took years to rethink and refine, to write and rewrite. Over the years, the story of the evolution of Iranian psychiatry simultaneously started telling the story of new cultural formations and situated attempts at making life intelligible in a clinical language. Through the lens of psychiatry, this book tells the story of how stories are told. My hope for it is to challenge some of what we assume we know.

Ethnographic Experiments across Sites and Disciplines

DIARIES ARE OUR ATTEMPT AT IMMORTALITY. Writing them, literally or metaphorically, online or offline, is almost always a precarious yet calculated choice to remember and be remembered. *Prozāk Diaries* tells the story of such acts of remembering, experiencing, interpreting, and articulating life in medicalized terms. To some extent, it is an ethnographic exploration into the stakes of ethnography itself.

As *depreshen* became the word on the street, I set out to investigate the pedagogical logics, historical moments, and cultural/linguistic modes of legitimation behind the epidemiological and ethnographic data that I was collecting between the years 2005 and 2010. In this analysis, I explore the lived experience of clinical diagnoses, such as depression, as well as the social life of epidemiological data in relation to them. This exploration necessitates rewinding and tracing the history of Iranian psychiatry itself, situating it in its own pedagogical trajectory and asking what specific academic orientations have dominated it. The result is a multilayered scene that reflects the mutability of historical and psychological experiences within a specific historical frame. It comprises available statistics, government and media reports, memoirs, works of art, participant observation, and extensive interviews with psychiatrists and a wide spectrum of individuals and families, as well as field notes from professional meetings and academic and nonacademic events. In this mosaic of long-term multisited ethnographic fieldwork, discourse analysis, clinical observations, and extended interviews with psychiatrists, psychoanalysts, young Iranians and bloggers (in Iran, the United States, the UK, and Canada), I look for individuals' explanatory models and the ways different generations account for and interpret their identification with psychiatry.[1]

A first step was to look for indices and evidence. Iranian media increasingly quote, circulate, and relay statistics to the public as *evidence* for the rise in psychiatric diagnoses and medication with psychotropic drugs. Even though rising rates of medication reflect global trends, they must be situated in their own cultural trajectories.[2] Further, one must critically examine the modes of construction and circulation of such evidence and look beyond them, not dismissively, but to reach for what they reveal or mask. In assembling and examining such data, my aim is to draw attention to how data are collected, accessed, interpreted, and internalized by experts and laypeople.

The place of statistics in my analysis is culturally significant. For one thing, fluency in the language of epidemiology served as an ethnographic resource; it validated my inquiry and critical reading of statistics among medical professionals. Additionally, the available epidemiological data were useful for what they revealed culturally and pedagogically; I therefore follow the lives behind statistical *evidence*. The statistical materials on prescriptions of antidepressants and Ritalin, in particular, belong to the 1997–2008 period, a decade in which the field of psychiatry itself experienced major pedagogical milestones and achievements. This is why I focus on two categories of illness, depression and attention deficit hyperactivity disorder (ADHD), as potential signifiers of shifting cultural interpretations.

Apart from epidemiological data,[3] I use ethnographic and cultural materials to assemble a prima facie account of how these two widely recognized diagnoses are discussed in the Iranian public arena. The various landscapes of media, policy, and cultural productions reveal how the psychiatric profession in Iran has defined and treated these diagnoses by adopting American clinical standards while situating them in an Iranian context. Even though my ethnography was divided between clinical and nonclinical groups, in my final analysis I do not separate medical discourse from lived historical experience, nor do I separate doctors from patients. Such binary formulations mask the ways practitioners create a *third* space of situated practice that incorporates both biomedical and cultural knowledge.

In the absence of a written historiography of Iranian psychiatry, I interviewed key figures including attendings/professors of psychiatry, psychiatric residents, and interns. I combine these oral histories with the few available memoirs penned by the founders of the field, in order to outline a historical overview of the psychiatric discipline and its pedagogical logics in Iran. These interviews took place in London, Los Angeles, the San Francisco Bay area, Tehran, Boston, Toronto, and Halifax as I followed doctors. I use this material to situate illness narratives in larger pedagogical and professional contexts. These contexts include my own clinical experience as a medical intern at Tehran University's Ruzbeh Psychiatric Hospital.

Similarly, I interviewed young Iranians who had either identified with or experienced psychiatric diagnoses (e.g., depression or PTSD), taken medication, or were keen to discuss generational memories and/or psychiatric medication. The point, as some clinically inclined readers may wonder, was not to confirm whether each individual qualified for clinical diagnosis, but to learn what their perception of illness (e.g., their self-mediation, their contemplations about their own and others' conditions) revealed about underlying social, psychological, and cultural processes. I had initially expected some reluctance, but was often pleasantly surprised by people's willingness to talk. Many were pleased about "breaking the taboo of talking about mental issues," while others emphasized collective memories, for instance reminding me that "the Iran-Iraq War ought to be documented," and encouraged me not to miss details. Over weeks and months—eventually years—I was occasionally contacted by people who had heard about my work and wanted to share their own stories. This overwhelming desire to present and make heard one's own version of history was itself a valuable ethnographic finding. Before long, I knew I had to seek out what was driving this eagerness.

Anecdotes, life stories, dreams, interviews, and past and present narratives provide better insight into individual experience than master narratives or epidemiological data.[4] Using them requires close attention to moments of language switching, where individuals exploit the fluidity of language boundaries, at times Persianizing English or other foreign words (e.g., *depreshen*) and situating them in their own psychological grammar, at other times substituting foreign words for Persian terms in order to lift their stigma or emotional charge. These moves are important, because they are part of the sociality that psychiatric terminologies have made possible. They also reflect the ways terminologies, language, and concepts gain a new social life when they travel. I sometimes complement these data with other cultural material, such as films or songs, which are not meant to be mere examples, but illustrations to give a sense of the creative environment and social settings in which individuals' stories are embedded. They create better historical and psychological attunement into the worlds these accounts come from.

Working through past experiences by witnessing and retrospective meaning making helps people to (re)imagine and (re)negotiate what has been felt, desired, feared, repressed, denied, remembered, or forgotten. For me, this act of "working through" was itself a mode of inquiry into the unfinished and unpolished nature of experience. What is at stake in such working through is the subjective and intersubjective operation of a sense of *affectedness* by, and endurance of, a burden invisible to others. This burden is diffused and incomplete, never whole, never within our grasp. For an anthropology of experience to become possible, this unfinishedness ought to be appreciated. Objective conditions, the processes of subjectivization—"none of these terms," anthropologist Veena Das has argued, "may be treated as a 'given' in anthropological analysis. Experience is not a transparent category, for its essential feature of opacity makes the work of tracking it much more difficult."[5] To track experience requires, in part, exploring the new affective modes of being that it leaves behind.

Throughout the book, when using the term *affect*, I am referring to what is felt—the psychological embodiment of what lived experiences and their memories leave behind. Unlike in psychiatry, here affect is not a symptomatic, singular manifestation of an emotion; rather it reflects a sustained and proactive mood or emotional state. This definition requires being sensitive to the agency and performativity of individuals in the process of perceiving their own emotional experiences and social encounters. It also renders affect, mood, and emotion intersubjective, at times visceral, processes that are neither static and passive nor whole. In other words, I draw attention to the *act* of feeling and experiencing what is lived, which encompasses possibilities for emotions to be interpreted and felt in retrospect, bit by bit, through various cultural negotiations within and between individuals. By underscoring these ongoing cultural processes of meaning making, I explicitly avoid approaches that regard emotion as pre-social, contained, and given.[6]

One of the ethnographic sites for analyzing such *acts* of feeling is the much-discussed Persian blogosphere or Weblogestān. Iranian blogs are far more diverse and far less politicized than is often represented in the English-language media and press. Clearly, though, the blog posts I examine do not represent the full diversity of the Iranian blogosphere; they also belong to the period before social media prevailed.[7] I have chosen blogs based on their generational themes and/or their identification with psychiatric categories. I read them as both ethnographic object and site. As an object of ethnographic enquiry, primarily, Iranian blogs operate as *affective* spaces: emotive, interpretive, and performative sites for ongoing examinations of lived experience, for the reconstruction of generational memories, and for working through unfinished pasts. Affective, here, refers to the interaction and introspection of different emotional experiences and ways of feeling. By "affective" I describe this space as saturated, almost burdened, by visceral sensations, emotive performances, introjections, projections, and moods; above all perhaps, by individuals' *desire* to be recognized for their predicament. This affective capacity of blogs relies on the forms of sociality they create by locating themselves historically and generationally. Kinships created in these spaces may be ephemeral, but they are intensely built around sharing incommensurable experiences.

As ethnographic sites, these blogs are situated in universal discourses of virtual life, analyzed in early formulations of the Internet (in science technology studies) as spaces of "possibilities," and projective spaces of make believe; and later on as new forms of temporality (recursive and self-reflexive), of accelerated exchange across traditional cultural boundaries, and of language (informal, emotive).[8] While the virtual space is categorically a projective space of "make believe," Iranian blogs also create social forms and multilevel dialogue that complement the gaps in bloggers' social lives and allow them to negotiate their emotional experiences and their meanings. They serve, foremost, as places to "make sense."[9]

Yet, the virtual and the social cannot be separated, nor can they be examined in terms of the discovery of a "real" subject. Bloggers' online and offline fragments of subjectivity are not aligned in a linear extended continuum of selfhood, but are scattered pieces that constantly morph in relation to each other and to outside social and political discourses. They go back and forth, in a constant and fractured act of editing and publishing. The fragmented, essayistic, and incomplete stylization of blogs corresponds to the fragmentations and complexities of memory and subjectivity. The projected online self, in this sense, is neither complete nor polished.

The stakes of virtual ethnography in understanding a medical entity such as depression are high in places where memory is ruptured. Virtual forms of ethnography seem inevitable today, but anthropology is constantly rethinking the boundaries of its fields of inquiry and its sites and para-sites, creating new communities of research and communication. Whether it is in experimental ethnography and cultural critique or in hyper-awareness of the "third spaces" in which it flows, ethnography as a method engages in a close reading of historical conditions.[10] But this Iranian, or perhaps Middle Eastern, historical moment and representational crisis call for an "ethnography attuned to its times," to use the words of anthropologist Kim Fortun—ethnography that is creative and interactive in its imagining the future.[11] This necessitates, on the one hand, moving beyond outdated structures and paradigms, concepts, and technologies. On the other hand, it requires reconsidering ethnographic strategies that respond to shifting socialities and ethics of engagement. My deterritorialized field site of blogs defined itself in its generational sensibilities. Reading blogs from within rather than as mere objects of inquiry also required thinking carefully about the ways emotional investment can generate, block, reveal, or mask. The reader as ethnographer, blogger, peer, and interviewer (in person, online, or through comments and fora) carries her own emotional, psychological, and linguistic trajectories. These can build cultural access and trust, but also necessitate reflexivity.[12]

To do "ethnography through thick and thin," to borrow from anthropologist George Marcus,[13] is to map, explain, or illuminate social problems, dynamics, or public issues in ways that standard methods cannot. Following communities along and across precarious territorial and virtual borders (real and imagined), much like traditional ethnography, entails participant observation (ethnographer), observant participation (blogger), and extended interviews (analyst) via the web or through blog comments. Much more than in traditional ethnography, the malleable contours of the field are constantly imagined, scrutinized, and negotiated. I could not enter the world of Iranian blogs without contextualizing it, as well as myself, in various emotional, psychological, and linguistic trajectories. Emotions became critical, not as distractions, but as conduits that enabled relating with bloggers' dynamic forms of life.

Crossing Assumptions of Class, Profession, and Language

Most of the accounts in this book take place in Tehran, and do not represent all social strata. Each transpires within a multitude of scenes that are at times contrasting and contradictory. Yet, contrasting scenes provide context for different cultural codes and ritualized spaces. Aside from senior psychiatrists, most of my interlocutors are young, urban, and educated. I have changed their names and occasionally details to protect their anonymity.

A question often raised is whether this psychiatric turn in language and thinking is a middle-class phenomenon, a question that implicitly suggests the phenomenon must be a marginal one. Indeed, the skepticism toward ethnographic engagements that focus solely on so-called middle-class phenomena is well justified. I share it insofar as it is rooted, in part, in the fact that some anthropological work on post-1990s Iran has prioritized middle-class representations at the expense of others, or has depicted middle-class youth cultures as acts of resistance against the establishment, a formulation that reduces youth to a monolithic entity and reflects the assumption that all change in society is top down.[14] But the Iranian psychiatric selfhood challenges this skepticism, for it underscores how new subjectivities, ideals of selfhood, and modernist aspirations of care for the self are discursively shaped and felt in their relation to the normalization of new forms of knowledge.

Of course, the appropriation of psychiatric interpretations initially became visible among educated and younger Iranians. However, the rapid distribution of psychiatric discussions by domestic and international media both reflects and facilitates the contagious nature of a language that sits well with individual desires. These desires blur the conventional boundaries of class. Psychiatric television talk shows, for instance, receive calls from both urban and rural areas. In other words, the reach of media (television, radio, print media, telephone, and the Internet) across urban and rural settings facilitates the distribution of information in ways that are not always hindered by socioeconomic standing. While the phenomena I am describing began among the middle classes, class, in this case, may not be a useful analytical category. Over the past few decades, education and economic status have become increasingly disjointed in Iran. Access to diverse forms of (psychiatric) knowledge is increasingly becoming less contingent upon socioeconomic status and more upon one's location in networks of information and communication. Today, what characterizes the growth and appropriation of psychiatric modes of articulation in Iran is a growing *cultural* middle class; one does not need to be well off to absorb media debates on depression or ADHD.[15]

To dismiss a cultural phenomenon as middle-class is also to dismiss the cultural trends and desires it generates. The symbolic capital, or the Weberian *stand* (cultural status), one can gain through adopting medical talk responds to people's desire for upward social mobility across different economic strata. Among Iranians, that desire has a long-standing link with how one is perceived in terms of education, knowledge, and credentials. Medical knowledge is privileged among superior forms of knowledge, especially where alternative modes of herbal and humoral discourses are commonsense, having once been integrated into philosophy and rational theology. Iranians do not need to read Bourdieu to rationalize their keen attitude toward medical fluency: knowledge, in the Iranian traditional mythology, is the ultimate form of wealth.[16]

I am very aware that this question of status inevitably relates to my own ethnographic position as a physician, or *khanom doctor*, as many medical colleagues still call me. Throughout this research, I was often immediately assigned a place in unspoken hierarchies of status and awarded subsequent assumptions and expectations. Even though I approached people as an ethnographer, my medical background was hardly lost on many Iranians for whom the weight of a clinical gaze can be reassuring even if unsettling. I soon noticed, however, that the combination of the clinical and the ethnographic gaze served to soften this assumed hierarchy, allow mutual vulnerability, and evoke curiosity. All along, I let people decide how to define my position, as outsider or as insider, doctor or ethnographer.

This raises questions about ethnographic feeling: how to remain deeply attached ethnographically and emotionally, while incorporating and engaging with other forms of knowledge (e.g., psychiatry) that are either our ethnographic object or have shaped the ethnographic subject in some way. I am a physician, scientist, anthropologist, and former blogger: What can these parallel epistemologies offer in terms of an openness that may lead to the coproduction of knowledge?[17]

Ethnography as both participant observation and observant participation inevitably relies on a sense of liminality that helps the anthropologist to listen with the *third* ear; that is, to be patient with narrative, and to go beyond narrative and explore the quiet that precedes it. Like the émigré, the ethnographer learns to speak different languages and adjusts to different linguistic mindsets and lifeworlds in her travels back and forth. Upon each return, the émigré learns to switch lenses and attune ears to alternative tones and signals and secrets and rumors, to understand and embody the local norms of each place, and, ideally, to feel each setting fully. Such was the recognition of my own code switching and traveling across disciplinary borders. As a former disciple, I had known some of the key figures of Iranian psychiatry and their patients in their clinical practices. When talking to physicians, mine was a return to a conceptual space (psychiatry) that was, pedagogically and ideologically, more influenced by an American spirit than an Iranian one and sometimes assumed a consensus about concepts such as modernity and progress. Even then, my critique did not mean that I could not sympathize with clinicians' logics of practice. Besides granting me access to relevant networks, these experiences helped me in reading between the lines of inter- and intra-disciplinary rivalries, negotiations, and trajectories of discipline formation. Engaging with the nuances of medical models, locating doctors in the same social contexts as their patients, and tuning in to the rites and rituals of psychiatric training helped me engage with practitioners' situated knowledge as well as with elements of biomedical rationality from which anthropology can benefit. The scientist in me, for instance, has repeatedly wondered to what extent long-term and incremental loss might possibly leave a mark on the nervous system. That is an empirical question for epigenetics and it is outside my inquiry here, but it is nonetheless a lingering point of rapport with psychiatrists' professional logic.

This hybrid position has been a learning experience, particularly when transference-like moments challenged ethnographic boundaries vis-à-vis my gender, my cross-disciplinary position, and my generational kinship with some of my interlocutors. Such challenges were inevitable. But each provided linguistic, generational, and professional access and helped me relate to a fragmented ethical landscape. On occasion, in this book, I use my own first-person voice, not as a self-indulgent vehicle, but as a third-person autobiographical "I" that is present only insofar as it locates my own ethnographic position and puts it in perspective.[18]

Similarly, at times during interviews, I point to complementing languages, references, and frameworks that individuals summon in order to communicate their experience of illness and their ways of inhabiting it. Consider, for example, people's frequent usage of poetry. For Iranians, poetry precedes literacy; it is carried "in the chest," an expression indicating that Iranians' poetic heritage lives on from one generation to the next, in hearts and in memory, shaping part of the cultural aesthetics of the literate and illiterate alike. Poetic references, recitations, and invocations are thus part and parcel of the daily experience of speaking Persian; so are associated rituals such as divination and bibliomancy. For the ethnographer, this necessitates an awareness of poetic code-switches and their underlying emotional meaning and cultural import. For example, Iranians have a long tradition of divination (commonly called *fāl, fāl gereftan,* or *tafaʾol*), a common practice of seeking spiritual inspiration and knowledge about the future by means of interpreting signs and omens from, among other sources, *Divān-e Hāfez* (the collection of mystic poems by Khājeh Hāfez-e Shirāzi).[19] One opens the book at random and seeks inspiration from the first *ghazal* (ode) one arrives upon. In the picture on the cover of this book, for instance, we see a page of *Divān-e Hāfez* displaying a widely memorized and recited *ghazal* that invites one to take heart, to endure with patience and with hope, a kind of "this too shall pass" consolation that complements the other various (medical and non-medical) ways people inhabit their experience of suffering. Verses of this particular *ghazal* have been recited to me by a number of young people when talking about depression, at various points, to remind me of their will to rise above:

> Oh grieving heart, you will mend, do not despair
> The mind in turmoil will calm again, do not despair
> If the turnings of the universe do not bow to our will today
> These tides of time will one day change, do not despair
> If the journey seems perilous and the destination out of reach
> Yet there are no paths without end, do not despair

Like this poem, all the blogs and interview materials used in this book were originally in Persian; therefore, this work has also been one of translation, with all the complexities of the task. Blog entries and interviews are anonymized to protect identities and their sources remain on file with me. All translations of interviews, cultural material, and Persian blogs are mine, as are indeed any associated translational shortcomings. I have specified when English terms are used in Persian conversation or when they are uttered in Persianized forms. All along, translation (between English, Persian, clinical, and generational vernaculars) has remained a key stimulating challenge, both for me and for those I have interviewed.

Equally challenging have been the complexities of experiences that defy rigid binaries of health and illness or conventional analyses of phenomena such as wars. Many, for example, imagine it impossible to have a happy childhood in times of war. But childhood has its own magic; images of dust and rubble coexist with the images of birthday parties, the first day of school, or the joy of feasting on strawberry ice cream on a hot summer day. The challenge at hand, then, would be to write about the health impact of a war (or its relationship with the development of psychiatry) without depicting a dark image of a people's childhood, without overlooking the everyday fragments of joy or solidarity, and without undermining the powerful agency and faith with which people remember, endure, and overcome. This, after all, is a tension at the heart of writing about subjectivity.

Or at the heart of language itself. At times, I struggled to reach for words (or choose a language) that wouldn't betray people's psychological experiences. Was it even possible, I wondered, to narrate in English affective states that were so deeply imbued with the Persian language and its semantics and emotional sensibilities? In the interaction of our voices, I had to confront the limits of language, the perils of transference, and what often seemed like the impossibility of translation. There are, of course, translational problems in the history of psychiatry itself (for instance, in the interchangeable use of *ruhi* [of the soul] and *ravāni* [of the psyche] to describe mental illnesses). But most significant were moments when translating the unspeakable into language itself seemed impossible.

The Narrative Arc of the Book

Crossing genres and voices, the following chapters serve as a mosaic and, together, are meant to reveal a larger picture. This is an ethnographic attempt to ask how one might inhabit worlds that are demarcated, interpreted, and transfigured by perceptions of illness. In juxtaposing patients' or doctors' historical reflections, I aim to look beyond their various interpretations of specific events as well as the oft-emphasized political frames in the study of Iranian society, and to focus instead on understanding the act of living through and within the experience of psychological distress, to penetrate the mundane that transcends, and to explore both the internalization of medical mindsets and the infusion of the past into one's lived life. That is, to live life as it embodies, in the same breath, loss and joy, pain and pleasure.

I set the stage, in Chapter 1, with mapping the conceptual premise, the temporal juncture, and the thematic structure of the book. Introducing the cultural shift that the book seeks to examine, namely the incorporation of psychiatric discourses into ordinary life in the 1990s, the chapter provides a historical pretext and raises questions about the semantic structures and cultural meaning of illness categories as well as how to formulate medicalization in this context. I continue, in Chapter 2, with the story of psychiatry itself, and its historical and pedagogical trajectory in Iran, focusing on the historical location of Ruzbeh hospital as the birthplace of academic psychiatry. Particularly for readers less familiar with contemporary Iranian history, the chapter provides an overview of temporalities through the vantage point of psychiatry as it arrived in Iran, and as it emerged and diverged in its approaches. The chapter also provides an overview of Iranian cultural discourses of affect and emotion and their interrelation with psychiatric mindsets. In Chapter 3, I trace the emergence of new psychiatric discourses and their modes of presentation in the public domain through five parallel frames and sets of data: mass education, media, statistical evidence, policy, and prescription patterns; through these frames, I explore the cultural forms, linguistic shifts, and epistemological possibilities that the consolidation of this clinical discourse created.

The middle chapters of the book are both generationally and thematically organized. They seek to investigate the lived experience of (psychiatric) illness and/or individuals' identification with it. In doing so, they reimagine the past through the eyes of different generations, reflecting particular cultural and generational sensibilities and understandings of so-called *depreshen* and ADHD, not solely as categories of illness, but also as symbolic structures through which individuals navigate the domain of ordinary life. These symbolic structures are intertwined with situated desires for medicalization and medication, and with the "pill" operating as a discursive symbol, an evocative object, and a technology for (re)making the self, the past, and the present. These interpretative frameworks are in conversation across chapters. Thematically and conceptually, Chapter 4 focuses on narratives of *depreshen* and the concept of psychiatric subjectivity. Chapter 5 explores memory, its generational aesthetics, and the cultural forms it creates, in order to provide a cultural critique of trauma theories and PTSD frameworks. I then turn in Chapter 6 to illness narrative itself, and provide a culturally and historically situated approach to parents' narratives of, and clinical decisions about, ADHD as a window onto shifting generational and moral frameworks. The last chapter returns us to the beginning, to Ruzbeh Psychiatric Hospital, where we revisit Iranian psychiatry's lived life, as it were, and juxtapose it with patients' narratives. Listening to psychiatrists' reflections, cultural debates, and explanatory models for medicalization and the rise of psychiatric talk, the chapter explores competing pedagogies and situated practices through a comparative perspective; in doing so, it aims to open a space for psychiatry, itself, as cultural critique.

Throughout the book, the characters I have interviewed operate as diagnosticians, social critics, and historians, providing a multi-voiced account. The chapters are separated by interludes in the form of snapshots of individual accounts that represent varying, at times competing, mindsets and interpretations. This structure is inspired by the online and offline narratives and diverse vantage points that inform the book and by the layers of linkage between personal accounts and analytical discussions: like hyperlinks in blogs, different voices intersect with chapters; each story differs and may yet refer to multiple other accounts of the same events. In these accounts, I look beyond any ideological leaning that each narrator may represent, and search instead for the psychological and cultural processes that are mobilized, allowed, or hindered in individuals' acts of remembering and working through. Each retelling is new and yet remains loyal to the task of defying forgetfulness. The repetitiveness of images and sounds and dreams invoked is a force of content rather than a form of writing, as I follow that same pulse that the owners of dreams and flashbacks convey to me.

Any contributions to theory and method, I hope, will emerge from the ethnography (rather than ethnography being a case illustration for theory) and from within the narrators' accounts. They harbor "storied implicitness," to use Michael Taussig's words, "as a way of making theory make itself," contesting and getting in the way of past theory and rebuilding it with new materials.[20] Their perspectives provide opportunities to reexamine some of the dominant conceptual frameworks and theories both in psychiatry and in anthropology. It is my hope that the reader will walk away from this book, as I do, with an appreciation for the open-ended and multifaceted nature of experience and subjectivity. I also leave this tapestry well aware of the need to weave in new material through future research by others. This is a start, I hope, for a project of listening, openly and inquisitively, to silences.

FIGURE 1: The Poet-Satirist

The Poet-Satirist

Tehran, 2010. The cover reads: "Be *depress*, and grand, and humble" (Figure 1). A playful tribute, one immediately notices, to the famous verse from the 1966 poem "Mosāfer" (Pilgrim/Traveler) penned by poet Sohrab Sepehri (1928–1980): "Be grand, and solitary, and humble, and strong."

This special section cover appeared in issue 292 of the weekly *Hamshahri-ye Javān*,[1] or *Hamshahri for the Young*. *Hamshahri* literally means "fellow citizen" or, even more literally, "fellow city resident," while *Javān* (young) carries connotations of courage, strength, and playfulness. *Hamshahri for the Young* is a popular youth-oriented weekly and a spin-off of the daily newspaper *Hamshahri*, published by the Tehran Municipality. This issue had its special subsection, *Café Javān*, dedicated to the topic of *afsordegi* (depression), with playful subsection titles like "This Collective Sorrow," "The Depression Gesture," and "Wikidepia," a satirical encyclopedia of some commonly used and some made-up *depreshen*-related terminology including *dep zadan*, *dep*-artement, *depress*, and Johnny *Dep*. As in English, the term "café" is often used for discussion forums, reminiscent of the eighteenth-century coffeehouse public sphere venues where newspapers were shared and the issues of the day debated. Transformations of this ideal of the public sphere (in the Habermasian sense) resonate among youth, as they do in this book; in actual cafés such as Café Shoukā (in Chapter 4), in the virtual café of the blogosphere (in Chapter 5), or in the Ruzbeh alumni blog *Café Analysis* (in Chapter 7). And of course, in this cover page of *Café Javān*.

The cover stands out and captures not only the everydayness of a (psychiatric) discourse, but also various cultural sensibilities in the image of a fellow citizen holding the thinker pose (mimicking *Le Penseur*, or *The Thinker*, by French sculptor Auguste Rodin). This young thinker, however, is humorous and satirical, far from stoic, embodying several other personas: the joker (face), the thinker (pose), the *depress* (mask), the poet (words). The classical Athenian comic and tragic masks are both performatively in play, reminding us to reflect on the performativity of language: what does it mean to be *depress*?

He invites us to *Café Javān*, a (print) café, for a generation of wordsmiths; words that reveal and conceal; words that bring together poetic common sense (the allusion to Sepehri's poem) and generational sensibilities, seamlessly weaving the word *depress* into the ordinary and the poetic.

CHAPTER 1

Mapping *Prozak Diaries* and Medicalization

MEDICINE HAS SEVERAL LIVES; it gains a new life in each language and creates new cultural forms in each temporality. In 1990s Iran, a cultural shift took place in public articulations of psychological well-being, manifest in the evolution of a psychiatric discourse in the media and a rise in psychiatric talk among people. By the end of the 1990s, a Persian psychiatric vernacular had emerged in society: *afsordegi* (depression), *depreshen, dep zadan* (becoming depressed), *toromā* (trauma), *esteress* (stress), *bish-faāli* (hyperactivity in children), and the Persianized catchall term for antidepressants, *Prozāk*.[1] This shift toward a clinical and psychiatric discourse for talking about psychological distress was indeed part of a broader historical and cultural change. Traditionally, one discussed psychological and psychiatric pathologies primarily in a concealed, private, poetic, or religious language. After all, in Persian poetics, Sufi traditions, and the Shi'ite ethos of conduct, stoicism had an elevated status. Far from medicalized, melancholic gravitas signaled depth of character achieved through spiritual transcendence, unrequited love, and unshaken faith.[2] Within the medical establishment too, psychiatry had historically been seen as the unwanted child of medicine, its image marred by its allegedly *less scientific* foundations and the close proximity many of its key figures had to the world of letters and the humanities—if not the stigma of madness itself. Throughout the twentieth century, Islamist and Marxist ideologies too had further regarded psychiatry and particularly its psychoanalytical legacies as Western constructs that contradicted the ethos and priorities of the revolution.[3] But this was all to change.

In the late 1980s, a psychiatric discourse began to enter the media; a space emerged where psychiatrists and psychologists began educating the public about mental health. They introduced signs and symptoms of mood and anxiety disorders, as well as clinical and diagnostic frames with which people could understand their psychological experiences. This was a new opportunity for psychiatry, as a discipline, to be claimed in a specifically Iranian context. Psychiatric talk was now public and explicit.

When we find ourselves embracing a particular form of knowledge—in this case, psychiatry—it is tempting to assume that certain forms of illness must have become either more common or more efficiently diagnosed than before. Real life is more complex. The narratives and languages we choose have as much, if not more, to say about the world we have lived in than about what we are telling. Our choices—of languages, of concepts, of frameworks, of the bodies of knowledge we draw upon—are truly ours only insofar as we choose from what is culturally, scientifically, psychologically, and historically legitimate, accessible, and available to us. The internalization of new articulations necessitates, and reflects, the internalization of mindsets that have made that particular language intelligible and instrumental for us. In doing so, it reveals historical, cultural, and epistemological possibilities and impossibilities that have made a particular form of knowledge fit for a particular people at a particular time and place. This book is meant to describe some of those possibilities and impossibilities that might easily be overlooked by purely biomedical explanations.

Indeed, recent developments of medical disciplines need to be situated in several historical contexts, including that of the Iran-Iraq War (1980–1988). Shortly after the 1979 Revolution, Iraq invaded Iran and ignited a destructive eight-year war that resulted in a large number of casualties and adverse health conditions, as elaborated in numerous studies conducted by Iranian clinicians and researchers who have documented the physical and mental health impact of the war among veterans and civilians alike.[4] The postwar years were also marred by economic sanctions imposed by Western governments, many of which continue to this day with health-care-related implications. Yet the Iran-Iraq War (officially, in Iran, the Sacred Defense) also engendered new societal norms and solidarity; it mobilized, through educational and media campaigns, the Shi'ite ethos of endurance and sacrifice for justice.

For clinicians and policymakers, wartime concerns with post-traumatic stress disorder (PTSD) and anxiety disorders were replaced, in the 1990s, with concerns about depression and dysphoria. A discourse of mental health (*salāmat-e ravāni*) began to emerge, with the primary focus on raising awareness about and destigmatizing psychological disorders. Gradually, growing numbers of mental health talk shows and newspaper columns on psychiatric topics introduced a new clinical vernacular that gave people a way to discuss the very real pain that lingered from the war. This clinical language was both validated and welcomed by doctors as well as policymakers because and insofar as it fit several other paradigms in the late 1980s. The biomedical, authoritative, and symptom-centered language of psychiatry indicated that the malaise so many were experiencing resided in the purview of medicine. In the absence of an alternative public discourse, psychiatry and *disorder* provided society with a legitimate language to channel psychological and social experiences after the war. However, while the war is an important historical context, it does not solely explain the growing popularity of psychiatric discourses among people.

As psychiatric terminologies and diagnoses moved outward from the privacy of clinical encounters, a shift began to appear in language. People began to speak more publicly and commonly of their prescriptions for *ghors-e aʾsāb* (nerve pills)[5] and of *depreshen*, jokingly, as an "epidemic," a "crisis," or a "national trait." Everyone allegedly knew someone who was *depress*. *Depreshen* became street slang, and gradually it became less surprising to hear individuals talk about depression or call themselves *depress*, or *afsordeh*. Media, art, literature, and blogs adopted an explicitly medicalizing discourse of *afsordegi/depreshen* and statistical reports on mental health began circulating in the media. By the early 2000s, websites and blogs dedicated to mental health flourished among Iran's growing educated and urban population.

This, of course, was in part an outcome of media and educational campaigns for destigmatizing mental illness (particularly mood disorders); but a certain kind of receptivity and readiness for this language ought to have been in place among people and practitioners alike. A decade after the end of the war, reports emerged of a surge in antidepressant (and later Ritalin) consumption. Doctors both welcome this as a step forward in raising awareness (and better illness detection) and speculate about possible overmedication, but explain that medication is usually the first line of intervention for a number of practical reasons: the lack of a well-funded mental health care infrastructure, the arbitrary distribution of patients among specialties, the lack of patients' compliance with psychotherapy, and a culture of quick fixes, as well as what they perceive as a clash of tradition and modernity. But they still advocate medication and insist that it provides relief, destigmatizes psychological problems, eliminates guilt, and projects modernist and educated attitudes. Above all, it provides hope.

Although these cultural shifts remained gradual and largely unacknowledged, a discourse of *salāmat-e ravāni* (mental health) was palpable in the 1990s. Psychiatrists were now provided with a platform to educate the public and to introduce a fluent psychiatric language into people's daily lives. The discourse was also implied in parallel shifts in mental health policy and the institution of new legislation, as well as in public policy behind television programs, city planning, and education reforms that aimed to reintroduce splashes of color and joy into the daily life of citizens. When addressing alleged mental health problems, experts and officials alternated between different and at times competing rationalizations. Whether explaining them in terms of neuropathology or lack of religious integrity, they were nevertheless participating in a public discourse on mental health and psychological well-being, albeit in a sanitized clinical language. Most important was the very emergence and existence of a medico-rational attitude toward governing society's mental health and well-being; its presence validated the predicament to which psychiatry was trying to respond. And in this emerging public discourse, pathology was increasingly becoming a given. The gradual normalization of this new psychiatric vernacular further created a new way of knowing, interpreting, and perceiving oneself in the world.

Of course, we do not need to look further than news headlines to notice a palpable increase in psychiatric diagnoses (particularly depression and ADHD) and medication in Iran and around the globe since the 1990s. Worldwide, there are cautionary discussions about the psychological impact of communication technologies, psychopharmacological interventions, and the changing psychological landscapes of family and interpersonal relations. Is it possible, one might ask, that urban lifestyles or shifting gender roles are leading to more dysphoria everywhere? Maybe. Is it scientifically imaginable, as some neuroscientists suggest, that the adverse effects of the war might leave a genetic imprint across generations? Maybe. Could Iranian children too be more prone to hyperactivity and inattention as a result of shifting familial, gender, and technological patterns? Perhaps. Would that mean their brains are changing in ways that lead to psychiatric diagnoses such as ADHD? Maybe and maybe not. Is it possible that not everyone who calls herself *depress* or takes antidepressants is clinically depressed? Yes.

While these questions are fascinating in their own right, they are not the focus of this book, nor are causal claims about mental illness, questions of whether depression has increased in society, or epidemiological surveys of psychiatric diagnoses. These questions could not be asked, much less answered, until concepts such as *depreshen* are clinically *and* culturally analyzed in their Iranian contexts. To investigate *depreshen*, attention to its psychological detailing is necessary. But so is an anthropological understanding of its historical and cultural trajectories.

What We Mean When We Talk about Depreshen

It is misleading to assume that the rise in *depreshen* talk or alarming statistics means that people must be *clinically* depressed. Medical anthropologists have always been interested in the meaning of illness and how patients account for their illness experience or their identification with it, thus creating a legacy of studying "illness narratives" that, in its initial formulations, aimed to confront the hegemonic universality of "explanatory models" that Western biomedicine provided.[6] Narratives of illness also reveal the historical and cultural trajectories that underlie health conditions. On the one hand, the political economy of health has become the focus of a critical branch of medical anthropology that asks how illnesses evolve, medically and socially, and what sociopolitical contexts and material conditions of power or inequality underlie their social construction.[7] On the other hand, influenced by anthropological traditions of cultural analysis and hermeneutics, another branch of medical anthropology has focused on an interpretive anthropological investigation into how illness experiences are culturally shaped, experienced, and made sense of by individuals.[8] Narratives are equally instrumental in understanding the subjective experience of illness, a topic of interest shared today with the fields of medical humanities and narrative psychiatry, both of which have successfully brought patient narratives to the attention of clinicians.[9] Both disciplines are, however, situated in wider Western traditions that tend to regard the self as a universal, whole entity. Anthropologists, instead, regard the self as situated in historical contexts and therefore subject to diverse interpretations of selfhood. Anthropology also cautions against the tendency to essentialize and universalize individual narratives of illness and suffering, and deems it important to appreciate the messiness and (dis)order of such narratives in order to grasp the ethical implications of clinical decisions. "The disordering of narrative," writes anthropologist Veena Das in her book *Affliction*, "is part of the sense of bewilderment about what it means to have *this* illness in *this* body,"[10] and in *this* moment.

Four decades ago, a classic study by anthropologists Byron Good and Mary-Jo Good and their colleagues laid the groundwork for analyzing how Iranians experienced depressive illness as an *interpreted* disorder whose symptoms were situated in the cultural context of Iranian affect.[11] B. Good's earlier work on *nārāhati*, depression, and anxiety (experienced as heart distress in the 1970s) had already shifted the conventional focus from cultural responses *to* illness toward its cultural interpretations and semantic networks—that is, experiences associated with illness through networks of meaning and social interactions. Importantly, in approaching narratives of illness, Good went beyond the narrative structure to explore how cultural and linguistic contexts shape our experience of a particular illness. "As new medical terms become known in the society," Good argued, "they find their way into existing semantic networks" and shape medical rationalities.[12] Among Iranians, these semantic networks are informed not only by medical rationalities, but also by traditions that include, but are not limited to, Zoroastrian, mystic, and Shi'ite symbolism. The work of anthropologist Michael Fischer in the 1970s identified the cultural cues and linguistic references for such rationalities by unpacking Shi'ite symbolism and its various cultural, psychological, and political interpretations of Iranian affectivity.[13] Fischer also provided a genealogy of the Iranian revolution and its emotional residues, followed by Fischer and Abedi's analysis of depression and cultural articulations of feeling blocked, caught, and suspended (*āvāreh*) between cultures, as was the fate of many Iranian émigrés in the United States.[14] These studies, alongside Lotfalian's research on psychological conditions among Iranian émigrés in California in the immediate postrevolutionary period,[15] laid important ground for my work.

Today, Iranian medical rationalities have changed immensely. What was once communicated in the double entendre of unrequited love in mystic poetry, sacrificial ethos in Shi'ism, self-denying melancholy in mysticism, or even clandestine political rebellion, can now be part of a public discourse of psychological and psychiatric distress. After almost four decades, I pick up where the above scholars left off, starting with an examination of the cultural and historical semantics of *depreshen* among Iranian youth. Another way of posing the question might be to ask how *depreshen* differs from clinical depression, and what the difference can tell us about Iranian society.

Iranian psychiatrists and general practitioners—who often fill in where there is no referral system from primary care to mental health specialists—use the fourth edition of the *Diagnostic and Statistical Manual of Mental Disorders* (*DSM-IV*) as their gold-standard diagnostic tool.[16] In the *DSM*, a time frame is set for the duration of symptoms. If a number of symptoms such as depressive mood persist beyond a certain period of time and cause functional impairment, diagnosis is confirmed. The *DSM* also regards loss as marked by a singular event; to be diagnosed, the patient ought to have experienced a particular number of symptoms for longer than a particular period (beyond what is considered "normal" reaction to the stressor), and ought to have experienced an impairment of function because of those symptoms. In Iran, generally speaking, a depression diagnosis often means that medication will follow.

But the *DSM*, embedded in a very specific American biomedical epistemology, takes for granted function as universal, time as linear, and loss as singular. It sees contextual factors as secondary to the essence of the illness.[17] At best, when considering the cultural aspects of illness, biomedical psychiatry treats culture as a static and secondary variant that intervenes upon the already-formed illness. But cultural, historical, and social contexts are not located outside of the realm of illness. Rather, illnesses are both biologically and socially constructed; their cultural contexts shape how we experience and relate to them.

Clinically speaking, in what is called *depreshen*, or afsordegi, the lines are blurred between situational depression, collective dysphoria, melancholy, clinical (major) depression, PTSD, anxiety disorder, and what psychologists call "learned helplessness." *Depreshen* problematizes global paradigms of mental health *and* provides a paradigmatic case (among many postwar societies), in part because of Iran's seventy-plus-year history of modern psychiatry and in part because it juxtaposes a largely individual-focused modern psychiatry (and the *DSM*) against the backdrop of a very particular social setting and its cultural experiences. These experiences, in 1980s Iran, also include the internalization of what psychologist-anthropologist Bateson and his colleagues call a double bind: a sense of emotional distress or defeat that individuals may experience in the face of contradictory or mutually exclusive imperatives.[18] The concept is useful to describe the chronic sense of loss that many individuals relate when they discuss depression, distress, or life in general.[19] These double binds, created by both large-scale societal dynamics (e.g., during the war or in the immediate cultural aftermath of the 1979 Revolution) and smaller-scale interpersonal ones (e.g., generational divides within the family), can overlap and interact. They consolidate cultural and historical elements that eventually become part of individuals' perceptions of themselves and their worlds.

In many respects, the double bind is a familiar story from prerevolutionary times: life had always been complicated by particular codes for conducting the private and public, inner and outer.[20] It perhaps took on a more charged ideological edge after the revolution with the institutionalization of particular moral codes of conduct in daily life. Evoking a state of internalized loss, double binds partially reflect the rupture in social norms, or the social anomie—to use Durkheim's term—that society experienced during and after the Iran-Iraq War. Put simply, one can speculate that rupture in social norms and orders could lead to double binds and Durkheimian anomic conditions.[21] Some have speculated that, to varying degrees and forms, double binds, along with the experience of the Iran-Iraq War, could lead to widespread dysphoria, and, perhaps in a very Durkheimian development, higher rates of depression.[22] But this assessment would be too simplistic, not least because it assumes universal responses; it also overlooks the simultaneous function and situated meaning of various cultural forms (e.g., Shi'ite ethos) and modes of cohesion that served to sustain the moral fabric of society during and after the war.

Juxtaposing Iranian *depreshen* with the diagnostic tenets of depression in *DSM-IV* confronts us with questions about the universality of diagnostic categories, a topic that has been debated globally. Several scholars have drawn attention to modes of subjectification facilitated by psychiatric apparatus and have investigated the discursive processes that legitimize psychiatric knowledge.[23] These processes are further complicated when the *DSM* travels East. For example, the assumption of a time frame for traumatic events and loss reflects not only a particular linear understanding of time, but also the cultural forms and health care infrastructures in which the *DSM-IV* was designed and evaluated. According to the *DSM-IV*, if symptoms persist beyond and despite that infrastructure, one can make a clinical diagnosis of depression. But what about when the *DSM* travels to a society harboring a different set of cultural and affective discourses, or one working through the aftermath of a war in its own terms? What if the social and spiritual meaning of loss challenges what psychiatrists know as due processes of mourning? What if mourning is arrested or delayed, as in the case of families who receive the bodies of loved ones decades after they went missing in action? What if loss is not a singular event or of a loved one, but a prolonged sense of lament?[24] And what if mourning for unrecognized losses has been stuttered over time?[25] These questions are meant to draw attention to the clinical and cross-cultural intricacies of diagnostic appropriations.

Psychiatry and Cultural Forms

Changing frameworks in relation to diagnoses such as depression and ADHD are indeed global phenomena, particularly since the 1980s and the globalization of Prozac and Ritalin. But their lived experience and interpretative processes need to be contextualized in their own cultural and generational trajectories of meaning. Young Iranians' reflections on their experiences of depressive mood and *depreshen* vary, indeed, but often entail a discussion of a range of affective states in highly situated ways. Many interpret and discuss their psychological distress not only as an ailment of the present, but also as one situated, directly or indirectly, in the emotional and cultural afterlife of a certain lingering past that may be far or near (thus further challenging the boundaries of what the *DSM* defines as mood disorders, anxiety disorders, or PTSD). Such historicization of psychological experience both relies on, and contributes to, specific generational formations depending on how individuals perceive their own place in the post-1980s Iranian cosmos. Understanding these generational demarcations is necessary for understanding individuals' affective references when talking about illness. Most notably, I had to learn early on that one could not discuss the life of psychiatry without an underlying understanding of the significant place that the 1980s and the Iran-Iraq War occupy in the memories and worldviews of Iranians.

The Iran-Iraq War, which is an inevitable part of the history of Iranian psychiatry, has been largely overlooked by the international community, both in terms of its health impact and in terms of the ethos, sacrifices, and values that it continues to symbolize for Iranians. In my interviews, individuals persistently underscore their generational relation to this particular history. These generational identities (and their ensuing labels) anchor themselves in the affective memories of childhood; for instance, in the aftermath of the Iran-Iraq War or the cultural transformations that followed the 1979 Revolution. The cultural and psychological significance of such generational identifications, however, has commonly been overshadowed in overly politicized analyses of Iranian youth or historical periods. But a nuanced examination of individuals' narratives of illness requires contextualizing them in their affective histories and the (psychocultural) meaning of such generational references. My approach to these memories is thus cultural rather than political: that is, I analyze individuals' reflections and nostalgias as moment-fragments that shape people's cultural imageries and psychological sensibilities and continually infuse themselves into the more tangible experiences of daily life.

Anthropologist Veena Das has defined *critical events* as those that institute new modes of historical action that redefine traditional categories and become inscribed in the psychosocial inventory of the event's afterlife.[26] I find such modalities in the afterlife and memories of historical events, in the consolidation of biomedical psychiatry as a form of thinking, and in the generational sensibilities of young Iranians. The 1990s normalization of psychiatric concepts and terminologies both helped to destigmatize mood disorders and created new possibilities for youth to connect the dots of individual, familial, and social forms of disorder and to situate their present-day emotional distress within historical, generational, and cultural contexts. It gave them a language of emotion and memory.

I intentionally refrain from calling wartime experiences *trauma*, in order to keep a distance both from disciplinary connotations that burden the term (for example, in relation to PTSD) and from the assumption of its universality.[27] The double binds of ordinary life can constitute subjective experiences that are not easily mappable or translatable to the term *trauma*. I use the word *rupture* instead. Rupture allows for the complexity of historical conditions and their emotional afterlife, as well as for the new cultural forms they generate. It also allows the conceptual capacity to convey the infusion, diffusion, and multiplicity of experiences across generations. My focus, thus, is not on the events per se, but on the consequent burden of remembering their residues that are bound to be overlooked by institutionalized memory—in other words, on their assimilation and inscription into the present and its cultural or artistic forms. I turn to everyday life, then, as the site where the ordinary can turn ruptured, and where the opacity of ordinary experience escapes a complete theoretical formulation.[28]

Today, the constant circulation of compelling accounts of the nostalgias as well as anomies of the past and the present is creating a new mode of self-recognition, a new sense of voice, and a new identity politics for young Iranians. Different generations since the Iranian revolution of 1979 have come to claim distinct generational identities, which they continually reconstruct, online and offline, in various ways including (but not limited to) the appropriation of psychiatric concepts.[29] Among these generational claims there are inabilities of intra- and intergenerational translation, making for accounts that are unpolished and in ongoing negotiation. These generations are created not necessarily through temporal junctures, but through (distinct) aesthetics of memory that are both psychiatrically and culturally informed. Each generation's imagination is imbued with distinct and incommensurable vocabularies, values, and visual imageries within a shared time frame. The same event may have been experienced as disruptive by some, but not others; thereby creating different cohorts of experience within the same age group. The sensibilities and worldviews that these generational cohorts harbor are marked by the particular aesthetics of memory that they create around cultural prompts, objects, sounds, and images of the past. These sensibilities need to be recognized, heard, and addressed in different emotional registers. To understand their stories, one would have to know how to imagine and live in multiple times and places.

Much is revealed in the making of generations in terms of the cultural aesthetics (visual, auditory, and textual) through which individuals construct memory and language, locate themselves in the order and disorder of historical change, and create explanatory models for their perception and experience of psychiatric disorders (e.g., depression or PTSD). Remembering, for those who performatively engage in it, emerges as an attempt to sort and work through disorder, to get a step closer to what one perceives as normal, as if to remember would be to overcome. Accessing these modes of remembering reveals the seemingly normal instillation of past ruptures in all ordinary things—in the order created within, and out of, (dis)order. A mode of being emerges in such remembering, one whose building blocks are every bit as social as they are psychological. These generational forms can thus serve as analytical categories to understand psychosocial and cultural change in ways that do not depend solely upon master narratives, biomedical models, or institutional histories. Even more important, they raise questions about the psychological and cultural import of self-naming.

Generational labels are abundant and contested: e.g., *daheh-ye shasti-hā* (the 1980s generation, or the 1360s in the Iranian calendar [*shast* meaning sixty]), *nasl-e sevvom* (the third generation), *khāmushi* (quiet, also referring to the electrical blackouts during missile attacks), or *sukhteh* (burnt) generation. Equally significant are the competitions over these labels and over which is the most affected and affective generation. Each is indeed ideologically and socioeconomically diverse. The boundaries of these generational definitions are blurry and constantly shifting—for example, in the interchangeable usage of the label "1980s generation" among those born in the 1980s and those who were in elementary school during the 1980s.[30] Competing and at times nostalgic claims over generational labels beg the question of what lies in a name and what kinds of historical, psychological, or cultural claims are made possible by self-naming.

It is, of course, impossible to capture the complexity and diversity of generational forms, in that these labels relay different meanings at different times and by different people. For the most part, *daheh-ye shasti-hā* (the children of the 1980s) have no memories from before the revolution; they grew up during the Iran-Iraq War and under the shadow of international sanctions imposed on Iran. Today, they constitute some three-quarters of the population and are highly dynamic and engaged in several scientific, cultural, and artistic domains. They also bore the brunt of the early 1980s population boom in their experience of education, employment, and polarization of polity. This self-identified 1980s generation charts its childhood psychology not just in the aftermath of the war but also in the cultural aesthetics of the 1980s. For this younger generation, psychiatry has provided a language and resource for (re)negotiating life itself. It also helps to signal upward class mobility or to project progressive and scientific mindsets—something that Iranians valorize immensely.

Compared to the younger generation, the older generation that came of age in the early 1980s distinguishes itself in the more immediate and gendered experience of wartime. As they became young adults, some experienced structural anxieties in the makeshift period of the *very* early 1980s, while some others identified with its spirit of revolutionary idealism and sense of social responsibility. Among those older, who readily sacrificed their lives fighting in the Iran-Iraq War, the more immediate health impact of the war as well as the transition from a decade of solidarity to one of rapidly moving on gave rise to an ecological niche for the incorporation of today's psychiatric discourses.[31] But more relevant here, some of them are now parents whose children may be medicated for another rising diagnosis, ADHD. I rediscovered them as parents as I researched the sharp increase in the prescription of Ritalin between 1997 and 2008. Their narratives of illness, at once medical and historical, serve as a lens for investigating generational transferences: as in many other societies, a seemingly clear-cut biomedical condition (ADHD) might also reflect shifting moral as well as biomedical imperatives shaping parents' perceptions of normality and healthy childhood.[32]

Psychiatry's engagement with memory (e.g., of war) is often dominated by the individual-centered paradigm of PTSD; but these generational narratives challenge such universalist frameworks by creating culturally generative spaces in acts of remembering. What is striking in generational narratives is the merging of the present with particular moments in a past that seem to have remained ever present. Below the surface of what happens now, it seems, the shadows of what one has lived are always lurking, seeping through the cracks of memory and everyday life. The ensuing generational cultures and memories matter not only because they narrate a different, more psychologically attuned account of history and culture, but also because they have a medico-cultural function. They reflect how a clinico-cultural category like *depreshen*, if not psychiatry at large, can operate as a cultural resource for negotiating life and (re)making the self. Conscious recollections aside, the unsaid, the unspeakable, and the unheard remain present among those for whom the possibility of reworking has been blocked. Such memories become tacit knowledge; they return in our dreams, in choices we make, and in (cultural and medical) desires we nurture. They also create a desire for retelling and sharing that, in turn, can make possible new forms of sociality and generational kinship. This desire, first in the 1980s generation and later in others, found refuge in at least two new possibilities among others: medicalization and blogging.

Needless to say, not all generational peers blog or identify with psychiatry; these accounts specifically come from those who do. In the *depreshen* that some members of the 1980s generation describe and the cultural meaning of ADHD among the children of the older generation, I seek a window into the global, historical, socio-ethical and generational contexts in which illness is interpreted and clinical decisions are made. They help us understand how medical choices are biomedically, culturally, and psychodynamically structured—while forming part of people's everyday explanations and psychological processes of meaning making. Looking through this window, I return to the question of how to account for the consolidation and normalization of psychiatric discourses among young Iranians. What kinds of claims are made possible when both individuals and (biomedical) institutions agree on medicalization?

Medicalization: A Conversation across Disciplines

Medicalization—the term anthropologists use to refer to the formulation of human conditions and social phenomena under the purview of biomedicine—is a double-edged sword.[33] On the one hand, it can be liberating and humanizing; it facilitates access to care for controversial or stigmatized illness categories; it can provide relief and lift the burden of guilt and shame.[34] On the other hand, anthropologists have argued that medicalization can be desocializing, depoliticizing, and abstracting. It can take away individuals' agency. It can reduce a range of sociohistorical conditions to clinical artifacts by generating fixed categories and defining normalcy in biomedical terms, thereby creating the impression that biomedicine is the only proper response to the problem. The medicalization of *depreshen* may have done both, but it also had a third function: it resocialized a culturally generative discourse of memory and affect.

There are several possibilities for understanding the medicalization of affective experiences. At first glance, can we see the promotion and consolidation of psychiatry and psychiatric discourse as a Foucauldian biopolitical phenomenon? Perhaps. What represents and maintains the psychiatric discourse is a knowledge-based language that, promoted by experts, also creates its own moral order. In other words, by defining the problems in its own language, biomedicine claims privileged access to truth. As in a Foucauldian framework, the biomedical discourse constituted pathology as a mode of thinking that was socially and scientifically legitimated and psychologically configured. Thus a particular biomedical mode of thought replaced and dominated others and consequently produced relevant forms of knowledge and practice (such as medication). The frequent use of institutional and social statistical research on depression as an index of social pathology can also be read in Durkheimian terms: as a means of (re)engineering the social structure to make it possible to measure, monitor, and remedy pathologies,[35] to treat society and render it both healthy and scientific/ modern.[36] Iran's great investment and success in gaining recognition as a techno-scientific and biotechnological power in the region can thus put the promotion of biomedical sciences (including neuroscience) in perspective.

The consolidation of a biomedical discourse also informs the shaping of illness for patients and normalizes and internalizes certain ways of understanding and experiencing a given condition.[37] This matters because who is diagnosed and who gets labeled as *depress* is as much a sociocultural question as it is a biomedical one. And psychiatry, theory often expects, desocializes etiological and diagnostic processes that are profoundly social, political, and cultural. However, a Foucauldian framework is only partially useful here, insofar as genealogies of discourse shed light on how new epistemes and mindsets become internalized through discursive processes and how psychiatry invokes a kind of utopian refuge from mental anguish.[38] But it does not sufficiently explain why and how ordinary individuals would performatively engage with psychiatric intervention and interpretations. What happened, one wonders, to the stigma of calling oneself *depress*? Indeed, public campaigns around destigmatizing mental illness and their biological reductionism initially reflected forms of [Foucauldian] governmentality that may have reshaped agency and internalized a particular discipline and mode of (biomedical) thought.[39] However, they also found a unique audience and reception among laypeople.

Singular focus on top-down formulations of medicalization and biological reductionism can miss two points.[40] First, Iranian health policies and initiatives
have not been static; they are constantly in the making and have taken different
approaches in responding to different public health conditions.[41] Second, while
cautioning against universalizing biomedical explanations, post-Foucauldian
medical anthropology also risks regarding medicalized individuals as passive.
The other side of the coin is that individuals performatively engage with biomedical models and find in them frameworks that make their psychological experiences intelligible. Without losing sight of the hegemonic forces of biomedicine, I
turn to individuals' intimate accounts, where we may find potential for a complementary bottom-up analysis of medicalization. The medicalization of *depreshen,*
for example, was partly an unusual function of performative self-expression and
agency. That is, it was partially driven by individuals' medicalizing *desires* that are,
in turn, situated and interpreted by them in a cultural and historical context. It is
in *their* diagnoses, not mine, that one discovers an urge toward the recognition
of their psychological and historical predicaments and finding their place in a
world that seems oblivious to their individual struggles. Investigating medicalization thus leads to investigating how people construct their (medical) choices and
practices at the intersection of biomedicine, ordinary life, and memory; thereby
turning medicalization into a cultural resource and generative process of meaning making. In validating experiences such as PTSD or *depreshen,* for example,
psychiatry provides them with a language to articulately remember yesteryears
filled with ruptures, most of which, one would expect, could have been reified in
the process of clinical diagnosis. Instead, it was precisely through the processes
of medicalization that the story of those ruptures came to be resocialized, and
turned into new cultural forms.

This focus on the medicalized is not meant to undermine or replace biomedical explanations or practitioners' accounts; they too should be actively included
in debates on medicalization. When and where informed clinical diagnoses are
made, biomedical interventions should not be simply negated in favor of, say, psychotherapy. Understanding the place and merit of medication can inform anthropological inquiry by letting the ethnographer inside the porous boundaries of the
experience of illness. In Iran, when people seek professional help, the lines between
psychiatry, psychology, psychoanalysis, and counseling remain blurred, resulting
in an arbitrary allocation of patients among the specialties. While psychological
discussions and incredibly widespread self-help discourses contribute to the formation of psychiatric forms of life, in this book my focus is only on psychiatry.

The explanatory models that doctors propose for medicalization or the surge in prescriptions of psychiatric medication vary depending on their pedagogical orientations (biomedical versus psychodynamic). In the juxtaposition of their explanatory models against those of their patients, it becomes clear that practioners' own cultural experiences shape part of their situated knowledge and practices. These situated worldviews should not be overlooked. Nor should attention to historical and biomedical meanings come at the cost of overlooking individual and psychological processes, defense mechanisms, recurrent dreams, or transferences. A preliminary dialogue between anthropology, psychiatry, psychoanalysis, and cultural analysis can unpack binaries of health and illness, tradition and modernity, biological and social worlds.[42] It can push each discipline to revisit its dominant frameworks and potential blind spots.[43]

As such, each character in this book is meant to raise the question of what possibilities might emerge from psychiatric ways of thinking. What forms of sociality, for example, can psychiatric medication or blogging about one's *depreshen* create? In locating medicalizing *desires* in people's shared and intersubjective (rather than individual) constructions of meaning, I ask how psychoanalysis might benefit from an anthropological understanding of desire. In turn, how can a psychoanalytic appreciation of transferences, returns, and compulsive repetitions (in dreams, blogs, and recollections) contribute to anthropological empathy? In this conversation, I hope to join others' efforts to trace the life of theoretical frameworks and conceptual tools (such as medicalization), knowledge forms (such as psychiatry), and diagnostic categories (such as depression) as they arrive and are molded to fit into a non-Western scaffold.

Freud

Sitting in his room in the doctors' quarter in St Luke's Woodside Hospital in London a few days after the victory of the 1979 Iranian revolution, thirty-four-year-old psychiatric registrar Mohammad Sanati was going through a patient's files. As he read, celebrations were underway in Iran's major cities, including in his hometown of Isfahan. BBC Persian radio, playing in the background, was broadcasting a young, passionate man rebuking "Westernization and its symbols." In the lecture, he used the metaphor of the Quranic "Golden Calf" of Samiri (*Gusāleh-ye Sāmeri*, worshiped by the Israelites), now a symbol of the cultural corruption threatening society. Describing one such symbol, he continued:

> In this new bourgeoisie, [he] armed himself against all moral and human values, against all high and ascending manifestations of the human soul and called it realism. . . . A prophet of the bourgeoisie, whose religion was *sexualism*. . . . This prophet was named Freud. His religion was sexuality; his temple, *Freudism*.[1]

Intrigued, Sanati turned up the radio. The *gusāleh* (calf) in question, it turned out, was none other than Austrian psychoanalyst Sigmund Freud, and the voice on the radio belonged to French-trained, Fanon-influenced, Islamist-Marxist sociologist Ali Shari'ati. And Sanati was listening to a rerun of some of his popular lectures. One of the influential ideologues of the Iranian revolution and a cultural icon with many young followers, Shari'ati was among the advocates of the anti-imperialist "return to self" paradigm in the 1960s. Freud, he believed, symbolized the moral corruption of bourgeoisie.

Having lived in London since 1974, Sanati was relatively distant from Shari'ati's widespread influence among young Iranians during prerevolutionary upheavals, though he had heard about his famous lecture series in the religious institution Hosseiniyeh-ye Ershād in Tehran. And even though it shocked Sanati, the *Gusāleh-ye Sāmeri* metaphor was quite well known in Iran. Freud, however, was being reinvented in the imagination of the masses. By mobilizing terms such as "Freudism" and "sexualism," Shari'ati portrayed Freud as a symbol of moral corruption. In two of his lectures, "Expectations of the Muslim Woman" (originally delivered on June 25, 1972), and "Fatima Is Fatima" (originally delivered on July 6, 1972), Shari'ati had famously said:

> One of the most important tools that has been created by this ruling power to dominate all intellectual, social, economic and moral aspects of modern life, is Freudism's sexuality [*jensiyat-e Freudism*]. This has become the communal social spirit of our age and has become the substitute for all values, virtues and liberties. It is not accidental that Freud's view of sexuality came to prominence after the Second World War and became the fundamental basis and foundation of art. Most motion pictures are based on only two elements: violence and sexuality.
>
> . . . From *Freudism* they [the bourgeoisie] built a supposedly scientific and humane religion. From sexuality they built an ethical conscience. Finally, from lust, a blessed temple was built. They built their place of worship and created a powerful servant class. And the first sacrifice on the threshold of this temple was women's human values.

The lectures later appeared in his widely read *Fatima Is Fatima*, which outlined the exploitation of women under the guise of modernization and sexual liberation. In it, Shari'ati blamed bourgeois cognition and "Freud's pseudo-science and ideal of sexual liberation" ("Freudism") for the exploitation (in a Marxian sense) of Muslim nations: "In the market of Freudism, the worship of the most abhorrent and wretched sex has been offered as an intellectual philosophy."[2]

After the 1979 Revolution, Freud's name would be removed from public media and print for years.

Although Shari'ati did not live to witness the fruition of the revolution that he helped foster, psychodynamic psychotherapist Mohammad Sanati returned to Iran in the 1980s. By the 1990s, he had established a psychoanalytically oriented psychiatric practice and an academic legacy. He was a participant in the discursive shift that led to the normalization of psychiatric modes of thinking and became a household name in Iranian media for pioneering psychiatric talk shows and literary criticism that engaged psychoanalysis and, later, initiated debates regarding Shari'ati's reading of Freud.[3] Neither Sanati nor Shari'ati could have foreseen in those days what would come in the 1990s: the normalization of a psychiatric language in Iranians' daily lives.

CHAPTER 2

Pedagogical and Cultural Histories
of Iranian Psychiatry

THERE ARE MANY WAYS to narrate institutional histories. It is often too easy, for example, to treat any given country as moving from a primitive lack of facilities to progressive, contemporary integration into global standards. But history is full of roads not taken, conflicts unresolved, good intentions blocked, and frames of reference transformed. Psychiatry was not a new arrival in postrevolutionary Iran. As an academic discipline, it had emerged in the 1930s. As a social institution, it had evolved, initially, as part of a century-long attempt at what historian Cyrus Schayegh has called scientific modernization,[1] and, later, as part of the establishment's public heath efforts for medical advancement and psychosocial reconstruction. The psychiatric turn of the 1990s had indeed cultural and social precursors in the history of psychiatry in Iran, as it did in self-help movements.[2] Add to that a long legacy of translations, competitions, negotiations, and rhetorical flows in training and practice that had shaped its cultural logics over the course of the twentieth century.

Psychiatry also evolved in conversation with historical and cultural debates over sadness and joy that stretched back to the 1930s, in the dialogue between Zoroastrianism, mysticism, and Shi'ism, and in Iranian affective discourses more deeply.[3] In other words, in entering the cultural and affective consciousness of Iranians, psychiatry has been in interaction with emotions as situated in a particular religio-cultural context. Variably, this context embodies particular conceptualizations of affective states such as contentment, joy, or sorrow. Consider for instance, well-known verses in mystic poetry such as Rumi's "Joy [shādi] is the sweet fruit of the garden of sorrow [gham] and heartache—this joy is a wound, and that heartache, its remedy"; or religious teachings such as the Shi'ite hadith from Imam Sādegh: "Hozn [melancholic gravitas] is the sign of the devout." To follow the life of psychiatry then, we need to first understand the cultural and religio-affective foundations upon which psychiatry arrived and thrived in Iran.

It is quite common, and tempting, to explain the rise of psychiatric talk or the perceived prevalence of depreshen as an artifact of mysticism and Shi'ism. But such claims to melancholy, as a distinctive taproot of philosophical Persian culture, need unpacking.[4] They should also be understood in their relation to equally contextualized conceptualizations of joy and contentment in both Sufism and Shi'ism. Rather than essentializing cultural expressions or overlooking the diversity of culturally situated affective states, we need to investigate what psychological and epistemological spaces these belief systems create, what cultural forms they produce, and how they have interacted over time with parallel epistemologies such as science and medicine. Surely, the Iranian discourse of emotions has a rich connection to melancholy, which, Good et al. have argued, "is grounded in a culturally shaped conception of selfhood, in a highly ritualized tradition of religious grieving, and in a tragic view of history and society shared by religious and secular thinkers in Iranian culture."[5] Pre-Islamic and Islamic grand tragedies not only inform the psychic structure of Iranian society, they also contribute to an affective value system in which melancholic inclinations are valorized. This is not to say Iranians are uniformly melancholic; on the contrary, it is to point out how such emotions are embedded in their own value system and affective structure, where the ideal self embodies and endures stoic suffering as an indicator of wisdom and depth of character.[6]

An appreciation of these contexts is necessary for understanding the historical and cultural life of psychiatry. Both Shi'ism and Sufism have been instrumental in shaping Iranians' affective epistemologies and valorizing melancholic gravitas.[7] For instance, martyrdom, as a valorized category of experience, is associated for Iranians with a complex tangle of emotional, political, and historical meanings, and it shapes part of the emotional structure of Iranian culture. Even though the framework of martyrdom predates Shi'ism and is part of Iran's pre-Islamic mythology and epic literature, contemporary formulations of martyrdom are primarily based on the Karbala paradigm.[8] Shaped around the moral tale of the uneven battle of Karbala (680 AD) in which Prophet Mohammad's grandson Imam Hussein, the third Shi'ite Imam, and his supporters sacrificed their lives and refused to bow to injustice, the story is a tragedy par excellence. Imam Hussein's martyrdom is a story of loyalty and betrayal, and it lingers in the Iranian psyche.[9] In the 1980s, the Iran-Iraq War engendered a communal spirit of solidarity among Iranians and rendered martyrdom not only a cultural resource in making the Sacred Defense intelligible, but also a formative criterion in the creation of war-related identities.[10] Mourning rituals and other acts of remembrance, in this sense, provided platforms for sociopolitical processes of making the self and locating it in the hierarchies of social identity. Meanwhile, in its creation of cultural meaning through the paradigm of Karbala, the Iran-Iraq War changed the politics of emotions in everyday life. An understanding of these nuances of emotions is therefore necessary for understanding the situated working of psychiatry.

It is important, however, to remember that, as far as analysis is concerned, these categories cannot be taken for granted. While understanding the cultural import of martyrdom or Shi'ism is crucial, it would be shortsighted to analyze categories such as depressive mood solely in their relation to religious categories. A myopic focus on religion or on Shi'ism can mask other discursive and dynamic processes that shape the social life of emotions and diagnostic categories. It also overlooks historical variations in the bearing of Shi'ite cultures over the course of the twentieth century. These historical variations inform the ways both doctors and laypeople conceptualize and relate to variations in mood and affect. Consider, for example, that in the early twentieth century, Reza Shah Pahlavi pursued a national campaign to rid Iran of Shi'ite rituals, replacing them with civic rituals and nationalistic symbols that emphasized Iran's Zoroastrian heritage. After the Islamic revolution, a counter-ideology relying on Shi'ite ethos expanded the Karbala paradigm to an imperative of endurance, stoicism, and fight for justice in a corrupt world. The 1990s discourse of emotions is thus situated in these histories as well as in the ensuing cultural shifts such as the elevation of stoicism in the public domain in the 1980s, followed by the reversal of several cultural policies in the 1990s. For example, in the very early 1980s, public celebrations changed form; Eid-Noruz (the celebration of the Persian New Year and the spring equinox) was briefly denounced as frivolous; music was initially prohibited (considered inappropriate, in part, for evoking *ghenā* [sexual provocation]) and was replaced by ideologically relevant martial anthems that suited the spirit of the time. This was followed, in the 1990s, by the growth of several music academies and the reemergence of pop music in the public domain. These cultural ebbs and flows, a characteristic shared in many postrevolutionary eras, shape the affective context that underlies the history of psychiatry as an academic and medical discipline.

Toward a Pedagogical History of Psychiatry

To push the history of psychiatry further back is the task of historians, but I use historical accounts to identify discursive shifts and pedagogical continuities, divergences, negotiations, and innovations. No formal historiography of Iranian psychiatry exists, but there are Persian memoirs and textbooks written by a number of the founding figures including Hossein Reza'i, Abdolhossein Mirsepāssi, Ebrāhim Chehrāzi, and Haratoun Dāvidiān.[11] Various themes are braided together in these works: the spirit of modernity and the role of physicians as mediators between popular culture and scientific expertise; the legacy of Galenic and Avicennian medical distinctions between diseases of the nerves and diseases of the soul; and the creation of mental health institutions.

A close reading of these works, alongside oral histories and extended interviews with psychiatrists, provides a partial map of the evolution of the field in relation to three overlapping domains: state-building, global trends in psychiatry, and other psy disciplines (psychoanalysis in particular).[12] These accounts shed light on the ways the formative years of the discipline shaped new epistemologies and how key actors' personal trajectories influenced the ways in which past and present, tradition and modernity, dogma and progress, and above all, self and other were and are dichotomized, juxtaposed, and interpreted.

The foundations of modern Iranian psychiatry were established in what later became Ruzbeh Hospital, in the 1930s and 1940s, by neurologists and neuropsychiatrists trained in France with a largely biological (i.e., non-psychodynamic) orientation. In the 1950s, a debate around Freud emerged (albeit outside of psychiatry), and, in the 1960s and 1970s, there was an important turn to Jung and a rediscovery of Iranian mystical traditions, meshing the psychological and anticolonial tenet of a "return to self" with cultural authenticity. In the 1970s, an influx of US-trained psychiatrists with a more psychodynamic, if not psychoanalytic, orientation introduced psychodynamics into psychiatric training.[13] But the Cultural Revolution of 1980–1983 created a detour, as many psychiatrists, including those who had introduced dynamic methods in the 1970s, emigrated or retreated into private practice. Some psychiatrists trained in the United Kingdom and the United States returned after the 1979 Islamic Revolution and contributed to new initiatives. Among these are the Board of Child Psychiatry (in 1997), the Psychodynamic Therapy and Human Studies Unit of Tehran University (in 2006), and the psychodynamic therapy rotation within the psychiatric residency program at Ruzbeh Hospital (in 1998).

As elsewhere in the world, Iranian psychiatry is split between the so-called dynamic (psychodynamic, psychoanalytic, and psychosocial) and so-called biomedical (neuro-centered and psychopharmacological) approaches. The latter has become dominant in Iran, but the former has retained strength and is recognized by the medical community; it promises approaches that connect social, cultural, and political-economic contexts with clinical ones. But from a comparative perspective, Iranian psychiatry has a distinctive feature: unlike in the United States, biomedical approaches have been dominant in Iran since the first French-trained neurologists and neuropsychiatrists set up facilities in the 1930s. This dominance took on a more "evidence-based" ideology in the 1990s as the efficacy of psychopharmaceuticals became more widely accepted. This modern psychiatry, however, had its roots in prior institutional and cultural histories of mental illness in the early twentieth century.

Let's rewind.

From Madhouse to Ruzbeh

While rapid modernization under Reza Shah Pahlavi (1878–1944) involved hospitals, orphanages, theaters, opera houses, and art academies in the early twentieth century, the affairs of the mentally ill remained ignored. In nineteenth-century Iran, before the birth of modern psychiatry and not unlike in Europe, the mental asylum was understood as a place of confinement for those engaging in dangerous behavior, often together with the poor and the homeless. Like many hospitals and poor houses, asylums had been funded by a charity endowment system called *vaqf*. More recently, asylums were mostly located in the suburbs or outskirts of cities, including Tehran, Shiraz, Isfahan, and Hamadan.[14] They were often managed by municipalities under poor conditions, and accommodated a range of poor, criminal, mad, mentally impaired, and handicapped individuals (e.g., those with cerebral palsy). In his novel *Dārolmajānin* (a Persianized Arabic term meaning madhouse), novelist Ali Akbar Jamalzadeh tells the story of Hedāyatollāh-khān, an asylum inmate tricked and betrayed by his own family and friends into a life of misery.[15] The novel is interesting not only for its depiction of the asylum, but also for putting an intellectual at its center. Hedāyatollāh-khān, whose character (and name) conspicuously echo those of Iranian writer and intellectual Sādegh Hedāyat (1903–1951), represents society's conscience, poking fun at the absurdity of authoritarianism and ignorance while challenging the boundaries of sanity.[16] The novel becomes a social commentary staged in the microcosm of a *dārolmajānin*, meant to represent a country on the cusp of broaching boundaries to embody new modes of thinking, while pushing the boundaries of madness.

Such cultural images of the psychiatric patient are historically shaped around the language forms and systems of knowledge that define him.[17] These forms, in Persian, carry a range of both stigmatizing and valorizing associations; the terms *divāneh* (mad) and *majnun* (a Persianized Arabic term meaning mad; also the name of archetypal Iranian "Romeo") have encompassed a range of Iranian behavioral and literary language games and ways of understanding. The *dārolmajānin* (asylum), then, can be seen as a space of differentiation associated with insanity and the need for care.[18] But various novels, memoirs, and oral accounts suggest inconsistency and a lack of discipline within the madhouse. The madness was more important than the house.

Elsewhere in Iranian literature, Hossein Reza'i's memoir echoes many portraits of Tehran in the early years of the twentieth century, in which madmen are described as homeless wanderers who are usually kept to the confines of a particular neighborhood, named by the residents, and subject to their mercy and charity or to their bullying.[19] Reza'i reports that, following a couple of violent incidents and murders, the young Reza Shah administration decided to accommodate madmen in a medical hospital, Tehran Hospital in Akbarābād, also known as Timārestān (asylum), under the direction of Loghmanossoltan Pezeshkian. A graduate of Dārolfonun, where medical training had been underway since 1851, Pezeshkian accepted the position out of charity.[20] The turnover of directors at the Timārestān reflected several feuds over management corruption and incompetence.[21] This hospital later dissolved; parts of it were absorbed, under the directorship of Abdolhossein Mirsepāssi, into a municipal-owned *Polyklinik* (a Persianized French term, *polyclinique*), which was renamed Ruzbeh Hospital in 1946. The remainders of Timārestān were transferred to Ray, a suburb south of Tehran, and renamed Rāzi Mental Hospital, after the Ray-born physician and scientist Rāzi (865–925 AD), known in the West as Rhazes.

Iran's first resident specializing in psychiatry, Haratoun Dāvidiān (1924–2009), recalled visiting as a medical student in the 1940s: the Timārestān, he contended, was still a dismal place, filled with the sounds of screaming and cursing, with a few white-coated doctors and many catatonic and melancholic patients.[22] Later on, he reports, the management attracted a variety of scientific, cultural, and public policy interests to Ruzbeh and other, later, teaching hospitals. Ruzbeh's two founders, Mirsepāssi (1907–1976) and Reza'i (1904–1993), secured funding, improved sanitation, and aimed to build a modern psychiatric hospital (see Figure 2).

Mirsepāssi played a significant role in transforming Ruzbeh. A former disciple of one of Joseph Babinski's students in France, he was influenced by Jean-Martin Charcot, Jean Piaget, and Pierre Janet, but he followed Babinski in believing in the power of suggestion and will.[23] Most significantly, he brought with him the French preoccupation with criminal law and heredity, and he played an important role in shaping the field of forensic psychiatry by incorporating toxicology, hematology, and chemistry into the landscape of crime and psychiatry. In 1951, Mirsepāssi coined the term *ravānpezeshki* (*ravān*, "psyche," *pezeshki*, "medicine"), and wrote the first Persian textbook of psychiatry, eponymously titled *Ravānpezeshki*. The founder of the first scientific journal of

FIGURE 2: Ruzbeh Hospital and the Training and Research Center at Ruzbeh, in the buzzing heart of Tehran. 2015. Photo by Kousha Ghorbani.

psychiatry, *Majalleh-ye Elmi-ye Ravānpezeshki* (1953), Mirsepāssi also authored a book on madness and law and translated relevant texts from French. His commitment to hereditary theories was coupled with his interest in the social contexts of crime. He also created the first ECT-like device, called a *dastgāh-e ghash-sāz*, or *dastgāh-e ghash-angiz*, or convulsion-inducer machine. During World War II, at the peak of ECT's popularity in the West, Iran struggled with importing machines. After the war, Reza'i and Chehrāzi bought ECT equipment from abroad, which they started using at Ruzbeh. But Mirsepāssi is famous for having made a patriotic point by building his machine by hand and giving it a Persian name.[24] Mirsepāssi's legacy remains wrapped in patriotic mythologies that grew even after he retired from the University of Tehran in 1969.[25]

In 1953, Ruzbeh received a site visit from the World Health Organization, which named it "the best psychiatric facility in the region."[26] The Iranian Psychiatric Association (IPA), however, was founded long after the establishment of psychiatric wards and hospitals, in 1966, and has since been a member of the World Psychiatric Association. In the 1970s, the Ministry of Health and Welfare began professional training in psychiatric nursing and introduced a comprehensive mental health care system including the rehabilitation of the disabled and the mentally ill. Modernizing campaigns for a healthy society, however, had begun much earlier, and shaped the core of psychiatry's pedagogical development.

Modernizing Crusaders and the Neuro Turn

The cultural capital and status of doctoring in Iranian politics present a point of historical continuity. Medicine has a long history of interrelations with politics, stretching back as early as *hakim-vazir* (doctor-viziers), who played an instrumental role in courts (including the father of early modern medicine, Avicenna [980–1037 AD]), and more recently, seen in a century-long intersection with nation-building and modern politics during the twentieth century. From the infiltration of clinical rhetoric in politics to doctors' active participation in national politics by holding government positions, doctor-politicians occupy a central place in the Iranian scientific and political imagination. Their language has always been a form of cultural capital, contributing to the shared desires and readiness of the cultural middle class to appropriate a psychiatric language in the late twentieth century. But more significantly, doctors were among key players in the modernization efforts of the early twentieth century.

Historian Cyrus Schayegh has shown that "modern Iranian society" after the 1910s relied on a rising "modernist" middle class educated in France and caught between traditional morals and a progressive ethos.[27] The first generation of psychiatrist returnees among them championed science as the path to modernizing Iran. As technocratic nationalists, they translated their scientific mindset and pragmatism into shifts in public policy: upon returning to Iran, Mirsepássi, Reza'i, and Chehrázi actively fought alcohol and opium addiction, improved living conditions in psychiatric hospitals, and drafted public health policies and national agendas for raising literacy rates. But they were caught in a quasi-colonial impasse: on the one hand promoting Western science and models of development and, on the other, claiming that the roots of Western science lay in *their* pre-Islamic, "authentic" history. The modernists applied Western science in the context of social problems, but also endeavored to contextualize those problems and concerns in local terms.[28] Theirs was a social reform mindset stressing education as both an individual goal and a goal for the good of the nation.[29]

There are striking continuities and departures in this history. Indeed, the clinical idioms modernizing professionals used for describing the maladies of society were already in place in the languages that developed during the Constitutional Revolution (1905–1911) and manifested in metaphors such as *jáme'eh dar tab-e jahl misuzad* (society burning in the fever of ignorance) and *jáme'eh dar bestar-e marg dar entezár-e nushdáru-ye tajaddod* (society on its deathbed waiting for the remedy of modernity). Part of such maladies was "mental," thus a new neuropsychiatric terminology started to infiltrate politics. In the teachings of Chehrázi and his peers, the mobilization of that language was sanctioned by nationalist agendas, not unlike how the clinico-engineering language of the Islamic Republic addressed mental health almost a hundred years later. There is one important difference though: the earlier modernist class of professionals could vocally emphasize and contextualize the maladies of society. For doctors in the 1980s, this was less possible; it could be seen as criticism, a turn that had already happened some twenty years earlier: Leftist writer and psychiatrist Gholámhossein Sá'edi mentions in his autobiographical essay *Sá'edi in Sá'edi's Voice* that during his residency at Ruzbeh Hospital in the 1960s he had tried to convince others that depression was not "solely the outcome of chemical imbalances in the brain" and to show that external social factors mattered in treatment. Eventually, he was imprisoned: "They thought I was advocating the [Tudeh] Communist Party's ideology. But I was just trying not to see things in only 'biochemical' terms."[30] However, what Sá'edi sees as a political intervention by the state was in fact also largely rooted in psychiatry's own prejudice and its history of privileging the brain.

Strikingly, since its inception, the hospital's pedagogy was characterized by the distinction made between *mental* and *nervous* diseases,[31] as reflected in the first curriculum for teaching theoretical courses in psychiatry in the medical school of Tehran University in 1937–1938. Psychiatric training was underway before Ruzbeh Hospital was founded, but in 1939, after the appointment of the French professor Charles Oberlin as the dean of the School of Medical Sciences (1939–1947), the core of today's medical curriculum was formed. In a six-year training period, including clinical internship, fifth-year medical students would read "mental illnesses" (*bimārihā-ye aghli*, or *amrāz-e demāghi*) and "nerves illnesses" (*bimārihā-ye a'sāb*, or *bimārihā-ye maghz va pay*, or *amrāz-e a'sāb*) in separate courses.

Nerve/brain illnesses were to be taught in the Neurology Faculty, founded by another French-trained returnee, Ebrāhim Chehrāzi (1908–2010).[32] Son of a doctor of traditional medicine (*hakim*) and raised in a middle-class family, the first teacher of "nerve diseases," Ebrāhim Chehrāzi was among the first ninety-eight students sent to France by Reza Shah on government scholarships.[33] Upon graduating from Dārolfonun, he went to Paris in 1929 and finished his training in neurology and medical pathology in 1936.[34] His strong neuropsychiatric and anti-psychoanalytic orientation is reflective of dominant trends in French psychiatry at the time. Upon his return, he served as a resident physician in the army hospital, where, according to his memoir, he gained insight into the ills of society.[35]

In 1937, at the time when Timārestān was in poor shape, struggling with bureaucracy and unsanitary conditions and fighting for volunteer nurses and psychiatric medication, Chehrāzi started training medical students in a small neurology ward in what later became Rāzi Hospital. In 1940, he was appointed the first Professor of Neurology and Diseases of the Brain and Nerves. The neurology ward was later transferred to Ruzbeh Hospital, and then again to the *Hezār Takhtekhābi* (1,000-bed) Hospital (later called Pahlavi, now Imam Khomeini Hospital). In 1941, he published the first Persian textbook on neural diseases. A close reading of his Persian neurology textbook reveals an emphatic tone and belief in the brain as the locus of personhood. Around the same time, the first ward of neurosurgery was established in Tehran's Firouzabadi Hospital, in 1946, and was later transferred to Pahlavi Hospital (formerly *Hezār Takhtekhābi*), joining the Department of Neurology. By 1951, the ward was equipped with the latest technologies of the time, including electroencephalography (EEG). Neurology enjoyed rapid advancement, but it would take another decade for psychiatry to be seen as a formal discipline. "The fate of the neurology patients," recalls Dāvidiān in his memoir, "was brighter and more promising during the early years of psychiatric training." Indeed, Chehrāzi's faith in neuropathology, neurophysiology, neuroanatomy, EEG, and neurosurgery was part of larger ideologies defining the orientation of modern medicine and public policy.

His was a generation of scientific, Francophile, can-do modernizers who returned to Iran with a mission beyond medical work. Promoting health, they believed, was part and parcel of the solution to the poverty, addiction, infection, and illiteracy that afflicted society. Chehrāzi called for attention to "cultural development"—educating people about scientific and modern advancements. In 1943, in the aftermath of foreign occupations during the Second World War, he founded the Association for Fighting Alcohol and Opium, while also running the magazine *Salāmat-e Fekr* (Healthy Thinking), which was published for two decades. His integral approach and his international mobility (representing Iran in the International Federation of Mental Health in London in 1948, for instance) further empowered Chehrāzi to become a crusader against "backwardness." Having written the first Persian textbook of neural diseases, he also left a huge impact on psychiatry as a discipline in the making.

Meanwhile, the first teacher of *mental* illnesses was Ghāsem Ghani (1893–1952), who was appointed Professor of Mental Illness in the Medical School and Professor of Psychology in the Theology Faculty of Tehran University.[36] A graduate of Dārolfonun, Ghani studied medicine at St. Joseph College in Beirut, but remains best known as a literary figure (for instance, recognized for having edited, with Mohammad Qazvini, the most accurate collection of Hāfez's poems). Fluent in Arabic, French, and English, he held various positions, from heading the Ministry of Culture to sitting on the Board of the Anthropological Institute and being a member of the Academy of Culture. Later, he was an ambassador to Turkey and Egypt. Ghani's appointment and cultural trajectory reflect deeper epistemologies in which the foundation of psychiatry was situated. At the time when a Freudian transformation was underway in American psychiatry, the sharp distinction in Iran between teaching neural disorders by a man of anatomy and mental illnesses by a man of letters created a specific pedagogical trajectory and hierarchy of knowledge in Iranian psychiatry.

The dominance of neuro-brain-centered approaches in psychiatry's public and pedagogical agendas connects Iran's eras of psychiatry. This is a distinctive feature: unlike American or British psychiatry, psychiatry in Iran never accommodated a strong psychodynamic moment from which to depart toward neuropsychiatry. In other words, Iranian psychiatry never believed in anything but the brain. Almost.

Freud Comes to Tehran

From the outset, psychoanalysis was placed outside the purview of psychiatry.[37] Freud had been introduced to the public in at least two radio programs and a few translations before he was written about in 1951 by sociologist and literary critic Amir-Hossein Aryanpoor (1925–2001), who published *Freudianism*.[38] But Iran's first psychoanalyst was Mahmud Sanā'i (1918–1985), who was trained in London and became the chair of the Department of Literature and Humanities at Tehran University upon his return in 1955.[39] Sanā'i established the Institute of Psychology at Tehran University. He did not train many psychoanalysts, but his most important contributions to psychoanalysis were his translation of Freud's work on dreams and the formulation of an innovative psychoanalytic interpretation of conflicts in the Iranian epic *Book of Kings* (*Shāhnāmeh*) penned by Hakim Abolghāsem Ferdowsi (935–1025 AD). In an article, "Ferdowsi, Master of Tragedy," which grew out of a lecture he gave at Tehran University in 1967, he formulated the notion of a "Rostam complex," or son-killing in Iranian cultural psychology, which contrasted with Freud's Oedipus complex.[40] In his 2014 lecture "Psychoanalysis in Iran: Changing Sociocultural Context," Mohammad Sanati underscores Sanā'i's role in the establishment of an academic approach to psychoanalysis, even though by the 1970s he had returned to work as an analyst in London, where he lived until his death in 1985.

Discussion about the conscious and unconscious dynamics of political activity remained in the air, particularly in the aftermath of the 1951 nationalization of the oil industry and the 1953 coup d'état.[41] But in the 1960s, a more dramatic cultural conversation occurred indirectly around the figure of Carl Jung's archetypes and explorations of mystical and alchemical traditions of ancient wisdom. At issue here was an identity politics that struggled between an Islamic and an ancient Iranian (Zoroastrian) wisdom and authenticity. A resolution was forged in an Iranian school of philosophy, facilitated through Jung's notion of deep archetypes;[42] the key term was "return to self." Meanwhile in the 1960s, with the exception of a couple of good translations, there was little *academic* attention to Freud. Sanati argues that most readings of psychoanalysis at the time were either too politicized (Marxism-oriented) or mystical (Sufism-oriented).[43] At a time when the concept of *gharbzadegi* (Westoxification) was gaining purchase among intellectuals, many saw psychoanalysis as a manifestation of it.[44] Many of those who attacked Freud, including sociologist Ali Shari'ati (1933–1977), assimilated him into a broader popular attack on (American) commercialism that manipulated desire through the advertising of sexual images. Freud thus became associated in this rhetoric with notions of promiscuity and adultery.[45] And the return to Iran's authentic cultural self was a potent call in the 1970s, both politically and perhaps as a tool for psychological self-training.

Shari'ati's teachings had an undeniable impact on the fate of psychoanalysis. The Islamist-Marxist revolutionary orator remains a controversial figure in Iranian scholarship; regardless, he is considered an influential ideologue of the revolution.[46] Yet his impact on psychoanalysis and psychiatry has often been overlooked. Psychodynamic psychotherapist Mohammad Sanati has described Shari'ati's rhetoric as mystical, prevailing at the time among both the masses and intellectuals, not to mention psychiatrists.[47] According to Sanati, Shari'ati's ill-educated sentiments about Freud, and the West in general, were misplaced as he provoked his audiences against psychoanalysis by introducing a "distorted impression of Freud." His anticolonial sentiments were indeed a reflection of larger negotiations among Iranian intellectuals. Nevertheless, his straightforward formulation of Freud's teachings as the causes of corruption in the "bourgeois West" gained a life of its own.[48]

But psychoanalysis's doom was not single-handedly created by anticolonial sentiments; it is important to remember that hostility toward psychoanalysis was also situated in broader contexts including that of psychiatry itself.

Psychiatry Meets Psychoanalysis

Iranian psychiatry experimented with psychoanalysis at two points in the twentieth century. Psychoanalysis, although translated and discussed, remained outside the territory of medicine until, in the 1970s, a new generation of returnee psychiatrists from the United States brought with them the legacy of psychoanalysis, which was a dominant influence in American psychiatry at the time. However, with a few exceptions, these doctors enjoyed little influence on academic training at Ruzbeh Hospital, the country's main center for psychiatric training. Most set up private practices, though some found places in psychiatry departments at the universities of Shiraz and Isfahan. Resistance at Ruzbeh contributed to the formation of a training center for "research and residency" programs, *Markaz-e Amuzeshi-ye Residency*, in the 1970s, under the purview of the Ministry of Health (as opposed to the Ministry of Science and Higher Education, which administered medical schools until they became a part of the Ministry of Health and Medical Education in 1985).[49] The center provided some training in dynamic methods, and pioneered the training of clinical psychologists (at both master's and Ph.D. levels) and psychiatric nurses. In 1980, it was renamed the Tehran Institute of Psychiatry and merged with the newly founded Iran University of Medical Sciences. The psychodynamic training program lasted only a few years, until the 1979 revolution, after which many of its leading members left Iran (or retired to private practice), and the Tehran Institute of Psychiatry increasingly abandoned psychodynamic methods and adopted the standardized training guidelines of medical schools. In 1996, it was recognized as the country's center for collaborations for mental health care with the World Health Organization, and, in 2001, the Ministry of Health recognized it as the "scientific, educational and research pole of psychiatry and psychology."

This short-lived and unofficial academic marriage of psychiatry and psychoanalysis can be seen as a precursor to psychiatry's second experiment with psychoanalysis: 1980s efforts to incorporate psychotherapy in the psychiatric residency program at Ruzbeh. But in the intervening years, the Cultural Revolution of 1980–1983 changed a few things.

The Cultural Revolution is often discussed in terms of the highly visible transformations that it brought to public spaces and to academia.[50] But more relevant to the story of academic psychiatry, psychology, and public health is the impact of the Cultural Revolution on medical pedagogies. At its outset, the Cultural Revolution embarked on the cleansing (*pāksāzi*) of academia. Universities had played a major role in the mobilization of the revolution; and now it was time to reform and remove the remainders of the past regime from their campuses. Universities were thus closed for almost three years, during which time a sizeable number of faculty members, including some of the psychiatrists who had pioneered psychodynamic training in the 1970s, either left or were dismissed. These changes in the makeup of medical faculties were situated, indeed, in broader cultural changes following the 1979 Revolution and the beginning of the Iran-Iraq War. The psychiatric mindset that emerged in public after the

1990s seemed like an afterthought for two forms of citizenship that were central to Iranian consciousness in the 1980s. One was formulated through the implementation of religious codes of conduct and a Shi'ite moral order in society.[51] The other, more relevant to medicine and not unlike during many other wars, evolved in the institutional formation of war-related categories of identification, such as martyrs (shahid), veterans (razmandeh), disabled veterans (jānbāz), returning POWs (āzādeh), and their respective wives, offspring, and other kin. A structure was meticulously crafted based on medical (including psychiatric) evaluations and compensatory calculations that, while legitimating rights and status, also defined responsibilities for those representing its moral values.[52]

Back on campuses, the Cultural Revolution had two goals. First was the project of reforming universities, both in terms of the implementation of Islamic codes of conduct and in the sense of affirmative-action admission for those demonstrating proper moral commitment.[53] Second was to transform academic curricula to reflect and suit the needs of an Islamic society. In these processes, the balance of power shifted back and forth between the poles of ta'ahhod (religious commitment) and takhassos (expertise and knowledge). Social sciences, humanities, and the arts were the first areas for reform, though other faculties were not exempt.[54] Indeed, none of the following changes occurred overnight. Many ebbed and flowed and remained contested. At the end of the day, many of the more technical faculties, including medicine, kept their teachings intact but saw, instead, their share of cleansing in the dismissal of faculty members who were deemed as lacking moral commitment or representing westernized and liberal values. This, for academic psychiatry, meant the reversal of the few nascent 1970s attempts for psychodynamic training in psychiatric residency.

The broader medical curriculum, however, remained largely unchanged, except that residency programs for gynecology became exclusive to women. Psychiatry, on the other hand, already located at the margins of medicine itself, was implicitly neglected early on, if not disdained, as either a bourgeois discipline or as inconsequential compared to other medical specialties. It eventually sustained, after a hiatus, as pragmatism prevailed in response to the immediacy of health matters, if not the return of war casualties and veterans and the increasing visibility of war traumas. Pedagogically speaking, psychiatry's teachings became increasingly biomedically and psychopharmacologically oriented during the 1980s (note that this timing also coincided with a different, global, reform in psychiatry worldwide and the consolidation of a biomedical turn via the DSM-III and the rise of Prozac in the United States).

The historically and scientifically (if not spiritually) elevated status of medicine at large served to exempt it from major *curricular* reform; although demographic shifts in the makeup of faculty members variably had an impact on pedagogy, as evident in the case of psychiatry. In the new era, medicine was also integral to the development of new public health priorities, particularly in rural areas. Doctors were needed more than ever before; and they reclaimed their place in the life of the society even more so during the war.[55] Within the conceptual frameworks of the Cultural Revolution too, it was asserted, *elm va dānesh* (science and knowledge) had been given priority in Islam; and medicine, historically seated high in the Iranian hierarchies of knowledge, went on to play a major role in several public health initiatives that followed. It continued to flourish, though this varied across specialties; during the war, for instance, medical fields like orthopedic surgery, general surgery, and ophthalmology made significant advances.[56] But psychiatry's fate was to unfold a decade later.

(Re)turning to the Brain

Psychiatry's prestige rose both within the medical community and in society at large in the 1990s, as a result of at least four factors: (1) a growing public awareness and discussion of dysfunction within families and the social fabric that emphasized anxiety disorders, and later depression, stemming from the Iran-Iraq War; (2) the use of a neuroscientific language as an explanatory and promotional tool for destigmatizing mental illness by psychiatrists in the media; (3) the return of several psychiatrists with the latest training from abroad and their participation in public media; and later, (4) the professionalization of child psychiatry and the emergence of ADHD as an illness category among children and the popularization of Ritalin. In particular, the ascendance of ADHD's diagnostic terrain helped mark the evolution of a new identity for psychiatry among medical disciplines and the wider public.[57]

Initially, postrevolution mental health policy was based on institutional care and the use of trained professionals in urban settings. In 1986, a National Mental Health Program (NMHP) was drafted by a multidisciplinary team of professionals and approved by the government, with the goal of incorporating mental health (especially in rural populations) into the national Primary Health Care (PHC) program.[58] This approach was part of a major reorganization of primary health care that included village-level initiatives carried out by village health workers. Most significant in the agenda of the NMHP was its call for media campaigns and raising public awareness about mental health, but it also called for mental health training for all health care personnel, a district-level mental health support system, and the recognition of a national mental health week.

The NMHP, which covered 21.7 percent of the urban population and 82.8 percent of the rural population, was officially launched in 1988 and helped revive the status of psychiatry.[59] In 1989, it was implemented as a successful pilot program in rural areas, with the aim of improving the quality of service delivery and public education about child mental health, drug use, and mental health and natural disasters; and in 1995, it was evaluated by WHO and the Tehran Institute of Psychiatry and recognized as one of the best programs in the region.[60] The program defined the hierarchal pyramid of the mental health referral system, with the *behvarz* (local health worker) at its base. Locals in urban and rural areas were trained to detect and refer the mentally ill and to pay home visits to the chronically ill.[61] Simultaneously, an unprecedented step was taken: the establishment of psychiatric wards in general hospitals, which increased the visibility of psychiatry.[62] Meanwhile, psychiatric and psychological research was widely popularized.[63] Today, a growing number of psychiatric training departments and psychiatric hospitals train psychiatrists.[64] The 1980s development of the NMHP and the integration of mental health into primary health care marked a successful reform in mental health care policy.

The media-based psychiatric turn of the 1990s was indeed born of these seeds. Doctors often speculate proudly that society's attitudes about psychiatric care have changed, pointing out that people are seeking help more from doctors than from traditional healers.[65] This seems to be a sign of success in raising awareness, an outcome of the medical community's destigmatizing campaigns, themselves situated in postrevolutionary nation-building and identity politics, as well as in larger political discourses that made the psychiatric turn possible. But they were also facilitated by a demographic change among psychiatrists. The returnees of the 1980s, primarily trained in the UK, brought new prestige to their field and introduced new, dynamic approaches in academic psychiatry. Through appearances on public television and radio, they provided a new language for laypeople to articulate psychological struggles, thereby contributing to the emergence of a public psychiatric discourse. Later, in the 1990s, another influential return, this time from the United States, with an emphatically biomedical orientation, resulted in the establishment of the first board-certified subspecialty in psychiatry for child and adolescent psychiatry. Gradually, more and more top-grade graduates entered residency programs in psychiatry, particularly at Ruzbeh. A fresh wave of self-esteem contributed to the recovery of psychiatry's image and its professional identity.

In the 1990s, the growing media visibility of psychiatrists, along with the popularization of two diagnostic categories, depression and ADHD, coincided with two reinforced and modernized, but countervailing, traditions of psychiatry: a biomedical-neuroscientific approach to childhood psychiatry, and a psychodynamic psychotherapeutic one integrated with both psychopharmacology and social medicine (or, at least, an acknowledgment of social causes of stress and mental health problems). This widespread attention to mental health also followed profound changes in the texture of everyday life after the war. The reshaping of psychiatry and the psychiatrization of daily life reflect, in part, the collaboration between history and medicine in creating a new public discourse.[66] This convergence was simultaneously a force behind the psychiatrization of social dysphoria and a response to historical conditions, while coinciding with two pedagogical milestones in academic psychiatry.

Introducing Dynamic Psychotherapy into Psychiatric Residency

Psychodynamic approaches have struggled, but survived, in academic psychiatry.[67] Unlike medication, psychotherapy promises longer-term retraining of behavioral and affective patterns, as well as engagements with broader discourses in society. But it first had to find its way back into academic psychiatry. The post-1990 revival of psychodynamics within psychiatry is intertwined with the career of psychiatrist and psychodynamic psychotherapist Mohammad Sanati (b. 1945).[68] Sanati returned to Iran from the UK in 1985, five years into the Iran-Iraq War and two years after the reopening of universities. By then, the visibility of war trauma was already calling for the attention of academic psychiatry, which, by now, had become less welcoming to psychoanalytically oriented psychiatrists who had worked in places such as the Tehran Institute of Psychiatry. This resistance to dynamic approaches was in part a reflection of global trends; American psychiatry too was undergoing a biological turn in the 1980s. The demand for psychiatric medication had also increased among people who, affected by the war and economic austerity, did not have the luxury of psychotherapy (particularly in 1984 and 1987, during the two intensive periods of missile attacks on Iran's major cities).

Sanati was among the first psychiatrists to appear on radio and television shows in the 1980s. He navigated media politics by using a sanitized clinical language, but also began to popularize psychodynamic interpretations in his analyses of well-known Persian literary works. Informally, he trained psychiatry residents in psychoanalysis at his home. Adamant in pursuing every available venue to promote dynamic psychotherapy, Sanati's main goal was to incorporate psychoanalysis into academic psychiatry. He was—and still is—insistent that psychoanalytical teachings should be brought under the umbrella of psychiatry. However, he worked toward a psychiatry that would not be medicalized American style with cognitive behavioral therapy (CBT) as a dominant approach, nor French style, where dynamic therapies and medicine were kept apart. In other words, he did not pose psychotherapy as a replacement for medication, but advocated a combination of medication and dynamic therapy.

Sanati found an eager audience among the residents of Ruzbeh Hospital. Perhaps a few words on the current structure of medical training are necessary. Although it is structured as a direct doctorate program (seven to eight years, starting immediately after high school), the current Iranian medical educational system is modeled after the American system and its content is mainly adopted from American textbooks. It includes a course on general psychology in the first two years, a course on psychiatry, a one-month clerkship rotation of psychiatry in the fourth year of medical school, and a psychiatric rotation during clinical internship in the final year. Like other residency programs, admission to psychiatric residency programs is based upon an annual national competition.[69] Lectures and courses on psychiatry follow reference textbooks such as Kaplan and Sadock's *Synopsis of Psychiatry, Comprehensive Textbook of Psychiatry*, and *New Oxford Textbook of Psychiatry*. American and British medical journals, as well as Persian psychiatric journals, are widely discussed during training.[70] Sanati's informal training was a welcome addition to this structure for interested residents.

By 1999, Sanati was teaching residents dynamic psychotherapy at his home, was a leader in CBT for chronic pain management, and had pioneered gender-segregated group therapy in Iran. But the most important contribution of his team to academic psychiatry came in 1996, when a new curriculum was designed for teaching dynamic psychotherapy to psychiatry residents. The grander ambition was to establish a fellowship and a degree program in dynamic psychotherapy; but change had to occur in incremental steps; first the creation of a small team (which included psychiatrist Mahdieh Moin) and the 1998 establishment of the analytical psychotherapy unit at Ruzbeh introduced a nine-month training program for residents. A long bureaucratic process then led to the 2006 formation and the 2008 national implementation of a four-year residency curriculum that included nine months of dynamic psychotherapy training. This coincided with the 2006 official birth of the Dynamic Psychotherapy and Human Studies Unit at the University of Tehran, whose aim was the creation of a fellowship in analytical psychotherapy. The fellowship struggled to materialize (in part due to several management shifts and internal contestations), but was eventually approved and launched in 2014. In the intervening years, Sanati's team established a practical training program in dynamic psychotherapy (including theory) for second- and third-year residents at Ruzbeh.[71] Today, several psychiatrists teach on the program and residents are required to complete a research project, participate in a rotation in neurology and a rotation in child psychiatry, and take part in psychotherapy training by the end of their residency.

This cornerstone in psychiatric training was not without opposition. Parallel to official reluctance to embrace psychoanalysis, the hierarchy within psychiatry, too, has used the argument of "scientific-ness" to put psychodynamic psychotherapy at the bottom of its pyramid. Psychiatrists' views on psychoanalysis vary; there is a spectrum of total approval (primarily among the few who practice it, as well as the younger generation of Ruzbeh trainees) to ambivalence, ignorance, or outright dismissal. I return to these debates in Chapter 7, but key here is the coincidence of this pedagogical moment with another one: the foundation of psychiatry's first subspecialty.

Child Psychiatry

Child psychiatry was for long an area of interest for many psychiatrists, most of whom were of the psychodynamic mindset, but it was hardly known to the public. ADHD, often diagnosed by pediatricians and adult psychiatrists, was still a professional's term in the 1990s and was only starting to make its way into "child expert" medical shows on television and the radio.[72] But as public discourses were transformed by psychiatrists using the media, ADHD became an important site for the socialization of psychiatric explanatory models for mental illness. The psychological residues of the war were being recognized in public discussions, and it naturally followed that children in families undergoing stress would also experience stress.

Although child psychiatry was officially established as a subspecialty in 1997, those more familiar with the Iranian psychiatric scene know well that it was psychiatrist Mohammad Vali Sahāmi (1944–2013) who, in the 1980s, brought child psychiatry into the consciousness of academic psychiatry, and that un-accredited child psychiatry wards were already active not only in Ruzbeh but also in a few other medical schools.[73] Trained in the UK, Sahāmi returned in 1991 and, through his presence in the media (along with his academic affiliation with Tehran University), he brought children's mental well-being (from a psychody-namic perspective) to the attention of the public.[74] But it took another decade for child psychiatry to become professionalized as psychiatry's first subspecialty, following a series of negotiations and contestations spearheaded by psychiatrist Javad Alāghband-Rād (b. 1964) and his colleagues. The founder and first chair of the Child and Adolescent Psychiatry Unit at Ruzbeh Hospital (1997–2007), Alāghband-Rād was trained at Ruzbeh (1989–1992) and the National Institute of Mental Health (NIMH) in the United States (1993–1996), bringing with him a passionate biomedical research focused mindset.[75] His return to Iran coincided with the first term of the reformist president Khātami (1997–2001), which brought a great deal of relative social liberties and facilitated academic exchange with the outside world. Upon his return, Alāghband-Rād mobilized these networks. With the approval of the Board of Child Psychiatry and its newly designed curriculum for a two-year fellowship, the first group of fellows was selected through a na-tional exam and began their training in 1998 in two accredited hospitals. Child psychiatry immediately attracted the top students from medical school classes. The advanced image of the field, along with the celebrity status of some of the regular psychiatrist commentators, helped.

There was now a "scientific" and "professional" authoritative language emerging. Psychiatry relied on the language of neuroscience, moving up the prestige ladder among other medical fields and distinguishing itself in its popularization of diag-nostics such as ADHD. Ruzbeh Hospital now seemed to host an array of talented, highly motivated, and research-minded young doctors, with a visibly growing number of female residents. In 2005, a second child psychiatry board was founded and approved at Isfahan University's Medical School. The first few rounds of child psychiatry fellows later established their own practices and began teaching in other major cities (often, where they had to serve their mandatory public service after graduation). Child psychiatry traveled to Mashad, Shiraz, Ilām, Shahr-e Kurd, Sāri, Tabriz, and other cities, and unaccredited spinoff wards sprang up.[76] Today, dozens of child psychiatrists work in major medical universities around the country.

In 2001, the Iranian Association for Child and Adolescent Psychiatry (IACAP) was founded, independently from the Iranian Psychiatric Association (IPA). In 2002, it held its first international conference on child psychiatry. The foundation of IACAP was a landmark, increasing the visibility of child psychiatry, giving doctors freedom to organize successful conferences, and inviting international guests from the United States. IACAP's visibility grew also through its publication of books, its newsletter, and its workshops for both experts and the public. Many ups and downs followed. But the professionalization and biomedicalization of child psychiatry was another pedagogical milestone in the history of Iranian psychiatry, one that consolidated a biomedical ethos that reflected a firm belief in the merits of cutting-edge laboratory-based research, presumably value-neutral scientific progress, and universal standards of behavior. As the founding fathers of psychiatry had once dreamed, child psychiatry put Ruzbeh at the heart of global trends in genetic and clinical psychiatric research. I shall return to Ruzbeh again, in Chapter 7, to elaborate on this legacy.

.   .   .

The professional and academic trajectory of psychiatry has indeed played an important role in the development of everyday discourses of mental health and the psychiatric turn that began in the 1990s. But it was the "public" life of psychiatry that shaped new language forms and categories of experience among laypeople. How did academic psychiatry enter the public domain? In the next chapter, I trace this public emergence through a series of interrelated frames and scenes.

The Counselor

Fast forward four decades from Ali Shari'ati's famous lecture on Freud. Sit at your computer and type in moshavere.org. You are now looking at the Center for Counseling and Guidance at the Imam Khomeini Institute of Research and Education at the Qom Seminary (*Hozeh-ye Elmiyeh*). Under the green and red logo, the introduction to psychological well-being reads,

> There is a new trend among contemporary psychologists and psychotherapists that focuses on the importance of social and human aspects of psychological illnesses. They consider religion a protective factor that balances personality and contributes to one's patience and endurance in the face of life's hardships. The Quran has taught us that faith, unconditional faith, protects the soul. When one has faith, one doesn't fear anything or anyone other than Almighty God. One will need very little from others. One will feel stronger. One of the cures the Quran recommends for tackling psychological disorders is connecting with other believers. Many psychotherapists have testified to the significance of human connections for one's mental health.

The piece then takes a more diagnostic and clinical turn, and a large section on psychiatric disorders follows. In "treatment of *afsordegi*" (depression), we read:

> In treating depression, many psychologists agree that a combination of psychotherapy and medication works best. But what has created a revolution in treatment of depression over the past forty years is the advent of medications such as those listed below.[1]

As I scroll down the comprehensive list of antidepressants and reach the section on the family of SSRI antidepressants, I am distracted by the inviting titles in the side menu. I click on one, *Āzmāyeshgāh-e Ravānshenāsi* (Psychology Lab), that takes me to a whole new range of articles on psychiatric disorders and introduces such topics as depression, anxiety, stress, marriage, creativity, and self-esteem. Under *depression*, we are introduced to the Beck Depression Inventory,[2] followed by a section titled "Depression and the Quran."

The website *Moshavere*, meaning "counseling," has published a series of bro-chures and pamphlets on depression. Reading through them feels like reading a psychiatry journal—perhaps not what some may expect from a "Center for Counseling and Guidance" based in the country's largest Shi'ite seminary, in the religious city of Qom. But today it is no longer a novelty to see young clergy ap-pear on Iranian television programs, revealing their fluency in clinical (and, at times, psychoanalytical) terminology in offering, say, marital or familial guid-ance. The openness of the clerical establishment to psychological discourses is both impressive and reflective of the broad reach of psychiatric discourses and languages.

Thirty years ago, clerical teaching would have been distinct from biomedical elaborations. Today, the article "Depression and the Quran" combines them in dis-cussions of personality and the soul. It calls on well-known verses such as, "The presence of the Almighty calms the heart," while also introducing antidepressants and closing with links to further articles on major depression, bipolar disorders type I and II, "30 signs of psychological cold (depression)," types of depression (including postpartum depression and seasonal affective disorders), treatments for depression, and antidepressant medications. The language of psychiatry—terms like "bipolar" or "depression"—would once have been an unimaginable part of the seminary's teachings. Today, the psychiatrically savvy clergy have eagerly joined a mental health campaign that educates, counsels, and keeps up with biomedical advances.

CHAPTER 3

An Emerging Psychiatric Discourse in Five Frames

T H I S   C H A P T E R uses five settings or frames—each set at a different angle—to make visible the emerging psychiatric discourse and clinical modes of talk that have found acceptability, popularity, and, at times, a kind of ordinary common sense status among Iranians. It begins with a popular public lecture series in which a psychiatrist educates the public about mental health. It then follows parallel destigmatizing efforts for raising awareness about mental health in order to trace the normalization of this clinical language in other related frames of legibility: educational efforts in the media, the circulation of epidemiological evidence and the public life of statistics, emerging health-related policy including destigmatizing attempts to medicalize suicide, and, finally, rates of medication prescription.

Psychiatry and Public Education

A pair of eyes stare out intently from a poster advertising a public lecture series. Now in its sixth year, the series *Āyin-e Behtar Zistan* (Principles for Living a Better Life) has also been broadcast, recorded (available in a DVD series), and advertised on television. In the ads, soothing music and Tehran's skyline appear on screen; then we see Tehran's Milad Hospital and interior shots of a large lecture hall filling with people: "Every Friday. Milad Hospital's Lecture Hall," the narrator intones. The lecturer is Dr. M., a renowned psychiatrist and professor of psychiatry in Tehran.[1]

The auditorium is packed and beautified with colorful flowers, bright backdrops and banners with large letters, conspicuously signifying joyfulness and enjoyment, one of Dr. M.'s favorite English terms (from here on, I will underline terms that experts use in their original English form). This colorful mise-en-scène is radically different from earlier 1980s television programs. Dr. M. speaks softly and slowly in the voice of a teacher, a common characteristic among psychiatrists. He sprinkles his speech with English terms, illustrative stories, and psychological insights expressed in Persian poetry, and implements a rhetorical style that is akin to that of preachers. In a performative moment of establishing rapport, he jokes about his rather careful choice of words, using the English term psychopath instead of *lāt* (thug) for instance, referring to instructions as to what terms "I have been told to use. . . . I will now speak in a way that none of you will be able to understand!" The audience laughs. Instantly, a shared consensus is established based on the tacit knowledge that public speech and media representations must be carefully strategized.

Anxiety is today's topic. He begins:

> *Ezterāb* or anxiety is an experience that everyone is familiar with. It is a natural experience. It is not always an illness. What happens is that something happens in our synapses, and it alarms us that at this very moment, we should feel this way. What a beautiful system!
>
> . . . We have chemicals in our brain, neuro-adrenaline, serotonin, and others, and they go up and down. They work instantaneously. You feel change, physically or psychologically; it changes your mood. Your mood changes are nothing but changes at the cellular level.

An advocate of psychotherapy and psychodynamic methods in the 1990s, and still insisting that anxiety is not necessarily an "illness," Dr. M. is now speaking in the language of organic biomedical, neurological, and psychopharmacological approaches. The audience carefully take notes, and within the first few minutes, are engaged with anxiety at a "cellular" level:

> Different factors are at play for changes at the cellular level. One factor is the history recorded in our cells: all that we have lived, heard, said; all that we have lost, remembered. The other factors are the external ones: both of this moment, and historical. Neuroserotonins warn us that something has changed. Anxiety is an intra-cellular reaction to all internal and external stressors; and in my experience,

mostly internal stressors. External factors include stresses, anything that changes the intracellular balance. . . . This is the definition of life itself.

An anecdote about a patient who, uncommonly it seems, sought psychotherapy is compelling:

> Mood switching occurs due to changes inside our cells. A young male patient once asked me if his obsessions and anxiety had a remedy. I said, "Yes of course, we have tools. Talking alone is not enough. There is a better fix." And then I wrote him a prescription for Sertraline. Two months later, he came back. He was in a good mood, his thoughts under control. . . . Anxiety is an unpleasant feeling where we always anticipate bad events. Where is my husband? Will my child come home safe? What if I fail the exam? Multiple questions that we have about life. These biological changes are now better understood than before. . . . Anxieties are mostly genetic. We need to have the anxiety genes to become prone to anxiety. . . . They don't come only from parents, but also from ancestors and generations of genetic heritage. Our environment can turn these genes on. Sometimes you have four genes on, but the environment turns them into sixteen on genes. External stressors mostly work on the awake on genes.

In the talk's multiple forays into genetics, epigenetics, neuroscience, and real-life scenarios, one notices the translation of anxiety into a desocialized chemical problem. But to the Iranian ear, this language is not as sanitized as it intends to be. There are inferred interpretations about codes of speech: among environmental stressors, Dr. M. briefly suggests, "What you wear matters too. You keep wearing black. All you were told is to wear dignified colors. No one told you to wear black." In "you were told," Dr. M. refers to dress codes instituted and promulgated under the Islamic order in the 1980s. Today, the import of lifestyle and color is frequently peppered among psychological discussions in the media.

Aside from such indirect allusions, another common feature of programs like this is how experts work poetics into their neuro-talk as a powerful rhetorical tool and a way of creating cultural/emotional rapport. Sometimes, however, they sound confusing even to the Iranian ear. If the founding fathers of Iranian psychiatry had tried in the 1930s to separate illnesses into *ravāni* (of the psyche) and *ruhi* (of the soul), giving the former a location in the brain and leaving the latter to psychologists and philosophers, today Dr. M. brings them back together: "I like to use the term *jān* [meaning both "soul/being" and "dear"] instead of *ravān* [mind]. *Jān* is psyche. It implies a capacity for love. And anxiety is caused by both psyche and body. . . . You should get help from the *jān* doctor! [*Audience laughs*.] I wish we would call psychiatrists *doctor-jān*." The double entendre (*jān* meaning both "dear" and "soul/being") makes the audience giggle.

It is easy to dismiss strategic poetic turns as an Iranian mannerism. The poetic, however, serves as a navigation strategy for media representation, particularly when legitimizing speech or when trying to get the psychiatrist's message across to patients and audiences. The strategic operates in everyday Iranian life as well, but is heightened when navigating a professional and ideological terrain that is unwelcoming to psychosocial approaches while always in favor of biological and scientific explanations. It is used, intuitively, to create a bond in the monologue-based relationship between the psychiatrist and the public. Most psychiatrists know that society expects them to be the kind of physician who has "cultural" and "literary" interests and is well read in literature (and thus able to speak with the educated) and folklore (and thus able to speak with the uneducated). In these interactions, however, neither the lecturer/clinician nor the public is static.

Today, poetics are merged with neuro-talk; far from incompatible, they blend together seamlessly:

> Avicenna [the physician, philosopher, poet] was the first person who linked depression to the thyroid, and called it *ghambād* [literally, swelling as result of profound sadness]. The thyroid can either start or block anxiety. Glands are controlled by genes. . . . There is a very close relation between our psyche and our heart, and this is manifested when anxiety induces increased heart rate. In fact, most anxiety patients are referred to us by cardiologists.

Health, he reminds, is associated with a healthy heart and long life. The semantics of the heart in Iranian psychological discourse are both physiological and psychological, thus "the heart of what's the matter," as Byron Good put it in the 1970s.[2] But in addition to mobilizing semantics, drawing on a combination of American positive psychology and cognitive behavioral therapy, this mass education is also meant to facilitate "cultural change":

> My message for you is to be *shād* [happy, joyful]. There is no guarantee that tomorrow will come. Our mood changes our perceptions. Laughter can reduce our anxiety. It is an anti-anxiety drug.

This public message—to be *shād* (happy)—in the media would have been hard to imagine in the 1980s. In the late 1980s, the media were still imbued with a sense of gravitas and the Sacred Defense was still a fresh wound. It still is, to some extent. But today, Dr. M. talks about prevention: healthy relationships, happy marriages, a *kānun-e garm-e khānevadeh* (a warm and healthy homelife), for which one may need psychiatric and psychological help. He also creates a mélange of analytical explanations to promote pharmacological treatments.

Let me be explicit: If you are having anxiety for no reason, please treat yourselves: take tranquilizers. I do the same. If you have anxiety it always has a reason, like pregnancy, marriage, etc., remember that it is normal and temporary. But, I prefer that you do not even have that kind of anxiety. Before giving birth for instance, you can treat the anxiety with tranquilizers. You can become anxiety-free before an exam. Before an important meeting with a loved one. You can cut these unnecessary anxieties. Things have become so much easier in our discipline now. We can help you go to the exam, anxiety-free. Like most people in the world. . . .

. . . You always ask me whether exercise, prayers, alternative medicine, and things like that work; "anything but medication, doc," you say. This is a polite way of insulting me [*audience laughs*] because I am a doctor and it is my job to treat you with medicine, with *dāru-darmāni* [medication therapy].

The mixed use of English and Persian terms, and of biological and cultural references, is meant to illustrate how physiology manifests itself in interpersonal relationships among couples, individuals, and society at large. At times, the lecture sounds like physiology seminars in medical school, with interludes of Rumi and Omar Khayyam. The lecture is long and includes a classification of depression, explaining one by one seasonal affective disorders, bipolar mood disorders, and major clinical depression.

In the question-and-answer period, audience members ask about the prevalence of depression in university dormitories, among the unemployed and the retired, thereby bringing the talk back to practical matters of everyday life. The audience reveals an impressive knowledge of symptomatologies and treatment options in their questions. By the end of the program, it seems not only had mutual rapport been successfully established, but also education en masse has reached a point of spectacular prominence, paralleling clerical teaching traditions of giving sermons. Dr. M. ends the session by announcing the contact number of his institute, in case people wish to get help.

The broadcast of Dr. M.'s "Anxiety" lecture serves as an exemplary manifestation of the ways in which the Iranian public has been and continues to be educated about mental health. It reflects a shift to a seemingly direct psychiatric discourse, albeit still marked by strategic modes and politics of performativity. It contributes to the very cultural change that it reflects, highlighting the dramatic turn from a revolutionary attitude toward psychiatry (culminated in the 1980–1983 Cultural Revolution) toward the pragmatic and explicit appropriation of its conceptual and linguistic possibilities. This postwar change was in part an inevitable and legitimate response, championed by practitioners and policymakers alike, to a perceived public health problem. Psychiatrists were indeed only one among a wide range of professional groups (such as the clergy, psychologists, policymakers, and academics) that shaped the media representations of what was perceived as a potential concern for *salāmat-e ravāni* (mental health).

Almost twenty years after the first mental health talk shows began to air on national television, Dr. M.'s public lecture marks continuities and departures in content and tonality: while presentational modes, manifest in stage design and the occasional acknowledgment of the social roots of collective dysphoria, have slightly changed over time, the core educational message remains centered on ridding society of illnesses of *jān* (the psyche) by way of biomedical intervention upon the working of the brain. "Over the past thirty years," Dr. M. tells the audience, "it has been my aim to provide people with purely scientific information. There is a lot of misinformation about mental health. I know that our lives are not perfect. My aim is to provide us with better choices, enjoyment, and pleasure. . . . I want to help you live a better life."

Psychiatrists have joined a mass education campaign that is culturally situated and widely embraced by society. The broadcast of *Āyin-e Behtar Zistan* brings out the interrelations between, and the merging of, different pedagogical orientations (and tensions) within the field of psychiatry. It also provides a point of entry into the complex and overlapping spheres of the public, the private, the psychological, and the educational. Above all, it highlights how the traditional roles of clergymen and physicians can reverse: the clergy can now medicalize (as manifest in the frequent incorporation of medical knowledge into clerical teachings), while the physician masters the art of the sermon. It is tempting to imagine Ali Shari'ati's response to this mass education. Would he too, by now, have mobilized psychiatric concepts in his teachings?

The Media, Medicine, and Destigmatizing Signs and Symptoms

Mental health talk shows began broadcasting toward the end of the Iran-Iraq War in the late 1980s, when PTSD and anxiety disorders had started to make their way into the public's consciousness. Newspaper columns and magazine features followed, either in the form of questions posed by the public to experts or practitioners writing short, accessible pieces on mental health topics. The early television and radio shows attracted call-ins from both urban and rural people, sharing symptoms, seeking advice, and finding relief in knowing that one's experiences were not idiosyncratic, nor simply a failure of will, faith, or character. The couching of psychological symptoms of trauma and depression as biological and treatable conditions worked to destigmatize mental distress and psychiatry at once.

The first figures to venture into radio and television on these topics were psychologists. Many Iranians remember psychologists Gholām-Ali Afruz and Simā Ferdowsi on lunchtime family talk shows aired after the noon call to prayer, focusing on creating a healthy family and society. They began to use a language that melded religious phrasing with the flavor of psychological terms, gradually normalizing the notion of counseling. Shortly after, psychiatrists joined in. When the media began to reach out to psychiatrists to appear on talk shows, many initially regarded the idea as below their status. However, it was not long before many recognized the potential for an educational campaign and joined the circle of psychiatric commentary on television and radio. Entering the landscape of already popular medical and (physical) health related programs, they began to stress a more biological and bodily interpretation of mental illness, addressing symptoms of mental illness and educating the public about when and where to seek help.[3]

During the 1990s, talk shows shifted their focus from PTSD and anxiety disorders to depression. Toward the end of the decade, child psychiatrists joined in, and a new discourse of ADHD emerged in conjunction with the professionalization of the field of child psychiatry (in 1997). This involved an increasingly biomedicalized discourse of mental health, introducing the brain as the site of illness and departing from what was previously perceived as mental anguish. Meanwhile, newspaper columns on mental health related topics grew, and popular health-oriented publications such as the weekly newspaper *Salāmat* (Health) and the magazine *DARD* (*dard* means pain, but in Persian *DARD* is also an acronym for "on the road to medical knowledge") emerged and gained audiences alongside newspaper columns and talk shows. Some dedicated regular sections to mental health; gradually it became normal to come across headlines such as "Depression among women four times more prevalent than normal" or "13 to 15 percent of people in society are depressed," often followed by a brief report citing this or that survey, or more commonly, quoting psychiatrists or relevant officials.[4] These were sometimes paralleled with question-and-answer columns where psychiatrists, often university professors, answered readers' queries.

Media presence provided a new opportunity for psychiatry, as a discipline, to be claimed in a specifically Iranian context. The psychiatry that evolved in the public imagination via a carefully composed media representation was legitimated primarily through organic explanations of the brain and the nervous system (as opposed to psychodynamics). Emerging in unexpected ways and places, this discourse was welcomed by policymakers and the medical community at large. Psychologists and psychiatrists who participated in the talk shows navigated through the maze of permissible and inadvisable language. But they were not too dismayed; a biological language served to destigmatize psychiatry itself, freeing it from the status anxiety provoked by other branches of medicine: one was advised to stay away from psychoanalytical discussions, and instead to focus on *scientific*, bodily, individual, and organic causes. By the same token, public advocacy of psychiatric medication (primarily tranquilizers and antidepressants) signaled scientific progress and pragmatism.

Indeed, this psychiatric turn was also the call of the times. The health impact of the Iran-Iraq War was becoming palpable. By the late 1980s and early 1990s, the war had left behind countless physical and psychological injuries, displaced several families, and changed the internal dynamics of many others; international sanctions had already left a mark on the economy; and dysphoria, psychiatrists reported, was creeping under the skin of society alongside physical injuries.[5] According to many practitioners, the most common psychiatric diagnoses during the war were anxiety disorders and PTSD; it was only after the war that depression and depressive mood disorders made an appearance in their practices. The Sacred Defense against the atrocities of Saddam Hussein, including his brutal use of chemical and nonchemical weapons on civilians, had united Iranians of all political persuasions; doctors report that solidarity, conviction, and faith demarcated the psychological landscape of the 1980s. Now, in the 1990s, they believe, society came to experience a postwar condition in psychiatric as well as in Durkheimian terms; and psychiatrists were the first to detect its signs and symptoms. While nationalistic and religious sentiments continued to lead the official discourse of a sacred defense, there was now a genuine need to talk about the adverse health effects of the war, and the most legitimate and useful language for that seemed to be a clinical one. Even psychodynamically oriented psychiatrists adopted it in their media appearances: "PTSD, anxiety, signs, symptoms, these were the key words: If you have this and that symptom, it is called this, so you should go get help."[6]

The very idea of media mental health shows was new to the Iranian public, whose experience with the state-run media in the preceding few years had primarily been war-related. Now they were learning a new vocabulary that was compatible with the Karbala paradigm, Shi'ite ethos, and the Sacred Defense against the brutality of Saddam Hussein's invasion and the superpowers that supported him. Gradually, doctors, like clergymen, became public speakers and spoke the unspoken, even though in a strikingly medical language. To many psychiatrists, this was the beginning of a never-ending educational campaign to raise awareness about mental health. To the Iranian people, this was a voice of relief and recognition of suffering that was previously not named. It allowed them to feel whatever it was they were feeling without guilt or shame.

Gradually, studios were flooded with phone calls from rural and urban areas, people of all ages, and particularly women, whose battle was no easier than that of the men at the front. One of the first psychiatrists who appeared on these shows, Mohammad Sanati, remembers a call from an elderly lady in a village in the vicinity of Shiraz:

> She said she heard my program on the radio. And she was almost crying when she said, "For long, I have had all the symptoms you mentioned. . . . I always thought it was normal; now I realize I am ill. And I can do something about it. You changed my life, Doctor!"[7]

This was still before policymakers began to discuss issues of *āsib-e ruhi* (psychological distress/pathology) and *āsib-e ejtemā'i* (social pathology) in the media. That discussion and terminology followed in the 1990s, when epidemiological evidence began to emerge for an impending mental health crisis that required public health interventions. Gradually, it became more common to publicly refer to emotions, anxieties, and interpersonal troubles as *zakhm* (physical wound or injury, lesion), *āsib* (psychological as well as physical injury or pathology), *nārāhati* (distress, nerves), *afsordegi* (depression), *toromā* (trauma), *esteress* (stress), *zarbeh-ye ruhi*, *āsib-e ruhi*, or *sadameh-ye ruhi* (psychological trauma). Today, mental distress is articulated with a range of explanatory terms on a continuum from clinical depression and PTSD, or diseases of the brain (*bimārihā-ye maghz*, *amrāz-e a'sāb*) or of the mind (*bimārihā-ye ravāni*), to an archive of philosophical and poetic expressions of melancholy as diseases of the soul (*amrāz-e ruhi*).[8]

This is not to say the media presented a uniform approach, but to underscore the introduction of a new clinical language to public discourse. The Islamic Republic of Iran Broadcasting (IRIB) still vacillated between discussing mental illness as a medical issue and as a consequence of deviation, and many interpretations in between. In 2008, for example, the IRIB produced and screened a documentary titled *The Shock: Satanism, Rap Cults, and Promiscuity* that included a range of psychological discussions. Psychologist Simā Ferdowsi appeared in it, commenting on youth engaged in deviant behavior around rock and rap music, who were, in her words "suffering from personality disorders and psychopathologies." A young psychiatrist in the same documentary drew attention to the needs and desires of adolescents as a starting point for engaging with what were represented as social anomalies. The gap between the epistemologies of these two commentators exemplifies the fragmented landscape of contesting clinical and professional views. What they share, however, is a flexible diagnostic and clinical language.

Nevertheless, pedagogical differences do not sufficiently explain the fluctuations of this discourse. Sometimes, the merging of professional and popular discourses provides a space for speculative, even questionable, remarks. In Dr. M.'s televised lecture, for example, his attempts to connect with his audience took an odd turn at times, for example when he gendered depression by assigning women fluid and labile moods that result in crying, while maintaining that in men, crying signified depression. There was, he suggested, a biological difference in the brain: "Women's brain hemispheres work independently, while men's are linked." This explicitly gendered formulation is not necessarily common in most psychiatrists' teachings. But Dr. M.'s use of it highlights how practitioners employ what *they* perceive as culturally appropriate in order to get their message across.

Whether in some experts' educational formulations or in their liberal use of figures and statistics, generalizations are not uncommon. In an interview with the newspaper *Salāmat* in December 2009, the then head of the Iranian Psychiatric Association said:

> Mental illnesses are in fact physical disorders, and are caused by changes in the body and the brain. Eighty percent of psychiatric treatment consists of medication. . . . For example depression, which is treatable with medication, is caused by imbalance in the chemicals of the brain. . . . It is wrong to call these disorders *bimāri-ye ruhi* [mental illness, of the soul]. This is a misunderstanding and a misconception. Psychiatric disorders are like diseases of the body; they are the outcome of imbalance in the brain's chemicals and it is wrong to link them with the mind and soul. They should be called *bimāri-e maghzi* [disease of the brain].

While the intention to destigmatize mental illness is central to commentaries like these, many psychiatrists worry that such statements can confuse as well as create false expectations. They also worry about instances where statistical data are conjured or mobilized uncritically. And for good reason. In a 2006 interview with daily newspaper *Hamshahri*, one of the well-known early commentators on ADHD in the public media urged parents to medicate their hyperactive children:

> These days we know about the gene that causes ADHD. As for treatment, 99% of these kids need medication. If we don't give them medication, we are criminals, we are cruel; it is like depriving a patient with a bacterial sore throat of antibiotics. If we don't medicate them, they usually get expelled from school (30–40% of cases) because teachers can't handle them. They end up with mood disorders, depression, and even criminal or antisocial behavior such as addiction.[9]

Today, mental health educational platforms have evolved, incrementally but surely, in content and form. In earlier days, the campaign was heavily invested in destigmatizing the profession of psychiatry. Gradually, the media helped the emergence of these psychiatric discourses that were constructed and validated by (and manifested in) a new language of everyday life. This media campaign relied, in large part, on increasing and widespread mobilization and circulation of epidemiological "evidence," primarily in the form of statistical data. But how is one to read these widely circulating figures?

Evidence and the Question of Quantitative Data

In a 2010 op-ed in the Iranian daily newspaper *Āftāb-e Yazd*, a journalist speculated that "Tehranis have become more irritable" and reported a 40 percent prevalence of anxiety disorders and *afsordegi* (depression) in Tehran (and 21 percent nationwide): "Psychiatrists suggest putting antidepressants in Tehran's water," the author wrote, since, quoting the head of the Bureau of Mental Health, "these are chronic problems of urban life and socioeconomic struggle. . . . Anxiety is a normal part of Tehrani lives."[10] Articles of this sort appear frequently in Iranian newspapers and relay a range of statistical indications to laypeople. Unlike the early 1980s, no eyebrows are raised today when, for example, reading in the morning paper that—according to a survey conducted in five major cities—42 percent of young Iranians suffer from "anxieties about the future" or reading on medical news websites that 21.3 percent of rural and 21.9 percent of urban youth suffer from mental illness, primarily depression.[11] Furthermore, it is as common for such figures to be taken at face value, as it is for their accompanying professional language to be casually used by laypeople.

But statistics (for example, on the prevalence of depression) and their media reportage can be misleading if read out of context, and thus need to be examined critically. Rather than taking figures at face value, I follow them as indices for underlying cultural change as well as shifts in public discourse and the ways that epidemiological studies are constructed, presented, circulated, and mobilized in public. Beyond these statistics lie competing cultural and professional discourses, knowledges, assumptions, and aspirations that are often overlooked by universalized estimations such as those proposed by WHO, which ranks depression as a soon-to-be most common global burden of disease. At issue are how evidence is interpreted, mobilized, and instrumentalized as both a clinical and cultural resource and how a particular mode of thinking and knowing becomes normalized in their usage. In other words, we ought to ask what these figures reveal by virtue of what they mask.

With its battery of quantitative data sets, biomedicine tends to rely on epidemiology to monitor the dynamics of epidemics, thereby reducing a variety of practices and understandings to a static variable such as culture, gender, or risk. The language of risk, culture, and prevention in epidemiology creates a meta-narrative that assumes its own legitimacy, gives false assurance of having dealt with the social aspects of illness, and neglects processes of meaning making that inform risky behavior or cultural practices.[12] This understanding is increasingly at odds with that of anthropologists, who consider culture to be highly situational, dynamic, and continually under negotiation.[13] Forced to exclude social and cultural pretexts and interpretations from both design and analysis, this understanding risks downplaying hierarchies of knowledge and negotiations among various professional groups, such as epidemiologists, pathologists, general physicians, virologists, clergy, policymakers, journalists, and others.[14] Indeed, quantitative and qualitative researchers concerned with social suffering can inform each other by engaging in methodological and theoretical exchange on "how social power relations propagate illness in identifiable patterns," problematizing unilateral consequences of public health interventions, and carving out space for a discussion of disciplinary power relations by bringing in ethnographic insight.[15] In other words, in expanding attention from a pathology-disease-patient perspective to broader social contexts that account for multiple causalities, we need a reflexive and critical approach that analyzes what statistics foreground or marginalize.

There is, indeed, the question of how statistical information is assembled and how certain knowledge forms are produced. The collection and distribution of these statistics call for critical examination in two domains: methodologically, in their use of particular standardized models and questionnaires that are almost uniformly translated from American and British protocols; and procedurally, in light of what Iranians tacitly refer to as *farhang-e adad-sāzi* or a "culture of making numbers." The term reflects, ironically, the simultaneous suspicion of official figures and their uncritical appropriation by people in everyday life. The social life of these statistics therefore lies not in the figures, but in the myths, rumors, stories, desires, and aspirations that they reveal and reflect. They serve as both text and context.[16]

One key contextual element in reading statistics is the situated knowledge of researchers and medical professionals who are socialized and taught to both rely on and be skeptical of "figures." While this skepticism does injustice to many carefully designed and conducted research projects, it nevertheless informs the ways in which future data are collected. On the other hand, the usage of statistics is part of practitioners' professionalization, in that it shapes an expert, authoritative, and evidence-based rhetoric that is situated in a tangle of professional cultures. For example, medical publications, which are largely limited to epidemiological surveys, performatively use a standardized language that is integral to the socialization and acculturation of medical professionals. That most epidemiological studies use standard questionnaires, often translated and adjusted from English, rarely seems to raise questions about cross-cultural applicability of universal models.

Problematic as statistics are, they are still important as data sets that are compiled by and cited by physicians, politicians, hospitals, and media as indices for public health issues. They are indicators that people refer to cautiously, mockingly, or with cynical recognition of their limitations. More significantly, they have a public life and are widely circulated in the news. The largest publicly cited epidemiological study on depression was conducted in 2004, on a sample of 35,014 individuals countrywide.[17] The prevalence of psychiatric disorders was reported in the study to be 21.3 percent in rural areas and 20.9 percent in urban areas. "Prevalence increased with age and was higher in married, widowed, divorced, unemployed, and retired people. Prevalence rates are comparable with international studies. There is a wide regional difference in the country, and women are at greater risk."[18] Various newspapers have reported depression rates varying from 8 percent (citing a 2008 report of the State Welfare Organization of Iran) to 20 percent (citing a 2006 WHO report). While most of the cited studies report a higher prevalence of depression among women, the State Welfare Organization has reported that the inpatient cases of chronic mental illness are mostly men (67 percent).[19] These variations in statistical data have triggered public discussions about data collection and their methodological variations.[20] Since the formalization of the discipline of child psychiatry in 1997, attention has also been shifting toward child mental health. Several studies have drawn attention to psychiatric disorders among children and adolescents, and thus, an increasing awareness among clinicians and policymakers about mental health in this age group.[21] Child and adolescent psychiatric research publications too have increased dramatically.[22]

These modes of reporting ought to be critically examined vis-à-vis two demographic statistics that have long been a fixture in social commentary, but are rarely evidenced or explored in any depth: first, that the majority of the population is under 30, and second, that university education has vastly expanded and women comprise 60 percent of university graduates (while the population has doubled since 1980, from some 35 million to over 75 million).[23] Such nuances are often overshadowed in these publications by immediate references to WHO estimates that report depression is the fourth—soon to be second—most common burden of disease, thus, a global phenomenon. I will return to these questions of cross-cultural psychiatry in the Conclusion; the point, here, is to underscore the public and cultural life of numbers.

Aside from the issue of data collection, the reading of statistical data is additionally situated in the varying modes and politics of their circulation and interpretation in different media, creating tensions between institutional, formal, and informal regimes of data collection and interpretation. These intricacies highlight the contribution of ethnography and situated productions of knowledge, providing the context in which one should carefully listen to, for example, doctors' anecdotal reports from their clinical practices. It is in the juxtaposition of the official and the unofficial that one can analyze the growing visibility and circulation of statistical data about mental health. At the most basic level, they reflect a cultural shift and the pragmatic recognition of the need to address a potential public health concern, which brings me to the third frame through which one can identify the emergence of a public psychiatric discourse.

Technoscientific Matters and Mental Health Policy

As explained in the previous chapter, biomedical psychiatry has thrived in recent decades, in large part because of the implementation of new mental health care policy since the late 1980s. This conceptual turn to (Western) psychiatry was part of broader technoscientific priorities and pragmatic stances (particularly in relation to public health) integral to Iranian health policies of the recent decades. They reflect a continuity of state-promoted trends toward technoscientific modernization throughout the twentieth century, rather than a radical departure from the past. Part pragmatism (e.g., it is common knowledge that, in Iran, medicine thrived in response to wartime afflictions), part realism, part technoscientific aspiration, and part globalization, the core impetus behind the 1990s psychiatric discourses lay in the fact that doctors and health policymakers were all embedded in a postwar public health condition that they were required to address. The psychiatric paradigm, in other words, emerged both as a symptom of and a response to an official public health concern with mental health.

The 1990s consolidation of an individual-brain-centered biomedical psychiatry and campaigns for destigmatizing mental illness fit the medical community's as well as the state's larger medico-rational and technoscientific ambitions, evident in the emphasis on scientific advancements from physics to neuroscience, from theoretical to applied sciences.[24] Iran's technoscientific pragmatism is historically rooted, in part, in proud aspirations for independence from "the West" since the early twentieth century. But equally significant in shaping these aspirations is seeking technoscientific distinction in relation to the rest of the Muslim world; and recent years have seen more of such efforts, particularly in public health.[25] An explicit rubric of science is evident in various reports on increasing numbers of Ph.D. programs and government-funded research activities in postwar years. Iran's 2005 "Twenty-Year Vision Document," for example, aimed at placing Iran in the first rank in the region for investment in science and technology.[26] The emphatic use of the term "region" reflects a preoccupation with local geopolitics of scientific advancement. If, under the Pahlavis, this pride was officially formulated in the glorification of a pre-Islamic past and the creation of modernized citizens, today's scientific aspirations toward knowledge as power are rendered synergic with the Islamic tenets of pursuit of knowledge and care for the self.

Understanding this context helps us understand, in part, the desires that justified the psychiatric turn of the 1990s. Psychiatry reemerged as a branch of medicine (thus *scientific*) and enjoyed an easier reception (both within the medical community and in public) than did psychoanalysis, insofar as it relied on biochemical and organic explanatory models and pharmaceutical interventions. As discussed in the previous chapter, this differentiation was largely rooted in the history of Iranian psychiatry itself. Subsequent policies for media representation of this psychiatry contributed to and facilitated further entrenchment of a biomedical, organic pedagogy in academic psychiatry. The focus in the media was on a rational approach to "medical" matters such as signs, symptoms, and treatment, and even more, on evidence. As such, today, topics such as suicide among married women, addiction among youth (with shifting patterns of drug use), the rise in medication with psychotropic drugs, and other psychosocial problems are widely recognized and addressed by the government, and the results of surveys on depression or anxiety disorders are frequently published in national newspapers.

Even without statistics, one can still make inferences about the rise of a rational psychiatric discourse from several changing policies. The end of the Iran-Iraq War marked a dramatic shift in modes of production and selection of material for media programs and educational materials. A close examination of children's programs on television in the 1980s and 1990s, for instance, shows a departure from stoic contents in the 1980s, to the more active use of colors and music in the 1990s. Unlike the 1980s, there is an emphasis now on attention to children's psychological well-being in relation to their environment. The idea of making school textbooks more colorful and fun evolved, in part, as a response to a perceived concern raised by psychologists and public health experts alike; new regulations also changed the color of school uniforms for elementary school girls, changing the color of head scarves from black and navy to white, and allowing color in the uniform itself. Part of the significance of these seemingly trivial details lies in the generational aesthetics that I shall discuss in future chapters. But they also reflect epistemological and pragmatic shifts toward the recognition of mental health, which also became manifest in new mental health care legislation in the 1990s and early 2000s.

The more recent legislations have incorporated integral approaches to mental health policy, but they also reflect variations over time and are embedded in their particular administrative contexts. In 2008, the Bureau of Mental Health of the Ministry of Health and Medical Education drafted a *ghānun* (law) for mental health, a plan for the documentation and prevention of suicide, as well as a program to integrate the mental health plan into the family-medicine initiative of the ministry.[27] A year later, the Ministry of Internal Affairs announced an initiative of *mohandesi-ye shādi* or "engineering happiness." Both terms reflect several layers of meaning. "Happiness" (*shādi*) taps into familiar affective tropes in both mysticism and in contemporary poetics: the former assigns the term a transcendental quality intermixed with stoic gravitas, as per Rumi's line *ghand-e shādi miveh-ye bāgh-e gham ast*, "happiness is the fruit of melancholy." The latter laments the scarcity of happiness in the public domain, as in the first line of a famous poem by the contemporary poet and scholar Mohammadreza Shafi'i Kadkani: "A child called Happiness has gone missing." Yet, more immediately, the choice of words in "engineering happiness" is symptomatic both of the recognition of "happiness" as a societal requisite and of the tensions regarding proposed formulations of said happiness and the static nature of such happiness to be engineered; the proposal, however, maintained that happiness reflected a state of mind that was radically different from conventional conceptualizations of happiness in the West (that is, not materialistic or this-worldly). This national project, it explained, should aspire to a culturally situated notion of happiness as rooted in a spiritual worldview and religious faith.

While "happiness" reflects epistemological tensions, "engineering" (*mohandesi*) reflects the pragmatic and technocratic mindset with which dysphoria is perceived and dealt with. Such efforts, though often transient, were not isolated (particularly during the period between 2005 and 2010), nor were they always ideologically charged. In November 2008, Tehran municipality, together with one of its many cultural centers called *Farhangsarā-ye Salāmat* (the Culture House *Salāmat*; *Salāmat* meaning "health"), announced the opening of a series of *bāshgāh-e khandeh* or "laughter workshops." At times, the transience and public perceptions of these initiatives as ephemeral or ironic undermine their significance in reflecting the sincerity or deep epistemological tensions inscribed in both their rhetoric and content. More importantly, they illustrate how institutional conceptualizations of what constitutes (culturally situated) happiness have changed and continue to change since the 1980s.

Culturally situated interpretations of happiness and contentment are often emphasized; they matter, indeed, for reading statistics and understanding other indices of mental health. But they also take various forms among experts and generate cultural and policy debates that reflect epistemological and administrative variations. For example, in 2009, the newspaper *Etemād* published a report on the preparation of a national happiness plan (*tarh-e neshāt-e melli*), quoting an official explaining that happiness and contentment were defined differently in different cultures and were shaped by religious and cultural teachings.[28] The official further explained that religious mourning rituals, for example, were part of society's cultural sense of self and thus "integral to *neshāt-e ejtemā'i*" (social and collective contentment): "We need to avoid spreading disappointing statistics and news in public. They cause distrust and insecurity." As part of such efforts, in May 2010 the Iranian Census Bureau issued an order to provincial municipalities, instructing them to reduce public reports of surveys that "agitate public opinion, particularly those on divorce and death rates."[29] The order indicated that public reports should highlight improvements such as birth and marriage rates, and that their goal should be "enhancing the level of happiness in society." Such moves can be seen as both an attempt at social engineering and a genuine concern with reducing the circulation of stressors among people. What was significant, nevertheless, was the very emergence of an official stance toward the question of happiness. Engineering happiness thus relied on a particular statistical representation that revealed more than it concealed; it helped make evidence and data intelligible.

Varying methodologies and mindsets across different administrative temporalities are to be expected and manifest over time, as they have in recent years. The organizing of the first National Symposium on Islam and Mental Health in April 2015, for example, indicates a move toward more concerted efforts and potential openings for a culturally and medically situated discourse of mental health. Broadly speaking, though, Iranian mental health-related policy attempts often employ WHO recommended protocols while endeavoring to formulate them in culturally situated frameworks.[30] They reflect global trends as well as competing priorities, mindsets, and ambivalence toward a mental health problem that both health experts and the establishment feel affected by, responsible for, and compelled to remedy. Public policy remains focused mainly on destigmatization of mental illness and educational campaigns for raising public awareness about psychological well-being.

It is important, however, to remember that mental health initiatives take different forms at different times, reflecting broader organizational shifts in priorities and contexts. In other words, mental health policies, much like the government itself (or any government), are far from monolithic, static, or linear.[31] At times mental health policy efforts have reflected convergences or rivalries within professional power structures; at other times, they have reflected pragmatic and effective responses to a perceived mental health crisis. They have been, regardless, the outcome of, and the force behind, the entrenchment of a profound cultural shift that has created new public discourses and biomedical perceptions, languages, and interpretations of what constitutes mental health. One of the domains in which such medicalization became instrumental was public discussions of suicide.

Suicide in Medical Terms: Destigmatizing and Raising Awareness

Suicide is a characteristic of depression. I don't mean all suicidal people are depressed. But it is a sign of major [in English] depression.

Dr. M., lecture in the *Āyin-e Behtar Zistan* seminar series, 2012

Suicide, this quintessential Iranian taboo, has transformed in the recent years from a hidden secret to a public and spectacular object of analysis. During my time in medical school in the 1990s, I knew of two students who committed suicide. One was a devout Muslim, Kurd (an ethnic minority), and the son of a martyr of the Iran-Iraq War, who, we later found out, had been admitted to a psychiatric hospital for depression a month before he killed himself. The other, the son of a secular, middle-class family in Tehran, committed suicide after a rough breakup and a few years of struggling with untreated depression, we were told. Shocking as they were, neither death was openly called *khodkoshi* (suicide). Nor were the other few that I recall, either during high school or during my friends' and siblings' experiences with school. Unlike today, in those days, the idea of hiring a school counselor was considered excessive. There were more important, "real" issues at hand; but there was also unease in talking about "mental" issues publicly.

Today, that discomfort is perceived by many educated people as outdated and backward. Like being on *dāru* (medication), suicide prevention is now discussed in the media, albeit in medicalized ways. When not medicalized, its official representation in the media comes in terms of nihilism, deviant behavior, and declining religiosity. Either way, suicide is more readily discussed now in the public domain. Many people readily report that they know someone in their circle who has committed suicide. Medical interns and residents frequently share stories of having admitted a handful of suicide cases in their ER rotations, for example, in Loghmān Hospital (Tehran's referral center for intoxication), of women who have committed suicide by ingesting what is known as *ghors-e berenj* or rice pills (aluminum phosphate pills used as pesticides for rice); such anecdotes often accompany expert commentaries or epidemiological reports in newspapers. Suicide has transformed from the occasional scandalous news headline, often in the context of love stories, into a public, medicalized, and spectacular object in the news. Medicalizing suicide has allowed for the emergence of a public health discourse of suicide, thereby creating a platform for its socialization.

The point here is not to ask whether suicide is on the rise (in Iran or globally), but to draw attention to a cultural shift toward a rational and medical discourse of suicide, and to the ways we talk about it, publicly and clinically. Good numbers are hard to come by (as in other countries), and suicide statistics are marred by unreliable family reports affected by the stigma attached to suicide and the condemnation of the act in Islam. But the existing data are still informative. The emergence of a medical discourse of suicide is first and foremost visible in the media circulation of a growing body of headlines, expert commentaries, and epidemiological and medical publications that contribute to alarming official reports.[32] Equally important are circulating media reports on recent shifts in suicide patterns as well as its modes of public representation.[33] Mental health experts have been at the forefront of these discussions, arguing that proper intervention requires open discussions of suicide as a public health matter. Significantly, these reports rely on rational biomedical and epidemiological frameworks and attention to public health measures for suicide prevention; thus reflecting global public health discourses: in 2010, for example, a representative of the National Welfare Organization announced that a crisis threshold had been reached, with an official suicide rate of 7 in 1,000 among individuals younger than 30 years of age.[34] In the same year, the Forensic Medicine Organization reported a 17 percent increase (compared to the previous year), warning of rising rates of suicide among women under 30 years of age in western and southern provinces.[35] Often, these reports mention that Iran still has lower suicide rates compared to developed countries such as the United States or Japan.[36] Experts and practitioners also warn that statistics are only the tip of the iceberg (a problem shared with many societies), citing for example a report published by university hospitals of Tehran University, which indicates that most suicides remain unrecorded, by request of the families, as a result of the stigma. Such reports and analyses echo both global debates around suicide and a growing medico-rational tendency to incorporate it into public health agendas and interventions.

As elsewhere, suicide has become an attractive topic for media reportage. The public imagination, too, is increasingly infiltrated with the topic: take the example of the circulation of special issues of the journal *Eynak-e Falsafeh* (The Lens of Philosophy; first issue) and the September 2005 issue of e-zine *7Sang* (7Stones),[37] both dedicated to suicide. The former contains a set of philosophical reflections accompanied by poems. The latter opens with an article calling for a departure from official denial of suicide, followed by a set of sociological glosses on etiologies, prevention, and literary and cinematic representations of suicide, as well as reflections on suicide notes. Most widely circulated in news headlines, though, are occasional reports of suicide among university students (often linked to drug use and dormitory life),[38] married women, and veterans, implicitly reflecting broader contextual elements perceived to be implicated in suicide.[39] The dominant narrative remains a clinical one that aims to destigmatize mental illness and raise awareness about it.

Among public accounts of suicide, those of war veterans (particularly among the *jānbāz* community) have attracted media as well as medical attention and contributed to a public health discourse of suicide. This discourse has also served to call on society for a deserved attention to the struggles of disabled veterans with psychiatric illnesses. Medical studies conducted by Iranian clinicians on the correlation between suicide and psychiatric illness among veterans have already underscored the importance of destigmatization and intervention, while some have also reported that suicide rates among Iranian veterans remain lower compared to those in other countries, attributing the difference to factors such as familial and marital support, spirituality, and faith.[40] Not unlike discussions of suicide among veterans in the United States and in Europe, these discussions have entered media and public health policy debates on psychiatric care and suicide prevention. In 2009, for example, newspapers reported that a disabled veteran committed suicide in front of the Veterans Organization building in protest of bureaucratic negligence of his medical and economic condition.[41] It appeared that, struggling with severe health conditions, the veteran's request for his injuries to be rated higher on the disability scale had been contested.[42] The verdict was that he lacked evidence to link his injuries to the war—a common problem in the evaluation of compensatory claims over time. Within weeks, a couple of other incidences of self-immolation by veterans in other cities made headlines in Iranian newspapers.[43] The media reports and medical discussions that followed these tragic incidences highlighted a genuine need for better recognition of chronic (physical and psychiatric) conditions among veterans and ignited official debates in the Iranian media and among the veteran community, public health experts, practitioners, and policymakers alike.

Psychiatry was instrumental to these debates, as were psychiatric disorders and mental health care paradigms, underscoring the need for destigmatizing the psychiatric conditions that many veterans have endured as well as for the improvement of their health care and welfare. The medicalization of suicide, in other words, made possible a broader public discussion of an otherwise unspeakable act, while the spectacular and public nature of what anthropologist Junko Kitanaka has called "suicide of resolve" turned such acts into a call for action.[44] More recently, for example, the Veterans Organization has introduced new initiatives for

FIGURE 3: Cover of the *Journal of Research in Behavioral Sciences*, issue 12, vol. 6, no. 2, 2009, a special issue of abstracts from the National Symposium on the Study of Suicide Behaviors and Prevention Strategies in Iran.

more integral models of mental health care that would focus on veterans with psychiatric illnesses as well as on their caretakers and family members.[45]

The organization of several conferences and symposia too reflects both the emergence of a clinical discourse of suicide and the underlying recognition of an impending public health issue. In one of the first of such attempts, the Iranian Psychiatric Association (IPA) held in Tehran the first National Symposium on the Study of Suicide Behaviors (*Raftārhā-ye Khodkoshi*) and Prevention Strategies (*Rāhkārhā-ye Pishgiri*), in February 2009 (see Figure 3), a year after the First International Conference on PTSD was held in the same city. The head of the Suicide Prevention Section of the Bureau of Mental Health in the Ministry of Health and Medical Education noted in the conference briefing that, not unlike in many other societies, more than 75 percent of suicides are not reported due to cultural beliefs and stigma. The papers presented at the conference covered a wide range of regional epidemiological studies that reported more suicide among married women and unemployed men, as well as changes in patterns of suicide.[46] More significantly, several of these symposia are often reported in the media, particularly in newspaper headlines, further circulating clinical and epidemiological data among the population.

Key to these public discussions is the participation of physicians, the clergy, policymakers, and officials, opening a space for multi-voiced debates on intervention and the consolidation of a public health discourse of suicide. These sporadic yet culturally generative debates continue to further evolve in the media.[47] Emerging policy initiatives, medicalizing or not, reflect a collective *sense* of a public health dilemma, one that has triggered several official proposals and has created a possibility for the public recognition of and intervention in suicide. The medicalization of suicide has indeed been a double-edged sword: it has biologized suicide by underscoring its purely clinical interpretations in relation to depression and mental illness; but it has also opened up a potential space for a public debate and open discussion of a growing, yet sinful and stigmatized, act. Psychiatry, in other words, has helped socialize a discourse of suicide.

Prozāk *and Ritalin by the Numbers*

Iranians take pills in abundance; one hears this from experts and laypeople alike. But frequent and often generalizing claims about increasing rates of medication with antidepressants ought to be unpacked and interpreted in context.

They are meant, in part, to reflect situational contingencies and, in part, to project medico-rational and progressive values and modernist aspirations of the cultural middle class.[48] However, the other side of the coin is media discussions around prescription patterns, illness detection, and what many newspaper reports have called *su'-e masraf-e dāru* (misuse and overuse of medication) due to "misinformed cultural habit" (*farhang-e ghalat*) or what most clinicians experience firsthand as a quick-fix culture among patients, often citing WHO for allegedly ranking Iran's medication usage twentieth worldwide. A glance at daily newspaper columns and news headlines reveals these concerns: unofficial reports claim that 40 percent of people self-prescribe; non-prescribed prescription-only painkillers and central nervous system (CNS) drugs are commonly purchased, in large quantities, not only at pharmacies but also occasionally in grocery stores; the Ministry of Health reports that the most common cause of intoxication admissions at hospitals is overdose of antidepressants and painkillers. In the midst of these speculations, the first task was to ask whether one could take these figures at face value: was there any evidence for an actual increase in prescription and sales of certain drugs. And if so, how was such evidence assembled and interpreted?

Both the National Statistics Organization and the Ministry of Health collect data that can help us understand possible shifts in patterns of medication. Since 1984, the ministry has published an annual report called the *āmārnāmeh*, or "statistical report," on drug sales.[49] The data I draw on are from these reports, which contained raw data. Although the data cover the years 1997 through the third trimester of 2008, there are gaps.[50] First, hospital/inpatient prescriptions are included in the annual report only after early 2008. This means that the earlier figures report only outpatient prescriptions. Second, some drugs that are prescribed in Iran are not listed in these tables.[51] Third, some drugs appear in one year's listing but not in another year's. The tables for each quarter, listing drug name, sales in units per year, and accumulative sales in units, show some variations of format, partly reflecting the turnover of executive teams in the ministry. That in itself reveals patterns of medium-term change in policy and priorities.[52]

Despite limitations, one can still puzzle out some longitudinal findings. In general, the figures show a rise in prescription rates between 1997 and 2008 (for instance, there is a 12 percent rise between 1999 and 2000). Among different families of drugs, CNS drugs (painkillers, tranquilizers, and antidepressants) had the highest rate of prescription, followed by antibiotics, and gastro and cardiovascular medication.[53]

I have chosen to focus only on antidepressants and Ritalin as I follow the discourse of depression and ADHD: the findings indicated a notable increase in the sales of antidepressants between 1997 and 2008, and the same decade saw a significant rise in the use of Ritalin.[54] Doctors explain this in terms of, first, the role of educational campaigns in destigmatizing psychiatric medication, and second, better detection of depression and ADHD by practitioners. Remarkably, this is also the first decade since the establishment of the subspecialty of child psychiatry in Iran (1997). During this decade, the Iranian Association for Child and Adolescent Psychiatry (IACAP) held the first two international conferences on child psychiatry in Tehran.

In lay discourse, I learned, *Prozāk* stands for a range of antidepressants. It is important, however, to remember that not all psychotropic medication is prescribed by psychiatrists; internists, neurologists, and even general practitioners commonly assert that antidepressants can help "anyway," since "most people" are suffering from "degrees of underlying depression." It is not uncommon for general practitioners to prescribe Prozac or Citalopram for chronic pain or for irritable bowel syndrome (IBS). They do so citing clinical studies that suggest the efficacy of SSRIs in the treatment of IBS. One young orthopedic surgeon confided in me that his newly established practice became successful because he knew psychiatry well—"more than half of the patients who visit orthopedic surgeons for back pain are eventually diagnosed with depression." In many of my conversations with psychiatrists, such anecdotal evidence was often seen as either representative of a dire need for medication, thus rendering medication "inevitable," or explained through infrastructural problems in the absence of a functional mental health referral system. Another internist told me, "I can't say there is an epidemic of clinical depression; but there is definitely an epidemic of dysphoria, which can still be helped by medication. And besides that, many patients ask for antidepressants, and if I don't prescribe them, they go to another doctor and get them."[55]

Indeed, the globalizing forces of the Big Pharma and the psychiatrization of life are not solely Iranian issues. Changing medication patterns reflect global trends, particularly since the 1980s, and there has been a global increase in the use of antidepressants and Ritalin during the same time frame. Whether these figures can possibly be taken at face value, or whether they reflect overmedication, overdiagnosis, better detection of emerging illnesses, or patterns of medication misuse, would be questions of another project. But more significantly, to ask whether these data reflect overmedication would be a misleading question, because it defines the problem in its own terms and in the framework of biomedical diagnoses: it assumes that diagnosis always justifies medication, thereby not only legitimizing biomedical assumptions but also obscuring other contributing forces. But ethnographically speaking, the data reveal much in terms of broader shifts in cultural contexts of and attitudes toward medication, as well as modes of data collection by epidemiologists, institutions, and public health experts. At the least, looking at the statistical graphs can help visualize underlying changes in cultural logic and medical rationalities.

An Iranian Psychiatric Niche

Suicide, overmedication, and growing diagnoses of depression or ADHD are not uniquely Iranian concerns; they are part of broader global discourses on mental health and globalization. The rise of brain talk in the Iranian media, however, was not solely an indication of importing global biomedicalizing trends. Nor was it solely the outcome of a top-down hegemonic biomedical discourse or seventy-plus years of a deep-seated neuropsychiatric legacy in Iranian psychiatry. The 1990s shift toward a destigmatizing language of organic symptoms was in part a situated medico-rational response to concerns with anxiety, depression, and children's mental health, providing an opportunity for psychiatry to reclaim its identity, both academically and culturally. In the 1990s, the marriage of media and mental health expertise further created new ways of understanding and conducting the self and contributed to the normalization of new language forms and categories of experience. Indeed, the outcomes (e.g., growing prescriptions of psychiatric medication) may seem conspicuously American. But Iran's case stands out in a number of ways, not just compared to the United States, but also compared to other non-Western societies, such as Japan, that have experienced a similar cultural shift in terms of psychiatric medicalization in the 1990s.[56] Such comparative perspectives help us track continuities and divergences, and enhance our understanding of each particular cultural setting and its discourses in their own right.

For one thing, the biomedical language served the double purpose of elevating psychiatry's status within medicine and in the eyes of the public, as well as offering a legitimized vehicle for social commentary in the aftermath of the Iran-Iraq War. This is a distinctive feature that in part relies on the particular trajectory of Iranian psychiatry and its historically rooted imperative of educating the masses (see Chapter 2), while also reflecting the intricacies of how public discourses emerge and become normalized. In postwar Iran, biomedical psychiatry and the Iranian media found in each other unlikely allies, each carefully demarcating the boundaries of public discourse. While in Japan, for instance, legal mechanisms and court cases led the way in representing the social causalities of depression among working men, in Iranian discussions, social commentary remained implicit in the discourse and secondary to biomedical explanations.

Another distinctive feature of the Iranian psychiatric discourse is that it has been precisely a biologizing and individualizing discourse of psychiatry that made possible a public discourse about mental health and its social elements. This can be seen as a strategic use of media and medicalization at once. In using an individualizing discourse of self-care, however, Iranian media are not alone. Aside from such dominant discourses in the United States, similar accounts also exist in the postsocialist era in the former Soviet Union with the creation of a new neoliberal "self" in the media through psychotherapy talk shows that promoted a discourse of "responsibilization."[57] In Iran, however, not only have psychodynamic debates been peripheral, but even biomedical psychiatric discourses have not been explicitly neoliberal (save for their implicitly liberal pedagogical trajectory). It is true that they are situated in a larger network of transnational discourses, a booming self-help industry, modernizing lifestyles, and aspirations for scientific modernization. But it is also true that they are embedded in the merging of various discourses of Iranian affect and identity politics (including Shi'ism and mysticism). More significantly, in their inception, the Iranian talk shows were situated in a tangled web of wartime anguish and an imperative of destigmatizing mental illness and raising public awareness about mental health (compared with Russian talk shows, where psychological training was initially perceived as that which "people take to be important for succeeding in a market society").[58] What came naturally to health experts and their audience was a smooth double entendre; that is, by making an *illness* that resided in the brain the legitimate target of analysis and intervention, they created a project of refashioning the self without engaging with its discourses.

This 1990s paradigm shift in the media was part of a larger story of the marriage between a specific ideological and cultural pretext and a rational appropriation and normalization of biomedical and psychiatric epistemologies and interventional modes; hence a new discourse of care for the self. But this discourse was hardly the outcome of an imported authoritative biomedical apparatus imposed from atop. Instead, it was a coproduction of top-down and bottom-up cultural change. In other words, the incorporation of brain talk into daily life both represents and shapes the Iranian discourse of mental health.

Similarly, the surge in the use of antidepressants, a seemingly global trend, offers a situated lens into shifting cultural desires, practices, and processes of meaning making through which individuals and physicians perceive pathology and manage it accordingly. These shifting discourses are dynamic and reflect equally dynamic processes of cultural change and work on the self. In the following chapters, I explore the cultural possibilities that this clinical discourse created; that is, the identifications and modes of legitimation that individuals employ in such work on the self. I start, in the next chapter, by asking those who identify as *depress* how they account for and experience *depreshen* and their trust in *Prozāk*. What is at stake when one identifies with *depreshen*? What is gained and what is lost?

The Student

"*Prozāk* helped me with my *depreshen*; I should have started sooner. . . . How long do we want to insist on backward thinking? Don't you take antibiotics for an infection? It's the same thing; *depreshen* has its own medication; simple as that," twenty-eight-year-old Samāneh told me in Café Shoukā in Tehran. Shoukā was a small, trendy café, frequently shut down by the morality police and best known for its eccentric owner, a writer himself, who also sold literary magazines and secondhand books. Shoukā once epitomized the fantasy of *café-neshini* (socializing in cafes) and of the old Café Nāderi—the nostalgic 1960s intellectuals' Café Maxime of Tehran that, in the imagination of Samāneh's generation, was populated with poets like Ahmad Shāmlu and Forough Farokhzād, and iconic authors such as Sā'edi and Hedāyat. [1] For sure, the fog of smoke, the sighs, and the lamentations made Shoukā seem like a pretentious pseudo-intellectual space. But the café was also filled with the restless young and, in the summer of 2005, we were sitting among them. Samāneh lit a cigarette and adjusted her black shawl; half-covering her long highlighted locks, the scarf brought out the color of her bright matte lipstick. She continued, "I come here at least once a week. It's the only place I can sit alone at a table and no one bothers me. *Injā hameh ham dardan*! [We are all suffering the same pangs here]."

Samāneh and I had met in the most unlikely of ways: we read each other's blogs. Mine was written from Oxford and hers from Tehran, but a fascination with Kundera's prose, the poetry of Akhavān-Sāless, and Hātamikia's films connected our blogs, and we eventually met at a bloggers' gathering in Tehran. Later, her blog posts became part of those I followed in my ethnography.

Samāneh was a recent graduate of a top-ranked engineering school in Tehran. She explained her *depreshen*:

My *depreshen* began to infect my life. I was too *bihoseleh* [down, blue]. Much has happened. My US visa application got rejected for the third time, my [Masters] admission [to . . .] will expire this autumn, and I don't know what to do with my life. [2] My relationship with [. . .] is over. And my parents just don't get it. They keep asking what's wrong with me and blaming me for being down, as if I don't want to be happy, as if it's my fault that life sucks. I can't stand it anymore, to live with their questions, and being single in this crazy city. . . . People have become jerks. I can't trust anyone I meet. . . . And now I'm *depress*. . . . *Dāru* [medication] is helping. That's what I need now. I can't change anything else, you see.

In an earlier interview, Samāneh had commented, "Everyone is *depress*. It's as if someone has splashed *gard-e marg* on the city." I have heard this from others too: *gard-e marg* (literally, the "dust of death,") or *gard-e gham* (the "dust of despair") allegedly smudging Tehran's face. In their emphatically exaggerating, generalizing, and lyrical wording, such phrases do not translate well. In Persian, they are not to be taken literally. Rather, they serve as proxies to convey a wide range of feeling states including dysphoria, a claustrophobic sense of being stuck, or hopelessness. They also reflect a kind of performativity in language that serves to anchor one's psychological experience in its relation to those of others and assign to it a shared meaning. More significantly, they relay the intensity of the affective and emotional states they spring from. Depression, for Samāneh, is scattered everywhere like dust. On the surface though, Tehran beams with colors and movement.

Back in Café Shoukā, Samāneh said she had not slept the night before; a nightmare had brought back disturbing memories:

I know I'm *depress*. . . . But who wouldn't be? Now that things look better on the outside, we forget that deep down, we're still stressed; we forget how anxious we were as kids. . . . I have so many good memories too. But all the hide and seek, the bombs and things I had to fear . . . and the war.

Just like that, Samāneh drifted back to the 1980s and the Iran-Iraq War. "Remember the red siren interrupting *barnāmeh-ye kudak* [children's TV programs]? I still panic when I recall that ear-piercing sound."

"But what makes you think about those things *now*?" I asked. Without hesitation, she said: "I still dream about them, like I did last night; sometimes I see missiles in my dreams, or hear that terrible siren and its announcement. . . . Can you believe it?"

I can.

CHAPTER 4

Depreshen Talk, the Pill,
and Psychiatric Subjectivities

SAMĀNEH IS NOT ALONE in insisting on telling the story of her generation, nor is she alone in choosing a clinical language to express her emotional
state. The psychiatric vernacular has helped her situate her present-day emotional distress within historical and social contexts. It has given her a situated
language of memory and affect. The *afsordegi* or *depreshen* that Samāneh suffers
from may or may not be a direct translation for clinical depression; many who
are medicated are not clinically qualified for a diagnosis of major depressive disorder or major depression. Symptomatically speaking, and as discussed before,
sometimes the lines are blurred between situational depression, dysphoria, depressive mood, clinical (major) depression, PTSD symptoms, anxiety disorders,
and what psychologists call "learned helplessness," thus challenging the diagnostic demarcation of the *DSM*. Nevertheless, the lived experience of her depression
is both real and situated in the psychiatric epistemology that defines it.

Language, anthropologist Veena Das has written, serves as both experience
and representation for the subject, letting us into the experience of those who
transcribe an experienced trauma into the ordinary domain of daily life, thereby
managing to remain in and to reconfigure the experience.[1] In her scholarship,
Das has carved out a space for a different kind of truth, an individual truth created by the merging of memory (private) and tradition (public). I seek to enter
that space, by investigating individual modes of identification with illness and

processes of meaning making. This chapter specifically engages with individuals who self-identify with *depreshen* in a particularly performative and generative mode of articulation; their accounts are thus not meant to be representative across their generation or of all experiences of clinical depression.

Let's Talk about Depreshen

Loss does not come to language as if it were an accident—as if it came later to language—but points to an essential dimension of what language is.

Jeffrey Sacks, *Iterations of Loss* (2015)

Psychiatric terminologies have almost become a given in many parts of the world; outside the clinical encounter, they increasingly populate the media, arts, and public culture. But in these travels, they find different meanings and take different forms in different languages. In the 1990s, young Iranians quickly picked up the psychiatric vernacular that was circulating the media. By the time young artist Amirali Ghasemi titled his 2004 photo exhibition in Tehran *Deep Depression* (see Figure 4) (followed in 2005 by *Deeper Depression*) and showcased faceless young people sitting in cafés smoking and socializing, the choice of words such as *depress* was not an oddity: "The concept:" the announcement of the exhibition read, "Deep depression and its relations with art is a main [theme] of the exhibition[.] It can be about depression only or it can be about people who are *depress* and this situation made them deep or artful."[2]

Bloggers, too, were talking about depression in clinical terms. Some shared their experiences with depression in order to help others, explaining their symptoms in biomedical terms similar to those promoted by psychiatrists and raising awareness about when and how to seek help. In online fora, others commonly recommended self-help books and medications, even referring each other to medical textbooks such as the *Oxford Textbook of Psychiatry*. In 2007, a blogger wrote a widely read post about his experience with *depreshen*. Wittily, he said:

> Just like a strep throat infection or food poisoning, the invasion of obsessively pessimistic thoughts and long hours of sleep into your day has physiological causes. Trust me; it is not an existential or philosophical malady; it is simply that your serotonin levels have dropped. . . . Now, who is this guy Serotonin? The key to mood disorders, your body's natural happiness inducer. This lovely chemical,

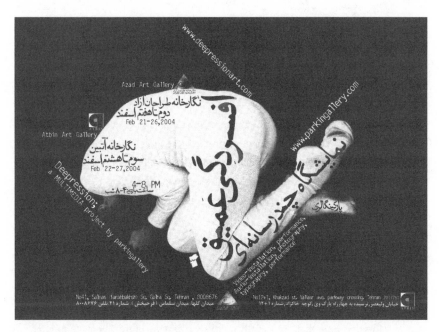

FIGURE 4: Poster of the photo exhibition *Deep Depression*, curated by Amirali Ghasemi. Parking Gallery, Tehran, February 2004.

whose low levels make you literally miserable . . . haven't you heard of iron deficiency? Like that, low <u>serotonin</u> is one of the major causes of depression.[3]

He continued with an impressively informed, but relatable, voice: "Funny, right? You would never connect a lifetime of misery with this tiny chemical imbalance," and ended by encouraging medical attention in an elaborate discussion of side effects:

Each person finds his or her own way of making it better. But seriously, if you feel too unwell, please do not skip the idea of pills. Try to fight this fear that forces you to find philosophical excuses. If you are among those who believe they have Proustian and Dostoyevskian depression and if you believe that treatment would have stopped those guys from creating masterpieces, then please be realistic. Ask yourself whether you have, so far in your depression, created your *À la recherche du temps perdu*? Who knows what those guys could have written if they had been treated? . . . Tell yourself loudly: "I need to inhibit the uptake of <u>serotonin</u>. I need to inhibit the uptake of <u>serotonin</u>."

Bringing to mind the public lecture from Chapter 3, the emphasis on "this lovely chemical," serotonin, is meant to undo several myths about mental illness. In many other blog posts, tensions between pathologization and the historicization/romanticizations of *depreshen* prevail. One blogger recalled her first episode of depression:

> It happened around the time of the *konkur* [the national university entrance exam]. I couldn't study at all. . . . Although I think the real roots of it were in my childhood. . . . It took me two years to get back in touch with life, thanks to my friends in the dorm. . . . But now I am sure that I was completely *depress* then. . . . It took me a year to seek help, after I hit rock bottom and realized I couldn't tackle it on my own. This wasn't about strength. . . . There is no merit in being sad, in crying. And going to a doctor only reflects your intellect.

She then explained how she treated her *depreshen*:

> Very, very slowly. I don't want to scare you all. But I want you to know you should be patient. If you are depressed now, you are probably really good at self-nagging and criticizing. Stop that. Apparently there are two types of treatment: counseling [*moshāvereh*] and medication. Both take time, because they have to fix the chemical imbalance in the brain. And when that is fixed, one day you'll wake up and you feel you are not depressed. It took two years for me.

Aside from distributing biomedical knowledge, bloggers' *depreshen* threads also functioned as primary support groups that aimed at educating, lifting stigma, and brainstorming coping strategies. Socializing in the blogosphere, she explained, helped her, as did living in the moment, having a pet, being patient, and being "realistic." In the comments, many readers asked for recommendations for therapists; others responded with lists of tests or hyperlinks to other bloggers' related posts on depression and professional advice. Some even said they took her advice on blogging about their condition.

Not all bloggers are so keen on biomedical explanatory models. Some *depreshen* narratives are intermixed with resilience, humor, and irony, and imbued with references to historical junctures or cultural practices with varying interpretations. Sometimes, for example, some narrators performatively link it to culture or religion, which they use as a catchall for a range of dominant beliefs and cultural practices ("if you have never been *depress*," one blogger joked, "try living as a Shi'ite for two weeks"), perhaps relevant here insofar as it relates to some young people's perception of their childhood as imbued with Shi'ite mourning rituals or encircled in a paradigm of stoicism in the early 1980s. This, some of them assert, serves as pretext for dealing with today's stresses of making ends meet or intergenerational transfers of anxiety that are "enough to drive you *depress.*" Many others, on the other hand, disagree and in fact find an antidote to depression in those very religious paradigms and cultural practices; faith, they assert, has helped them overcome depression.

Blogs that engage with *depreshen* in either self-reporting or interventional modes are as filled with humorous meditations as they are with reflexive, at times poetic, social commentary on matters such as the impact of international sanctions. The significance of these assertions lies in their performative use of language, rather than mere content. A handful of these often-generalizing, at times lyrical and at others witty, explanatory models from blog posts reveal the performativity of these mediations on what, in *their* views, underlies *depreshen*:

- When you are isolated from the world, when everywhere you look you see *depreshen*, when your friends leave the country leaving you behind; you must be a potato not to become *depress.*

- Where endless running is the fate of those who never win the race, and where winning is for those who never run, how can you not be *depress*?

- Depression is contagious. When you are surrounded by *depress* people, you become *depress* too.

- When I was in college, I was *depress.* So were many of my friends. But it felt normal back then. Now I study in India; people are poor but they have so many celebrations, so many places to go and things to do to have a good time. There is so much color and so much music and dance. And I realized why we were all *depress.* In hindsight, it breaks my heart. Why did we have to be so gloomy?

- *Depreshen*—like oxygen—is present in every Iranian household.

Other blogs point to living "where laughing is frowned upon," "where the future is uncertain and hope is elusive," "where everyone else is *depress*," and, most commonly, "where you are always worried about tomorrow."

One does not have to agree with these interpretations in order to appreciate their ethnographic significance; and to judge them at face value would be misleading. These generalizations are situated in the tacit knowledge of several nuances (including a particular socioeconomic timing in the mid-to-late

2000s), and are meant to convey what is beyond their literal meaning. They need to be historically contextualized and psychologically unpacked for the affective desires that underlie them. Listening, anthropologically and clinically, to individual reflections on *depreshen* alerted me to both the anxieties of the present and the still-consuming narratives of the war, of childhoods lost, symptoms evolved, and hopes stolen. To listen was to be vulnerable to history, to strip myself both of a listener's distance or judgment and of medicalization theories. Yet, I learned that, as performative contributors to their own processes of medicalization, these narrators actively resist allowing victimization and suffering to become the primary categories of their lives. Instead, they create in such medicalization new social forms and cultural spaces; and often, humor shines through.

Numerous examples of such performativity with language are found in many periodicals; for example, the appearance of a section titled "Café Afsordegi" (Café Depression) in the weekly *Hamshahri-ye Javān* opens a space for expanding the domain of *depreshen* beyond the individual, mixing reflexivity with humor and social commentary with resilience (see Figures 5 and 6). The issue includes "Wikidepia," a satirical encyclopedia of *depreshen*-related terminology that introduced to readers expressions such as *dep zadan*, *departemān*, *depress*, and *Johnny Dep*. A compelling example of language as both experience and representation (see Figure 5). Another section in the same issue, titled "This Collective Melancholy: Invitation to a Gathering of *Dep-zadegan*" (satirical term for "those struck by depression"), features several reflections and commentaries on the week's topic: *trip-e afsordegi*, a slang term describing a person's feigning or giving the appearance of depression (see Figure 6). One commentary belongs to a young woman describing her experience of depression as "an illness that needs to be treated. When I was young, I used to rejoice in it, I drowned myself in its depth, self-destructively. . . . Refusing to see the beauty of life, I immersed myself in its sorrows. . . . It took me years to learn that life had much beauty to offer, and that one can live a better life if she wants to."

The same space that language opens for performativity, however, simultaneously evokes critical debate. In an adjacent commentary to the one above (Figure 6), a psychologist writes: "I take issue with this title [*trip-e afsordegi*], because it implies pretension. What you want to hear me say as a psychologist is that this is different from 'real' depression defined by such and such symptoms. This kind of judgment prevents us from investigating the phenomenon with the attention it deserves [. . .]. But now let me say what I think: What we suspiciously call *trip-e afsordegi* is in fact collective and social depression [*afsordegi-ye ejtemā'i*]. It is a feature of us *nasl-e sevvomi-hā* [the third generation]. We are depressed for social reasons; you can tell from the songs we listen to, the films we like, the way we think about the future." He then goes on to argue that his generation's cultural aesthetics are in fact a reaction to contextual issues: "Look at our generation's bitter experiences with divorce and unemployment. This is not an illness per se. We are not 'sick'; we live with our *afsordegi*, we go to work with it, we go to school with it; it's part of our lives, we experience it in occasional bouts. We even coin the very term *trip-e afsordegi* to describe it. . . . Which one of you has never experienced it, seriously, which one of you?"

This third generation, as the psychologist put it, or the self-named 1980s generation (*daheh-ye shasti-hā*), insists on demarcating its generational identity. Its members are indeed diverse in their worldviews and their interpretations of the past (i.e., being the children of the 1980s), but they are hardly indifferent to their history. They stand out for their preoccupation with particular cultural aesthetics that draw on visual, auditory, linguistic, and sensory prompts from the 1980s as a decade of war, anomie, solidarity, innocence, and perplexity all at once. They taught me that to ask how pathology becomes one's language and how one comes to call oneself *depress* required not only an exploration of the uncertainties of the present but also a rewinding and revisiting of the ruptures of their childhood. To ask what is remembered, in turn, means understanding generational demarcations and the kinds of historical and psychological claims they underscore. I followed their lead, sketching out generational boundaries—however blurred they might be—and listened to their narratives of mutually medicalizing life and humanizing illness.

Today, compelling accounts of daily life in the 1980s are persistently circulated among young Iranians, creating a new mode of self-recognition, sense of voice, and politics of the everyday. Nostalgia for the 1980s has only grown in the years since my interviews; today books, magazines, and websites increasingly memorialize the material culture of those who were children in the 1980s. Before returning to Samāneh, a few words seem necessary about what it means to call oneself a member of the 1980s generation, and why the 1980s have gained such significance in the Iranian psyche as a key decade of moral ideals, historical claims, hopes, losses, anxieties, and solidarity. Why are such seemingly mundane recollections of the childhood memories of *daheh-ye shast* (the 1980s) significant in the construction of medicalized narratives?

FIGURE 5: Two consecutive pages of the special section *Café Javān* (Café for the Young) in the weekly *Hamshahri-ye Javān* (issue 292, 04/10/1389 AP—25/12/2010). This week's Café is dedicated to the topic of *trip-e afsordegi*, or "feigning depression." The title on the right-hand page reads: "*Wikidepia*: An Encyclopedia of Depression," and entries provide satirical definitions of made-up terms such as *depology* (depressive epistemology), described as one culminating in "so what" [in English], *dep-marg* (depressed with

suicidal ideations), *deptor* (depression doctor), *afsor-dep* (combining *afsordeh* [depressed] with *dep*), Johnny *Dep* (posh kid pretending to be depressed to look cool), *departemān* (Persianized "department," referring to the apartment where the depressed young live), *depkadeh* (depressive village; for example, university dormitories), as well as more commonly used terms such as *depress* and *dep* (depressed person).

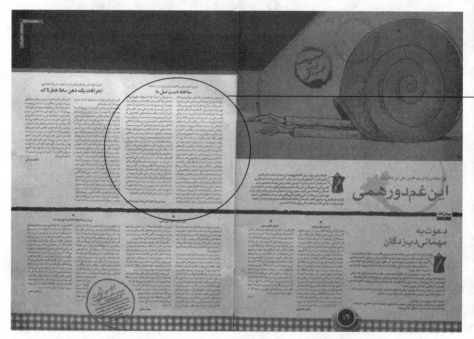

FIGURE 6: Two facing pages from *Hamshahri-ye Javān* (issue 292, 04/10/1389 AP—25/12/2010), titled "This Collective Melancholy: Invitation to a Gathering of *Dep-zadegān*" (satirical term for "those struck by depression"). The section features various reflections on *trip-e afsordegi*, including a column (enlarged on the facing page), titled "Our Generation's Making," written by a psychologist.

ساخته دست نسل ما

راستش را بخواهید من کلا با این دو تا موضوع کافه جوان که اولشان خورده «تریپ» یعنی «تریپ غرغر» و «تریپ افسردگی» حال نکردم؛ چون همین کلمه اول عبارت از همان بار اول کار قضاوت آخر کار رانشان می‌دهد. این قضاوت که غرغر کردن بد است و ادای افسردگی را در آوردن بد است. همین نگاه قضاوتگر از بالا به پایین است که نمی‌گذارد ما این پدیده‌های اجتماعی را به رسمیت بشناسیم و درست و درمان تحلیلش کنیم. در راستای همین نگاه است که به من روان‌شناس سفارش می‌دهند که تو فرق افسردگی واقعی را بگو. اگر این کافی است. باشد: «آن طور که ویلیام ساروبان نویسنده می‌گوید چیزی مثل گیر کردن بین سگ‌های سیاه است؛ ترکیبی از نشانه‌های درداوری مثل ناامیدی، اندوه، مشکل در تصمیم‌گیری، پایین آمدن انرژی، بی‌خوابی یا پرخوابی، کم شدن وزن یا اضافه وزن، بی‌اشتهایی یا پراشتهایی، احساس گناه و فکر کردن به مرگ (به شکل فکر کردن یا اقدام به خودکشی). شما اگر در طول دو هفته پنج تا از این نه تا نشانه را داشته باشید یعنی اینکه یک حمله افسردگی را تجربه کرده‌اید اما تریپ افسردگی مسلما این نشانه‌ها را ندارد. ما به میل خودمان چند روزی دپ می‌زنیم. برای اینکه دیگران هم از دپ بزنند ما با خبر شوند چند روزی ریشمان را نمی‌زنیم یا به خودمان نمی‌رسیم، بیشتر از معمول می‌خوابیم، لبخند نمی‌زنیم، بی حوصله می‌شویم و ترجیح می‌دهیم خیلی از خانه بیرون نزنیم و خیلی از کارهایی را که به طور معمول انجام می‌دهیم انجام ندهیم. تریپ افسردگی بیشتر یک اداست تا یک

مشکل واقعی. خبا حالا که وظیفه مطبوعاتی‌ام را به عنوان یک کارشناس انجام دادم می‌خواهم حرف خودم را بزنم؛ چیزی که ما بناگاه قضاوت‌گرانه‌مان به آن می‌گوییم تریپ افسردگی همان «افسردگی اجتماعی» است؛ یک پدیده اجتماعی کاملا بومی که مال ما نسل سومی‌هاست. ما به صورت پیش فرض و به دلایل اجتماعی غمگینیم. این را می‌شود از ترانه‌هایی که گوش می‌دهیم، از فیلم‌هایی که می‌پسندیم، از یادداشت‌هایی که نماینده گلمان در نشریه‌های جوانانه نوشته‌اند از محتوای حرف‌های روزمرّهمان و از نگاهی که به آینده داریم فهمید. بعضی از روان‌شناس‌ها پیش‌تر رفته‌اند و گفته‌اند حتی شیوه پوشش ما یک جورهایی اعتراض پنهان به دلایل اجتماعی همین افسردگی است. فقط کافی است تا تجربه‌های ناکام کننده نسل ما در تحصیل و اشتغال و ازدواج را مرور کنید تا دلایل این افسردگی همه‌گیر دستتان بیاید. افسردگی اجتماعی بیماری نیست. ما بیمار نیستیم. ما با این افسردگی زندگی می‌کنیم، دانشگاه می‌رویم، سر کار می‌رویم، برمی‌گردیم به خانه و نشانه‌هایش آن قدر با ما آمیخته‌اند که دیگر نمی‌توانیم از یک زندگی واقعی تشخیصشان دهیم. واژه «تریپ افسردگی» هم نسل ما ساخته است. شاید بیشتر برای توصیف همین نشانه‌هایی که شکل‌های حادتر بروزش را در یک قرارداد نانوشته به صورت شیفتی تجربه می‌کنیم. کدام یک از شما تا به حال تریپ افسردگی نگرفته‌اید؟ هان؟ کدامتان؟

سعید بی‌نیاز / کارشناس ارشد روان‌شناسی

این تریپ افسردگی لعنتی

یک روز صبح که رفتم دانشگاه دیدم هفت، هشت تا از بچه‌ها دور یک نفر حلقه زده‌اند. جلوتر رفتم و دیدم دوست صمیمی خودم بوداشک می‌ریخت و سوال های بچه‌ها که چی شده عزیزم؟ آخی بمیرم.. یکی دستش را می گرفت، یکی بغلش می کرد و هم گریه می کرد. من که خوب می شناختمش بیشتر نگران شدم. تا دیروز

برایش شدم فقط یک همکلاسی.. تنهایی را ترجیح می‌دادم. بعد دیدم بچه‌های کلاس با من سردتر و سرد‌تر می‌شوند. گاهی کنار کسی می‌نشستم و می‌دیدم که با بغض و وحشتناکی حرف می‌زند. یک روز که دیگر تنهای تنها مانده بودم و یکی از بچه‌های کلاس آمد و گفت چرا با بهترین

در مقطع ارشد می‌خواند اما کا بود؛ حتی در ف وقتی هیچ راهی افسردگی زدم؛ سنگ صبور یک

Looking Back through the Child's Eyes

Attention! Attention!

The siren you are about to hear,

Is the sign of a [red] state of danger.

It indicates that an air strike will imminently take place.

Please leave your place of work

And seek shelter.

"Red siren," radio announcement of air strikes on civilians during the Iran-Iraq War[4]

For many Iranians, wartime announcements of missile attacks, urging them to seek shelter, are a distinct relic. "Attention! Attention! The siren you are about to hear is the sign of . . ." and the screeching sound following still send shivers down the spines of many. Equally uncanny is what it evokes when circulated on the Internet, two decades later, or when it is recycled in art and cultural productions. Intermixing nostalgia and terror, it signals a shared meaning—that is, the experience of intense air raids targeting civilians during the Iran-Iraq War, known as the War of Cities, as well as the embodied and visceral experiences of racing hearts or running down to basements.[5] The children of the 1980s return to the siren, aesthetically, psychologically, and performatively, again and again. Consider this radio podcast:

Attention! Attention!

What you are about to hear [pause] is Radio Khāmushi . . . [*The sound of a siren follows*].

We are the 1980s generation, now scattered around the world. We wear colorful clothes but our insides are black, dark, and *depress*. . . . We want to extract this bitterness from life and show it to you, the way the work of Gholāmhossein Sā'edi did.[6] We are the most affected generation. . . . We are the *khāmushi* generation, born and raised under those periods of city bombing and *khāmushi*. [. . .] We want to have a voice. (Opening announcement of a Radio Khāmushi podcast, Spring 2009)[7]

This *khāmushi* generation provides a culturally useful platform from which to see the contrasts between numerous cultural streams and to underscore shifting cultural economies of the Internet and new media.[8] The word *khāmushi* means, variously, turning off (as in turning off a light), extinguishing (as in extinguishing a candle), and silencing. During the Iraqi bombings of Tehran, the word was used to denote the periods of silent (*khāmushi*) hush between the red siren and the all-clear white siren, as well as, more commonly, of the electricity blackouts meant to prevent Iraqi aviators from detecting residential buildings. Families sheltering in basements would clutch portable radios; thus the Radio Khāmushi of 2009 is also a reminder of anxious, huddled families. And much more.

Wars are always perceived differently through the eyes of children than through those of adults. Until the Iran-Iraq War ended in 1988, the spirit of Sacred Defense had dominated every aspect of Iranian life. Wartime solidarity and Shi'ite ethos were implied in most cultural productions, including children's programs and school textbooks.[9] Most of the fathers in textbook stories were now on the battlefield, while moral instructions, many now recall, also inscribed deep emotional states and a sense of vigilance among children. In real life, several children lost their fathers or other male relatives who sacrificed their lives to defend the country. Several others feared losing them. In the 1980s, state-run television had only two channels, and domestic programs were often related to the Sacred Defense. War conditions, particularly in periods of city bombings, generated homebound lifestyles, so people's imaginations were infused with what was shown on those two channels. What is ethnographically and psychologically significant is that today, the 1980s generation is conspicuously preoccupied with the children's programs of the earlier 1980s, persistently referencing cartoons—such as post–World War II Japanese or Korean ones dubbed into Persian, usually telling stories of children who had lost or were searching for their parents—and describing their characters—such as Nell, the Parisian girl searching for her mother who had gone to a place curiously dubbed *Pārādāis*, or the little orphan honeybee Hāch, also searching for his. The 1980s generation often seeks distinction from those older and younger by meticulously highlighting such memories. They remember, for example, when children's television programs began to lighten up in the later 1980s with happier characters, and how on programs such as the popular puppet show Red Hat Boy (*Kolāh Ghermezi*), moods changed. Trivial as they may seem, distinction-seeking references like these have come to shape their generational and cultural sensibilities. These seeds of future recollections also seem to be culturally and psychologically consequential as spaces where children would internalize wartime anxieties while creating in them new cultural forms. These fractional and gendered sensibilities are deeply inscribed in the body, producing feeling states and efforts at repression and rechanneling. Psychologically speaking, while many today consciously recall the childhood fear of, for instance, losing their parents, some others may have internalized those anxieties into catastrophic thinking or obsessive traits as adults.

Of course, this is not to say all was bleak nor that everyone was affected the same way, but rather to ask why the bleak moments are remembered differently and persistently by some today, and what they might have left behind, psychologically, in the imagination of the child. In fact, the 1980s produced a rich set of cultural products. Iranian cinema and art flourished. Despite the constraints of wartime austerity and international sanctions, radio and television saw timeless new productions, and talented voice artists delivered foreign shows with dubbed dialogue to Iranians. Some of the most prominent Iranian actors appeared in period dramas and tele-theaters, as well as in puppet and sketch shows for children. The creators of these programs were revolutionary idealists genuinely striving to instill authentic values in a decade of hopes and principles. The puppet show *Mice School* (*Madreseh-ye Mush-hā*) and the sketch show *The Happening Neighborhood* (*Mahalleh-ye Boro-biā*), for instance, told tales of camaraderie, loyalty, and honesty and continue to live in the fond memory of their now-adult audiences. Like peers elsewhere, *daheh-ye shasti-hā* also have fond memories of storybooks and story cassettes (*navār-e ghesseh*) that charmingly preserved folktales and children's poetry. Young parents among them often lament that today's productions are no longer as profound or meaningful as what they grew up with. Still, many report, the other side of this idealism was that children's programs, even when not bleak, were too dry and saturated with *pand va andarz* (moral advice). In the media's return to themes of family, asceticism, solidarity, and pastoral values, they recall a prevailing sense of dysphoria. More vividly, they recall the imprint of war on children's programs. News, roundtables, and the siren essentially all said the same thing: The nation was in a sacred war with the Great Satan, a moral defense against Saddam Hussein's brutal invasion, and a genuine struggle for justice.

Then, in 1988, the war ended.

When Iran accepted the ceasefire (aka United Nations Security Council Resolution 598), children were too young to understand why the war had happened. As they came of age, they found new appreciation for its sacrifices and values, but also learned about its losses; what was lost was many lives, homes, and families, and for some, part of a generation's childhood. Experiences of coming of age varied, of course, but generally speaking, as the society stepped into a new era, the 1990s witnessed both dysphoria and a gust of fresh air under the reconstruction administration. The late 1990s saw a relative return of social liberties under the reformist government; and the media embraced a move towards more colorful and uplifting content. Perhaps urban women and young people, students like Samāneh in particular, were the main beneficiaries of this period: independent of one's political judgment, many youngsters of the late 1990s remember how the media, press, publishing houses, cinema, and theater flourished and codes of conduct relaxed. They remember regaining international recognition, a sense of new beginnings, and, above all, hope. And *that*, they insist, *did* make a difference. *Daheh-ye shast*, however, never left them.

Various reflections on these themes began to emerge in the 1990s among Iranians and were later picked up by bloggers. The decade of 1980s became emblematic of moral values, solidarity, and affective experiences that continue to unite its children, even if in different emotional registers. There was now time to reflect, and much to be perceived, processed, appreciated, mourned, and interpreted, collectively as well as individually, online and offline. And there now was a new clinical language available with which to think and articulate what was left behind and what lay ahead. This was when psychiatric terminology, already popularized by educational campaigns in the media, began to appear in film, music, literature, and other artistic and cultural productions. By the late 1990s, this clinical language was consolidated in the media and had merged into the Persian lexicon, and the 1980s generation was among its first speakers. *Dep zadan* (made-up slang term meaning "being struck by dep[ression]"), it seemed, was now an acceptable mode of talk.

The point in attending to generational trajectories here is to underscore the generative function of (clinical) language in relation to the meaning of individuals' cultural references (as opposed to a simplistic and short-sighted argument of causality for an alleged illness among a generation, or other such commonly pathologizing assertions about Iranian youth). In other words, the point is to contextualize narratives of illness in their affective histories, to understand their emotional references, and to ask why individuals (or psychologists, as the one in the *Hamshahri-ye Javān* commentary) choose to *persistently* underscore their generational identity in their elaborations on what they call *afsordegi* or *depreshen*.

Patients as Historians and Diagnosticians

TEHRAN'S DUSTY FACE: SAMĀNEH. TEHRAN, LOS ANGELES, 2005–2009

Many people avoid talking about *depreshen*, because they are either scared or in denial. Talking about *depreshen* is the first step toward dealing with it.

Samāneh, interview with author, 2005

Like many others in her predicament, Samāneh used neurochemical, brain-centered explanations (often learned via media experts or doctors) while situating her feelings in a broader social malaise. Diagnosis, she recalled, provided her with the relief of knowing that what she was feeling was not her fault. Through her *Prozāk*, she found progress and passage to a different way of feeling. For her, *Prozāk* functioned as an "evocative object," to use Sherry Turkle's terms; i.e., it shaped her identity as a patient, it embodied power and evoked emotions, it transformed her from "unhappy" to a "broken biological mechanism" that psychiatry could fix.[10] And not just any psychiatry, but one endorsed by what is perceived as progressive and cutting-edge science: "You can get the Iranian pill for one-tenth of the price of the American one," she told me, "but, it makes sense; the made-in-Iran one is just chalk."[11] A world of aspirational readings seems to be packed in one pill.

Back in Café Shoukā, Samāneh's reflections alternated between individual and collective identifications: between the story of her ex and her frustration with her parents, to "everyone is *depress*," and the dust of despair on the face of Tehran. Neither polemic nor uncommon, her emphatically generalizing and exaggerated references reflect not only the intensity of her feeling state but also her reliance on collective perceptions and strategies of "getting on with life," strategies that are by no means limited to medicine. "I did a *fāl* [divination] last night," she said with an ambivalent smile, "and Hāfez lifted my spirits; turns out I have to be patient."[12] She sounded exhausted. "Who wouldn't be?" she repeated. "There is only so much we can fix in our lives. Just look at how our generation grew up."

"What do you mean 'how your generation grew up'?" I asked sheepishly. I am expected, perhaps tested, to know what her usage of *nasl-e man* (my generation) or *nasl-e mā* (our generation) implies. She put down her cigarette and gave me a knowing look: "all the duplicities." The implicit reference is to the 1980s, the "hide and seek," fearing the bombs, the school principal, the morality police, parents even. And that was when she brought up *barnāmeh-ye kudak* (children's TV programs) and the uninvited return of sounds and images in her dreams. In children's cartoons and television programs, she recounted the sad, anxious, and somber feelings of her childhood. And those, in turn, reminded her of the red siren interrupting those programs (According to the *DSM*, one could speculate, she was reporting symptoms of PTSD).

A few years and several Skype interviews later, Samāneh told me about a *khāb-e bad*, bad dream:

> You see, we internalized the war. Though Tehrani kids were the lucky ones! We only
> got to see destroyed buildings, the ruins left after air attacks, the hasty phone calls

after the white siren to see which relative's house was hit, who was dead and who was alive. . . . But it wasn't as horrible as it sounds now; at that age, one only knew that when the red siren went off, everyone had to run to the basements. It felt as though we had a tree house in the basement, just like in the movies!. . . . And that's the thing, even if it felt almost normal back then, it seems to have scarred me for life.

. . . So, it was the same in my dream; we were running away, everything around me was crashing and crumbling, I was so scared and kept running; but it felt as though I was an observer from outside. An observer who could feel my heart pounding.

Aside from dissociative mechanisms in her "observing" her own dream, Samāneh's description of her dream shares several generational, war-related, and embodied features with others I have collected: running for one's life; driving or running through tunnels; dark nights; the sound of missile attacks; being stuck in a house, or being sent on forced family trips to the safer outskirts of Tehran. They often entail detailed descriptions of environment, colors, smells, and sounds. But more striking is that these recollections usually pop up during ordinary conversations, unrelated to the war or the past. Later, in 2009, Samāneh shared with me two more disturbing dreams haunting her sleep even on the other side of the Atlantic.

In 2008 and 2009, Samāneh was earning a master's in fine arts in Los Angeles, where we met up again. She had found her way into "building a future" of her own away from her home and in pursuing her passion—art—rather than an engineering degree. "Living alone wasn't easy at first; I wish I could have this independence without having to leave my country." She had kept the blog going, albeit with a new design, less nostalgia for Café Nāderi and more engagement with life in the liminal spaces of migration and graduate school in a foreign country. And yet, the past persisted: "It was only after I left that I got to see the wounds, the gaps, the paradoxes. They felt semi-normal back then. Now they don't. I think about them. I think I can now see that the way my generation grew up explains a lot of my anxieties today."

Samāneh's insistence on a generational identification as a *daheh-ye shasti* is psychologically and culturally instrumental, helping her anchor herself and find meaning in an ecology of uncertainty. In his classic essay "The Problem of Generations," Karl Mannheim argued that generations form based on the consciousness of having experienced in their youth a particular generational location in historical events.[13] For the children of the 1980s, cultural and sensory prompts that remind them of shared historical experiences serve as generational markers.

This symbolic, rather than chronological, demarcation partially explains why those born in the 1980s as well as those, older, who remember growing up in the 1980s, all self-identify, or compete to identify, as the 1980s generation. Such remembering, for Samāneh and many others, takes various forms, social, virtual, private and public, turning them into "global generations," in the words of sociologists Edmunds and Turner, who have described global generations in terms of their increasing interactivity via communication technologies.[14] It is precisely in such online and offline interactions, both with other generations and among themselves, that I trace the discursive formation of *daheh-ye shasti-hā* as a particularly self-constructed generation.

In these interactions I also discovered their psychiatric subjectivity, i.e., internalizing psychiatric modes of thinking in the formation of the self and as a signifier of their generational sensibility. Samāneh's *depreshen* humanized and recognized genuine emotional anguish, as diagnoses often do. But it persistently went beyond the individual—it provided, and continues to provide, a space for underscoring what she perceives as her generation's shared cultural experiences. Theme songs, slogans, television programs, or clothing codes, of course, shifted and varied across the 1980s, but the sensibilities they created remain psychologically present today.

Samāneh's constant switching between "me" and "my generation," between "I" and "we" is significant and common in many accounts of the 1980s generation, on- and offline. Individual narratives persistently merge with collective ones, seeking occasional distinction or status in "I," while taking comfort and seeking recognition in the multitude of "we." The "we" is exclusive and inevitably self-constructed out of shared experiences:

> I envy those my age who don't obsess over these memories. I know many people just a little younger than me who are living their lives as if nothing went wrong. Maybe they're made from a different cloth. This is lonely-making, you see, for some in my generation. . . . Here, there are very few people with whom I can share how I grew up, and why sometimes I feel so *depress*.

Inevitably, a large part of the "we" is constructed out of the experience of the Iran-Iraq War. Children like her, Samāneh says, "internalized" the war. "We were too close to death at a very young age, without even realizing it," Samāneh and many others tell me. In my interviews, I am often given visual and visceral elaborations such as this one from Rāmin: "They took away our school playgrounds, and built [bomb] shelters in their place. There was construction work in our elementary school for as long as I remember. Young as I was, I knew exactly what that meant."

PROZĀK AND BRIGHT YOUNG THINGS: RĀMIN. TEHRAN, 2008

When women are *depress*, they will raise *depress* children. *Afsordegi* is contagious. When you're surrounded by *depress* people, you become *depress* too.

Rāmin, interview with author, 2008

Rāmin's sweeping generalizations about everyone being *depress* are reflective not only of a particular performativity among youth, but also of the clinical and diagnostic language many in his generation have adopted. Rāmin is among the cynics, however, mocking psychiatry and psychiatrists, calling them oblivious: "If you ask me why I am *depress*, I can tell you of very simple reasons: all my close friends, my buddies, are leaving this country. I have no one to talk to. I can't communicate with my parents; they don't get who I am." "Conditions of impossibility" is the term thirty-two-year-old Rāmin uses in his story of living on *"Prozāk* and whisky" and going against his parents' wishes by quitting university. As we talk in 2008, he is a freelance photojournalist in Tehran. He has experienced episodes of clinical depression and is on medication. His symptoms wax and wane. He lives with his parents, both retired teachers, and speaks passionately about his photography.

For Rāmin, *depreshen* is an "existential condition of impossibility" rooted in a mélange of past/present; this is, after all, Rāmin reminds me, a postwar society. Often when I am told that common stress (of making ends meet or conflicts with parents) is "enough to drive you *depress*," the memory of the Iran-Iraq War surfaces in one way or another. Even if, as a Tehrani kid, he felt relatively unaffected by the war, Rāmin still witnessed how it made his parents anxious. "We were kids, we had the ability to live in our own imagination; but we ended up being raised by *asabi* (anxious) parents who were suffering from profound anxieties." In a rapid contagion then, the war and its consequences underscored further generational differentiations.

Unlike Samāneh, Rāmin has refused to leave Iran, even though his siblings and several of his friends are doing postgraduate studies or working abroad. "Those who leave can't make any claim to knowing anything about Iran. If you care and choose to stay in your own country, you have to accept the fact that you'll suffer like me." Hints of judgment flow my way. Rāmin resents his siblings, who, like me, left Iran. But with me, there is an additional gendered tone. It is not the first time that I have encountered transference-like moments that challenge ethnographic boundaries. In Rāmin's comments, relationships with women surface often as a symptom of social anomie:

> Little things, you see. I have nowhere to go to meet like-minded people, except for parties. But people in these parties are not from my world. There is no relaxed social space. Little things, you see. And every day, one of my friends leaves. I'm extremely lonely. And if you are not privileged or middle class, then of course you also struggle with making ends meet.

A year later, Rāmin told me about an autobiographic documentary, *My Sad Face* (*Chehreh-ye Ghamgin-e Man*), directed by Farahnaz Sharifi (2008), and suggested it was a great illustration of his argument about *depreshen* being part and parcel of living in conditions of impossibility.[15] The theme of dysphoria had already populated Iranian cinema by the late 1990s, particularly among the growing numbers of female filmmakers attempting to bridge private and public lifeworlds. But Sharifi's, Rāmin informed me, was the first explicit and intimate autobiographical articulation of *clinical* depression. The title of the film comes from a short story by the German Nobel laureate writer Heinrich Böll (1917–1985) and its Persian translation. Böll's is the story of a man who, living under a totalitarian regime, is sentenced to ten years in prison for having a sad face against the official mandate for everyone to have a happy face. When the order is reversed, he is sentenced again, this time to five years, for having a happy face. Eventually, he ends up adopting a poker face to get by. Sharifi's film tells the story of her *afsordegi* (*depreshen*) by bringing Böll's story into her own, both directly narrating it and using it as a scaffold for her own rendition of depression as experienced by a newly married woman. Rāmin related to Sharifi's depiction of her experience as a "condition of impossibility": "everyone instructs you to be happy, and Sharifi shows how absurd these efforts are." Rāmin discussed these efforts—rapid reprinting and sale of self-help publications, the creation of laughter workshops, or parents' and partners' well-meaning demand that one act cheerful—arguing that none of them could make up for the human conditions in which depression is rooted.

Over our several following conversations, Rāmin emphasizes these mundane yet impossible conditions. He returns to Sharifi's film several times in order to elaborate on them, insisting that while most people talk about the social roots of depression or dysphoria, Sharifi was among the few who got it right: one is *depress* not because of what society is, but because of what it is not. *Depreshen*, Rāmin argues, is not simply the direct offspring of war, unemployment, sanctions, or other social ills—one can always find ways to cope with those. Rather, *depreshen* results from the lack of things that could have helped one cope and create balance: displays of joy, color, cheer, play, laughter. It is about *living through* "conditions of impossibility," conditions that are certainly not remedied by laughter workshops or self-help books.[16] Rāmin uses Sharifi's film as a testimony to his analysis, but the choice also serves to display his artistic sensibility, his sense of loneliness, and his mistrust of psychiatry.

I try to bring us back to the latter; isn't he himself on psychiatric medication? I ask. Suspicious as he is of psychiatry as an enterprise, he still believes that *Prozāk* has helped him:

> You see, I can't change the time and place I was born into. These are conditions of impossibility. When, in only three decades, a country undergoes every event that one reads about in history books, from revolution to war, earthquakes, economic crisis, international sanctions, then even the simplest and most trivial realities will have different meanings—meanings that are exclusive to that very time and place. There is nothing I can do to fix this situation, nothing. The only thing I can do is to numb myself with *Prozāk*.

Rāmin juxtaposes psychological pain with historical fate, and his sense of loneliness with sociohistorical anomie, thereby challenging biomedical psychiatry's assumption of the individuality of illness.[17] But his is as much a story of hope as it is of pathology. Rāmin's cynicism makes the construction of his psychiatric selfhood complex; it confronts us with the limits of individual choice, particularly when there are not many choices available. Instead, Rāmin's choices lie in a multitude of sociohistorical conditions and cultural desires, dispersed across and embodied in contradictory life moments. This dilemma of choice, this "condition of impossibility," in part explains why he would surrender to the phantastic persuasion of *Prozāk*—that is, to biomedicine and psychiatry's spectacular capacity and power to reawaken in the mind of individuals a utopian dream of health, to convince them to believe, to hope, and to trust in the phantasy of recovery. The use of *phantasy* here, instead of *fantasy*, is meant to evoke the notion of phantasy as used in psychoanalysis as well as phantasmagoria and spectacle as per Walter Benjamin: in this case, as what psychiatry projects onto the individual who is experiencing mental anguish.

The concept requires some deliberation. Like Rāmin, anthropologists too are often consciously critical of hegemonic biomedical ideologies, which, coupled with the stigmatization of psychopharmacological interventions, should presumably make us suspicious of the very idea of being medicated. But individuals' choices to be medicated are also shaped by their very personal psychological experiences. Standing *inside* the experience of illness, or what one perceives as illness, changes perception and heightens intuition, giving way to a desire, if not an urge, to break free and through that experience. Once diagnosed or in angst, even the cynics among us may surrender to the promise of medication or anything else that might help. On the other hand, as authoritative objects, medical language, technology (medication), statistics, figures, and images can render biomedicine a *spectacle*, in Benjamin's sense of the word, and give it an illusionary effect.[18] People, particularly those experiencing immediate illness or what they perceive as illness, can internalize this spectacle because it operates upon unconscious processes, tapping into a utopian pain-free dream, thereby lowering their resistance to, say, psychiatric medication. This spectacular capacity can convince individuals to trust in a phantasy of recovery.[19] In the case of psychiatry and its technologies, the phantastic dream would be to make sense of the (dis)order of the outside world and its inside embodiment. For Rāmin, *Prozāk* evokes both the phantasy of a future without pain and the utopia that, informed by the intuitive knowledge of the past, attempts to evade past anxieties that cause illness.

The spectacular nature of medical discourses is also useful when thinking about the media dissemination, democratization, and popularization of psychiatric terms and imageries; think of publications, public reports, media representations, promises, graphs, sophisticated words and gene talk, or authoritative representations and seductive images of chemicals and molecules that are generously circulated in public.[20] It is only fitting then that biomedicine's privileged spectacle would find a niche among those seeking hope and salvation in health, in breaking free. *Prozāk*—the discursive symbol, if not always the pill—relocates hope for Rāmin by evoking a possibility of recovery from *depreshen* as much as from the past; as if recovering from this *depreshen* would equal overcoming a historical condition.

But this recovery, I learned, necessitated both remembering and becoming a new kind of patient: one who explains her *depreshen*, at least in part, in the language of history. Overcoming *depreshen*, whether through antidepressants or street drugs or blogging, involves an increasingly articulate witnessing to a decade that, in their words, "took away our souls" or "wounded our sense of self." Like many (urban or somewhat middle-class) others, Rāmin reflects on the 1980s vulgarization or "regulation of pleasure," the mundane, the ordinary, and what he sums up as "bright young things" that should have marked youth. His generation, he asserts, came of age with a sense of scrutiny (societal, familial, and interpersonal) and within particular institutional conceptualizations and demarcations of the body and its conduct, wartime anxieties, childhood aesthetics, and pleasure and play. Childhood, he believes, shaped his sense of adult self. This is not to reduce Iranian youth to a static subjugated category or to imply that all generational peers share these sentiments; on the contrary, Rāmin reflects on gender in terms of gendering and gendered languages and practices that are inscribed in aspects of one's perception of the self. At issue is to ask how such experiences influence the discursive formation of gender and subjects, psychiatric or not.[21] Perhaps Samāneh's description of this intersection of youth and gender provides a glimpse of these intergenerational and structural tensions: "as if our parents, too, were in with the morality police. . . . No one defended our childhood, our youth. If the morality police stopped me for my short manteaux, my parents would blame *me* for provoking the police and giving them a *bahāneh* [excuse]! Even our parents treated us like criminals."[22]

Rāmin does not agree. *Depress*, yes, but Rāmin says he is not a victim: "This is an existential struggle, the human condition; one has to find a way to live, to be, to endure." This is a key feature. For many of his peers, this urge to live, to tell, to come through, to overcome, and to experience joy (*shādi*) is as much a distinct generational feature as are claims to *depreshen*. This paradoxical performativity is best summed up in a few 2008 posts by a female blogger in Tehran:

> We squeeze pleasure and joy from Google Reader, from blogs, staring at this monitor, and [parents] think we are wasting time, but we are having the time of our lives in these pages; we travel, we go places, we fall in love, we see the world; and no one can stop us. . . . We dig up every rock to extract some joy from it. . . . Why can't [parents] understand. I get bored sitting with them while they preach, as if they were saints and martyrs when they were young. Someone should tell them: you had fun when you were young, and now that we have to deal with the world that you created for us, you brag about your own youth and blame us for wanting to have fun.

Perhaps Rāmin's diagnostic speculations can shed light on what is at stake here. More than mere lamentations about the stifling of bright young things, they compel us to ask what it means to *perceive* one's youth as deprived of trivialized pleasure or to feel helpless in the face of double binds and generational divides. This particular segment of the 1980s generation self-consciously charts its psychology not just in the memory of the inscription of ideologies in private life, but also in generational differentiations. For them, *depreshen* writes the story of larger social and intergenerational predicaments that underlie individual struggles.

A few months earlier, the same blogger had written, in a comment on another blog, about how many times she had changed her antidepressants. She listed Prozac and other medications before saying, "Reboxetin seemed to be working. I know because I am not constantly fighting my father about late night outings." Rāmin's Prozac and her Reboxetin, sites for intergenerational conciliation and navigation, help and convince them to embody the possibility of a world where not only illness, but also resentment and anomie can be cured.

Taking (in) the Pill

One's relationship with the psychiatric pill remaps and washes off the boundaries of selfhood. The medicated status alters one's sense of self.[23] While for Samāneh, *Prozāk* is a locus of hope and agency, for Rāmin it is part of a human condition. Both a transitional and a transformative object, the pill constructs new identities for them, moving the individual over a threshold, chemically "fixing" the inner while signaling modernist attitudes and social capital for the outer. At the most functionalist level, medication helps one to cope, nodding to the possibility that the social brain too, after all, might have been affected by past and present anomies. It also conforms to century-old modernizing forces; yet, in its conformity, it contributes to challenging the "conditions of impossibility" on behalf of the individual. In its intimate relationship with one's inner body, *Prozāk* interrogates and reconfigures what it means to be modern: to, literally, *take in* the individuality and Western-ness that the pill represents; to redefine the boundaries of choice; and to negotiate one's affect in relation to loss. To ingest the pill is to ingest the world that it comes from and to mold it into one's existing world.[24]

"Zoloft never replaced the processes of mourning," thirty-one-year-old poet and designer Sara told me, recalling her episode of *depreshen* following the loss of an aunt who was like a mother to her. "But it worked for me, in the sense that a few weeks later, I was able to eat and get out of bed. I even left home and went hiking to clear my head. In a way, I was relieved when I was diagnosed; I wasn't being weak or weird, I was ill." In the language of the *DSM-IV*, the impairment of Sara's "function" differentiated diagnosis and illness from "normal" grief. Regaining function, then, is clinical success. For Sara, though, this success created a perplexing remorse:

> Part of me felt I was betraying my aunt, myself, and whatever due process of mourning that I was escaping. Another part of me was frustrated that I was numb,

that I could no longer write painful, to-the-marrow-consuming poems. . . . I now realize why we have these rituals of commemoration on the third, seventh, and fortieth days after one's passing.[25] I used to find them annoying, but now I see how long it takes to mourn. *Dāru* [medication] fast-forwarded some of that for me.

Sara internalizes both the pill (as an evocative object) and her relationship with it consciously and unconsciously, as she takes in the world that the pill comes from.[26] Not all losses, however, are singular or legitimated like Sara's (for many, loss has endured, while for others, underneath each individual loss lingers the ghost of collective losses, of loved ones, of integrity, of the social fabric of life itself); nor does medication always work for everyone. Several scholars have raised questions about the efficacy of antidepressants, underscoring the lack of transparency in the pharmaceutical enterprise and randomized clinical trials; others have criticized the increasing pharmaceuticalization of sadness and grief.[27] But these often-valid debates usually take place in isolation from a discussion of the nonchemical processes and lived conditions that compel individuals like Rāmin and Sara to medicate themselves. The medicalized, in these debates, often adopt the role of survivor, if not victim, of psychiatry. But far from a value-neutral biomedical intervention, the ingestion and introjection of the pill is a profoundly personal and political act that shifts the demarcations of the body. Samāneh, Rāmin, and Sara urge us to pay attention to their inner struggles, hesitations, fragmented choices, and desires to embody the phantastic persuasion of *Prozāk* by assigning to it not only a chemical, but also a sociohistorical responsibility to recognize, legitimate, and, in a wishful way, remedy their experience of anomie.[28]

Located at the intersection of a triumphant narrative of biomedicine and internalized anxieties, uncertainties, and stigmas, *Prozāk* evokes mixed feelings for them, from remorse to liberation, from helplessness to progress. It serves to defy mortality and to resist posterity. Its working manifests in various tones, from sarcastic to resilient, from value-neutral and objective to witty and nuanced. *Prozāk* "helps us get on with our lives against all odds," as the thirty-one-year-old Lidā, a young engineer working for a tourism company, tells me: "We find a way to live, we don't give in." As if the inner voice of longings and desires, *Prozāk* becomes the physical device, the technology, through which and with which individuals think and interpret the world around them.[29] Carrying the authority of biomedicine, it empowers and makes vulnerable at once, invading the self, opening it up, like a surgical tool opening the body, implanting hope, and making one dependent. *Prozāk*, above all, evokes the dream of a better place (socially, medically, historically, psychologically) and of breaking through and beyond mental anguish.

Depreshen *as a Cultural Resource: Psychiatric Subjectivity*

There is something inherently humanistic about what is to be theorized or analyzed in the making of mental angst and individual and social suffering. Evidently, the individuals discussed in this chapter are embedded in specific social locations; their interpretations thus do not reflect everyone's experience or interpretation of depression. Investigating the lived experience of their particular articulation of illness and medication, however, helps us understand the psychocultural processes their choice of *language* reflects.

The theoretical apparatus here is used only in the hope that readers, myself included, come away from this work with the ability to imagine parts of human experience that may otherwise be inaccessible to us. Several years of listening to *Prozāk* diaries have confronted me with the limitations of both diagnostic categories and our theories of medicalization. For one thing, the undifferentiated translation of clinical depression, PTSD symptoms, anxiety disorders, situational depression, adjustment disorders (following grief, for instance), learned hopelessness, and social dysphoria into the shorthand *depreshen* or *afsordegi* challenges common critiques of medicalization that may fail to take into consideration linguistic nuances and cultural desires. Psychiatrically medicalized individuals such as Samāneh and Rāmin, far from being recipients of top-down biologizing processes, performatively create their own biomedical and social truth in a very specific historical context. Their *depreshen* as representation, as a category of experience, and as a site for meaning making serves as a cultural critique of standardized diagnostics by juxtaposing the *DSM-IV* against that historical context. Biomedical and pharmaceutical hegemonies that have led to overmedication elsewhere cannot solely account for their relationship with their so-called *Prozāk*.[30] Nor do they themselves perceive *depreshen* as silencing or marginalizing in the way that psychiatric diagnoses elsewhere have denied individuals' experience or agency.[31]

Unlike clinical depression or any top-down biomedical construct, *depreshen* here is actively constructed in the juxtaposition of psychiatry with various discourses of social and generational affect. In postwar Iran, psychiatry created a politico-affective impasse *and* resource at once: psychiatrization of dysphoria initially sanitized and biologized mental anguish, with the almost unintended outcome of making possible an otherwise muted social discourse around it. As evident in the psychologist's commentary in the magazine column mentioned in this chapter, it was medicalization that allowed young people's stories of malaise to be reattached to social causations. Psychiatry thus facilitated the *resocializa-*

tion of loss by creating a platform for integrating social conditions into individuals' explanatory models for emotional distress.

The emerging discourse of *āsib-e ruhi* (distress/pathology of the soul) in the 1990s necessitated and contributed to a discourse of *āsib-e ejtemā'i* (social pathology) in public media. On- and offline, private and public accounts of *daheh-ye shasti-hā* reveal how psychological distress persistently underscores its historical context and social memory. It is therefore in the marriage of biology with history that this *depreshen* is constructed. As I spoke to more and more young people who identified with *depreshen*, it became evident that daily life and its ordinary corners are the loci in which *depreshen*, often understood as pathology of the mind, emerges as a mode of "being" in the historical present. The normalization of *depreshen* talk also provides a space for reconfiguration of coping strategies such as humor. These narratives—at once narratives of illness and voices of affective memory—compel us to listen with an ear attuned to desires for clinical legitimation and historical accountability. They demand that we understand individuals' medicalizing *desires* vis-à-vis the psychological and historical claims that underlie them. A purely biomedical approach fails to capture this assimilation of ruptures into lived experience, the embodiment of its cultural prompts, and the normalization of broken narratives in one's life.[32] What is needed is an intimate and situated ethnographic look at how history shapes medicalizing desires and informs the ongoing processes of creating a way of inhabiting the world and the making of psychiatric subjects.[33]

Psychiatric subjectivity explains the bottom-up desire for, and the internalization of, psychiatric mindsets as a mode of thinking and a way of understanding, interpreting, and articulating individual and collective experience.[34] This new Iranian psychiatric subjectivity is characterized by individuals' simultaneous attempts at medicalization, historicization, and recursive articulation. In other words, individuals submit to a psychiatric diagnosis and yet performatively situate their malaise in collective experiences: one's illness becomes a language that renders life meaningful in the aftermath of a shared or unspeakable past. Such psychiatric interpretation of individual emotion and historical experience turns illness into a site of pathology, historical conciliation, *and* witnessing. Psychiatric subjectivity, therefore, suggests a bottom-up trajectory for medicalizing narratives that are situated in their specific social contexts, thereby allowing for theory, for new explanatory structures, and for new social psychologies to arise from the heart of sociohistorical ruptures—from below—making possible fundamentally different incarnations of medicalized selves.

Two key characteristics stand out: first, psychiatric subjectivity is expressly performed by the medicalized individual; she mobilizes several strategies of living through the everyday (from irony to pragmatism) in order to articulate her condition, both personally and socially.[35] Second, psychiatric subjectivity relies on, and facilitates, a *generational* conception of the self. Samāneh and Rāmin construct their *depreshen* in its relation to their affective memory and generational aesthetics; that is, to the ways they perceive their being in the world as tightly linked to the ways they remember and (re)construct certain pieces of the past. Their historical recollections are literally diagnostic (calling themselves *depress*) while their clinical reflections are historically informed. Memories of childhoods resurface in the (alleged) collective *depreshen* that they diagnose for themselves and their peers. Diagnosis and medication, for them, offer an "alternate universe of references," a possibility that contributes to their generational identification.[36]

These narratives—written though they may be in the language of *Prozāk*—are not meant to pathologize an entire generation. On the contrary, they underscore the internalization of clinical languages and explanatory models as cultural resources that help some individuals make their feeling states intelligible. These accounts situate the discourse of Iranian *depreshen* in an alternative reading of symptoms. They make *depreshen* a site not only for the making of psychiatric subjectivity, but also for processes of meaning making, breaking free, and working through. Rather than myopically focusing on whether or not depression (the illness) is on the rise, they remind us that memory-work ought to be at the heart of any meaningful investigation into the construction of psychiatric selfhood. Below the surface of *depreshen,* the shadows of what one has or has not lived always lurk.

Depreshen, in a way, points to broken processes. The overflow of shards of collective and individual memories makes Iranian psychiatric subjectivity an embodied site of psychological and cultural negotiation. The "I" seeks legitimation for its *depreshen* in the meaning that it shares with the "we." Their pasts and presents trespass, infect, invade, haunt, interrupt, interrogate, and rewrite one another. *Depreshen* looks backward and forward at the same time. As if to "be" in present and future spaces, one has to work through pasts that are simultaneously far and near: pasts infused with conflicting nostalgia for the good and the bad, for warmth and solidarity and hope intermixed with fear and anxiety. It is the very anticipatory and desire-textured capacity of this nostalgic present moment that leads the 1980s generation to look back.

Depreshen thus is not (only) an illness category; it is also a cultural critique of (American) psychiatry and its privileged epistemologies. It destabilizes the assumption of individual choice; it renders choice performed and fragmented, fleeting, and, at times, created at the limits of choice. As a site for subject formation, *depreshen* is a paradoxical domain of exclusion and inclusion: it humanizes anguish, provides the relief of recognition and explanation, and yet testifies, persistently, to generational claims. Its language both represents and shapes experience; it also lets one remain in and reconfigure it.[37] *Prozāk* gives individuals a language of remembering and renders psychiatry more than an overdetermining form of biopower that takes away subjects' ability to interpret and/or draw on their pain as a cultural resource: here, medicalized subjects mobilize multiple languages of desire and pain—including, but not exclusive to, psychiatry—into rich accounts of lived life.

Perhaps there is a space here for psychiatry of postwar societies and for an alternative reading of psychological trauma.[38] Generational experiences of childhood ruptures (such as wartime memories) cannot be summed up as trauma or reduced to diagnostic categories such as depression or PTSD, nor can they fit into orthodox debates regarding the medicalization of mental illnesses. Psychiatry is only one of the many ways Iranians reveal and negotiate their psychological predicaments. A purely biomedical interpretation of the aftermath of ruptures can thus reify and medicalize its experience into an individual diagnosis, which, from the clinical perspective, is to be individually cured and erased. But an anthropological shift away from the clinical register toward gaps, escapes, pauses, silences, and cultural constructions of shared meaning may guide us to a world of new therapeutic possibilities. *Daheh-ye shasti-hā*'s construction of psychiatric subjectivity, in the broadest sense, is a way of navigating ruptured pasts, slippery presents, and uncertain futures. Through the language of psychiatry, they create new cultural forms. Following what has become *their* language ensures we will not fall into the trap of psychologizing a complex Iranian society by imposing on them universalizing clinical categories (like depression) that would erase individual agency and cultural histories. As the next chapter will illustrate, they also urge us to listen to what, and how, they remember.

The Blogger

In art class at school, we used to draw red tulips with blood dripping from their petals, like the blood of our martyrs. From each drop, a red tulip would grow. Martyrs never died. I always prayed for them and their families. After school, I'd run all the way home, take off my *maghna'eh* [headscarf], throw my *rupush* [school uniform] on my bed, sit in front of the TV and the Betamax video player. I would press the play button to watch a cartoon (my favorite was *Cinderella*), as my mom brought my snack, a tray of bread, butter, jam, and sweetened tea. At five o'clock, I would switch to the children's program on Channel 1. There was no Cinderella there, no tiaras, no silver shoes, no happy ending. There was Little Ali waiting for his father; Nell and others looking for their dead mothers. I felt very sad for them. There was a lot of heartache in their lives. I always wanted to be brave like Little Ali, but I never liked Nell. The hour-long children's program used to be interrupted with martial announcements of latest developments at the front, or in those darker days, with the red siren and then we had to run to the basement; sometimes I imagined myself in the tiara and the puffy pink Cinderella dress, and we would all run down the stairs. I don't remember a lot of things, but these have stayed with me. Younger people won't understand any of this; they have no idea. Swinging between Disney and anthems, between Nell and Little Ali, felt normal back then. I didn't know any other way.

. . . Western people think we must have had a miserable childhood! But I have a lot of good memories too! Most of us, at least in Tehran, were fine, thanks to those brave men who put their lives on the line for us. . . . We got to have imaginary friends and play hide-and-seek away from the battlefield. We got to play with our classmates and fill the gap between missile attacks with cartoons and birthday cakes. I mean, of course, I remember the siren, the bombs, the funerals, the fear. But things kept changing, getting better and then getting worse again. . . . And here we are now; we will be the last generation to remember the war.

Neda, thirty-year-old blogger in Tehran
(Letter to the author, 2007)

CHAPTER 5

Material Remains, Cultural Aesthetics, and Generational Forms

In these alternative voices and memories, we have found a new, shared appreciation for what that war meant. This has brought us closer as a generation.

Interview with artist Golrokh Nafisi, 2012

BIOMEDICAL PSYCHIATRY has a peculiar relationship with remembering, particularly with regard to the psychological effects of wars. Increasingly, it has treated them by defining normative stages of symptoms to demarcate "normal" and "pathological" reactions. Identifying memories as traumatic, psychiatry's objective is to erase excessive memory and relieve its symptoms. Tension arises, then, when individuals insist on both remembering *and* medicalizing their memory.

Let's not forget that such a clinical rendition of memory is itself situated in a century-long history that resulted in the consolidation of trauma as a universal, event-based concept and of post-traumatic stress disorder (PTSD) as a diagnostic category in Western psychiatry.[1] To say this is not to undermine the individual's experience of suffering, but to underscore its cultural forms of recognition and entry into both medical and lay discourse.[2] Diagnostic categories and labels such as trauma and PTSD are culturally situated; as are, indeed, critical debates over their validity set in their own cultural histories. In what follows, I turn to the psychological afterlife of the Iran-Iraq War among the children of the 1980s, in order to ask what cultural and psychological possibilities may lie in the reconstruction (or medicalization) of their childhood memories. The analytical focus here is not on the events themselves, the historical accuracy of their recollections, or the ideological persuasion or interpretation of their narrators. Rather, the point is to understand cultural references, emotional themes, and languages with which the childhood experience of events is internalized, reconstructed, and interpreted. These accounts do not speak for everyone across a generation, but are meant to capture a sense of generative affectedness among those who actively underscore these generational demarcations and engage in such modes of remembering and retelling: they open a space for a cultural critique of trauma theories and the paradigm of PTSD.

The highly self-reflexive ways in which young generations discuss affective states such as *depreshen* provide an opportunity to explore debates about the appropriate cross-cultural translation of diagnostic labels. Many *daheh-ye shasti-hā* (the 1980s generation) refer to their wartime childhood memories as *toromātik*, a term only recently incorporated into Persian. But the social meaning and cultural hermeneutics of *toromā* do not map onto single events or psychological trauma. Rather, the term raises questions about how history is psychologically "lived," infusing itself in the present, in the afterlife of past ruptures, causing further ruptures in living through and remembering them. I use the term *rupture*, rather than trauma, in my analysis of such embodied pasts. The term *rupture* surpasses the limitations of the concept of trauma; it allows Persian terms such as *toromā, khātereh* (memory), *khoreh-ye ruhi* (psychological canker-like wound), *āsib-e ravāni* (loosely, "psychological damage"), *zarbeh-ye ruhi* (blow to the soul), and *feshār-e ruhi* (distress and pressure on the soul/psyche) to emerge within their own trajectories of meaning. Rupture also allows for the diffused nature of the psychological experience of historical conditions and their aftermath. If trauma is individual, ruptures are shared; they are intersubjectively interpreted, legitimized, and reconstructed as part of the makeup of generational demarcations. Ruptures disrupt the order of one's world and create anomie. They live on in the social mind. Trauma's territory is psychological. But ruptures can be culturally generative in that they create new social forms, voices, cultural aesthetics, and identifications.

Not only is the generational temporality of ruptures distinctive for *daheh-ye shasti-hā*, so too is their insistence on simultaneous remembering and medicalizing—more precisely, adopting medicalization as both therapy and politics of identity. As one of the many affective strategies for navigating the present, medicalization then can voice a generational demand for historical accountability. Understanding ruptures, in this case, also requires understanding the historical and psychological significations of the cultural and material memorabilia of the 1980s. The triviality of these objects and mementos reveals the mundane conditions of possibility underlying individuals' identification with psychiatric diagnoses. But beyond accounting for alleged *depreshen* or PTSD, *daheh-ye shasti-hā* are aspiring historians writing the fragmented stories of a generation, online and offline.

In psychoanalytic terms, unrecognized loss can endure for decades in various forms of hyper-remembering and compulsive retelling.[3] *Daheh-ye shasti-hā*'s retellings are characterized by the normalization of a diagnostic mode of thought as well as persistent revival and mobilization of wartime cultural relics. This active historicization is part of a larger attempt at historical conciliation and witnessing to the 1980s as the decade that they believe shaped their childhood and was neglected by the outside world, and to losses for which mourning was interdicted. What is at stake in the recovery of their generational voice, however, is individual attempts at creating one's truth by virtue of having lived through particular historical moments.[4] "Individual lives are defined by context," Das wrote in "The Act of Witnessing," "but they are also generative of new contexts."[5] Here, I explore some of the culturally generative venues for the compulsive return of the 1980s: in the interrelations between online and offline lives, between blogs and works of art, between dreams and waking life. In them, I look for recursive processes of remembering or forgetting that produce new cultural contexts and generational identities.[6]

A Never-Ending War: Dina. Los Angeles, 2008–2009

"We share a messed-up history that younger people won't understand," twenty-eight-year-old Dina tells me, laughing, using English for "messed up." We are at her home in Los Angeles, where she has lived since her family left Iran a decade ago. "What do you mean?" I ask.

> I doubt if I'm the only one, but when I was little I was obsessed with the thought of my parents dying; everyone was worried about the next missile attack. And when I began school, I became even more obsessed, especially worrying about my mom. There was this time in first grade when our *tarbiati* [moral education] teacher told us that women who wore perfume in public would burn in the flames of fire in hell. For weeks I had this consuming thought that my mom was one of the sinners and couldn't stop imagining her burning. Now, you tell me: if that's not messed up, what is?

Dina laughs. I imagine her in one of those elementary school classes, a tiny girl sitting in a row of three on a bench-desk, in a black *maghna'eh* (headscarf) and a navy *rupush* (front-buttoned uniform). *Tarbiati* teachers, often young pious women responsible for the moral guidance of children, had a short-lived existence and varied in their approaches; some are even remembered fondly. But this particular one, along with wartime childhood anxieties, lives on in Dina's memory. "These things are important," she continues.

And that's why I know my *depreshen* is not the same today. It's different now. I may be homesick, or sad, or down, and I know that's a mood thing. Only now do I realize that when I was *depress* back then, I was in fact anxious [*asabi*], you know, I had a lot of anxiety as a child, especially during the war.

She jokingly continues, "I think we were *depress* kids, seriously, just look at this," she says, turning to her computer. She shows me a blog post depicting an Iranian children's comedy called *The Fat Man and the Thin Man* (*Chāgh-o Lāghar*) from the 1980s. Aired annually during *daheh-ye fajr* (celebration of the February anniversary of the revolution), it was the story of two clumsy SAVAK detectives,[7] played by actors in puppet masks and white gloves, who consistently failed to block revolutionary activities in the 1970s, particularly those performed by a wily ten-year-old boy. We sipped tea and looked at the monitor. The post, along with its picture of the two detectives directing readers to YouTube clips, had been widely circulated in 2008. The entry read:

I had buried [the detectives] in my unconscious for a very long time. The scary detective pair that we knew from Channel 2 . . . I never had a good feeling about them. Like most cartoons we used to watch, it was very gloomy . . . All we knew was orphans who had either lost a parent or spent their lives searching for them. And at the end of the day, they never found anything! All the cartoons were basically saying: this world is nothing but misery. . . . And that is who we are: the lamenting generation [*nasl-e hasrat*]. We lament, and we lament.[8]

That a seemingly comic clip would prompt such emotional and exaggerated self-identification with misery is striking. Not everyone feels that way, indeed, nor were all children's television shows about orphans. But this tendency to generalize and to pluralize one's experience is itself psychologically and ethnographically significant. Dina agrees: the only child of former leftist revolutionary students, her uncle was a pilot in the air force. She was only a toddler when he was defending the country during the war, but she grew up in the shadow of his stories and those of her parents' activism in the late 1970s. Her uncle's reminiscences were patriotic; her parents' filled with utopian desires and the loss of friends to war or exile. Her parents had also experienced firsthand the Cultural Revolution: as young professionals, they failed ideological background checks when seeking employment. Despite it all, Dina's childhood and disposition remained happy. Her wide smile still brightens the room, but her wit conceals only so much. She says she was somewhat *depress* toward the end of high school in Tehran. In Los Angeles, she finally spoke to a therapist, "to resolve my issues; I realized how many of them were rooted in the childhood we all had." The "we" again.

This constructed "we" is not historically representative. Still, for Dina, the shared nature of said childhood serves to legitimate her *depreshen*, which she also traces in "feeling extremely suffocated" in her "strict" high school. It was just as children like Dina were becoming young adults that mental health experts started to be seen on television and heard on the radio, talking about anxiety disorders, depression, PTSD, and when and how to seek help. Dina, like many others, is unsurprisingly comfortable with incorporating a psychiatric language into her identity politics and acts of remembering. Her historical reflexivity, in other words, is knowledge-based and affective at once.

Reading the blog post together stimulated cascades of memory for Dina. Perhaps the stakes of remembering are higher for those who have left Iran. Particularly when it comes to the 1980s, maintaining generational kinship still depends on whether one "was there" when the collective "we" experienced a particular moment. Dina belonged to a time when the war was integral to many of the stories of school textbooks. In real life, many children lost their fathers or homes while many others feared losing them. From a child's perspective, death seemed to be a fact of life. Today, countless nostalgic accounts of those childhoods populate print media and the Internet alike, recalling warmth and solidarity and anxiety all at once, and often reminding the younger readers that this was a moment in history "you don't remember." Dina wittily reminisced about morning ceremonies at school, lining up in queues, listening to recitations of the Holy Quran, doing exercises, reciting slogans, and then marching to class. "Marg bar Amrikā!" they would shout. "Death to" Israel, to *Englis* (England), to "imperialism," to all the enemies, she recalled one by one. I imagine Dina in that queue, a restless bundle of energy, mouth wide open, perhaps shouting louder than everyone else. "We obviously took death very seriously as children!" she jokes.

Not everyone agrees, of course; these interpretations vary depending on one's beliefs and affiliations. In many devout families, the private family sphere was not distinct from the public sphere in the way it was for Dina; and state codes of conduct were in harmony with those of many families whose children did *not* experience the same kind of double binds that Dina did. But, psychologically speaking, the question is whether for children, wartime cultures might have instilled particular feeling states or private anxieties—a point that Iranian researchers and practitioners have already raised in their studies of the impact of the war on children's health.[9] Powerful teachings and public displays of cultural reform found an impressionable audience in children; they also found new meanings in the magic of their imaginations when no one was looking. In a genuine attempt to instill moral values, for example, wartime murals, circulating footage from the war front, school trips to martyrs' cemeteries and sites of commemoration, or material residues (such as the oft-mentioned school-distributed piggy banks in the shape of a grenade) could also internalize new affective states in children.[10] As the anxieties and symbolics of war continued to infiltrate society's imagination, even later in peace, they might have reconfigured, for some children, interpersonal dynamics and ways of living in the world.

Unlike Dina, for whom the war is primarily highlighted in the memory of school rituals and missile attacks on Tehran, her thirty-one-year-old cousin Arash is the child of a *jang-zadeh* (war-refugee) family who relocated from the south to the capital. Dina connected me with Arash, then working as a postdoc researcher in biology at a London university. "As a child, I don't remember much from the eighties, but what is left of those days is a sense that I shouldn't take anything for granted; that nothing was stable." Arash avoids "sentimentality"; he favors an "objective outlook" and tries to explain why "*depreshen* is so common. It's rooted in so many places. Our Iranian mindset is infiltrated with despair and confused between tradition and modernity. But I think the most important root of our *depreshen* is socioeconomic problems." Yet, he adds, people overmedicate themselves in part because they are not well-informed, something that has to do with the "tradition/modernity" problem: "We're not prepared for an integral approach to depression; we don't even know what kind of specialist to go to. Though eventually, they all do the same: prescribe pills."

Despite himself, Arash's observations drift into his family's relocation and "the *jang-zadeh* kid," who hardly remembers the war itself. Arash recalled anticipating his father's return from the front, and this memory brought back a popular theme song from children's programs: "Oh star! Oh star! Haven't you seen my daddy? Yes I have; he was up there, in heaven, a guest of Almighty God." This theme song, closing with "I won't cry, I won't make the enemy happy," was for many children, the Iranian version of "Twinkle, Twinkle, Little Star," except it reminded them—and still does—of the imminence of death. Arash continues: "The war made us older children mature beyond our years. Of course, the root of most young people's *depreshen* is, indeed, socioeconomic problems. But if you think about it, those are in large part the outcome of the war and sanctions." Arash was once diagnosed with clinical depression and took antidepressants for less than a year before he finished his military service, found a "really good" therapist, and gradually felt better. "The pill helped a little, but wasn't the ultimate solution," he told me. But it has worked for several of his friends, "at least two of whom, I'm sure, are *really* depressed."

Back in Los Angeles, of the so far thirty-six comments on the blog post Dina showed me, some joked while others recalled fears and anxieties (most prominently, the fear of losing a parent) provoked by other wartime cartoon characters: from Little Ali to the Japanese or Korean orphans *Pesar-e Shojā'* (The Brave Little Beaver), Hāch, and the ever-so-melancholic Nell. Each time Nell comes up in my interviews—and she does a lot—she triggers the memory of the melancholic melody and gloomy colors and cities that looked dark and haunted. Nell, as the Iranian dubbed version of the story had it, looked for her mother, who presumably lived in a place called *Pārādāis*. Even without knowing enough English to decode the double meaning, most children intuitively knew that Nell's mother was dead. At the end of each episode, Nell's mysterious grandfather picked her up in a carriage and rode into the sunset. "I was scared only of Nell's grandfather with that long beard and scary face," one comment read.

Trivial as they may seem, such comments circulate on Facebook and are found in print media too: In a special section dedicated nostalgically to children's television programs of the 1980s in the weekly *Hamshahri-ye Javān* (issue 300, 03/11/1389 AP—23/01/2011), Nell was featured, along with several other more cheerful characters, in a column that read ". . . I don't want to cry. I don't want to think about my childhood with Nell in it and with that darkness and panic that clouded my lens. . . . They have an irreversible magic, they make you feel miserable and remain miserable. I don't want to think about Nell. It makes me think about the gloomy parts of my own life, even if the story reaches a happy ending at a mother's grave!" With his face invisible behind a mantle of gray beard and hair, Nell's grandfather seems to remain one of the intimidating characters in the memories of *daheh-ye shasti-hā*. For Neda, the blogger who wrote the letter that appears in the interlude preceding this chapter, the message was different:

> In my childhood imagination, happiness had something to do with blue eyes and blond hair, with Postman Pat in his red Royal Mail van, with Madonna and Michael Jackson smuggled to us by the undercover Mr. *Filmi* who'd arrive every Thursday with his Samsonite full of Betamax videos and his triumphant smile for not having been caught. Whatever it was, that bright and colorful sense of jolly was not for us.

Many disagree with Neda, for example, by fondly recalling Iranian versions of such stories, among which was "Little Ali," or *Ali Kuchulu*, a photo-animation series comprising sequences of still photos that, half-toned and somber, moved against the background of drawings and told the story of Ali and his mother. Most Iranians who grew up in the 1980s can recall the opening theme song by heart: "Little Ali, the little man of the house / He doesn't belong in stories / He is just like you and me / Not a hero, not too weak, not too shy, not too bold / Their house is like every other house / with a door and a garden and a pond / Lā lā lā / This is his mom / His lovely mom is kind / and he knows it / This is his father / He is so missed / He is on the frontline, may God protect him / Ali is such a lovely boy / Today he has a new story for us."

What is striking today is the powerful return of these cultural references in the process of generational identification. Consider, for instance, the online re-cycling and circulation of the melody of Little Ali by *daheh-ye shasti-hā* in 2010. The new lyrics read: "Little Ali is no longer little / No longer do good grades make him happy / He has a diploma, he has done his military service / And he looks for a job every week / His mother is in debt / Trying to make ends meet / She cleans houses / She threads eyebrows / She has a heavy heart / Loaded with much pain / But she copes / And her only dream is that / Ali would be in first grade again / Vāy, Vāy, Vāy." In this version, "hands empty, heart loaded," Ali has been suspended from university (for his activism), and "wanders the Internet," instead of the narrow alley, "breaking filters on blocked websites." Samāneh once told me that the two songs, two decades apart, summed up the story of Ali's generation and the sense of uncertainty it grapples with.

The point here is not whether these sentiments are shared across the board or whether Neda or Dina speak for everyone; they do not, and individual inter-pretations and ideologies vary indeed. But the emotional stakes of remember-ing remain high. Short-lived as allegedly depressing cartoons might have been, both nostalgia and lamentation prevail in this corner of the Persian blogosphere. "As kids, our delights were small," reads another blog post, "collecting erasers or chewing gum wrappers, or having one of those double-layered plastic footballs. But our fears were big: what if a bomb hits our house? What if the war makes you an orphan? . . . As teenagers, our delights became sins . . . Our fears though, remained big: What if I fail the *konkur* and never make it to university, when one's fate is decided over a three-hour-long exam with multiple-choice ques-tions? Is it surprising, then, if as adults, we find relief in drugs?"

Such free associations and generalizations are common in blog posts and in conversations, linking objects, imageries, and anxieties of childhood to the present day in order to account for one's feeling state. They point to contrasting spaces of seemingly trivial, but increasingly instrumental, pronunciations of desire that underlie, but are often overlooked in, top-down formulations of subjects or cultures. The juxtaposition of Dina's story with these blogs is intentional and crucial, as I further discuss the Persian blogosphere as an extremely diverse and situated ethnographic site—a site for performative and affective reconstructions of memories—and its place in the medicalizing and historicizing of emotions. The point is to problematize the binary of virtual and real, and to show why Iranian blogs should not be read, as they often are, in isolation from the offline and lived lives of those who write and read them.

Wartime memories, like *depreshen* talk, are not always doom and gloom; they also carry recollections of the sense of solidarity, purity, and idealism that defined the 1980s. Like Dina, many other individuals utilize a variety of affective strategies, from humor to irony. These differentiate *depreshen* from clinical depression or from PTSD, and serve as tools for dissociation from the past. Moreover, what evokes a *toromātik* memory for some may affect others differently. One brighter comment on the blog post that Dina showed me read, "I used to love the detective pair: I loved their old colorful *Zhiān* that could fly; I was a boy fascinated with cars back then."[11] Others sprinkled their reflections with humor, irony, and wit: "The 1980s generation is fundamentally a doomed generation; when we were infants, milk was rationed; now that we are adults, gasoline is"; or, "We watched *Othello* televised without getting a glimpse of Desdemona until she lay dead, but Anthony Quinn's face in repeated screenings [of the 1976 movie *Mohammad, Messenger of God*] was a fixture of our childhood!"; or, "Those cartoons, the war, the bombs . . . Great timing being born, guys!"

Humor and irony, as in the following 2008 entry on an online forum, have become a generational particularity. Dina and I arrived at it a few hours after our first cup of tea, one hyperlink leading to another, time flying back and forth between 2008 and the 1980s. "There is no end to this! Our childhood on the Internet!" Dina reads aloud:

All my childhood was spent in wartime. The war was an obvious fact of life, one of the world's principles. Media told us that we were in *sharāyet-e bohrāni* [times of crisis]. After the war, we were advised to live austerely, because the war had just ended and we were living, again, in times of crisis. Then we grew up, Smiling Seyyed was elected and we celebrated;[12] but quickly, crisis followed, and this time, we didn't need the media to discover that, well, we were living in times of crisis. . . . Everyone believes *their* time was a time of crisis. . . . It is always "times of crisis" . . . . And the world will go on, not giving a damn about our struggles. . . . So, maybe after we got over winning the World Cup for misery, we could perhaps swim like a fish into the maze of life, and live. This is our way of being a *rend* [libertine].[13] We will learn living one day. Until that day, let's sing. . . .

I don't fight; I don't fight; I don't fight [*Man nemijangam*];
. . . Let's hold on to each other . . .
Let's forget about tomorrow; let's sing together:
The world is our oyster
. . . Let's take shots; haven't you seen the news headlines?
It's all nonsense
. . . We will all end up six feet under
So *what the fuck* [in English]
Let's dance to some *rock* [in English]
The future is ours; we are a bunch that was tricked
So who cares about what comes next?[14]

The song the author quotes, titled "Jang" (War), is charged with references to a generation that feels skipped, but its apparent nihilism and fatalism should not mask its powerful mobilization of cultural claims. "We will all end up six feet under" is, in part, a response to the idealism of their parents. Saying that they have been tricked reflects a consensus on shared meaning of lost promises. An adamantly antiwar generation, this one looks for peace and pleasure in the very mundane junctions of the everyday. I click on the next entry as Dina taps on her desk, singing along, "*Man nemijangam, nemijangam. . . .*"

A Virtual Café Nāderi: Weblogestān as an Affective Virtual Space[15]

The fantasy of a complete record for all time—a kind of immortality—is part of the seduction of digital capture. But memoir, clinical writing, and ethnography are not only about capturing events but also about remembering and forgetting, choice and interpretation. . . . The human act of remembrance puts events into shifting camps of meaning.

Sherry Turkle, *Inner History of Devices* (2008)

In their first decade, the Persian blogosphere, or *Weblogestān*, primarily provided young people with a space to tell stories and to indulge in an individual and social performativity that was lacking in their offline lives. This was the era before social media. In those days, "being a blogger" was a process of identification and individuation. To blog was to be able to edit one's selfhood, to delete and cut and paste, to rearrange, to replace, to fantasize, to explore, to express, to experiment, to construct and reconstruct oneself, generationally, psychologically— historically even.

Iranian youth quickly became one of the world's largest and fastest-growing populations of bloggers; Persian blogs have alternately been listed as constituting the third or fourth largest blogosphere worldwide. In their early days, much attention was drawn to Iranian blogs as a space of resisting censorship (itself often understood as top-down and monolithic, as opposed to diffused in a range of cultural practices and othering attitudes), and a Habermasian public sphere that presumably promised the birth of an Iranian practice of democracy.[16] Beyond its assumptions of universal access to the Internet and universal virtual selfhood, such myopic focus on a politicized reading of blogs reduces the diverse, heterogenic, fragmented, and dynamic Iranian blogosphere to a static site of linear resistance.[17] It also masks the multitude of forms and voices whose dynamic interactions are as much affective and horizontal as they were political and vertical.

The dialogical format and interactivity of blogs connected generational peers, particularly before social media. In the late 1990s and early 2000s, bloggers made friends, met like-minded people through hyperlinks and comments, and occasionally arranged bloggers' meetups. Blogs even connected those writing from inside and outside of Iran. The children of the 1980s had created their virtual Café Nāderi, the sanctuary that they had always romanticized in what was left of the actual Café Nāderi in the 1990s: an old restaurant in the crowded heart of Tehran, with a poorly maintained backyard that no longer hosted poetry nights and literary debates as it had in the 1960s. The blogosphere was now *their* table, with chairs located in Tabriz, Paris, Tehran, Isfahan, Qom, and Toronto. This sociality provided a space to imagine, to escape to, to be, in the same way that some members of group therapies in Tehran regard their weekly meetings as, among other things, a part of their social life. Unlike publishing in print, blogging also held the possibility of instantaneous interaction, being read, and being heard. Its links bypassed time, space, and scrutiny and thrived in diversity and multivocality. These kinships might have been transient, but they were intensely built around sharing and articulating memories. This virtual community is a transformative feature of contemporary Iranian life and communicative circumstances.

The blogs hosted lively debates, helped internalize larger social and psychological discourses, and constituted new social norms and networks.[18] The imagined community of *daheh-ye shasti-hā*, to use Benedict Anderson's term, transformed blogs into a culturally and psychologically situated entity.[19] Blogging made possible new narratives of belonging and community; there was room in it for everyone from secular youth and young women to devout veterans and the clergy. It secularized, mobilized, and democratized the autobiographical voice. It gave room to and made accessible a fluid and scattered space (in both form and content) for an alternative history to arise. In a world of double binds, blogging offered an alternative way of telling. As transitional spaces, blogs blurred the boundaries and binaries of the Iranian public and private, the online and offline.

It is this transitional, affective (i.e., saturated with emotive performances), and generative capacity, rather than mere content, that leads my reading of generational blogs. While some are topically dedicated to the memories of the 1980s, in many others the specters of the past emerge and reappear in the middle of mundane chatter. I only draw attention here to the generationally organized ones that are characterized by their creation of an affective arena for the reconstruction of memories and for reworking and working through unprocessed emotions—that is, those meant to experiment with allowing oneself to be, and to feel, outside double binds; to experiment with voice; to bring the (Persian) spoken form into the more formal written one, and to push formal boundaries of language and conceptualization. The essayistic and often fragmentary journal-like style of their entries corresponds to the fragmented nature of these memories and subjectivities. But it also reproduces social forms that rely on exchanging and sharing, in pieces and parts, in a manner that is very similar to group therapy sessions. Facilitating the circulation of the unsaid, these blogs have challenged the privilege of certain metanarratives over others. A purely politicized reading and interpretation could obscure these forms of telling and the cultures they create.

The children of the 1980s employ various strategies for editing, reconstructing memory, and rewriting history. They also make strategic use of available languages and conceptual tools, including psychiatry, in order to make the construction of their self meaningful.[20] Their performativity relies, in part, on distinct emotions and desires, reflecting the high stakes of remembering. These stakes in the present are the ability to get on with healthy, successful lives, to not wallow in the difficulties that history has bestowed on them, and to turn those histories into strengths and even into demands for accountability and recognition. *Daheh-ye shasti-hā*'s desire to be recognized for these histories, along with the particular forms of sociality their blogs produce, situates "the virtual" in a particular psychological context. Hardly polished or aligned, this projected virtual self is fragmented, malleable, dynamic, and in constant exchange with its offline lived life.

Early scholarship on the Internet, particularly in science and technology studies, regarded it primarily as a projective space of possibilities and of "make-believe."[21] These blogs serve both as a space of make-believe and as one filled with the desire to "make sense" of the past and the present. In this laboratory of experimentation in constructing the self, to use Turkle's words,[22] the fragments of the virtual self not only perform but also *feel* differently. The Iranian blogosphere, in other words, has been a particularly affective space for experiments in working through ruptured pasts and for organizing one's reflections on life experiences.[23] In the process, the virtual Café Nāderi has made possible social forms and interactions that would otherwise be constrained.

Weblog-e Daheh-ye Shasti-hā: *Childhood and Its Objects*

We left our souls in the 1980s. We grew up when no one was looking.

The world looked the other way when Saddam was bombing us.

Quotes from a *Daheh-ye Shasti-hā* blog entry

Daheh-ye shasti-hā's online and offline recollections give us a glimpse into often nostalgic wartime memories, as well as how the war returns and haunts, how individuals mobilize available concepts and languages to make its experience intelligible years later. Archiving the 1980s songs, lyrics, and visual traces of childhoods would be a task of enormous scope. But it is one that the 1980s generation has already embarked upon, starting in the early days of the Iranian blogosphere. My use of blogs as generationally organized sources is meant to highlight the psychological and cultural processes of generation and subgeneration formation; being born only a few years apart and yet remembering different "small delights," to use one blogger's words, or cultural objects that carry "big fears" can allow one to lay claim to being a member of the *daheh-ye shasti-hā*. Of course, these experiences differ by social positioning. But their urge to defy forgetfulness is situated in a larger shared sentiment: that the 1980s and particularly the Iran-Iraq War remain unrecognized, unacknowledged, unaccounted for, by the world. Whether implicitly or explicitly, the 1980s-generation bloggers put historical accountability at the heart of how generational psychologies and their cultural sensibilities are constructed.

One of these is the group blog *Daheh-ye Shasti-hā* (Children of the 1980s) and its several spin-off groups on Facebook. The blog entries include anecdotes, memories, and stories of preteens and teenagers of the 1980s who remember the war and the early 1980s in direct and indirect ways. Prevailing themes include documentation of both the experience of wartime solidarity and the memories of double binds; the need to navigate opposed imperatives, for instance, or the realization that parents, too, were under a double-bind pressure to protect their children, sometimes by lying to them. But austerity and solidarity remain common themes. Pictures of the most banal commodities and brands of the 1980s are fervently uploaded as reminders of wartime camaraderie under economic hardship and international sanctions: bottles of Dārugar shampoo (the iconic domestic brand; some even made it their profile picture on Facebook for a while), the infamous illegal Betamax video player, the newsprint-quality notebooks that came in forty and sixty and a hundred matte pages, Khersi chewing gums, and of course, the cartoon characters. Next to them, one would find pictures of "alternative" objects of fascination that only some had access to: colorful collections of *khāreji* (foreign) erasers that smelled nice—collecting erasers in the shape of shoes, houses, animals, and objects was a common hobby—scarce "foreign" items like pink Barbie pencil boxes, ankle sneakers, or Disney-themed stationery sets that were not deemed proper for school.[24] Many of the objects and memories mobilized here are indeed relational markers of class. Even the symbols of austerity (for example, Dārugar shampoo) become significant precisely because of one's access (either then or over the following decades) to alternative goods and a knowledge of what was available in the outside world—not everyone had this kind of access or knowledge.

Even though objects often map socioeconomic boundaries, in these blogs they coexist in service of a shared historical and psychological claim. Wartime ration coupons for basic goods and pink ankle sneakers sit next to each other, and they serve almost the same purpose of documenting a historical moment that is otherwise at risk of being forgotten. In those days, and for those who could know of such things, souvenirs like Pepsi cans or foreign chocolate bars internalized a sense of conflict and contrast. Neda's middle-class obsession with Cinderella (as in the interlude preceding this chapter) may sound indulgent or exclude peers who did not have the same attitude toward certain commodities and cultural products; but there is more to these objects than meets the eye. They reveal part of the psychological and material desires that society struggled with and aspired to after the war ended. Beyond their materiality, for Neda, these were objects to imagine with, to escape with, to fantasize with, and to make sense of and keep safe from the world that was falling apart around her:

> They connected us to the outside world. The moment of opening the suitcase of a returning traveler was bliss; the splash of that exhilarating smell on one's face: the smell of colorful foreign magazines with glossy pages, the smell of Nestlé Nescafe and Lindt chocolate, the smell of cleanness and the shining image of a beautiful woman holding a bottle of Chanel No. 5.

It is Neda's situated *desires*, rather than the frivolousness of the objects she draws on, that I would like to focus on. While Neda reminisces over foreign goods, many other children, like Arash, recall a similar relationship with domestically manufactured plastic guns, soccer balls, or other cheaper toys. In *Evocative Objects*, Sherry Turkle describes a sensual relationship with objects as one that evokes deep emotions and that intellectual memory has protectively bypassed. Our relationship with evocative objects, she maintains, provokes a sense of what Freud called "the uncanny"; it marks "a complex boundary that both draws us in and repels."[25] The point here is to recognize the function of these wartime memorabilia as objects creating and carrying potential desires, envies, resentments, anxieties, and fantasies. Variably, the same object evokes a range of emotions in different people, from deep nostalgia to perplexity or even guilt. Take the example of a picture of a Betamax video player from the early 1980s; one comment by a female blogger reads: "Our *tarbiati* teacher once asked us whether anyone had a video player set at home. Having videos was a sin back then and I knew it. I knew I had to lie, which, she had taught us, was another sin. And that meant feeling very, very guilty. Not just for lying, but also for my parents having the video set at home in the first place." For another commentator, the same image was a jolly reminder of "how many times I watched the Robin Hood cartoon on that machine!" If the image of Cinderella reflects underlying middle-class desires, the pictures of ration coupons tell the story of camaraderie and solidarity despite wartime hardship. The sensual relationship with reminders of a so-called *toromātik* wartime past can evoke mixed feelings, but it primarily helps generation(s) to anchor themselves in time. Each object, along with jokes and anecdotes posted in reaction to it, is an attempt at immortality.

Today, images and sounds keep coming back in the media. For example, three special issues of the weekly *Hamshahri-ye Javān* in 2006, 2008, and 2011 were dedicated to "The Cartoons of the 1980s," reviving "the makeup of who we are now."[26] The 2008 one, titled *Yārān-e Dabestāni-ye Man!* (My Grade School

Friends!), included reprints of pages from elementary school textbooks of the 1980s and familiar characters in stories and television cartoons, while the individual accounts accompanying them served as the glue that still holds generational peers together. The *1980s Children* blog, too, presents individual accounts as both text and context in order to make uploaded pictures meaningful. It revives a sense of awe in its reconstruction of those years of sanctions, solidarity, and scarcity of goods. The tone of the entries is at times sarcastic: "Look what an amazing childhood we lived!" Yet, there is a sense of nostalgia, of wanting so badly to hold onto this aesthetic as what defines their sense of self. In reading post after post, what stands out is an inescapable urge to document pieces of a history that people deeply fear will be forgotten and overlooked: "The world looked the other way when Saddam was bombing us."

The apparent lamentation in these entries ("We didn't want much; we were happy as long as no one would pick on our clothes") should not mask the resilience and endurance the entries project: "Yet we lived," and one of my favorite entries, "We found joy in eating pizza and reading *Waiting for Godot.*" Each post is followed by a large number of comments, mostly sympathetic, recalling the writers' own memory and, at times, mixing irony and wit. In most, however, nostalgic romanticization prevails. One would not want to go back, but one cannot help the pull of nostalgia. Uncanny indeed.

Commonly, depression and a host of (psychiatric) diagnostic signifiers are mentioned wittily as "our heritage" or as testimony to damage done and hopes lost. Sometimes they serve as anchors for holding onto and keeping alive the memories that, according to the overall impression of these blogs, are implied at the heart of what is perceived as *depreshen.* The seeming resignation in these accounts, however, is simultaneously contradicted by the strategies invoked for getting on with life (including, but not limited to, humor, irony, and/or psychiatric medication). These strategies reflect a rational tendency, commonly articulated as "being modern," which is manifest, in part, in the very act of blogging and exposing one's feelings to public scrutiny.

The virtual space also serves as a platform for marking generational boundaries by drawing a distinction between what is and what is not remembered. These boundaries are fluid, but they reflect the urge to seek distinction from older (parents') generations, as well as among mini-generations. For one thing, the 1980s and the 1990s witnessed rapid changes, leaving young people only a few years apart in age with extremely different cultural sensibilities. "You should have seen how subdued and stoic the presenter guy [in the children's show] looked in *our* time," one blogger joked, commenting on *Amu-ghannād* (Uncle Ghannād), a famous presenter whose children's show aired a few years after *Chāgh-o-Lāghar* was on air; "Now he almost dances for children on television."

More significant distinctions claimed by *daheh-ye shasti-hā* draw on the broader sociohistorical contexts in which they have come of age. In 2009, for instance, the 1980s generation reclaimed a voice in virtual space and responded to long-standing accusations of being—in the eyes of those born in the early 1970s and the 1960s—a generation bereft of ideals. A few weeks before the presidential election, the leitmotif of hope in all campaigns had lifted spirits. The 1980s and its triumphs were mobilized in election campaigns by all candidates in various ways. Generational references resurfaced and created lively debates. Independent of the contentious, and undoubtedly tragic, events that followed, these prior debates were culturally generative; and no word was more powerfully used, by all parties, than the word *generation*. Various factions of the children of the 1980s, from *basij* to reformist, extended their networking in blogs and on Facebook, Twitter, FriendFeed, and Google Reader, to real life, mobilizing references to *daheh-ye shast* (the 1980s) and incorporating its colors and sounds and imageries. Culturally speaking, this allowed for *āshti* (reconciliation) between generations that had previously been in a state of *qahr* (dispute where communication stops), unable to communicate due to the lack of shared experiential referent points. Until then, even for some of the children of the Iran-Iraq War martyrs and veterans, '80s *soruds* (anthems) and slogans seemed outdated and nostalgic; they were the past and belonged to parents who didn't blog. Now young people revived, borrowed, reworked, and recycled revolutionary *soruds*, images, slogans, and cultural references to the 1980s, including the Karbala paradigm.[27] Common approaches that study the virtual space primarily through the lens of political frames risk overlooking this psychocultural functioning of the virtual.

The psychological and cultural significance of such performativities lies, for all parties involved, in what they revealed about generational forms (e.g., connecting the Iran-Iraq War veterans with their children), in their "affective" capacity for reworking emotions, and in the kinds of situated sociality they created in two domains: first, across generations; and second, by situating online performativity in offline shared experiences and vice versa. The Internet offers, as Turkle has argued in her *Life on the Screen*, "the value of approaching one's 'story' in several ways and with fluid access to one's different aspects,"[28] and thus ethnographic possibilities for an alternative reading of generational histories. Ethnographically speaking, to understand generational blogs in terms of their own symbolic structures and works of culture means seeing them as not only situated in but also shaping the context in which bloggers live their lives. It requires us to extend our ethnographic attention to the texture of the everyday, to the multiple cultural forms and relationships circulating among online and offline lives.

Processes of forgetting and remembering reflect social and cultural change. The *daheh-ye shasti-hā* and their "communities of memory," in the words of Avishai Margalit in *Ethics of Memory*, reflect more than a "duty" to remember or an agenda for the creation of the new subject category.[29] Rather, they remember as part of broader psychosocial processes and possibilities of legitimation for different generational and subjective forms to evolve. They perceive themselves as, in Neda's words, the last generation who will remember the war—hence their urge to document its affective experience. Their overlapping, competing, or complementing voices across genres and factions can help untangle the changing cultural landscapes within which different generations of Iranians have experienced their being in the world. In their compulsive repetitions and recollections, the narratives also reveal unspoken and unspeakable wounds. This is why repetitions matter. Pleasure in recognition, rather than avoidance of repetition, renders their retellings powerful and meaningful.

Childhood and Its Colors

The contents of generational blogs resonate with many other cultural productions. One of the most widespread visual forms can be found in paintings of Iranian artist Golrokh Nafisi, initially posted on her blog and later on Facebook and other social media. The blog . . . *Was Born in 1981* dedicated each post to one painting, each of which depicted a moment from life in *her* Tehran. Mixed with cultural traces of childhood memories, Nafisi's art aims to structure a voice for *her* generation.[30] Her generation includes those slightly younger than Samāneh, born in the 1980s, and teenagers of the reform era. There is a palpable sense of esteem, at times seemingly naïve confidence that differentiates them from Samāneh and Rāmin, let alone those born in the early 1970s. But so does their outspoken, louder autobiographical voice, as evident in Nafisi's self-portraits and expressive captions. As visual works of culture, her paintings operate as entries into processes of remembering that are beyond conscious control, both in the evocative revelations, projections, and recollections that they make possible and in their belated constructions of the past.[31] But this engagement with the past is forward looking; persistent and purposeful acts of recollection, rather than lamentation, provide a passage to a future that embraces life with all its shades and colors. Among her older paintings, one can pick up fragments of the past filling the gaps of the present as she claims the shaky ground of her generation's memories and symbolism. A famous depiction of schoolgirls, for instance, underscores the "color aversion" of the 1980s: the girls are marked not only by navy and gray uniforms and headscarves, but also by a powerful transmission of their affective state.[32] Sleepy little girls on a school bus, holding innocently on to their school bags, provoke and confront those who have once themselves been little girls on those buses. The painting transmits the tedious motion of the school bus, the agony of going to school at the crack of dawn—one can almost feel the impending morning ceremony, the anthems, the restless queuing, all marking her generational location in time. The specificity of depicted objects, too, speaks to a specific generation: this was a time of double-buckled brown or black leather Cambridge-style briefcases that represented the austerity of the era (see Figure 7).

FIGURE 7: Painting titled *Before the Morning Ceremony*, by Golrokh Nafisi. The caption on the blog posting reads: "The color of elementary school uniforms has changed, but the color of my childhood has not." Posted on Nafisi's blog . . . *Was Born in 1981* (http://golrokhn.blogspot.com/), December 2, 2008.

There is a world of difference, the powerful caption seems to say, between those who wore the brighter uniforms and white headscarves of the 1990s and those who came before. The implication is that only *proper* peers can possibly understand this generational location, though near-peers also add to before-and-after narratives in their comments on her work: "You know, nothing can ever give us our childhood back," one reads. "We didn't ask for much, we didn't ask for water parks, *khāreji* [foreign] pencil boxes, or LEGOs. No, all I wanted was peace and serenity. We learned to keep running but never arriving."

The following painting (Figure 8) complements the scene. This time the contrast is both generational and historical. As the little girl's navy headscarf frames her face in the mirror, the women of her mother's and perhaps her grandmother's generation are depicted in vintage black and whites, some without headscarves, some in tasteful school uniforms, all framed on a wallpaper covered with falling autumn leaves dancing in the wind. Gone with the wind, perhaps, are bygone days; what is inherited are stories in black and white. The girl's genuine struggle to make sense of contrasts is reflected in her perplexed face and the innocence of her clumsy effort to fix her headscarf.

The changing colors and styles of school uniforms are commonly used as markers of generational shifts. The oil paintings of another painter and graphic

FIGURE 8: Painting titled *You, Who Look in the Mirror*, by Golrokh Nafisi. The caption on the blog posting reads: "Remember everything that happened to you. Take it all in." Posted on Nafisi's blog ... *Was Born in 1981* (http://golrokhn.blogspot.com/), December 2, 2008.

designer, Shohreh Mehran, reveal such distinctions. For the older generation who came of age in the 1980s, the prevailing perception is that ordinary life was drained of color and filled with monotone imageries. Mehran takes photos of her subjects and then paints them.[33] Her reproduction of the original, the real, the personal, is quietly polemic; thus underscoring another generational distinction. In a series of paintings of female high school students, older than Nafisi, in gray uniforms, Mehran depicts the public images of the girls in "in between" spaces on the streets. The girls' faces are generally out of frame; when they are shown, they are covered or shy away. Yet, their coverage is challenged by the fluidity of their movements and the life behind the image: we see the bodies in motion, walking, chattering, as well as still, leaning on a car or sitting in groups of three or four. They all look the same on the outside, as though a testimony to their generational location. They bring to mind the accumulated energy of the young, waiting for something to happen. The monotone coloring also conveys a sense of stuckness during wartime; one can feel the heaviness in the air (the "dust of despair," Samāneh would say), the colorlessness of the city, and yet simultaneously, the anticipation, the excitement within, the aura of something about to happen (Figure 9a&b).

In Nafisi's *Frame* (Figure 10) we are looking at her version of a similar story: a little girl in a school uniform with angelic wings, shouting slogans with her mouth wide open, then growing into a teenager, again in a school uniform but now carrying a backpack (a marker of new times, as backpacks slowly became commonplace in schools), her headscarf loosening. As she grows up, the wings shrink and horns grow; fleeting innocent years disappear, and her face loses the smile. Then we see her older, perhaps in university, holding a half-read book, searching the world of letters, wandering. As she steps into her twenties, we see the headscarf fallen onto her shoulders, face stoic, looking out, uniform gone, horizons unknown. We soon learn that she must have been contemplating a departure from the home and from the past (neither would prove possible, would it?) and from "the frame," holding a suitcase, escaping the margins of the frame, face invisible, into the skies. The black-and-white line drawing resonates with the wandering, while the fiery red and orange color of the background is reminiscent of Akhavān-Sāless's famous poem, written after the 1953 coup: "My house is on fire. Oh spectating men and women! My house is on fire, a heart-wrenching fire." For the artist, there seems to be an inevitable sense of uncanny in her relation with the home, the frame, and "her Tehran."

FIGURE 9 (A & B): Untitled oil paintings from the *Schoolgirls* series, by Shohreh Mehran. 2009. Reproduced with permission of the artist. © Shohreh Mehran.

FIGURE 10: *Frame* by Golrokh Nafisi. The caption on the blog posting reads: "I was born in a frame . . ." Posted on Nafisi's blog . . . *Was Born in 1981* (http://golrokhn.blog spot.com/), April 27, 2009.

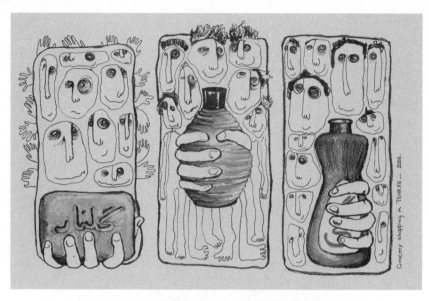

FIGURE 11 (A & B): Paintings by Golrokh Nafisi: *A Wartime Memento* (top), *Happiness . . .* (bottom). The caption to the first reads: "Kings of the market . . . wartime memorabilia"; and the second: "I remember . . . We had a balcony . . ." Posted on Nafisi's blog . . . *Was Born in 1981* (http://golrokhn.blogspot.com/), December 2, 2008, and March 2, 2009, respectively.

Leaving, however, does not mean escaping the past. Like the *1980s Children* blog, Nafisi's paintings are also concerned with material aspects of memory. In *A Wartime Memento* (Figure 11, *top*) we see a bottle of the infamous canary yellow Dārugar shampoo next to a bar of the green Iranian Golnar soap, both markers of wartime austerity, both distinguished by their distinct smell etched into her generation's childhood memories. Finally, in *Happiness . . .* (Figure 11, *bottom*), a party on the balcony of a flat in Tehran is marked with bright interior colors, laughter, smoking, snacks, and drinks. It reminds viewers of scattered spaces in wartime life where small pleasures persisted. In the black-and-white background, though, missiles are falling upon *Tehran-e man*, Nafisi's "my Tehran," to which many of her paintings are dedicated. An expressly romanticizing signature indeed.

When we met in Amsterdam in 2012, I shared my readings of her work before we discussed *depreshen*. First, she told me that the way I could read the stories behind her paintings illustrated that her work belongs to all who remember the 1980s. "Why the 1980s?" I asked. She responded, later in an e-mail, "Our return to the 1980s is the return to an unfinished past that continues to determine our present's rules of engagement." The unworked and unfinished keep returning. But, more significantly, Nafisi believes, "for my generation [*nasl-e man*], this is also a historical responsibility to document narratives and experiences that were overlooked in metanarratives, particularly about the war. Now that alternative voices have emerged, we have found a new, shared appreciation for what that war meant. This has brought us closer as a generation."[34] We also discussed color and mood. Although she has never been clinically diagnosed, Nafisi believes that "*afsordegi* [depression] is part of the life of Tehran and is only made possible in its juxtaposition with extreme mania—the kind of mania that is *only* possible in Tehran." She makes an important point, one that highlights the cultural particularity of this condition that is commonly called depression (or implied as such by statistics). She has many friends who are on antidepressants, but "since moving to Europe, I have started to doubt that our *afsordegi* is really depression; I think it is rather an outcome of repressed or accumulated energies of a large young generation." When I ask her to elaborate, she sums up *depreshen* as a collective sense (reminiscent of the psychologist's commentary in the previous chapter), as opposed to individuals experiencing depression in Europe as an illness. While her analysis may be generalizing or partial, it remains ethnographically significant: "Sometimes *afsordegi* even brings us together and closer. It is shared." And shared it is, indeed. Online and offline. Consciously and unconsciously.

Dreaming the War: The Unconscious Life of Memory

Besides artistic expressions, many generational recollections come in the form of dreams and flashbacks. In some, young Iranians recall being chased or caught. Others bring back the Iran-Iraq War. "Silencing," writes Michael Taussig in his *Nervous System*, "serves not only to preserve memory as nightmare within the fastness of the individual but to prevent the collective harnessing of the magical power of . . . the restless souls that return again and again to haunt the living."[35] Sometimes people tell me that they dream of incidents they had not personally experienced, but that they know others who had. Yet the dreams feel real.

Unlike an ordinary dream (*khāb, royā*), a nightmare (*kābus, khāb-e bad*) can cause feelings of suffocation, weight on one's chest, paralysis, and panic attacks. They disturb in different ways. Whether anxious and disruptive dreaming (*khāb-e āshofteh*) or dreams that bring sadness (*ghamāsā, khāb-e nārāhat va gham afzā*), they perplex and mute. A common reference among Iranians for describing the impossibility of narration is Rumi's *Gong-e Khāb Dideh*, the mute dreamer, attempting to decipher the images of the dream in waking life and separate the present feeling of the dream from the waking sense of present-ness.[36] In so many of the over one hundred and thirty, often bewildering, dreams that I collected from young Iranians, the enormity of the psychic pain of the dream escaped language.

My aim here is by no means to interpret dreams in a psychoanalytical manner but to listen to how individuals *themselves* interpret, justify, and make sense of their dreams as informed, if not shaped, by their particular generational experiences.[37] While not losing sight of psychoanalytical notions of displacement and dissociation, or the sensibility of belated and delayed perception, I hope to trace in these dreams intuition, as formulated by Adorno: intuition that tracks historically grounded contradictions that shape one's sensory perceptions or fleeting states of mind.[38] Cultural embodiments that go beyond what is conscious and controllable, in other words, can shed light on the historical grounds of distress. For example, generational references, concepts, slang, or points of reference return in these dreams and reflect cultural sensibilities of different generations that are deeply inscribed in the body, producing not only feeling states but also efforts at repression and rechanneling them. These (cultural) details of experience are important in listening to dreams, as is the psychoanalytical sensibility of remembering stressful and intense experiences "as if we were not there," "as if I were looking at it through the lens of a camera. I was a witness only," and "I was only a child and could not make sense of things."

Several themes stand out in these first-person accounts: motion and stuck-ness; uncertainties about the future; death (e.g., plane crashes); injustice (fights or a prevailing frustration with being misjudged by parents or a higher author-ity); Odyssey-like fantasies (of return to a home that is now "burnt down," "no longer there," "no longer safe"); re-living major stressors (the anxiety of failing the national university exam); and detailed descriptions of "location" and décor, colors, and environment (reflecting, in part, Iranian culture's clear boundaries between private and public culture and architecture).

These feeling states and their references fit into larger collective contexts of memory. They amplify the experience of historical ruptures that dislodge life expectations and create anxiety, guilt, or helplessness. Much of this is not only personal but also social. Not unlike their blog posts, the flashbacks and dreams of *daheh-ye shasti-hā* are filled with cultural bits and bytes: war anthems and wartime radio sirens that inscribe generational differences into the depths of the autonomous reflexes of the body. They are situated in waking life.

In waking life, individuals' tapping into the repository of cultural traces and historical experiences are widely found in blogs, in YouTube videos, in televi-sion psychology talk shows, and in young people's creative and expressive cul-tural productions. On YouTube, for instance, videos of interviews with soldiers in the Iran-Iraq War formatted as religious *nouheh* (mourning chants) are found next to music compilations with recycled and remixed old *nouheh* and *soruds* (anthems) and occasionally the Goth-like recycling of black apparel for the Shi'ite annual commemoration of Ashura. Such recycling can be seen as both conscious or unconscious attempts at working through and rewriting, if not righting, unworked memories.[39]

In dreams, sometimes the sense of unreality or bewilderment is described in the form of a meta-dream (e.g., "I dreamt I was dreaming" [*khāb didam ke khāb mididam*]). Sometimes, they come in the form of catastrophic disruptions of ordinary life plans and old feelings of being unsettled. At still other times, flashbacks remix traditional imagery or wartime sounds and images. There are also direct references: "I dreamt I was dead: people were wearing shrouds, people were lost and wandering"; "I dreamt I was running in a subway tunnel and the train was chasing me like a missile"; "I dreamt it was the day of resurrection"; "In my dream, we were all in high school, and suddenly a group of people broke in with guns"; "I dreamt of my twenty-first birthday when the morality police arrested me;" "I dreamt Bush attacked Iran; the sounds were those of the Iran-Iraq War"; and "I dream a lot about air raids." Even among those who had not experienced firsthand loss, the first encounter with a bombed house was often frozen in time, repeatedly experienced in dreams. As Omid, a physicist in his thirties, vividly recalled:

> I was ten years old. My mother had gone to the local store, and had left my five-year-old sister with me. Then there was an air attack. I was so scared, because I felt I had to save my sister's life in case we got bombed. We almost did. There was a missile a few blocks down from our house. But the main thing I remember is not the bombing itself, but the moment when the white siren went off and I went to the window and looked outside. Suddenly I saw our neighbor's house damaged by the shock wave of the missile. Their windows were broken, part of the wall was knocked down. There was dust and loud screams. My first thought at that moment was to protect my sister and not let her see that scene. I took her to the other room. But I was shaken. There was death across the street. Too close. I sometimes see it in my dreams. And I feel the same anxiety to protect my little sister.

The war for Kaveh, a graduate student in engineering, lives on in recurrent dreams about his grandmother's house in the northwestern city of Ardebil, where he lived until age 9, away from the effects of the war before his family moved to Tehran. "I dream that I'm back in my grandma's house, where I love and I long to be. But once there, I feel awkward and stuck; it feels as though I'm in our Tehran house. I desperately want to get out." Grandmother's house remains the only safe home in his dreams. The distinction between the two houses he describes is reflected in how he feels in each, the songs sung in each, the sound of sirens and the darkness of bombing episodes in Tehran. These images however, are not isolated from other anxieties of ordinary life, among which many young people underscore the anxiety of failing the *konkur*, the highly competitive national exam for university admission, which, for male candidates, would bring forward their mandatory military service. Kaveh recalls:

> That pathological competition that messed up our minds and souls with so much stress. . . . Sometimes in my dream, I have a Ph.D., but I still have to take the *konkur*, I don't know why! And I fail. The anxiety takes my breath away. It's horrible. Sometimes, the place where I'm taking the exams is bombed. And while bombs are falling on our heads, I keep trying to focus and write my exam!

The anxieties of the past merge into the anxieties of a present where he too, like many of his peers, asserts that "the war never ended. It never will." As Kaveh links the *konkur* to the war, I am reminded of men older than him, for some of whom failing the *konkur* during the war meant serving at the front, and of others who longed to join the front before taking the *konkur*.

For those who lost loved ones during the war, the images are starker. "My mother went inside to get me out to the basement," said a young man who lost his mother during air raids. "She never made it out; there was chaos. She died because of me; I was eleven, and the guilt has not left me since. Flashbacks, though, started years later, when I neared her age when she died. And got worse since I outlived her." In his dreams, "the giant missile comes back, filling half the yard. Everything buried in dust. And loud, loud screams."

The burden of the unspoken and the unspeakable does not dissipate with the passage of time, or even when one leaves. If anything, images become bleaker, and often reflect one's anxieties in relation to the present as well as the past. In one of the more disturbing dreams narrated by a thirty-one-year-old female who left Iran at the age twenty-seven and now lives in the United States, the fear of war was palpable in 2007:

> In the dream I was on a bus, then another bus comes next to ours, and we go side by side, very fast. Then, slowly, the two buses merge. They mesh into each other. Suddenly they're full of cadavers, piles of cadavers. We have cadavers on our laps. Everyone is wearing olive green, like soldiers. All I could see was masses, masses of faceless death. And suddenly there's a boy on my lap, around ten years old, very thin, I don't remember his face, but I feel his bones, alive, and moving, and I realize, "Oh my God, he's alive and I can save him." But instead, I'm so scared and disgusted that, you know, I just push him away . . . [*pause*] I keep pushing him away. And I wake up trembling. How could I push him away? I felt stuck on the bus with the boy for how long? Forever. But the bus is going so fast. Too fast. The speed is unbelievable. We can't stop it. I felt crushed by stuckness.

One could speculate that at a surface level, the émigré feels at home neither here nor there, and the concept of home becomes fluid, liminal, ungrounded, and elusive. But many *daheh-ye shasti-hā* who entered the United States in the aftermath of the 9/11 attacks suffer such anxieties because of their immigration status. Given only single-entry visas, they are unable to leave the United States without risking their return to their jobs and schools. In the emotional stuckness, the young woman who described her dream about the bus feels the acceleration, the speed, an image of being stuck in a slowed time warp. In both Iran and the diaspora, worlds speed on, leaving her hanging in between. In the bus dream, she is located in a mesh of life and death, and her fear—so internalized and so inscribed—outweighs her intuition. She pushes the boy away. Yet, beneath the contemporary context of the dream there are imageries and cultural interpretations and feeling states. The war, even if not experienced firsthand, remains a cultural and generational legacy. "I don't go about my life thinking about the Iran-Iraq War! No. But it's as if my dreams borrow images and memories from the war and use them in a different story. . . . I never really thought about the war like that. Isn't that strange?"

In another dream, she sees George W. Bush and his wife, around the same time when talk of a US military attack on Iran was a fixture of daily news headlines:

> They're in our house in Tehran! My parents are going out of their way to be hospitable. We're in the old house where I grew up. It's summer. We're sitting outside. I'm annoyed that my parents are so kind to the Bush couple. As if they don't know why they're here. Bush asks me to take a photo of them in our garden. I take the camera and look through the lens. Shocking! They both smile, but behind them, instead of flowers and trees and the swing, I see airplanes pouring bombs on the house. Everything is sepia and dark and dusty. I take my eye from the camera and look over it, and I see the garden again. I look through the lens again. I see airplanes behind the smiling couple. I'm terrified, but no one else can see what I see. This was one of the most horrifying nightmares I ever had.

Each look through the camera shifts time between past and present. The fear of an American attack merges uneasily with both the imagery of Iraqi bombs falling on Tehran in the 1980s and the uncanny terror of a US intervention in Iran. However, not all dreams are disturbing. Some are wishful; others are even ironic and yet still point to the ruptures at the root of their working. A dream from a male graduate student in the United States transposes everyday anxieties of being stuck between worlds. Shortly after the election of Barack Obama, which for many Iranians seemed a promising departure from the Bush era, this dream was circulated on the Internet in a blog post:

> We were talking, he and I. He was very nice. He asked me why I was sad. I said, "President Obama! Do you remember when your grandmother was ill and you flew to Hawaii to see her before she died?" He said yes. I said, "You know, we all have grandmothers who are getting old, who we love so much, but we cannot see them before they die." He looked at me and extended his hand to me and pointed to my passport. I gave it to him. He opened it and wrote something in it, and then handed it back to me, and smiled and said: "You are all set [in English]."

From Dina's joking about a "messed up" childhood to this blogger's fantasy of "being all set" (both terms uttered in English), humor and language serve to displace the emotional charge of one's recollection. In both, one can trace intimate generational and cultural desires that too often escape the clinical gaze of psychiatry and the psychoanalytical frame of trauma.

Trauma Theory and Its Discontents

There are certain wounds in life that, like a canker, continue to gnaw at the soul and eat it away in solitude. . . . It is not possible to reveal them to anyone. . . . As yet man has not found a remedy for these wounds; the only remedy now is forgetfulness brought by wine or sleep induced by opium and other narcotics. . . . The effect of these drugs, however, is transitory, only leaving one with more pain. . . . I shall try to write down whatever I recall, whatever has remained in my memory of the relations that connect the events.

Sādegh Hedāyat, *The Blind Owl* (1971 [1937])

Remembering is an anthropological and a psychoanalytical concern. In telling their stories, Dina and her peers reveal the situatedness of the Western paradigm of trauma in its particular cultural and historical contexts and trajectory.[40] They remind us that discursive terms such as *toromā, āsib-e ruhi, zarbeh-ye ruhi, āsib-e ravāni*, and *sadameh-ye ruhi* (all loosely translated as "psychological trauma") need to be understood in the very particular psychological grammar and cultural and historical context within which they evolved and were made meaningful. Those contexts are hardly captured by current trauma theories nor by much of the existing critiques of those theories. But there are useful insights in both cultural critiques and psychoanalytical theories of trauma.

Critics of the trauma paradigm have drawn attention to the outer structures, the institutional globalizing interventions that universalize trauma and privilege certain forms of knowledge over others. Derek Summerfield has criticized international organizations offering programs for "posttraumatic stress" in war zones, for reflecting "a globalization of Western cultural trends towards the medicalization of distress and the rise of psychological therapies."[41] Fassin and Rechtman, in *The Empire of Trauma*, provided a powerful Foucauldian analysis of the genealogy of the category of trauma victim through various modes of truth production and the construction of individual trauma and its political implications.[42] Although these critiques inform my analysis, the Iranian context is quite different. Unlike the case of humanitarian relief in war-torn areas, wherein international organizations step in and universalize or individualize trauma, the Iranian discourses of *āsib-e ravāni* and *āsib-e ejtemā'i* are not the work of an outside authoritative, let alone foreign, biomedical discourse. Rather, they evolved hand in hand, out of the historical conditions and institutional (medical and psychiatric) discourses that emerged in postwar Iran. In fact, the discourse of *āsib-e ejtemā'i* (social trauma or social pathology) owes its social existence to psychiatric medicalization and emerging discourses of *āsib-e ravāni* (psychological trauma).

Anthropological listening, on the other hand, can both inform and benefit from psychoanalytical modes of listening to inner wounds inscribed by ruptures, for example, in listening for compulsive (generational) archiving of memories in this chapter. This mosaic of charged words, images, and sounds requires close attention not only to contents but also to their modes of dissemination and interpretation, and to the intense emotional reactions they elicit, for instance when people hear the red siren on the Internet. Cultural symbolism, historical references, and delayed circulations are thus indispensible for understanding the affective structures of different generations. Problems arise, therefore, when theory (primarily the dominant North American trauma theory) assumes trauma is a universal, singular, or total *event*.[43]

Among the texts that have established the relevance of trauma theory in the humanities are Caruth's 1995 edited collection *Trauma: Explorations in Memory* and her 1996 monograph *Unclaimed Experience: Trauma, Narrative, and History*, based on the Freudian premise that psychic trauma is not locatable in one's past but rather "in the way that its very unassimilated nature . . . returns to haunt the survivor."[44] Trauma manifests, the theory holds, in delayed rearticulations that outline the traumatic event in our language and actions. The traumatic, in this sense, results from the "incomprehensibility" of what is not fully grasped or assimilated at the time of the event, and thus results in a narrative of belated experience.[45] This delayed narrative, in turn and in sequence, becomes traumatic, turning into "a wound that cries out, that addresses us in the attempt to tell us of a reality or truth that is not otherwise available."[46] The process of reconstructing traumatic memory, then, is composed of two core elements: dialogue and delay. In this dialogical construction, history may arise "where immediate understanding may not."[47] The departure from the silence imposed (on language) by unspeakability is at once liberating and exiling. This has also been a long-standing theme in anthropology,[48] which is also concerned with the impossibility of history as a grand narrative, but raises questions about the cross-cultural translations of such dialogue, as well as the hierarchical relationship between voice and listener.

Furthermore, if trauma is not simply located in the destructiveness of the event, then, the theory holds, in order to grasp what was not fully experienced at the time, there will be an urge, an "inherent necessity," for belated repetitions that can themselves be traumatizing and destructive. This is useful, here, in listening for the compulsive repetition of generational memories and in capturing the retraumatizing effect of remembering (particularly in dreams, where, for example, we see in Samāneh's dreams her struggle to grasp and reconstruct). But a solely psychoanalytical approach may not only overlook the culturally generative capacity of retellings (i.e., creating new identities and artistic forms) but can also overlook what is beyond repressive mechanisms—for example, the inarticulation caused by cultural silencing and intra- and intergenerational dynamics of suspicion or stigmatization.

If for Caruth it is the traumatic event that returns and haunts and traumatizes (and is eventually meant to be re-assimilated and recovered in the analytical process), for Laplanchian and British theories it is the belated processes of association and meaning making that render memory traumatic.[49] Synergistic with much ethnographic work in anthropology, this school of psychoanalytical thought can contribute to anthropology in three ways: First, by allowing the integration of the social context in which remembering is enabled, forced, or forbidden. Second, by un-universalizing trauma and foregrounding its linguistic and cultural symbolics as well as the incommensurability of experiences across different factions of a generation.[50] Third, by prioritizing the interpretations evoked by narrators *themselves*, thereby allowing voices to emerge from within cultural sensibilities and ethnographic fidelity to local discourses.

The 1980s generation continually endeavors to reconstruct a workable past in order to create a passage into the future.[51] For them, individual and shared processes of meaning making shape substantial parts of their strategies for living in the world. They also reflect larger sociohistorical discourses (including psychiatry, modernization, and globalization) that discursively shape their subjectivities. Their memory-work is culturally generative. As if weaving in new threads while ripping out the old ones, they account for the (dis)order of the present by recounting the (dis)order and ruptures of the past. Sometimes that past invades the present like a corrosive wound. Several young people quoted, in their reflections on depression, the opening line of Sādegh Hedāyat's timeless novella *The Blind Owl*: "There are certain wounds in life that, like a canker [*khoreh*], continue to gnaw at the soul and eat it away in solitude."[52] Hedāyat, whose life and work have been extensively psychologized by literary critics and psychoanalysts alike, was the diagnostician par excellence when it came to his time's social malaise and experiences, often inaccessible to non-peers or peers who lacked his cultural sensibility.[53] The Persian word *khoreh*, a corrosive canker-like wound, is also an old name for leprosy; and as in English, in Persian too this corrosiveness sometimes evokes references to cancer. *Khoreh* is not a scar but an open wound (*zakhm*); not a lifeless remnant of tragedy but an invading, consuming, intoxicating presence. For Dina and Samāneh, there is no escape from this embodied and *poisonous knowledge* (in Veena Das's terms) of having lived through, nor can one evade what remembering the past infuses in the present.[54] Theirs is an embodied experience that flows into the present in waves and tides, creating language forms, reflexive practices, cultural productions, and ways of life that include, but are not limited to, *depreshen* talk. The viscerality with which Hedāyat describes his pain resonates in *daheh-ye shasti-hā*'s modes of working through. However, unlike theirs, Hedāyat's wound remained invisible to the outside world, unacknowledged, unrecognized, and unaccounted for, resulting in a sense of isolation and alienation, which culminated in his suicide in 1951.

Today, the enormous volume of individual dream accounts, memories, and flashbacks and the pace with which *daheh-ye shasti-hā* circulate new material are driven by the compulsion to break through the past, to step into the future. They turn ruptures into culturally generative spaces of meaning making and continue to translate the embodied experience of the past into the present in ways that are hardly captured by diagnostic labels such as PTSD. In doing so, they create language forms that differentiate their translations across mini-generations of those just a few years younger or older. I turn to the older generation in the next chapter to explore this translational divide in relation to their medicalizing choices. For me, translating their translations has meant walking a delicate line. I find consolation in the fact that translation is, at best, an incomplete task—as, of course, is the ongoing work of interpreting the self.

The Mother

Tehran, 1998. "When you see an ADHD child, you'll know," said Ahmad Siädati (1936–2009). The prominent professor of pediatrics was speaking at a ward seminar in the Children's Hospital of Tehran University. A disciple of Mohammad Gharib (1909–1975), the founder of modern pediatrics in Iran, Siädati told the interns in his typically gentle demeanor, "The child comes into your office, and the next thing you know is that the scale is upside down, the bed's sheet is unrolled, there is stuff all over the place before you get a chance to make rapport with the child, and the mother is looking at you desperately." We, interns of Tehran Children's Medical Centre, dutifully wrote in our notebooks: It was often pediatricians who detected ADHD. The primary line of inquiry was ruling out underlying organic pathologies, looking into the child's diet, sugar intake, exercise, and other activities. Energy release was key. *Should* medication be necessary, Ritalin was the drug of choice. This was 1998.

Los Angeles, 2008. A decade later, I am sitting at the dinner table with an Iranian couple. Recent immigrants to Los Angeles, they have invited me to a family dinner with their ten-year-old daughter, Shirin, who is being medicated for ADHD. The conversation flows from politics to life in Tehrangeles and occasionally includes Shirin and her medication. I've told the parents I didn't intend to discuss Shirin's condition in her presence; they disagreed: "Nonsense; Shirin knows everything about her medication now." The interrogating look in her eyes makes me wonder what, in her impenetrable reticence, she made of what she was told about ADHD. At this table, it is understood that Shirin's good behavior is not to be taken for granted; how "well" she has behaved today, at school, at home, at the dinner table, is noted several times.

Shirin's behavior has been open to sharing, commentary, measurement, and praise all day long. Around 6:00 pm, when Shirin "came back to" her off-Ritalin state, she left the sofa where she had been watching TV. She was hungry, ran to the kitchen, asked when dinner was ready, went to find her father, returned to the kitchen chattering loudly, and, finally, joined us at the table. I remember Siädati's "typical" clinical portrait of the ADHD child and try to map that image onto the girl sitting across the table.

A decade ago, it would have been possible to miss Shirin's ADHD, which psychiatrists warn, might have meant the misery of unsuccessful schooling: she might not have fit in or performed well, and that could adversely affect her *e'temād-be-nafs* (self-esteem) and her future. Ten years ago, her parents might have resisted the idea of medicating her out of shame or fear of stigma. Back then, she probably wouldn't have been chosen to lead a musical play for the international fair at school; perhaps she would not be in school in California in the first place, if her parents hadn't joined the growing number of professionals leaving Iran in the late 2000s. Another possibility, though, is that her symptoms might have worn off over time: recovery by the teenage years is common in the absence of medication. Still, doctors recommend treatment: damage to a child's self-confidence and sense of social acceptance is too high a price to pay, and treatment is about improving "executive function" in the brain. A decade ago, I imagine, there would have been blame for Shirin and it would have been unlikely for her parents to label her an "ADHD child" the way that the label defines her now. That's who she is and what she should overcome.

Emeryville. 2009. On a mild February afternoon, we meet at a café not far from the shore of San Francisco Bay: Shirin, her mother Leila, Dr. N., and myself. Dr. N., Shirin's former psychiatrist from Tehran (though not the one who diagnosed her initially), is in the Bay Area for a week, as is Shirin's family. Shirin had been Dr. N.'s patient in Tehran for a short time, before her mother decided to switch to another (third) doctor. Then the family moved to the United States. The issue, Leila had told me, was Dr. N.'s attitude; hardly talking to Shirin, he had been cold and bossy. Yet, she still believed in his *savād* (knowledge), if not his bedside manner.

I had seen Dr. N. only once, years ago on a television talk show. Dr. N. is in his early fifties, tall, balding, with a goatee fit for the stereotypical image of psychiatrists. Dr. N. knew little about me—only that I was a family friend researching ADHD, "Not as a doctor, though, but as an anthropologist, am I right?" he asks, grinning. Before I can put a word in, he continues: "I used to be very interested in the humanities [*olum-e ensāni*]; I was also an amateur poet in my youth." As was every other Iranian, I imagine.

I start asking about Dr. N.'s visit and how things are back in Tehran. I emphasize that I am not here to discuss research, subtly pointing to Shirin who has sunk deep into the leather sofa. Dr. N. pounces on my discomfort, "It's exactly attitudes like yours that are the problem in Iran; there's nothing wrong with talking openly. This discomfort doesn't help anyone." He explains that Shirin should know about her condition and about her responsibility (*mas'uliyat*) toward it, rather than feeling stigmatized. If *we* talked *objectively*, he says, using "objectively" in English, and comfortably, she would feel the same, too. He then jokes about anthropologists "relating everything to everything; even a neurological problem is somehow related to everything that's happening in the world!" The implication is that ADHD is a neurological problem, and thus needs to be understood "scientifically." I change the subject. Shirin seems restless; I get up and take her to order her a hot chocolate. When I ask how she feels about Dr. N., she shrugs and looks away. When we get back, the conversation has moved on to other matters.

Done with her hot chocolate an hour later, Shirin is now sitting back, arms crossed, looking back and forth between our mouths from a corner, then fidgeting, occasionally whispering to her mom, insisting on leaving. She is clearly bored and could not care less about upsetting her mom by being rude and "hyperactive." She is "acting ADHD," while the adults follow the parenting rules recommended by child psychiatrists: not rewarding impulsive behavior, but ignoring it. No one is to be blamed. After all, as Dr. N. has taught everyone, ADHD resides in the brain.

CHAPTER 6

Tending ADHD, Shifting Moralities, and Generational Perceptions

THE CATEGORY OF *kudak-e bish-fa'āl* (*kudak* meaning "child"; *bish-fa'āl* meaning "hyperactive")—"the ADHD child"—and its easy use, are quite new to Iranian discourse, as are its implications for family dynamics. At issue is how to understand the discourse of ADHD in terms of its undeniable interrelation with modes of parenting and perceptions of the self. The medicalization of hyperactivity followed the medicalization of depression and can be seen as part of the larger psychiatric paradigm shift among Iranians. There was a significant increase in the use of Ritalin between 1997 and 2008.[1] Not coincidentally, this was the decade following the formal recognition of child psychiatry as a certified subspecialty in 1997 and the rise of ADHD in new educational platforms in the media. In the same years, Tehran hosted two major international conferences on child psychiatry. As in many other countries, by the late 1990s, a public discourse of ADHD had emerged and brain-centered models were integrated into how parents were encouraged to understand child behavior.[2]

In the 1990s, the rapid spread of ADHD discourse introduced it into households by way of daytime television and radio shows, Internet fora, and newspaper articles and Q&A columns (see Chapter 3). As mentioned earlier, for the growing Iranian "cultural" middle class, psychiatric modes of thinking can signify progressive attitudes, provide possibilities for relief from pain or shame, legitimize what is perceived as disorder, and offer new ways to adjust to it. This cultural middle class is gendered in its relation to ADHD, insofar as mothers constitute a more inquisitive and accessible audience, and are usually more involved in the day-to-day implications of children's behavioral issues. Today, more and more mothers (in Iran and globally) wonder whether their child "has ADHD," and doctors report that they are diagnosing ADHD more efficiently. They note that these children would have been missed or misdiagnosed some ten years ago. A new form of knowledge is thus settling parents' long-standing conundrums of shame, guilt, and self-blame with regard to their child's hyperactivity. But what is the significance of these discursive shifts?

Narratives of illness, whether told by doctors, patients, or caretakers, reveal much about one's historically and culturally constructed choices, competing moralities, and projected desires. ADHD and the ways Leila makes it intelligible serve as a window into her family's medicalizing rationalities. These dynamics vary, of course, across families and cultural locations; indeed, many mothers may not relate to Leila's modes of meaning making or cultural perceptions. Leila admittedly belongs to an educated middle class with strong modernist aspirations; but her story cannot be dismissed, not least because it can shed light on emerging trends and desires. To some extent, Leila's family dynamics in relation to ADHD reflect global trends and tensions, particularly in relation to those highlighted in universal debates on overmedicalization of behavior. But through her story, we can also identify some of the generational sensibilities and transferences that differentiate Leila, born in 1970, from her mother's generation as well as from *daheh-ye shasti-hā* (for example, Samāneh and Dina). In other words, this chapter is not about Shirin, but Leila.[3]

To investigate these generational forms is by no means to suggest a simplistic causation for complex illness categories, nor to cast doubt on the reality of illness and the psychological experience of patients and their caretakers or undermine instances where medication has its merit. Rather, exploring interpretations of illness and asking how cultural experiences become personal and psychological allow for intimate accounts that can complement biomedical explanations. These narratives are thus not substitutes for biomedical and brain-centered models of explaining ADHD (e.g., the final common pathway model discussed in Chapter 7); instead they are meant to add a complementary ethnographic element to those models.

I got to know Leila's family (first in Iran and then abroad) over a five-year span (2005–2010) of participant observation, extended in-person and Skype interviews, and e-mail exchanges. Shirin had been diagnosed a year before we met. Her chief symptoms were hyperactivity (*bish-faāli*), an inability to concentrate (*tamarkoz*) in class, and impulsivity that came out in occasional tantrums when she was younger. Some of the symptoms were mild, others more disruptive. Despite being an intelligent and opinionated little girl, she sometimes missed homework or stubbornly refused to pay attention in school. A couple of teachers described her as a "difficult kid" (*bacheh-ye sakht*). The decision to put her on medication came after a number of psychiatric consultations. And it helped.

Leila engages with explanatory models by mobilizing psychiatric knowledge and her cultural readings of it. This is not to say she characterizes all mothers, nor do I approach her choices thorough the lens of ongoing debates (in Western scholarship) on the medicalization of ADHD.[4] Rather, in what follows, I zoom in on one family's narratives to trace changing generational desires and moral frameworks that continue to take different forms. Leila's stories of motherhood, in part told in the language of Ritalin, operate as a kind of microhistory through which we can access and compare some of the underlying cultural and historical changes, generational reflexivities, and transferences that precede the medicalization of children's behavior.

Many parents rely on doctors' instructions and see medicating their children as a moral imperative, a way to be a "good," "modern" parent. The biomedical language with which Leila and many others interpret psychiatry lets them articulate their cultural desires, while they explain these desires by historicizing and situating them in their own generational experiences of the past. Psychiatry, in other words, becomes part of the process of destigmatizing a child's behavior *and* (re)negotiating parents' perceptions of normalcy. This modern mother medicalizes desire, accommodates psychiatric interpretations, and invites biomedical interventions toward a healthier future for herself and her child. Yet in its emergence, ADHD is shaping new subjective configurations and highlighting the tensions between old and new ways of managing the self. It also juxtaposes the individual-focused maxim of the *DSM* with shifting generational cultures and psychological dynamics that are not always conscious, but urge us to understand ADHD against the backdrop of how parents make illness intelligible. Let's begin with the *DSM*.

The DSM and Cultural (In)competence: Contextualizing "Function"

Many social critics have challenged the ideological underpinnings of the *DSM-IV*, and ADHD is already the subject of numerous critical debates in Western scholarship, particularly those concerning the medicalization of childhood.[5] But the underlying assumptions of the *DSM* are additionally problematic when juxtaposed with the cultural semantics of diagnosis. For one thing, the concept of "function" is culturally situated. The *DSM-IV* provides a detailed list of behavioral symptoms; required for an ADHD diagnosis is a combination of symptoms of inattention or of impulsivity and hyperactivity over a sustained period of time. The *DSM-IV* establishes the demarcation of what constitutes pathology at the *impairment of function*: "There must be clear evidence of clinically significant impairment in social, academic, or occupational functioning."[6]

However, a pedagogical and historical understanding of the bricolage of traditional wisdom and modernized thinking that Iranians operate in highlights points of contention in collective and individual conceptualizations of health, illness, and normality. Children's appropriate conduct, for example, is primarily formulated in terms of conformity, diffidence, and reserve.[7] (A common saying in Persian describes the well-behaved child as "not making the slightest noise," or "you could hear noise from the wall, but not from him/her.") Yet, as elsewhere, school performance is a primary site for measuring a child's function. To be sure, the cultural status quo of this social setting is also challenged by increasingly shifting gender roles that are undermining patriarchal values. This fractured landscape raises questions about the direct applicability of the (American) cultural tenets of the *DSM* (a healthy child as happy, self-confident, and outspoken) to Iranian or other non-Western practices.

Cultural and conceptual incongruities are but one side of the coin; there are also practical matters that may confuse diagnosis. Clinically and diagnostically speaking, anxiety can be conflated with ADHD, particularly when it is the main cause that interrupts concentration and focus or triggers impulsiveness.[8] While the *DSM-IV* indicates that anxiety disorders should be ruled out when diagnosing ADHD, anxiety is frequently regarded as a secondary or coexisting factor, or seen as an inevitable symptom of "exam stress" or "family conflicts." That aside, the more important question is how to approach anxieties that are embedded in both the child's and parent's lived experience. How and in the context of what emotional experiences do parents measure a child's function to present it to the psychiatrist? How do they interpret anxiety in themselves and in their children?

As a response to the limitations of the *DSM-IV*, the *Diagnostic and Statistical Manual for Primary Care* (*DSM-PC*) added to the criteria, in 1996, a contextual element: "Both activity and impulsivity must be judged in the context of the caregiver's expectations and the level of stress experienced by the caregiver. When expectations are unreasonable, the stress level is high, and/or the parent has an emotional disorder (especially depression), the adult may exaggerate the child's level of activity/impulsivity."[9] Clinicians acknowledge that, as elsewhere, Iranian parents often bring with them, in the words of Dr. N., a strong "pre-occupation with success," baggage of "past failures," and "social and historical insecurities." Clinicians also emphasize the parent-child unit as one, but still, caregivers' personal experiences, projected anxieties, and situated desires are too often neglected in practice. At best, they are described as the stereotypical dynamic of overbearing and demanding parents.

But if psychiatry draws the line between normal and pathological at the "impairment of function," we must ask whether the caregiver's perception of the child's function is universal and static. What if this perception is historically and developmentally shaped in an ecology of double binds and changing understandings of the self? What are the stakes in parents negotiating ADHD as a medical and social category? This is not a normative question; nor does it imply that the parents are wrong in their assessments or that they are simply projecting their desires onto their children. Rather, it is an exploration of how desires and perceptions of self, health, past, and future are culturally, psychologically, and clinically situated. Asking about parents' trajectories is also an attempt at ethnographic and clinical empathy. It was Leila herself who raised the question very early on in my research.

I therefore turn to Leila to find some answers. Why, I ask, does she choose to underscore her own experiences in order to narrate a coherent account of psychiatric illness? Why does it matter to her to remember her own childhood or to seek fluency in the language of psychiatry? What can Ritalin offer that conventional wisdom cannot? And what has Ritalin got to do with good mothering? Neither overlooking symptoms nor suggesting a myopic argument of causality, these questions are meant to explore how individual narratives of illness may help us understand the underlying desires and cultural processes in the construction of clinical decisions.

Talking ADHD and Self-Esteem across Generations

Leila insists from the outset on the importance of destigmatizing mental illness and adopting an objective and rational approach to life. In one of our initial conversations, she tells me that her brother, Sāmi, then in his twenties, must have had ADHD. "Now that I look back, he totally had ADHD. He didn't do well in school, was very distracted and absent-minded, messed with teachers, typical ADHD." I cannot help noticing the commonality of this depiction, especially of schoolboys.

For many Iranians, successful parenting is tightly linked to children's educational trajectories, which are themselves major anxiety-provoking sites shaping part of a family's social and symbolic capital in the "well-raised" child. Across social strata, many families prioritize and invest in schooling, extra classes, and tutors. There is a running joke that when one meets a child at a party, instead of asking how they are, one often asks "*Mo'adellet chandeh, azizam?*" (What's your GPA, darling?). Such projected anxieties leave little room for imagining out-of-school futures. Those children who do not make top grades are at risk of being shamed as dysfunctional. Variably, they undergo anxiety, stress, or shame. Even though her brother earned a business degree, Leila clarifies, it was from one of the newly opened, lower-tiered, private universities (ironically called nonprofit universities: *dānehshgāh-e gheyr-e entefā'i*).

Despite Leila's perception of academic shortcoming, Sāmi took a successful job in import-export, which suited him:

> He loves traveling; he should have been a geographer or something! He had this crazy idea of going backpacking abroad when he was younger. And you know how it is in Iran: who would want their son to hang around aimlessly [*ātel-o-bātel*]? Now it sounds cool; but at the time, the idea was more like a joke. So, there were many fights with my parents.

Leila lowers her voice, "Who knows? Maybe he could have become a travel writer or guide or something and had a different life had he not been born in Iran."

Or in that family, I thought. Such family dynamics are quite common though, especially among the more educated families. I met Sāmi a year later; he lived with his parents in Tehran. He stood out for his humor, starting with jokes about "nerds" and "well-behaved" geeks. It was immediately evident how much his family adored him, yet always tried to fix his life. I also met Leila and Sāmi's mother, a retired elementary school teacher, who, watching Shirin grow up, laments, "Back then, we didn't have your knowledge. What did we know about ADHD?" She seems to believe that if Sāmi's (alleged) ADHD had been treated at an early age, he would have done better in school, would have grown up with less drama and higher *e'temād-be-nafs* (self-esteem). Grandma looks up to her daughter as the modern mother: "Leila does a lot of research on ADHD; she takes amazing care of Shirin's nutrition; she is always in the car, taking her to language classes, music, dance, art, you name it."

In her words, there is a lingering sense of guilt for not having known what her daughter knows today—a typical and perhaps global intergenerational tension. To me though, Sāmi seems to be all right—successful, happy, relaxed. When I ask what could have been different for Sāmi, she is quick to answer:

> He'd have done better, like his cousins who are all doctors and engineers now.
> [Me: So, this is about education (*tahsiālt*)?]
> No! Don't get me wrong; I thank God that he is healthy and happy. But he is very intelligent; he could have done better and been happier.

The commonality of such dynamics among educated families is striking. Grandma's contradictory interpretations, reflecting a series of projections and conflicting normative agendas, are further complicated by the fact that, in lay and popular discourse, ADHD is often misrepresented as mere hyperactivity or inattention, and at times conflated with poor performance in school. Leila, though, disagrees and says there is more to her speculation about Sāmi having ADHD. For example, Sāmi is not focused or responsible "as a man should be; he's very rebellious" ("rebellious" being a common shorthand for intergenerational conflicts). Their father, a self-made retired civil engineer who served at the front during the war, believes his son was not disciplined enough: "My wife always spoiled him; she never let me take care of the matter properly." Characteristic of his cultural middle-class generation, the father's stance on medication is quite predictable: "Children need discipline, not pills. This pill talk is ridiculous. If you let them, they'd force me to take *Prozāk* too!" As it turns out, Leila and her husband are both on Zoloft.

Negotiating Ambivalent Moralities across Generations

When we met again in California in 2008, Leila and I discussed her antidepressant medication. She sees speaking out about medication as a starting point for overcoming stigma, oblivion, and outdated modes of thinking:

> I can't be a good person, a good mother if I don't take care of my own health. A depressed mother can't be a good mother. And yes, Zoloft has helped me be that; I feel better, I feel healthier. I don't believe in suffering in the name of sacrifice, nor

that I should be a sacrifice like my own mom, who had no life for herself because we were her entire life.

In finding her place among shifting cultural ideals of motherhood, Leila is pursuing an individual responsibility to care for herself and her child in biomedically legitimized ways, fighting depression, ADHD, and dated mothering patterns all at once. The emotional stakes of this knowledge-based performativity are high: it relies on navigating contradictory desires, always with an awareness of what is gained and what is lost. When Leila was a young child, her grandparents lived in an old house with a garden and a little pond and any number of relatives around at any given time. Her aunts and extended family were a big part of her upbringing. Leila has fond memories of her grandmother, the typical traditional grandma who cooked the way no one else could and who was always home. This is just how old houses were, before high rises mushroomed and grandmothers moved to apartments. Now, Leila's retired parents live in an apartment in the expanding western wing of Tehran. When they were in Tehran, every other Friday or so the family gathered at Leila's mother's apartment for dinner; the trip took at least two hours through Tehran's traffic. Of course, Grandma took Shirin to her apartment every chance she got, but that became increasingly difficult with Shirin's extracurricular schedule. Back when they were in Tehran, Grandma worried about Shirin and Leila:

> Leila is always stressed. Poor thing; these days, running a family is like running a firm. Children have very full schedules these days. They're tired, too anxious if you ask me. I know I'm not so knowledgeable like her, but I have experience [*tajrobeh*]. These kids are too tired. So is my poor daughter herself. And her husband is never home; he has to work hard to afford all of this. But if you ask me, I think he's happier going on long business trips than being home and dealing with all this.

Still, this doesn't stop Grandma from valorizing Leila's *savād* (literacy, knowledge): "I always wonder how different it would have been for Sāmi if we knew about ADHD in those days." (Over the course of our conversations, Leila's brother has turned from a "possible" case of ADHD to a confirmed one.) Grandma worries constantly about Leila, about Shirin, about her son, about me interpreting her words as criticism of Leila's mothering. In her soft, cautious words, she lays out the paradoxes that inform the Iranian ADHD landscape. At times, she reminisces about the old days without explicitly passing judgment on "today's mothers"; at others, she boasts about her own impressive medical knowledge of ADHD underneath an air of self-deprecation ("What do I know?"). Occasionally, she hints at deeper moral dilemmas:

> Back then, I always used nicknames for my girl [Leila], always hugging her, encircling her, spoiling her. You see, I was a hundred percent hers, at her service. God forbid, I don't mean to question my daughter as a mother; she is so *ba-savād* [well-read] and more knowledgeable than I was; she is an exemplary mother. I'm just saying that things have changed; young parents are less patient these days. . . . I ask you, how come Shirin is less hyperactive when she stays with me?

There. She pokes at the elephant in the room. The truth is, Shirin has a very special relationship with her grandmother. Shirin and Leila, though, are more like friends; they fight, they make up, they discuss things, they talk a lot. "To be counted, to be asked what she thought, to make her feel her opinion mattered" is what Leila wants for Shirin. "I'm not one to make a huge fuss about things; I just want to make sure she grows up confident." "And how does Ritalin help?" I ask.

"ADHD can take away Shirin's confidence. I don't want her to be picked on in school or in the family. I want her to grow into a confident woman, not like how we were, shy and insecure."[10] Repeatedly called "modern," Leila's proposition complements Grandma's pouring affection: "You know, it's the grandmother's job to spoil the kid," I am reminded. Yet Leila's emphasis on self-care challenges Grandma's narrative of selflessness as the core of motherhood. Both Leila and her mother feel their ways of mothering are under constant scrutiny based on how their child behaves. And it is into these competing pedagogies and moralities that the normative apparatus of modern psychiatry enters, promoting particular technologies of the self (e.g., medication) and parenting models.[11]

Today, shifting moral grounds have also shifted the ground of masculinity. As men like Hamid, Leila's husband, move toward more progressive lifestyles, living with working (at times even more educated) wives, many struggle to make ends meet and negotiate gender roles. Many are torn between the pressure of being the modern man who sees his wife as an equal and society's expectations of men as breadwinners. Many of the more-educated men feel that they are not rewarded for their skills, that corruption doesn't leave room for their success. Many have to work two jobs to pay for their children's tuition and extracurricular activities. Their anxieties about the future are extended to their children's futures. Many among the cultural middle class also feel pressured to decide between staying or leaving Iran.

The decision to leave came to Leila and her husband relatively late, in 2008, and it was not an easy one. There was too much to leave behind, and they are close to their families. But as Shirin grew older, Leila tells me, they became more and more concerned about her future. Quickly, she adds, the move wasn't entirely because of her daughter:

> I don't want to make this all about her; that would be the rhetoric of our mothers who say they made every sacrifice for our sakes, putting so much pressure on us. No. I mean, of course, your child is your priority. But I came to the decision also thinking about myself. I was becoming increasingly unhappy. It took my husband longer to come to that conclusion, but eventually we knew we wanted to leave.

During their last couple of years in Tehran, Leila says, it was increasingly difficult for them to escape frustration with the economy, their careers, and the sense that "things had changed dramatically," all references based on the tacit assumption among some of the educated middle class that one can leave to make better use of one's skills and pursue a more secure future. (This was a particular socioeconomic timing (2005–2010) during which many who had never contemplated immigration began to entertain the idea). In listening to her words, it is hard to parse out individual dissatisfactions from social ones, but the emotional burden of feeling stuck remains palpable. Being stuck in a tangle of struggles, primarily economic concerns and uncertainties, she recalls, felt like they had to exert themselves to maintain their lives.

The last time we met, Leila told me that Shirin had improved greatly (*kheili behtar shodeh*). It is not clear, however, Leila agrees, whether she might have improved without medication, as many ADHD children do toward their teens. Mostly though, Leila takes an instrumental approach toward Ritalin as a means to an end. It is simple: psychiatry tells her that ADHD is about loss of "executive function in the brain," which can of course result from genetic or environmental causes. Ritalin's job is to fix the brain pathways responsible for that. Her knowledge is, in large part, shaped by Iranian media and experts focused on destigmatizing and medicating ADHD, which are themselves situated in discursive processes of cultural work.[12]

Back in Tehran, Grandma had raised issues about Ritalin's side effects:

> It hurts to watch Shirin when medicated. You know, she suddenly becomes quiet, very *mazlum* [docile, subservient]. She sits in front of the TV all day. I bring her food, but she has no appetite. This breaks my heart. Her mother doesn't know

this, but sometimes when she stays with me, I skip the pill; I say I will have more *sabr-o-hoseleh* [patience and tolerance] with her today.

Despite Grandma's impression, the truth is ADHD is far from an invention by impatient parents. Even though doctors agree that overmedication is a valid concern, this doesn't take away from the fact that, in many cases, medication has its place. But the key question is how affective and sociocultural contexts shape doctors' and families' relationship with and decisions about medication. In evaluating parenting, biomedical psychiatry and its normative measures sit next to the culturally constructed meanings of particular moral imperatives such as parents' patience (*sabr-o-hoseleh*) and children's self-esteem (*e'temād-be-nafs*). Such moral frameworks are situated in shifting generational perceptions of the past and desires for the future, as well as in the ways in which the former shapes the latter. Today's ADHD children have more-educated mothers who are better read and more present in the job market. Many of these mothers are going through a transitional moment when an explicit focus on one's self is no longer taboo. Leila is on watch against "becoming like my mother," while wanting a happy, different, childhood for Shirin; but that double standard brings her mixed feelings: while "selflessness" turns from a virtue to a symptom of outdated value systems, Leila still sees her child as the measuring rod of her self-worth. Leila is also conscious of any possibility that Shirin's sense of esteem or worth might become scarred: "I don't want Shirin to grow up like we did; I want her to be happy and confident." So if something like ADHD were to threaten her child's confidence, she believes it would be foolish not to remedy it. Leila's desire is for Shirin to have a different, better childhood than her own—perhaps a desire shared globally by parents. But her insistence on a "happier" childhood is emphatically generational, wanting Shirin to grow up "Not like how we grew up." The "we" again. But what was so different, I ask, about *her* childhood?

Looking Back as They Depart

Leila's childhood and adolescence, she says, were shaped during the war and belong to the time of an ideological turn in the *very early* 1980s. In the quiet domain of daily life, her perception of herself was affected as she internalized a complex moral economy that entrenched specific strategies of conduct.[13] She talks about wartime anxieties, her perplexity, and the world turning upside down. Leila identifies as part of the *nasl-e sukhteh*, a generation that remembers childhood before the revolution and coming of age in the 1980s. The term *sukhteh*, often translated as "burnt," has several meaning trajectories in Persian, including: barren (as in *zamin-e sukhteh*, or barren land), done away with, no longer useful (as in *mohreh-ye sukhteh*, or defeated chessman in chess), burnt and wasted (as in *omr-e sukhteh*, or wasted life), and finally, the mystic poetic reference *parvāneh-ye sukhteh*, which describes sacrificing oneself for the beloved or for a higher cause (*parvāneh* [butterfly] signifies the lover, circling a candle's flame [symbolizing love and the beloved]; the butterfly is not afraid to be consumed by the flame, as that would symbolize union with the beloved). In the term *nasl-e sukhteh*, all of these references resonate. This generation perceives itself as caught in the current of history without the opportunity to process it. Many of them have moved on to productive family and professional lives, keeping their pasts ticking away under wraps.

Wherever the lines may be drawn, Leila's generation, some of whom are parenting "ADHD kids," have a strong and exclusive claim on the label *sukhteh*. They had an immediate experience of the Iran-Iraq War, either as young men fighting or as young men and women coming of age in a remarkably gendered and unstable historical moment. Like the 1980s generation, their memories are imbued with both a sense of wartime solidarity and a residue of childhood anxiety. Unlike *daheh-ye shasti-hā*, however, their generational sensibilities are primarily organized in a *before and after* mode, and with an emphasis on, in the words of Iranian novelist Goli Taraghi in her *Scattered Memories*, "being thrown from one era to another."[14] Their poisonous knowledge, in Veena Das's terms,[15] of things they know but cannot articulate, ought to be recognized in a different emotional register than that of *daheh-ye shasti-hā* and explored in its own variations of experience. Although different moments were experienced differently by different peers depending on time, place, and socioeconomic position, many perceive their childhood and teen years as interrupted. It is this psychological sense of disjoint among children, rather than oft-emphasized political readings of this era, that my analysis focuses on. Now their adult explanatory models for illness are in part shaped by transferences—that is, attempts to gain control over and make sense of what made them feel perplexed as children.

Leila elaborates on her childhood relationship with outside chaos with humor and wit. But sadness lingers: as a young girl in the early 1980s, she carried grief for incremental losses during the war and confusions caused by contradictory imperatives. She felt "thrown from one era to another" when she changed school.

There were compelling moments during the war that stayed in her adolescent mind: in a school trip to *Behesht-e Zahra* (Martyrs' Cemetery) she had her first encounter with dead bodies, "not bodies, but plastic bags containing pieces of a body—a boot, a leg, and pieces of cloth, thrown in a grave. Today, I admire those men for their sacrifices, but back then, I was too young to understand and process; I couldn't sleep for weeks."

Today, policymakers and psychologists are increasingly attentive to the impact of the environment on children's well-being. But in those very early days in the 1980s, children and adolescents absorbed the war and watched grown-ups "being thrown from one era to another," too. From where children were standing, things were happening too fast. Many professionals fled the country during the 1980–1983 Cultural Revolution. Those who stayed endured major losses and sacrifices to defend it. Home life too was changing form. Children (from secular families) witnessed their parents' frantic housecleaning, getting rid of music cassettes, videos, or earlier on, anything that carried the wrong seal linking them to the previous era. Others from devout families witnessed departures they couldn't comprehend. Many lost parents or witnessed their parents losing friends to the war. Many went through hurried farewells with cousins, family friends, or neighbors who packed up and left overnight; with fathers or brothers who joined the volunteer army; with teachers who disappeared to the front to defend the country; with war-refugee classmates who would come and go. One didn't need to belong to a particular socioeconomic class or ideological leaning to be affected by the war or the fast-changing order of things and the anomie that took over, in schools, on the streets, on schoolbook pages, and in their parents' transition into a new era. Experiences varied of course across social strata and political affiliations, but coming of age in the early 1980s was, for many, like entering a world in which grown-ups (whether perplexed observers, devout revolutionaries, or anxious mourners of the past) were themselves trying to figure out life after a major shift. How did *children* perceive all that?

Leila found herself in a rather strict all-girls' school, and insists on reminding me of the new uniforms: knee-length navy manteaux, matching trousers, and black headscarves. To focus on the clothes may seem trivial, but, not unlike *daheh-ye shasti-hā*, she summons details with precision. Leila persistently reminds me that the earlier dress codes were stricter and were replaced with looser ones shortly after; "younger people can't remember, they don't understand what I am talking about." These seemingly trivial details surface powerfully in generational narratives, differentiating symbolics and aesthetics that are meant to demarcate different generational locations and make possible distinct generational claims. That is what it means to be a member of the burnt generation, Leila insists: to belong to a time that no one else (i.e., the younger generation) can understand or remember.

Many of Leila's peers, however, disagree with her sentiments. The same dress code that made Leila feel uneasy served as a new opening for many others. The Islamization of schools provided an opportunity for many girls from more traditional families to pursue their education (an important factor accounting for Iranian women being more educated today than men). The process, however, was unregulated in its early stages and sometimes violated personal boundaries, for example, with some headmistresses reportedly checking students' faces for plucked brows or searching their bags for makeup or love letters. Short-lived as they were, these attempts were meant to internalize piety, but some teenagers also seem to have internalized ambivalent feeling states and anxieties; "Humiliation hurts. We were made to feel *zesht* [ugly] and subdued, or guilty otherwise," Leila repeats several times. Today, many teenagers would have a hard time relating to her experience, which makes these recollections even more vocal and powerful.

The compulsive repetition of such mundane details is hard to dismiss, regardless of whether or not one shares their accompanying sentiments. What is psychologically and culturally striking is why one would persistently mobilize such seemingly trivial past themes in reflections on the present time. They cannot be dismissed as insignificant, precisely because they keep returning, as they do in mothers' recollections of their sense of self-worth as teenagers, and inform their perceptions of health and aspirations for their children's future. If for younger *daheh-ye shasti-hā* the impact of wartime was on childhood feeling states, for the adolescent Leila those years also shaped her experience of her gender. Nevertheless, Leila's generation got on with life, pursued education, got married, found jobs. Today, some of them have come to incorporate psychiatry as a technology of selfhood that both heals and facilitates performative practices and transferences that distinguish them from their mothers.

The war dominates Leila's memories, "Everything was gory, even on television. The cities were being bombed, and everything was in flux. I never forget, my uncle's wife suffered a miscarriage after their house was hit." She lowers her gaze and pauses, then adds with a smile, "But we also had the illegal Movie Guy, who'd come to our house weekly with his suitcase full of Betamax videos . . . and we were scared to death! . . . It now sounds like a comedy but this was the highlight of our week: the joy of watching Michael Jackson's latest video, and half of the joy was because it was illegal! . . . I'm not saying everyone my age had the same experience, but most of us—rich, poor, religious, secular—did go through a very confusing time as teenagers. You wouldn't understand any of this unless you could remember those *very* early years and the intensity of those feelings."

Leila's memories are embedded in an admittedly middle-class sensibility that may not be shared across different social affiliations. But the *affective* impulse of her generational reflections (fears, anxieties, intense emotional responses) and the insistence on differentiating them from those of younger people resonate among many others who, during the same period, lost their families, were displaced during the War of Cities, or faithfully waited for their *basiji* brothers or fiancés who had volunteered to fight.

To uncover the emotional and affective afterlife of generational experiences, thus, requires an attention to these differentiations and demarcations of experience. The changes that followed (e.g., the re-emergence of music in the public domain or the variations of dress codes) only a few years later were dramatic enough that siblings only five years apart report they experienced two different social worlds—hence the ensuing incommensurability of their generational sensibilities. Things, Leila asserts, did change not only with the end of the war but also when the Internet arrived, e-mail reconnected peers, and phone cards made it possible to communicate with cousins and friends and relatives abroad. Many members of the diaspora began to travel back to Iran in the 1990s. There was now time to compare notes. Leila tells me:

> I saw Noor after almost twenty years. She had come back to Tehran to see her dying father. We used to go to the same elementary school; we looked at my photo albums. I hadn't looked at them in years. It was strange, as if I was looking at someone else's photos, but then again, I remembered everything like it was yesterday. We looked nice. . . . Noor wouldn't be able to fathom what came after she left. . . . I never thought about these things until Noor visited. We're the same age. She's still single; she is now an artist in London. I think she's lonely, but who isn't? I felt old; she still seemed young.

Of course, Noor might find Leila's experience unfathomable. But Leila too would perhaps be unable to fathom Noor's experience. When I finally met Noor in London in 2009, she recalled her visit to Tehran as bittersweet: "It reminded me of how much I had left behind, that when growing up I never had an extended family around, never experienced a weekend at my grandma's." Noor's losses are different from Leila's. Even though she has spent most of her life in London, Noor too grew up immersed in daily news reports and television footage of the eight-year-long war between Iraq and Iran. She remembers how she experienced the 1979 Revolution as a child: "I remember a family member had gone to the city and had seen a protest downtown. He came back home and said that he had seen a cut-off head. It was freaky, and you heard stuff like that everywhere." Whether true or false, rumors were amplified in her childhood imagination. She had nightmares of a "huge worm that had eaten up my mother, and my dad and I are marching in the street and mourning," and her grandmother "cleaning up vomit so that the local police could not see the evidence of a party my brother had thrown, during which another boy had thrown up," and overhearing in the background that the boy had died. "Vomit and illness and all these associations were really horrible. . . . My imagination was obviously open. I was receiving a lot of information that I didn't have the capacity to process. And I was feeling very unprotected." The order of life was disrupted, and no one could explain to her the logic of events. Noor remembers, "There was a headline story . . . of a boy named Mehdi who was kidnapped during a riot and was found dead in a well." Noor suffered many death nightmares, including that her brother had been kidnapped and stabbed. She reflects that "death was a major thing, always a major thing, especially the fear of my parents' death," and still today, "there is always this somberness in the air when I recall those days or talk about them with my mother; it's gritty, very real."

Noor's anxiety structures are layered also with the anxieties of exile and with her parents' anxieties. Two years into the war, her family fled with almost nothing. In England, where she had an uncle, Noor was sent to a boarding school, and her parents returned to Iran five years later. Boarding school was a second exile from the family, even if only on weekdays, and Noor responded with superstitious rituals to "keep her parents alive" while she was away: she wore the same clothing, ate exactly the same amount each day in between phone calls from her mother. Although she had been a good student in Iran, language problems interfered in England. As many immigrant teenagers report, "When you're twelve or thirteen, you're too embarrassed to raise your hand and ask what a word means." Still, though she had to repeat some of her O-levels, she went on to university. Around that time, her brother, having suffered a nervous breakdown and been diagnosed with depression, committed suicide. Noor says that she avoids medication for her occasional bouts of depression because her brother had been on so many medications. Noor still has "the repetitive dreams" in which "if something flies over my head—airplanes, balloons, and such—they always crash." Between her generation and the 1980s generation of Chapter 4, there are conspicuous parallels in the return of wartime imageries in dreams. The war, it seems, lives on in the minds of those touched by it in one way or another. And no one knows that better than the men of her generation who experienced it firsthand.

The War They Lived: Medicine, Memory, and Cultural Products

. . . Tell me what happened to our generation [nasl-e mā]

The generation who wanted to

Plant the earth in the sky,

Has got its sky fenced in

. . . One of us got stars [on his shoulders] in exchange

For his hands and legs

One didn't even get stars for them

Another was torn to pieces [pāreh-pāreh]

One remained lost [nimeh kāreh, "unfinished"]

Another went back to the trenches, to fetch

His remains

. . . Those whose bodies shielded this land

Are now searching for a piece of home

Some left home on foot; some did well; some lost their lives; some became stars.

Kaveh Yaghmaei, "Nasl-e Sukhteh" (2008)

The war, in Leila's and Noor's narratives, is a gendered, as well as a generational, experience. Leila's husband, Hamid, born in 1964, did his military service during the Iran-Iraq War. He went to university after his service, worked in an engineering firm during the 1990s, and established his own firm in 2001. Like Leila's, his parenting is informed by generational sensibilities and, whether directly or indirectly, by the war. Hamid is still haunted by the story of his friend's death on the battlefield. It was not even crossfire that killed him: "I woke up one morning in the tent, and there he was, dead. He was killed by a scorpion. I was unable to breathe. I lost my voice. I stared at him in shock."

Stories like this are common and have a gendering effect, as soldiers' accounts often do, by adding to their generational elements the physicality of being a soldier and graphic descriptions of what they have witnessed, as well as the sense of solidarity and brotherhood they shared in their fight for a higher cause, as evident in the song above. Rock singer Kaveh Yaghmaei (b. 1968) is the son of iconic 1970s singer Kourosh Yaghmaei. He studied music in Iran (with a few year-long interruptions during the Cultural Revolution and the closure of music academies, during which time he was home schooled). His work is largely located in the juxtaposition of his as well as his father's experience of the Cultural Revolution. In "Nasl-e Sukhteh," Yaghmaei uses the generation as an experiential framework for identification and differentiation. His generation cannot escape the war, nor can they forget its promises and ideals. *Nasl-e mā* (*our* generation) is not a temporality but an emphatically shared representational strategy for constructing the self, for negotiating converging or diverging historical claims that still hurt: those of the young soldiers who fought a war that is now forgotten by the world; those of veterans who experienced others' resentment; those of the forgotten veterans who "don't even have those stars" (indicating status and rank); those of the friends of the martyred; those of the young *basijis* who joined the front (*jebheh*), to "become pure";[16] those of the ones who left; those of the ones who stayed and got on with life. The lyrics echo other fathers I have interviewed; they too, like Leila, remember being "thrown from one era to another" in the very early 1980s. Classmates or neighborhood football-mates were suddenly forced apart as it emerged that one's father was a *tāghuti* (linked to the monarchy, literally an "idol worshipper") or *tudeh-i* (belonging to Tudeh, the Communist Party). Some friends volunteered to fight at the front, some left the country. Among those who stayed, many joined the volunteer army, *basij*, and put their lives on the line. Many longed to run away to *jebheh* despite being underage; many did go to fight and came back disabled but felt unappreciated. Many still long for the purity, the faith, and the solidarity that the war had engendered. Many others, on the other hand, remember being arrested for wearing jeans, pulled from school for having long hair, or stopped and searched for carrying cassette tapes—incidents that would become unimaginable some years later. What connects them across ideological divisions is a mixed adolescent sense of solidarity and perplexity. *No one*, they tell me, can understand the feel of those very first years of the war unless he was there.

The official video clip for the song quoted above opens with rhythmic martial drumbeats and throughout uses minimal instrumentality, an oblique tribute to the 1980s lack of music in any form but martial anthems. It recycles familiar imagery and footage from the Iran-Iraq War, as well as symbolics of *before* and *after*, such as a multiplication of the singer across a barren field, or disturbing images of drugs, amputated legs, cigarettes, syringes, and explosions, all mixed with martial beats and electric guitar. The angst feels visceral and immediate. The song is emblematic of the generation's reflexive subjectivity-work in the aftermath of the war. But its most powerful feature is the ideological diversity of its fans, many of them devout veterans, and the reviews they write on the Internet; from pious to secular, everyone deeply appreciates the sacrifices of those who fought for justice, the ambivalence of those who are left behind, and the grief for ideals lost and legs amputated.

Almost thirty years later, many veterans continue to struggle with chronic health conditions or with adjusting to the outside world, including to their own children who, as younger *daheh-ye shasti-hā*, may not directly relate to their fathers' wartime sacrifices. They returned to a society that had moved on from solidarity and austerity to reconstruction and privatization in the 1990s. Disabled veterans, who comprise a large percentage of bloggers too, sometimes experience resentment from those who were not directly affected by the war. Feeling forgotten, abandoned, and misunderstood, some feel stigmatized by their title *jānbāz* (disabled veteran), "as if they were compensated beyond what they deserved." They are left to work through lives that are quite different from what most people think.

For many veterans, the most pressing issue in their day-to-day life remains health care, regulated by the Veterans Organization.[17] Numerous Iranian epidemiological studies provide indicators for the challenges that veterans and clinicians face decades after chemical warfare and civilian injuries took place.[18] According to official reports, there are 400,000 registered *jānbāz* in Iran, 120,000 of whom were injured by the chemical attacks that Saddam Hussein inflicted on Iranians. In January 2015, the Fars News Agency quoted the head of the Mental Health Bureau of the Veterans Organization that there were 43,000 documented psychiatric patients and 7,200 patients with serious psychiatric disorders, with ten hospitals to serve them countrywide. The report introduced a new "initiative of endurance" (*tarh-e tab-āvary*) that would be implemented to help veterans, caretakers, and family members cope.[19] Aside from the efforts of the Veterans Organization, the health issues many veterans struggle with have not received enough attention outside the clinical setting. The lived experiences of such health issues are best depicted in Narges Bajoghli's ethnographic documentary, *The Skin That Burns*.[20] Bajoghli presents a compelling account of the daily life of disabled veterans who, despite their struggle thirty years on, refuse to identify with bitterness or defeat.

Even when the wounds were fresher, parts of society remained oblivious to them. Accounts such as the following, from a disabled veteran I met in the clinic, provide ethnographic complements to existing data in medical publications.

> Most people don't remember us now. No one cares. No one understands. Some people resent us. They think we were compensated with university seats and jobs and things we didn't deserve. And even if they don't think that, they don't respect us. My son, who doesn't remember anything of the war, thinks I was gullible. You tell me, what can compensate for the nights I can't breathe? We had masks, you know, but I didn't recognize the chemical attack when I should have. I breathed. I realized that I was chemically injured [shimiyāyi] when it was too late. People have no idea.

He had come to the clinic because of an infection, perhaps a minor complication compared to other chronic health conditions he struggled with. "I'd still go back to *jebheh* if anyone were to attack us; of course I would. As Imam Khomeini once said, it was our duty and our responsibility to fight for justice." Yet, what really hurt was being "alienated from my own son, my own blood [*pāreh-ye tanam*], who doesn't get it." Years later, his words were echoed by another *jānbāz* I met in 2008 in a medical conference on chemical injuries. His increasingly inflamed respiratory tract had made him a valuable educational case. He barely had a voice, and I could hear the wheezing from across the table, but he generously agreed to be interviewed. He was in his fifties, but looked older. His sunburnt skin had deep cracks around the eyes. His faith unshaken, he recounted all the health conditions he had developed over the years. In the manner of religious Muslim men, he initially did not look me directly in the eye, but gradually became more comfortable. He confided at the end of our interview that he was extremely saddened after talking to me: "Khanom doctor, I look at you and I can't help thinking of my wife and my seventeen-year-old daughter. I thought things would get better after I married. My wife married a *jānbāz* out of faith; but she is now *depress*. She takes pills. My daughter, too, is very *depress*. They are paying the price of being my family." His coarse, hushed voice struggled at the mention of his daughter, and uncontrollable coughs excused him from our conversation.

His pain was contagious and infused not only his present life but also his family's affective structures. For him, his wife's *depreshen* was relational, capturing many layers of a ruptured experience that rippled into her daughter's life too. These layers have been captured in the genre of Sacred Defense in Iranian cinema, which provides a window into this generation's experience of loss, solidarity, pride, and patriotism. Initially wartime publicity, the genre later offered a projective screen for more critical examinations of the social experience of war (later extended to the blogosphere and its many veteran bloggers).

The veteran's memory-wound is best exposed in Mohsen Makhmalbaf's 1989 film *Marriage of the Blessed (Arusi-ye Khubān)*,[21] the story of a young shell-shocked veteran's encounter with society after the war. The opening scene shows the veteran in a psychiatric institute, sedated and bedridden. When he is discharged to join his fiancée, who has faithfully waited for his return, he struggles to come to terms with the society he fought for. As a former photojournalist, he returns to his newspaper job only to learn that his impassioned photos of social ills have lost their media appeal. His boss asks for *happier* photos: "That is what people want to see." His camera shutter's click toggles him between the past and the present. Struggling with repeated attacks of PTSD and depression, he is again admitted to the hospital, where sedation and medication eventually put an end to his nightmares.[22] In the last scene, he lies in the garden of the institution, heavily sedated. A young photojournalist sees him through the fence and stops to photograph the scene. In an incredibly moving final close-up, the camera frames his pale face as he turns his head and covers his face with his hand. As each click of the camera juxtaposes past and present, the cinematic modality circulates in his technological unconscious, as if yesterday's socially committed photojournalist has become today's object for both photography and psychiatry.[23]

Marriage of the Blessed was among the earliest artistic expressions of PTSD.[24] More narratives emerged over the following decade. Like the blogs of the 1980s generation, these productions confronted their generation with reflections, refractions, and interruptions of their own experiences, in the sense used by Michael Fischer of mirrors set at angles, refracting and reflecting and allowing distancing, comparisons, and critiques from within their own cultural spaces and judgments.[25] These refractions, in turn, caused their own ruptures, interruptive breaks, and spaces for new judgment. Most significantly, the cultural space of the genre of Sacred Defense in cinema and literature both made visible the health impact of the war and further demarcated generational boundaries of experience. Much of this work is created by veterans themselves, who have turned to ordinary life as a space for deconstructing the war and reconstructing life out of torn pieces. These works also provide a bridge to other comparative references and stories they tell in pieces: the West, from which they borrow filmic technologies; postwar Iran, where their distinct expressions are articulated; wartime Iran, where they came of age on the war front; and prerevolutionary Iran, where their childhoods, imaginations, and families are rooted.[26]

Like cinematic recollections, earlier war novels' idealism was often represented in triumphant narratives, with the exception of a few early works such as Esmā'il Fasih's *Winter 1981* (*Zemestān-e 62*).[27] Post-1990s works gradually engaged with complexities of survival and ambivalence. In an award-winning novel by Hossein Mortezaeian-Abkenar, the fate of a soldier depends on whether he gets on a train delivering the injured to the city. If he remains behind, he might well be killed. *A Scorpion on the Steps of Andimeshk Railroad Station* locates the war in the affective liminality of survival, in an in-between space between life and death.[28] In a word play with conventional disclaimers in works of fiction, an author's note insists that the novel is based on real events, corresponding to yet another generational anxiety: the looming threat of forgetfulness if one's experiences fail to be translated for and believed by other generations. It is as though being heard and recognized somehow helps one work through. What differentiates the new wave of war literature and cinema from the productions of the 1980s is a conscious departure from the battlefield toward bringing home the human aspect of war experiences.[29] Today, appreciation of these sacrifices and hardships is growing among the young. As the previous chapter illustrated, there is a constant revival of wartime sounds and images, by both this generation and those younger, on YouTube and in blogs, increasingly remixed with new accompaniments or contexts.[30]

Men, however, are not the only storytellers of this generation. In the 1990s, poetry, literature, and film began to serve women as sites of subjectivity work, in which their affective introjections shaped their artistic expressions. In the new millennium, reflections on the contrasts between generations and between *now* and *then*, again, a before-and-after modality, populated the work of numerous writers and filmmakers, many of whom were women born during the 1960s and 1970s. Now there was time and ample distance to look back, to remember, and to consider what, in Leila's words, "could be had." Markedly since the 1990s, Leila's generation has turned to writing, blogging, filmmaking, and various other culturally constructed expressions of affect, in ways that their mothers never did.

Post-1970s intergenerational shifts are of course not unique to Iran. But what marks Leila's generation is an affective memory-work that compels them to retell, witness, and search for narrative and meaning. Like those of the *daheh-ye shasti-hā*, these generational testimonies create their own cultural aesthetics. They seek distinction in *their* construction of historical truth against the truths of those who came before and after.[31] Unlike previously male-dominated fiction, women's novels are increasingly preoccupied with urban women and their everyday lives, unspoken desires, hopes, and anxieties. Authors like Zoya Pirzad (b. 1952), for example, made up a cohort of postrevolutionary Iranian Virginia Woolfs and Sylvia Plaths, and in response to the trivialization of ordinary urban women's ordeals, they focus on the angst of the ordinary.[32] Yet, they skillfully refrain from sentimentality or cliché (that, they believe, would be a marker of the older generations). In unpacking the afterlife of the war, the genre is also strongly antiwar and socially conscious. The authors make life itself the plot of affective contestations and negotiation.[33]

These cultural productions have received, and call for, more in-depth readings beyond the scope of this chapter. I only invoke them here for the chords they strike culturally and generationally, and to give a sense of the psychological structures that Leila's narratives are embedded in. Their thematic trajectory serves to situate mothers like Leila in gendered and gendering psychosocial contexts. This narrativity complements the ways in which Leila's medicalizing narratives help in remedying the present and the future. In other words, psychiatry too serves as a vehicle for narrative making. Meanwhile, many veteran and war-inflicted families who settled on the shaky ground of adjustment are working through memories that still linger in many households, where children are reminded how privileged their lives are in comparison to those of their parents.[34] Shirin is one of those children. When her parents are tending her "ADHD," the war still lingers in their generational memories, as do their generational projections of anxiety, desire, and modernist modes of thought.

Medicalization, Narrative Psychiatry, and New Moral Forms

As a diagnostic category, ADHD serves as a window into cultural and social change and the consolidation of biomedical conceptualizations of health. It opens a third space between life and illness, allowing a psychiatric subjectivity to emerge and create explanatory models that assimilate both biology and history in the functioning of the brain. It renders the self generational. In combining these clinical plots with cultural forms, I hope to let these multiple narratives and cartographies of desire lead us to better comparative and situated understanding and therapeutic interventions. While Ritalin gains its legitimacy in the premise of "treating" a dysfunction in the brain, Leila's deliberations on the past remind us of other, historically justified modes of legitimation. In other words, her therapeutic choices are legitimated and made meaningful through biomedically *and* culturally constructed narratives.[35]

ADHD is indeed biomedically rooted, while igniting ongoing global debates among psychiatrists and social critics alike, raising questions about medication and medicalization of child behavior.[36] Its lived experience, however, is embedded in several semantic networks and cultural layers of meaning in each cultural setting. On the one hand, Ritalin is understood to function as a facilitator of focus, direction, and discipline, sitting well with traditionally valorized symbolics and semiotics of Iranian parenting. On the other hand, medication with Ritalin is also understood as something that protects a child's self-esteem in the face of ADHD. The brain discourse and its universalist parenting principles constitute a progressive attitude and validate the imperative to pursue a pharmaceutical response to children's behavior. Of course, purposeful focus on the future is not unique to Iranian parents. But Leila's conceptualization of her child's future is both medically, historically, and culturally situated. And medication (as a discursive symbol) is meant to protect that future from (dis)order. It can be argued that, for Leila, more than just the "behavior" of her child is at stake. There is a new regime of being that defines and projects future health and happiness and self-esteem, as if attempting to work through, or gain control over, what was once taken away. Meanwhile, the authority of a brain discourse makes it possible to focus on "behavior" and a set of brain-based skills that keep the stigma of illness at bay. Leila's projected will to "happiness" is also deeply gendered, as are Iranian psychiatric forms of life and their narratives. These gendered aspects call for further investigation. In my preliminary research, many mothers underscore their generational experiences as tightly linked to their gendering significance; gender is thus implied in their interactions with medicine and the seemingly value-neutral and scientific framework of psychiatry.

Psychiatry, on the other hand, is situated in and shaped by narrative. The field of "narrative psychiatry," which incorporates humanities into psychiatry, developed in the United States with the aim of empowering patients by helping them find and choose functional narrative frameworks that work for them.[37] Narrative psychiatry requires skills in narrative competence and listening, hence an emphasis on individual narrative as an end in itself.[38] Leila and many of her peers seem to have employed medicalization as a narrative framework, while performatively taking to storytelling and vivid reconstructions of their generational histories. History, in its ruptured and stuttered reconstruction, provides the plot to their narratives of illness, while biopsychiatry, promoted by expert voices, offers a language for making the stuttering of historical experiences intelligible. Understanding their perception of illness thus requires understanding the historical claims that underlie it. An illness narrative, for Leila, is not merely an end in itself, but also a means to historical and generational recognition and differentiation.[39]

The narratives and the performativity with which Leila simultaneously historicizes biomedical models and medicalizes history help us understand what underlies her strategic choices of frameworks and what contexts psychiatry operates in. Beyond mere metaphors, they reflect historical experiences and the desire for new moral forms and perceptions of health. They challenge the brain-culture binary by highlighting the porous boundaries of both biomedical and sociocultural interpretations of disorder. Leila renders history embodied, while diagnoses and medications provide relief, lift the burden of stigma and victimhood, help account for anxieties, project modernization and progress, and provide hope.

For Leila, the sense of individual responsibility for self-care takes shape against the backdrop of a generational shift (from her mother) in moral systems. The term *modern* (often pronounced in Persian like the French *moderne*, and often conflated with the concept of "modernized") is frequently used to signify a particular understanding of mental health and personhood as biologically embodied. ADHD, then, is located in this merging of [gendered] historical witnessing of the past with biomedically reconciled narratives of the present. Its discourse is a byproduct of the availability and promotion of such psychiatry in 1990s Iran and ensuing moral imperatives about healthier futures.[40] The progressive projection of psychiatric intervention (Zoloft for her, Ritalin for her child) facilitates, for Leila, the passage through a moral impasse: it makes possible the creation of a psychiatrically approved and generationally organized self for both herself and her child. This remedied self feels both compelled and able to overcome. Her moral responsibility is sociohistorically constructed and psychosocially negotiated, creating an altogether different operational framework for individual choice. And as she utilizes psychiatry to find her place in the world, her generationally formed desires continue to escape its biomedical tenets.

These competing contexts, of generational desires, of biomedical discourses, and of historical ruptures, shape part of the platform on which Iranian psychiatry operates. In the next chapter, I turn to this situated operation of psychiatric knowledge and practice, in order to complement these accounts with the narratives and explanatory models of Iranian psychiatry itself. Starting with where I had my very first encounters with it, and to pick up where I left off in Chapter 2, I return to Ruzbeh.

The Medical Intern

"Let me tell you one thing," the professor opened his lecture,

> if you expect cheerleading and gratitude from your patients, don't become psychiatrists. None of your patients will say hello if they see you in a party; they'll instead look the other way and pretend they never met you. Whereas if you're a gynecologist, everyone will come to you in parties and say "Oh, doctor! Look, this is my son whom you delivered twenty years ago! He's in college now!" As psychiatrists, you'll never get that type of acknowledgment; no one wants to be known as *your* patient! . . . Plus, as you well know, many people believe that psychiatrists are sort of *khol-o chel* [crazy] themselves! [laughter] But joking aside, psychiatry is both a skill and an art. It requires an open mind and a capacity to care deeply for people.

This was what we were told, in March 1997, on the first day of our psychiatric rotation in Ruzbeh Hospital's grand hall. Enthusiastic medical students in brand-new white coats, we were starting our month-long rotation in awe, feeling privileged to be part of the historic experience that Ruzbeh was. Later, as clinical interns, we anticipated a most extraordinary world of myths and mystique, jokes and rumors and heartaches. Among the first modern psychiatric hospitals in the Middle East, Ruzbeh housed a range of psychiatric patients as well as clinical and research projects. But Ruzbeh was more than just a hospital. For us, medical students and interns, walking in the hallways of Ruzbeh was like walking down the lane of history. Ruzbeh's architecture, fittingly reflecting the French legacy of its founders, was among the old landmarks of a Tehran that, in our eyes, belonged to memoirs and period dramas.

Ruzbeh thrived in the sense of historicity that it evoked; a history that started with the return of a generation of French-trained students in the 1930s to the Iran of the Reza Shah era. They had founded modern medical specialties and disciplines at a time when the majority of the country's population was illiterate. History for us began in 1934 and the foundation of *Dāneshgāh-e Mādar*, the

"Mother University," the University of Tehran. For decades, disciples had taken pride in walking in gardens where once upon a time, dignitaries such as Professor Reza'i and Professor Mirsepāssi had set foot; we were privileged to be taught by those who were their direct intellectual heirs. In seminars, we were reminded of the legacy of these founding fathers, whose images were wrapped in an aura of grace. But what distinguished *Maktab-e Ruzbeh* ("the Ruzbeh school"), as Ruzbeh's alumni call it, was the fact that it had remained a relatively safe haven for alternative debates to emerge and grow. Its senior professors had preserved the intellectual legacy of its dignitaries through the tides of time, and had helped Ruzbeh become a center of excellence. The institute's conceptual conversation with literary criticism too, made—and still makes—Ruzbeh a unique space between medicine and the world of letters.

Ruzbeh bred stories. I can still see my young artist-turned-messiah patient, walking under the Judas trees in his sky-blue uniform. Sedated and shrunken, his handsome eyes no longer confronted our questions the way they did the night he was admitted for a violent delusional episode. He was now Mahdi, the twelfth Shi'ite Imam. "The past and the future are *jabr* [fate]; the present is *ekhtiār* [free will]," he told me. It was he who made me wonder why we assumed we knew what he was going through. His will to escape to the other side found a different meaning at Ruzbeh, eliciting discussions that surpassed the *DSM*. Ruzbeh stood out for allowing those different meanings.

CHAPTER 7

The Many Minds of Psychiatry, or Psychiatry as Cultural Critique

I N T H E I R *Anthropology as Cultural Critique* (1999 [1986]), Marcus and Fischer historicized and emphasized anthropology's responsibility for critique through cross-cultural juxtapositions and a serious reexamination of our assumptions and what we take for granted. Such cross-cultural juxtapositions require giving up familiar forms of knowing, seeing, listening, and feeling; they necessitate a two-way collaborative openness and experimental engagement with what is to be analyzed and understood. I have so far tried to provide an ethnographic cultural critique of some such assumed concepts in our reading of individual symptoms and experiences. But what about psychiatry itself? Can psychiatry too serve as cultural critique by revealing aspects of the worlds it operates in?

Iranian psychiatry provides not only a primary prism through which to understand the 1990s psychiatric turn, but also a compelling case for comparative analysis. In its particular trajectories of knowledge and forms of practice, it disrupts some of our familiar assumptions about psychiatry's local histories, ethical and political implications, and biomedical tenets. In this last chapter, I lay out some of these historical, practical, and pedagogical particularities by way of a cultural critique. The identity of Iranian psychiatry as a discipline is historically situated in layers of cultural work in various sites such as media, training, and practice, and in negotiations between and among different orientations of psychiatry. The practice and conceptualization of this psychiatry provides an example of a medical infrastructure that, while skewed toward biomedical approaches, provides interesting spaces for psychodynamic approaches. It also coexists with a growing popular interest in self-help psychological discourses, a bottom-up desire for medicalization, and century-old modernizing aspirations that follow global trends. The various explanatory models that Iranian psychiatrists offer also reveal nuances, language games, gaps, and conflicts that distinguish their practices from global standard models.[1]

In a way, Iran presents a reverse history of academic psychiatry from that in the United States. In the American case, psychodynamics dominated psychiatry during the first half of the twentieth century and was replaced by psychopharmacological trends after the *DSM-III* was in place. In Iran, however, neurological and thus psychopharmacological views had always dominated and marginalized psychodynamic ones until a short-lived burst in the 1970s. It was only in the 1980s that psychodynamic approaches made their way into the core of academic psychiatry.[2] If in the United States the turning point was the advent of psychopharmaceuticals and the biomedical "coup" that resulted in the ideological departure of *DSM-III* from the psychodynamic spirit of *DSM-II*, in Iran it was a revolutionary storm of professional ideologies that, significantly, never connected with the anti-psychiatry movement of the United States and the UK nor with the anti-institutional movement in French psychiatry.[3]

Although psychotherapeutic language has become strikingly popular among Iranians in ways unimaginable twenty years ago, in medical professional training, psychodynamic psychotherapy struggled to be implemented in the national curriculum of psychiatric residency programs. Today, despite concerns with and general interest in helping people learn new parenting skills or adult interpersonal affective relations, many psychiatrists see little therapeutic use for psychodynamic methods due to practical limitations. At best, cognitive behavioral therapy (CBT) is endorsed as effective. Still, psychodynamic methods have survived on the margins of academic psychiatry through both informal and formal training, particularly in one institution, namely Ruzbeh Hospital.

As the birthplace of academic psychiatry and home to several pedagogical negotiations, Ruzbeh has informed and shaped both biomedical and psychodynamic mindsets, each representing distinct configurations of knowledge. The pluralism that is aspired to at Ruzbeh is rarely reproduced elsewhere. Psychiatrists' mass education and cultural work seems to be largely focused on destigmatization and getting people to seek psychiatric care. For most biomedically oriented psychiatrists, the "cultural" seems limiting and old fashioned, not evidence-based and falsifiable—an impression often based on inappropriate reductionist formulations of culture as people's nonscientific beliefs. This results in not adequately crediting behavioral, role-structured, family systems, or cognitive-emotional working in what they would define as fundamentally neurological, biochemical issues.

But there is another sense of "the cultural" that this limited understanding fails to explore, and that creative psychodynamic therapists use to uncover lost capacities, modes of self-understanding, and new social interactional patterns. Sustained group therapy, recovered mystic paths, literary and cinematic models of (and for) affect management are such cultural methodologies.[4] At Ruzbeh, it is understood that while psychiatry can engage larger cultural currents in society, this does not mean that there are not indications and conditions for psychotropic medications, nor does it mean that the destigmatization campaign should stop. Even though categories such as depression and ADHD seem to have become more accepted by people, other diagnoses such as schizophrenia and bipolar disorders are still stigmatized. Psychodynamic therapies and frameworks are therefore offered not as substitutes for medication or behavioral therapies such as CBT, but as models to complement, and—more importantly—widen the discourse, bringing pluralism to a place where no single answer dominates.

"Cultural" also applies to the professional and disciplinary cultures and mindsets experts harbor. Pluralism thus inversely also might mean that psychoanalysis should be brought back under the umbrella of medicine, an ambitious goal already underway at Ruzbeh. Since one lives in so many parallel worlds—the biomedical, the psychological, the social, the political, and the historical—one naturally exploits relevant discourses and rituals in order to make each world meaningful in relation to others. Psychiatrists are already engaged in a cultural discourse as they make biomedical interventions (specifically psychiatric medications) intelligible through processes of interpretation and work of culture, in Michael Fischer's words; i.e., they are literally weaving meaning into the (at times) contradictory contexts in which they live.[5] Each of these assemblages requires a contextual analysis. These debates are ongoing at Ruzbeh and in Iranian psychiatry at large, and are often taken up when I ask psychiatrists the same questions I asked young Iranians about the normalization of psychiatric discourses or the changing patterns of medication. In these parallel discussions I will highlight commonalities, convergences and divergences among them as well as between psychiatrists and their patients.[6]

Comparative Reflections on Psychiatry: A Cultural Critique

Today, much of the critical literature on psychiatrization in Western social medicine and anthropology is focused on three domains: first, psychiatry's reliance on psychopharmaceutical intervention, as well as the opacity of pharmaceutical companies, growing controversy around overmedicating children, and the legacy of psychiatry's relationship with institutions.[7] Several scholars have underscored the role of pharmaceutical companies in transforming psychiatric diagnoses and treatment, and further ideologies behind self-fashioning though psychiatric medication.[8] The second area of criticism is psychiatry's alleged oblivion to larger contextual issues, a criticism that hardly applies to Iranian psychiatrists, who, as I have already explained in earlier chapters, are acutely aware of and embedded in the contexts in which they live and practice. The third domain of criticism is the (in)appropriateness of the *DSM* as a diagnostic guideline. Here I will focus on the last.

Psychiatry's biomedical hegemony in the United States started with the shift from the *DSM-II* to the *DSM-III*.[9] Since then, the pharmaceutical industry and contestations between the advocates of dynamic and biomedical methods have shaped the social life of psychiatric practice, resulting in a notable increase in and dependence on pharmaceutical prescriptions. Critics like David Healy in his *Antidepressant Era* have argued that these forces influence the way psychiatric textbooks and classifications are revised, and have wondered if "it can reasonably be asked whether biological language offers more in the line of marketing copy than it offers in terms of clinical meaning."[10]

In Iran, internal rivalries among different orientations of psychiatry (primarily psychodynamic and biomedical) and its status anxiety in relation with the rest of medicine have increasingly moved the field toward biopsychiatry. The standard diagnostic model, as explained earlier, is the *DSM-IV-TR*. Despite psychiatrists' acknowledgment of transactional models and contextual differences, the status of the *DSM* has hardly been questioned. Most Iranian psychiatrists do acknowledge that the *DSM*'s criteria have not been designed with the cultural history and social psychology of Iranians in mind. But they rarely question its underlying assumptions beyond a consideration of so-called culture-bound syndromes. They argue, for example, that alcoholism and anorexia are pressing issues in the West, but not in Iran.

That anorexia and alcoholism do not have a public face in Iran is often interpreted as "cultural" difference between Iran and "the West." Such statements can create a false assurance about being aware of cultural differences when it comes to diagnosis and treatment. Most doctors fail or refuse to engage with how illness categories are not only biologically, but also culturally shaped, experienced, and manifested. As one psychiatrist told me, "When you have a diagnosis, it doesn't really make a difference what culture we're talking about, the brain image of the patients would be the same."

This blind faith in neuroscience overlooks the ways that Iranian *depreshen* or ADHD are perceived, experienced, and interpreted, culturally, by people. What seems to be lacking is a cultural critique of the *DSM*'s underlying assumptions such as "function" and "loss" (see Chapters 4 and 6). Psychodynamic psychiatrists have been at the forefront of this criticism, and have pointed out that relying on the cultural adjustments of the *DSM* (primarily the inclusion of culture-bound syndromes) is not enough for dealing with the cultural meanings of "function." The same applies to the usage of standardized questionnaires, where, even though translations often include cultural adjustments, they hardly raise questions about the cultural assumptions and epistemological contexts that underlie the construction of standard categories. Take the example of adjustment mood disorders: the *DSM* gives the patient a set period of time to adjust to a particular stressor or loss, and if symptoms persist beyond that and lead to impairment of function, major depressive disorder is diagnosed, which is often an indication for medication. But these criteria and timelines are evidence-based within the American health care system, with the assumption that specific support services are available after crisis, and where "impairment of function" means a set of specific things that may not apply to the Iranian patient. Not to mention that symptoms may persist beyond the end of crisis conditions that are sociohistorically formed.

Biomedical psychiatrists, however, argue that in evaluating patients' functionality, it doesn't matter what task it is that one considers important, what is crucial is the loss of ability to *perform* it. They also remind me that the *DSM* and *ICD* have been tested cross-culturally and have shown similar epidemiologic outcomes. For them, normal and pathological remain standardized and universal. Whether symptoms vary across cultures, they argue, is irrelevant: intervention should target the brain pathways responsible for those (varying) symptoms. In other words, the pathology is the same even if the presentation varies. The dominance of this biomedical mindset indeed reflects global trends in psychiatry; but it is also culturally situated. Iranian psychiatrists have long been engaged in a cultural campaign against stigma and misinformed societal beliefs about mental illness, requiring the emphasis on the brain in an attempt to fight such beliefs. Add to that the historical separation of Iranian psychiatry as a medical field from psychoanalysis as an intellectual domain, each harboring its own distinct culture.

The Cultures of Iranian Psychiatry

Psychiatry's professional and cultural assumptions vary and rely on a variety of trajectories, including how psychiatrists and neuroscientists may unintentionally bring their own cultural assumptions about social contexts into their practice.[11] In engaging with psychiatrists and their experiences, few social science scholars have explored the training experience of psychiatrists in order to understand the tensions that shape their own moralities and selfhood even before their practices are formed.[12] Even in works that have explored the training of psychiatrists, most of the core subject matter is located in Western societies and in conversation with a presumptive dualistic Cartesian rationality that puts the body at the center of analysis. This privileging of the body facilitates a type of academic critique in the West that is not easily applicable in places where the contours of body and mind are differently configured. Additionally, the significance of pharmaceutical and insurance companies in the United States (or the socialized National Health System in the UK) presents different historical and structural contexts for critiques of overmedication than those in Iran. The structural particularities of the Iranian mental health care system, psychiatrists believe, locate them in a pragmatic impasse and gives lesser weight to the role of pharmaceutical companies in dictating medication trends. While professional and Western biomedical epistemologies can migrate—as they have broadly—it is crucial to follow how they morph and adapt in distinct social and historical scaffolds. To understand these professional cultures requires asking what happens to diagnostic criteria and psychiatric mindsets as they travel east.

The competing professional cultures of Iranian psychiatry are in constant formation in several sites including training, practice, media, and personal and social lives. Cultural and medical concepts and meanings constantly interact, reject, negotiate, and shape each other. Practitioners' own life trajectories too contribute to the social contexts they practice in, because they place them in a continuum with the generational experiences of their patients and compel them to customize their practice. For example, as I discussed in Chapter 2, a cursory juxtaposition of NIMH-trained child psychiatrist Javad Alāghband-Rād (first chair and a co-founder of the Board of Child Psychiatry in 1997) and London-trained psychiatrist and psychodynamic psychotherapist Mohammad Sanati (the champion of psychodynamic training in psychiatry since the 1980s and the director of the Psychotherapy Fellowship at Ruzbeh Hospital), reveals different kinds of scientific stardom and success, contingent on institutional and ideological conflicts in establishing new disciplines. Alāghband-Rād's subdiscipline required careful navigation through institutional norms and politics. Sanati's, politicized and ostracized, was, by necessity, initially reconstructed in a heterotopic venue beyond the medical arena (see Chapter 2, notes 68 and 75). If each individual's psychiatric expertise develops differently, so too does psychiatric practice at large.

Iranian psychiatry's two distinct orientations and their corresponding explanatory models reveal distinct moralities—different notions of care, responsibility, and medical intervention. I ask each group to elaborate on the psychiatric turn among laypeople. How, I ask, do they account for rising rates of psychiatric medication such as antidepressants? Although most psychiatrists agree that psychopharmacology and psychotherapy ideally work best in combination, they also agree that today psychopharmacology leads the way. Psychodynamically oriented psychiatrists believe this is due to structural circumstances. Biomedically oriented psychiatrists agree, but also argue that medication corresponds to a neuroscientific understanding of illness, and that psychoanalytically oriented therapy is not as "evidence-based" and is being superseded by other, "scientific" approaches.

Disagreement between advocates of biomedical and psychodynamic approaches reminds us that there is a lingering status anxiety among psychiatrists of all trajectories. There are nuanced views on both sides, but most commonly, they disapprove of each other's dogma. In a nutshell, while some biomedically inclined psychiatrists might have a personal interest in psychoanalysis, they dismiss it as a reliable basis for *therapeutic* interventions, saying it is not measurable, scientific, evidence-based, falsifiable, or empirical—all key terms and used emphatically. The exception is CBT, which is accepted as evidence-based and effective. A common catchphrase among the biomedical faction is "falsifiability."[13] Striking in my conversations was when a younger psychiatrist put self-help and psychoanalysis in the same box and dismissed psychoanalysis as a combination of Freud, the unconscious, and "something to do with sexuality." None of it, a wave of the hand indicated, was falsifiable, and thus not science.

The feeling is in a way mutual. Followers of the psychodynamic orientation believe writing prescriptions is a quick fix for doctors, too. They are concerned about possible overmedication and overdiagnosis. They also raise concerns about treatment efficacy, arguing that child psychiatry, for instance, has become con-spicuously preoccupied with ADHD and that its treatment is reduced to medi-cation coupled with a limited universalist parenting model. Without proper engagement with family dynamics, they argue, the magic bullet of medication may do more harm than good. To understand these professional logics, I first explore each camp's interpretations and explanatory models and compare them with those discussed in previous chapters, before examining how situated knowl-edge and practices evolve in the two domains of training and practice. Let's listen.

BIOMEDICAL MODELS

When I ask psychiatrists to comment on the rise in medication and the possibil-ity of overmedication, they initially have a ready answer: early detection and di-agnosis have improved and people's awareness has increased help seeking. Thus more people who need medication are getting treatment these days. "I'm not sure if what we see in Iran is overmedication," said one child psychiatrist; "maybe compared to the past we're medicating more. I think medication has helped the paradigm shift in laypeople's views: even if we have overmedication, this over-medication has changed people's understanding of psychiatry."[14] But as our con-versations evolve, they often make causal connections to what they perceive as modernity or modernization, or lack thereof. They frequently point to Iranian society being in a "transition from tradition to modernity" and that if there are patterns of medication misuse, it has to do with "cultural" habits: "Medication is a tool to demystify psychiatry and also [to make intelligible] the brain and be-havior paradigm. So, it has a positive side effect. This has happened in the West too, a shift from a magical to a scientific discipline."

It may seem that in making such comments doctors are simply projecting and shifting the focus of responsibility and blame, but even when stereotyping, their explanations cannot easily be dismissed as the clichéd attitudes of a Westernized elite. Many are keen to engage in social commentary, while a few others prefer to focus on clinical and therapeutic possibilities. It usually takes longer into our rela-tionship for some of them to engage self-critically. And when they do, their com-ments reflect the deeper tensions that they experience in their different capacities as citizens and doctors. These are a few of the themes they frequently draw on.

INFRASTRUCTURE   For one thing, the public's confused perception of psy-chiatry, psychotherapy, psychoanalysis, neurology, and psychology has practical implications for help-seeking patterns. When psychiatry gained a different social and clinical status in the 1990s, the absence of a referral system increased pressure on psychiatric practitioners. Most patients come to the psychiatrist in crisis-like conditions. Thus, psychiatrists are flooded with patients who frequently demand quick fixes rather than more extended therapies and interventions. Biomedical practitioners are often forced to ignore psychosocial contexts for reasons of time, the inability to "change society," and the necessity of dealing with crises as presented in the clinic. They believe that infrastructural circumstances force them to medicate. These include an insufficient mental health care budget, the absence of a referral system (for example, manifest in the shortage of psychiatric nurses), and patients' insistence on quick fixes, all of which, to many doctors, reflect underdevelopment and lack of social progress. Overmedication, if there is any, ought to be understood as an "infrastructural and systematic problem."

THE TRANSACTIONAL MODEL   Practitioners acknowledge the importance of the social, familial, and environmental aspects of mental health, confirming that, for instance, more people are diagnosed and medicated with depression because people's threshold of referral seeking has changed. They seek help more commonly today when noticing symptoms of depression, both because they are more aware and because they have lower thresholds. Or, in an arc that brings to mind Leila's mother and daughter, discussed in Chapter 6, child psychiatrists agree that life was simpler before and today's parents have lower thresholds for the anarchy of childhood. Parents are also more likely now to know about ADHD and bring their children to doctors sooner and with less hesitation.

Psychiatrists appreciate that medication should not be the sole intervention and that the discipline has to engage with interpersonal and social dynamics. An example of this engagement is the application of the transactional model, which, for example, provides parents with a list of do's and don'ts in managing their interactions with their child. The idea is that, for ADHD, medication and therapy that educates parents should work in combination. But there is a caveat: "Parenting is universal and should have universal models."[15] The IACAP, for instance, is proud of its parenting model initiative for an integral approach in child psychiatry; it is also proud of its international collaborations in this initiative. Of course, this stands in contrast to how anthropologists approach parenting: as a historically and culturally negotiated dynamic. Critics within the profession too, often psychodynamically oriented psychiatrists, have raised questions about the direct applicability of British or Australian models in Iranian parenting. The late Vali Sahāmi, for instance, the child psychiatrist I introduced in Chapter 2, adopted a more accommodating language in his frequent appearances on TV and in the newspapers, addressing the very "cultural" issues that universalist practitioners dismissed as a nuisance. He promoted guidelines for engagement with children and teenagers in the cultural terms of the conflicts within families. The difference between the culturalist and universalist languages, therefore, is more than just a repetition of "traditional versus modern" explanations. The former engages in culturally situated scenarios; the latter emphasizes the need to do away with and press beyond limited cultural beliefs and expectations.

THE FINAL COMMON PATHWAY MODEL   Debates between more culturally attuned and more universal models of psychiatric practice amuse psychiatrists. But at the end of the day, they remind me, no matter what "social" circumstances are behind it, illness manifests through a neurobiological final common pathway, or through synapses in the brain, as psychiatrist Dr. M. told his audience in the televised public lecture discussed in Chapter 3.[16] In ADHD, for example, many child psychiatrists tell me, it is the *executive function* that is flawed, and we know where that is located in the brain. Despite debates and controversies over evidence, there is unconditional faith in neuroscience. Medication, cognitive behavioral therapy, and social circumstances, they tell me, all do something to the relationship between brain and behavior; and that is what matters. Some psychiatrists invoke gene expression and the promise of epigenetics to argue that they are not oblivious to social and environmental factors. "Neuroscience," one told me, "is totally compatible with social explanations. When we advise certain behavior in CBT or in our parenting models, our aim is to activate the relevant circuits in the brain." Neuroplasticity, in other words, brings the biological and the social together.

Today, Ruzbeh is heavily focused on what many advocates refer to as a "research mindset." Everything is neurochemical in the end, but this doesn't mean intervention should be "only chemical." By stripping mental illness of blame, guilt, and shame, neuroscience offers psychiatrists a tool for reaching out to more patients. In the aftermath of the Iran-Iraq War, neuroscience has also offered a relief paradigm for reconciliation with a sense of infliction and a wide spectrum of emotions, from dysphoria and helplessness to conviction or rage. The brain and behavior mindset resonates, when you think about it, with the reflections of Samāneh and Rāmin and many others who find in medication the possibility of soothing the pain of what cannot be otherwise fixed.

HOPE   Pharmacodynamics is not the only merit of medication though, bio-medical psychiatrists tell me. Beyond necessity, instilling hope is a compelling rationale behind their therapeutic choices. Psychiatry is a skill and an art, they say. It takes wisdom. Medication is important and makes a significant difference, they argue, especially when it's the only resource available. Its rapid impact is considered to give patients hope and an incentive to pursue further treatment options or to motivate them to improve their quality of life. This is where many of our conversations take a U-turn and reveal a key element of situated practice. After all, the doctors muse, it is life conditions and uncertainties that cause most mental health issues.

The bottom line is "medication gives hope, and this is what patients need most, no matter what problems they have. I think of ways to increase the patient's sense of confidence and competence. There are many situations we can't cure or treat optimally, but we can always increase their sense of competence."[17] Indeed, this situated perspective varies across the board, but is an important element in understanding the nuances of psychiatric practice in Iran. Many speculate, when they prescribe antidepressants for instance, that most of their patients do not suffer from "clinical" depression, but from "learned helplessness," dysphoria, general lack of hope. One child psychiatrist told me, "When parents are desperate, or don't really understand the concept of ADHD, medication becomes the first line of intervention. When you start medication, you see some changes soon. Parents start trusting you and come back and you can then start therapy. They find hope. It's the same when you have a family crisis on your hands; you need to manage the crisis first."[18] But the changes are so dramatic that most people are unlikely to come back for therapy, due to fear of stigma or lack of time or financial resources. Upon feeling better, it is common for patients to simply stop taking the medication, which means they will be back again with recurring symptoms.

Still, many psychiatrists caution me and insist they always make sure to tell parents and patients that medication is only one part of treatment—perhaps the most important one—but that it also needs to be complemented with other options such as psychotherapy. All along, when medicating, they create meaning—often positive meaning—in the imperfect conditions in which they practice. Hope is, after all, what shapes the core of the doctor-patient relationship; the magic bullet of the pill serves to persuade and sustain hope in the face of situational contingencies. Psychiatrists speculate that fulfilling patients' desire for medication will also make patients more resilient and empowered to seek additional care.[19] The pill will bring them around to more holistic psychotherapeutic care.

PSYCHODYNAMIC REFLECTIONS

Psychodynamic psychiatrists have a different take on hope in relation to rising rates of medication in society. They explain it not only in terms of social and infrastructural matters, but also in psychoanalytic terms and in the sense of a roller coaster of hope over time, a kind of meta-analysis: the hopes of the revolution, wartime solidarities and utopias, and the hopes of the reform era (1997–2005) were all followed by reality checks. Many psychiatrists report that in wartime, the major condition they dealt with in their clinical practice was anxiety (crisis was in the making), replaced in the 1990s with dysphoria and depressive moods (critical thinking in the making). There is, of course, good reason for dysphoria after any war. Mental anguish manifests differently during and after crisis; and wartime anxieties are understandably replaced with postwar losses and individuals' retrospective reflections.[20]

These retrospective readings were, of course, variously informed across social strata. In the 1990s and during the reform era, an additional stream of critical thinking in the form of publications, translations of Western thinkers, and cinema, along with new communication technologies (the Internet, satellite TV, international phone cards) swept the thinking of the middle classes. There was now time for reflection, and with alternative tools. Meanwhile, for those severely affected by the war, and for the working-class displaced masses who watched society rapidly moving on, there was a growing sense that wartime sacrifices had been undone and the blood of martyrs disrespected. Wartime solidarity, patriotism, and hope, these analysts argue, gave way to disillusionment. Later, they argue, the psychological roller coaster continued; the hope for economic reform during the reconstruction era (1989–1997) was dampened by class divisions and inequalities; the hope in the promises of the reform era (1997–2005) for civil liberties and a better economy was followed by the stifling of both. For psychoanalysts and psychoanalytically oriented psychiatrists, this entanglement of hope and dysphoria is more than a neuro-manifestation of environmental factors.

In analyzing the perceived sense of rising dysphoria or antidepressant medications, they also take into consideration the psychodynamic implications of mysticism, Sufism, Shi'ite rituals, and other Iranian cultural discourses that inform the cultural meanings of affective states. Psychodynamic psychotherapist Mohammad Sanati regards Iranians' wartime engagement with death as more than an ideological temporality; rather, the valorization of martyrdom is part of a historically internalized and culturally formulated construction of Iranian affect—with psychodynamic implications. In "Practicing Psychoanalysis in a Death-Conscious Society" (2004) and *Sādegh Hedāyat and the Fear of Death* (2001), he explores this theme through the work and suicide of modernist literary icon Sādegh Hedāyat, as well as an analysis of mythological figures of *Shāhnāmeh* and commentary on contemporary cinema and painting.[21] He argues for the need of a transition to a construct that embraces life. This, of course, is something that self-help traditions of positive psychology, such as PANA, have begun to introduce to people. But Sanati uses Lacan to draw a distinction and to highlight positive mystical discourses that generate desire through a lack, a separation from the beloved, a forward-moving deferral of gratification, and perhaps even sublimation in productivity. This, he argues, is very different from the notion of depression that is experienced as loss-induced hopelessness. This is a neat distinction between the feeling states of the 1980s and the 1990s.[22]

The sense of social helplessness, or, as one analyst put it, the "emotional exhaustion" of society after the war, should be differentiated from clinical depression. For psychoanalysts this distinction is essential. The difference resonates with what Samāneh narrated for instance in Chapter 4, situating her experience of *depreshen* in the sense of uncertainty about the future and life in general. Of course, psychodynamic psychiatrists, like their biomedical colleagues, believe that the mass education campaign about mental health should continue and that people are still reluctant to seek psychiatric help. But they also lament that somewhere between expert talk in the media and lay interpretations of social disaffection, a misguided message has formed that defines medication as a shortcut. This does not mean they are against medication; advocates of psychodynamic approaches, including Sanati, prescribe medication, but insist on approaching it with attention to contextual factors and in combination with therapy. Like their biomedically inclined colleagues, they too medicate knowing that many of their patients do not have the luxury of committing to therapy. When people seek help, they have a more comfortable relationship with medications than with psychotherapy. This can be explained in terms of stigma: Sanati believes that for most people, visiting a psychoanalyst is associated with the stigma of *bimāri-ye ravāni* (mental illness, and sometimes with the negative connotation of insanity), while being on psychiatric medication only reflects having a *bimāri-ye a'sāb* (disease of the nerves).[23] But seeking immediate relief is also explained in terms of a "culture of quick fix," which Sanati formulates in psychoanalytical terms as pre-Oedipal behavior. On the dilemma of quick fix both groups seem to agree.

Explanatory models are indeed at times generalizing on both sides; but comparing them is informative. Their convergences and divergences, themselves reflective of the field's historical and pedagogical trajectories, shed light on the particular historical and cultural circumstances in which psychiatrists are trained, initiated, and socialized. To trace the production of their knowledge requires unpacking moments of uncertainty and ambivalence, as well as the double binds that "intellectual histories" of the field can miss or obscure. These moments are to be found in both psychiatric training and practice, and call for further ethnographic investigation. But here is a preliminary exploration.

Of Many Minds: Becoming Psychiatrists

As a medical student, one is often told that doctors learn by doing. The anthropologist in me is interested in the reverse: how doctors *do* by learning. That is, how doctors' practices are shaped by the pedagogical cultures they are professionalized in. As in any initiation, the rites and rituals of becoming a psychiatrist reflect underlying discourses of knowledge and power. But they are also embedded in the residents' own generational histories and extracurricular experiences, as both citizens and trainees. Much of their knowledge, in other words, is gained beyond the lecture hall.

In thinking about training trajectories, I have been inspired by the term "of two minds" from Tanya Luhrmann's 2001 ethnography, *Of Two Minds: The Growing Disorder in American Psychiatry*.[24] The title captures the struggle and ambivalence of training, and the tension between models of psychiatry in the United States, where, by the 1990s, psychopharmacology had all but pushed psychoanalysis out of the medical profession. Luhrmann analyzed how psychiatry residents developed new ways of seeing, listening, understanding, interpreting, and articulating mental illness and the world around them. In other words, how biomedical mindsets become and function as *culture*.

Let's start with the curriculum. The current curriculum for residency programs in psychiatry, known as "Program Requirements for Psychiatric Residency and Objectives of Psychiatric Residency" (in Persian), is quite impressive on paper. First, it provides a perfectly inclusive approach to mental health (albeit giving more importance to neuroscientific elements). The inclusion of a nine-month rotation in "dynamic psychotherapy" and the emphasis on holistic and integral models and a Meyerian bio-psycho-social model is promising.[25]

"Residents should excel during their training, in physical, biological, psychological, psychopharmacological, interpersonal, familial and bio-psycho-social approaches." Within the program, residents should collaborate with a team of occupational therapists, psychologists, and psychiatric nurses. Finally, the curriculum demands familiarity with the country's subcultures, religious beliefs, and mystical (*erfāni*), mythological, and ethnic beliefs and practices so as to differentiate them from pathology.

The guidelines go on to include mandatory training in the history of psychiatry; basic psychology; psychiatry and its social, cultural, and anthropological contexts; research methodology and epidemiology; diagnosis classification (*DSM* and *ICD* and their limitations); psychopathology; psychiatric examination; child psychiatry; geriatric psychiatry; addiction and its management (in a required two-month rotation) and counseling; neurological disorders; ECT; psychotherapy; crisis intervention and emergency triage; psychiatric rehabilitation; and community psychiatry. Add to these the "cultural understandings of modernity and postmodernity, history of social theories, social and anthropological aspects of illness, financial and cultural impact of mental illness, culture-bound syndromes, cross-cultural syndromes, alternative medicine, sociological concepts of socialization, stratification, globalization, urbanization, gender, old age, violence, as well as evolutionary psychology, medical anthropology and comparative study of health care models." Among the more recent additions to these requirements and objectives are rotations in "dynamic psychotherapy" and "social and community psychiatry" (*ravānpezeshki-ye jāme'eh-negar*, literally meaning psychiatry attuned to society).[26]

There is, however, a gulf between theory and practice. Particularly, the marginality and the crisis of legitimation in social sciences and humanities beg the question of how interdisciplinary measures such as social theory or anthropological aspects of illness would be systematically taught and what they would entail if they are implemented. Furthermore, active academic engagement with psychodynamics largely remains limited to Tehran and other big cities. And even though in theory residents can choose their orientation between psychodynamic psychotherapy and CBT, even at Ruzbeh, training for CBT is in far greater demand. Although Ruzbeh stands out because of its integrated dynamic psychotherapy and CBT training, elsewhere the allocation of residents across the fields remains uneven.

Curricular matters aside, it is important to keep in mind the developmental stage in which residents are located. Having made it to the other side of several competitive exams, most are of the age when the stresses of making ends meet and consolidating their careers prevail. These elements surface in their discussions of growing medicating trends and the rise of *depreshen* talk. As such, while explaining the possibility of overmedication in terms of structural health care issues, recent graduates are sometimes refreshingly honest about the larger picture: "You can't blame the psychiatrist [for alleged overmedication]; how can you expect someone to sacrifice their career [by going out of their way] when they are not given possibilities [or infrastructure] and have to build a career while they themselves are struggling with financial issues?" The world, in other words, is a different place when one leaves training.

Many residents are critical of the way mainstream psychiatry is often based on medicating patients with little investment in psychodynamic methods. Some take issue with "mechanistic" patient-doctor relationships, others with the strong hold of pharmaceutical companies on the industry and doctors linked to them. There are disagreements. When debating among themselves, the argument also springs up in favor of biomedical explanatory models. I am told, "when someone is depressed after losing his or her job, or losing a loved one, we need to treat the depression first. Sometimes, it's exactly the very medication that you're all calling 'mechanistic' that brings the miracle, changes the patient's worldview, helps find a job or get over the loss. Often those tiny changes in brain chemicals can do the work of a good social system by changing our attitude." Medication, again, is meant to compensate for infrastructural shortcomings. Psychiatrists do what they can do (primarily medicating), and not in vain, they argue, by forwarding biological psychiatry's brain and behavior models.

Many former Ruzbeh interns and residents think of their time there as the high point of their medical training. They say Ruzbeh is where they could "learn from interesting and well-rounded people and have amazing conversations." When I probe what is limiting training in psychodynamic orientations in general, residents point to an infrastructural lack of resources as a broader problem across "medical"—not just "psychiatric"—health care. But at a more practical level, training in dynamic psychotherapy requires additional time and resources, and is hardly compatible with the intense structure of psychiatric residency and its exams, evaluations, and demanding responsibilities; it is more efficient to teach psychopharmacology during residency. After all, psychopharmacology is more likely to be useful when serving outside of big cities; that is, when training ends and actual practice begins. In a blog post in the short-lived group blog *Café Analysis* run by Ruzbeh trainees and alumni, one of them had once lamented the increasing hold of standardized models in training: "Contradictions are all over the place. It is in Ruzbeh where they teach you not to limit yourself to one specific diagnostic classification, yet they push you into the dogma of OSCE [objective structured clinical examination]! Where they teach you about 'empathy' and then they expect you not to see the suffering of our patients when they are on the other side of these fences." Another responded: "Do you feel the same? We are changing into machines. Maybe this is Ruzbeh's way of preparing us for the outside world."

Of Many Minds: The Making of Situated Practices and Moralities

An anthropological evaluation of psychiatric practice calls for a situated critique of medicalization. Comparatively speaking, unlike the more clear-cut divide between organic and dynamic arguments elsewhere, in Iran the sharp contrast between the two camps has been blurred, in part, due to practitioners' embeddedness in the postwar experiences of the Iranian people and in the ways this context shaped the nuances of their practice over time.[27] On the one hand, the medical establishment's attitude toward psychoanalysis oscillates perplexingly between acknowledgment and rejection.[28] On the other, psychodynamic psychiatry, neither absent nor holding a deserved status, continues to inform Iranian psychiatry in creative ways. In this picture, even psychoanalytically oriented psychiatrists practice in an "in-between" space within psychiatry: a conceptual space where psychiatric medication becomes incorporated into their analytical logic because, often, it has to. This is a radically different social and experiential context than the American *antidepressant era* or *age of Prozac*, in which pharmaceutical companies join forces with the ethos of the pursuit of happiness in order to make people "feel better than well."[29] Today, advocates of both orientations cohabit in a liminal conceptual and medical territory, where tensions both inform and situate their practice in broader social discourses. This liminality also offers them possibilities for dialogue in addressing similar immediate concerns; they do not function in binary form, but in a hybrid space necessitated, in part, by pragmatism and infrastructural contingencies.

Iranian psychiatry is of two minds and more. Indeed, it reflects global trends in training and practice, including the so-called defeat of psychoanalysis.[30] These globalizing trends are part of the working of international markets for psychiatric medication and enterprise, arguably influencing psychiatric pedagogy and practice globally. Furthermore, individualistic biopolitics and neoliberal discourses of "psy" disciplines, too, prevail in Iranian psychiatry; they manifest in what has become known globally as a discourse of "responsibilization,"[31] and in the emergence of psychiatry as a technology of self in the sense explained by Faubion in his *An Anthropology of Ethics*: that Foucault's analysis of the technologies of self relied on the ways in which the self relates to the rules (to the practice of which it feels obligated), and, further, on the ways in which individuals are "incited to recognize their moral obligations."[32]

In Iranian psychiatry, too, the discourse of moral responsibility and care of the self is implied. Simultaneously, it is challenged by doctors' and patients' tacit knowledge that illness is, in part, rooted in broader (dis)orders that are impossible to cure. Patients accept and, at times, insist on quick fixes, but this doesn't mean they turn down other possibilities. Of course, narratives of moral impasse are hardly uniform. Often, more strategic combinations of explanatory models and coping mechanisms emerge; and whether or not medically, politically, religiously or traditionally constructed, they almost always invoke fate and faith.

Furthermore, the historical trajectory of the discipline, too, suggests a distinct moral dynamic. Psychiatry, both a medical field and an elite modernizing force in its inception, ought to be understood in juxtaposition to the volatile Iranian landscape of a century-long social and cultural change. In this light, it harbors a dual sense of moral responsibilization: first, in the Foucauldian trope of "care of the self," constituting ways of being in the world;[33] second, and more specifically, in cultural and politico-psychological discourses of not only modernization throughout the twentieth century, but also today's identity politics.

Maktab-e Ruzbeh

I opened and close this chapter with *Maktab-e Ruzbeh*, to bring us back to where it all started and where the many minds of psychiatry continue to interact and debate (see Figure 12). This unique and fragile pluralism, a kind of heterotopia, was once captured among the network of trainees and alumni in two blogs called *Maktab-e Ruzbeh* (*Maktab* meaning "school of thought") and *Café Analysis*. Before it became the nostalgic name for an alumni blog, Café Analysis was a nickname for the space where, as one of the blog contributors described in an entry, residents at Ruzbeh took a break for coffee and talk. Sometimes, the attending would stop by and ignite conversation. Later, the blogs provided a similar space

FIGURE 12: Training and Research Center at Ruzbeh, Tehran. Photo by Kousha
Ghorbani.

for alumni.[34] A former resident recalled: "For me *Maktab-e Ruzbeh* was not just
a discipline, it was a symbol of pluralism, the true meaning of academia. It used
to be the place for the meeting of curious minds and generous sharing of ideas."

Nostalgia and appreciation for this pluralism remind us that Iranian psychiatry has come a long way, and that it continues to negotiate the boundaries of its
situatedness in the face of globalizing forces. But reading these blogs also makes
me think of the affectivity of the generational blogs I discussed in previous chapters. These entries too echo double binds, albeit of a different nature: Ruzbeh
teaches one thing and practice expects another. They also echo the idea of a
roller coaster of hope; the desire for authenticity and more nuanced reflections;
and the hopes of new generations of psychiatrists who demand from academia
conceptual explorations, combinations, and contestations of different ideas. They
make me remember Ruzbeh as the place that urged me to question assumptions,
listen to patients' narratives and silences, and cherish the informal conversations
that survived the positivist hold of biological psychiatry.

Reflections on Mental Health and Interdisciplinary Conversations across Cultures

---

The way that things come to mind, I feel that they are more as fragments. They are strange. They don't come in order any more, so the happy moments and the sad moments climb over each other: our home in Baghdad with the roof where we would sleep [during] summer nights and we would go down when we [heard] the sound of the siren; the simple heater in the middle of our living room that was called Aladdin, and, on it, that pot of tea with cardamom. . . . And I remember my father dying in front of my eyes. I remember the windows of our classrooms shaking from explosions. You know, the war was like the norm. . . . We all feel alienated because of this continuous violence in the world. We feel alone, but we feel also together. So we resort to poetry as a possibility for survival. However, to say I survived is not so final as to say, for example, I'm alive. We wake up to find that the war survived with us.

Iraqi poet Dunya Mikhail, 2013[1]

WE MAKE SENSE OF LIFE in stories we tell, in words we choose, in the way we narrate, in silences and gaps and slips. Sometimes we are in charge of our stories; sometimes they piece themselves together, triggered by historical turns and tides. Sometimes we adopt languages that soothe and help make sense (e.g., that of psychiatry), words that lift the burden of uncertainty and shame, and accents that best project our desires. Gradually those languages, accents, and silences change the ways we understand our story, ourselves, and the world that moves on.

Iranian psychiatry performs within a nexus of material and moral conditions wherein psychiatric medication can facilitate medicalization of experience while also providing relief. Today, somewhere at the intersection of the institutional self, the neurochemical self, the public self, the private self, and the generational self, a psychiatric form of self has emerged that relocates hope and shifts the psychocultural interpretations of one's life. These processes of self-creation and realization are not passive or merely encrypted or memorialized; they rely on active performativity by tapping into, reflecting upon, and working through dreams, nostalgias, aspirations, language forms, and embodied inscriptions. They seek, embody, internalize, and modify psychiatric and other psy discourses and their varying approaches to connect the dots of life. These psychiatric forms of selfhood ought to be understood in their own sociohistorical contexts. The ways in which *daheh-ye shasti-hā*, for instance, mobilize particular generational aesthetics of the 1980s and the Iran-Iraq War and meld them with the language of psychiatry reflect a fluid construction of choice. Choice exists insofar as it legitimizes their location within competing economies of truth and knowledge and hierarchies of biomedical and historical claims. Such choice is not taken for granted—nor is it an all-or-nothing possibility.

I have tried to assemble a historical account in a set of juxtaposing landscapes to create a baseline of knowledge upon which future work will surely build. These narratives of biomedicine, of brain and behavior, of psychoanalysis, of historical ruptures, of youth, and of hope can be perplexing. They are interrupted and incomplete. But if recognized, heard, and retold, they can shed light on doctors' and patients' interpretations of and justifications for their therapeutic choices. Above all, they help us think more critically about cross-cultural and interdisciplinary interpretations of mental well-being. Anthropology, psychoanalysis, other psy disciplines, and the field of narrative psychiatry together provide a matrix for such interpretations and their interactions with cultural particularities.

Conversations across Disciplines

An overly or predominantly biomedical approach to the afterlife of ruptures risks reifying affective memory into a diagnostic category such as PTSD, which is treated as only something to be cured, erased, and cleansed. Such pathologization of memory leaves little room for incorporating experience as a part of lived life and as a culturally generative space for new possibilities of working through. Such memory wounds cannot easily be translated to biomedical diagnostic categories. They are not depression or PTSD; nor do they fit into orthodox critical debates regarding top-down medicalization.

While psychoanalysis and psychodynamic approaches in psychiatry allow for interpersonal retelling of traumatic memory, they often focus on the individual's *lived affect*; anthropologists, on the other hand, underscore *lived life* and the kind of affective experiences that are culturally structured, historically shared, and intersubjectively configured. The merging of clinical and anthropological listening thus helps to liaise between the individual and the generational, the inner and the outer, the biological and the cultural, not as binaries, but as a tangle of interconnective tissue.

Even at a basic level, a conceptual conversation between cultural analysis and psychiatry can be mutually beneficial. New possibilities lie in bringing psychoanalytical sensibilities of retelling and listening into ethnography, and in bringing anthropological understandings of shared historical meanings into psychoanalytical understandings of memory or into narrative psychiatry. "Illness narratives," of course, do not substitute for biomedical and brain-centered models of explaining depression or ADHD. Rather, they complement those models by revealing the lived experience of illness and its cultural and historical meanings. One of these biomedical explanatory models that psychiatrists propose, for instance, is the final common pathway model, arguing that psychiatric disorders represent a *final common pathway* change in an area of the brain, thus leaving room for considering that environmental circumstances can make their mark by eventually manipulating neural pathways in the brain. Today, advances are being made in the field of epigenetics toward understanding generational transfers of traumatic experiences via genetic mutations. Illness narratives can contribute to or challenge those advances.

The power of illness narratives lies both in making alternative articulations of ruptured experiences possible and in suggesting alternative interventions to remedy their residues. One implication is that by opening a conversation between anthropology and narrative psychiatry, the meaning and function of narrative are broadened beyond the individual. In other words, treating narrative not as an end in itself (as is often the case in the field of narrative psychiatry) but as a means to contextualizing illness in its cultural history requires examining narratives of illness for their alternative references and for the social resources or impasses they may create. Equally important are the narratives of medicine itself, of doctors' lives, and of their experiences of professionalization, acculturation, and socialization.

The making of Iranian psychiatric selves opens a window into historical, cultural, and generational formations and processes. It also highlights three interrelated arguments. First, in explaining medicalization, a myopic focus on biological reductionism and top-down forms of biomedicalization masks the cultural meaning and generative capacities of categories such as *depreshen*. *Depreshen* here is constructed in the juxtaposition of biomedical tenets with various discourses of Iranian affect: from mysticism to war-related feeling states, from stoicism to institutionalized codes of conduct, from poetic intricacies to globalizing desires for happiness.

Second, anthropology has illustrated how medicalization can desocialize the lived experiences of illness by masking its social and cultural meaning. In Iran however, it was the medicalization of individual and psychological distress that allowed those experiences into the media, making possible a public cultural discourse. The psychiatric discourse of the 1990s, in other words, facilitated the *re*socialization of wartime loss and gave Iranians a language for articulating and working through its affective experiences.

Third, psychiatrically medicalized individuals are far from passive recipients of top-down forces of a hegemonic biomedical apparatus. Pills do not always medicalize away their agency nor do diagnoses always silence them. They urge us to see the medicalized as performative actors in the medical and social construction of illness categories. They construe these categories in relation to cultural discourses and historical memory. Understanding them requires rewinding and revisiting the past and the (shared) medicalizing desires of young Iranians for whom a medical diagnosis allows specific types of discursive truth. At once narratives of illness and voices of social diagnosis, their narratives reflect desires for clinical legitimation and historical accountability. Like the mobilization and commemoration of wartime cultural forms and memories, medicalization becomes one of their *many* strategies of being in the world.

Frequently, friends and colleagues from other parts of the region helped my comparative thinking by pointing out parallels or divergences of experience. From self-medication and modes of remembering among Beiruti youth, to the superimposition of new wars and wounds on the memories of the Iraqi side of the Iran-Iraq War, they underscore the significance of cultural and generational sensibilities in mental health, particularly in the complex region we have come to call the Middle East. My hope is for this book to make a humble contribution to such comparative lines of inquiry.

Conversations across Cultural Frontiers in the Middle East[2]

The Iranian psychiatric discourse and the afterlife of the Iran-Iraq War provide a rich opportunity for analyzing how new forms of self and generational voice can emerge from multiple entangled threads such as historical embeddedness, institutional legitimations, cross-generational transferences, and discourses of morality, medicine, psychiatry, and identity. This has implications beyond Iran, especially when thinking about the psychological afterlife of the ruptures occurring across the Middle East, from Afghanistan and Pakistan to Iraq, Syria, Lebanon, and Yemen. The Iran-Iraq War also provides a case study of how ruptures live on, across generations, in what is perceived, sensed, shared, experienced, remembered, forgotten, taken away, imposed, embraced, resisted, neglected, negotiated, desired, feared, and dreamed, not just individually, but also by creating new forms of sociality. To think seriously about mental health in the region over the coming decades requires a turn away from abstractions of psychological trauma toward an understanding of how ruptures become infused in everyday life and its cultural texture. We must, in other words, broaden our focus from individual health and illness to concerns about sustaining individual *and* social integrity.

What follows is meant as a set of provocations and reflections on the need for rethinking the psychopolitics of mental health in the region and what we assume we know about it. To ask what forms of life and ways of knowing and feeling emerge in different settings raises questions about cross-cultural pedagogies. Such inquiry starts with, first, identifying challenges and opportunities in psychiatry's encounter with different Middle Eastern societies and commonalities and differences in their health care infrastructures. There is also a need for incorporating other forms of mental health care, narrativity, accountability, and collective acts of remembering into therapeutic interventions. Furthermore, we ought to ask what therapeutic possibilities a historically informed cultural analysis might make available to psychiatry, and how psychiatry can benefit from collective narratives and experiences of war, as well as from a serious *conceptual* engagement with social science and the humanities. Above all, it is essential not to take lightly the ethical stakes in researching, listening to, treating, and representing the pain of others, particularly in today's representational landscape where Middle Eastern people are too commonly misunderstood, misrepresented, and intervened upon.

It is necessary to learn more about existing mental health care infrastructures, not just as deficits and lacks, but the diverse local and localized ways mental well-being is interpreted, practiced, conceptualized, and dealt with in different parts of the region. This is not to focus solely on cultural folkways but on active healing practices and cultures. Iran and Iraq, for instance, provide an example of deep, shared histories and recent wars, yet are structured differently, and have quite different institutional histories and health care pedagogies. There are valuable lessons about culturally situated practice forms in the various health care systems that are already in place or that have been destroyed by foreign military interventions, for example in Iraq or Afghanistan.

When attended to, local knowledges in the Middle East have often been translated to or summed up and dismissed as local belief systems, tested against the grounds of the biomedical enterprise.[3] Shifting our focus toward the embeddedness of psychiatric practice in historical and cultural processes is the alternative put forth by cross-cultural psychiatry.[4] Instead of reducing cultural differences to "culture-bound-syndromes" as the *DSM* does, it is crucial to move beyond binaries of the local and the universal by acknowledging the local moral worlds in which illness categories create their own social history (that is, the social and clinical constructions of pathology as finely formulated by medical anthropologists in the concept of "local biologies").[5] It is equally necessary to investigate how those processes are interpreted and articulated by laypeople as well as experts, thereby recognizing the social as well as the biological life of illness.

In Iran and in the Middle East, statistical and epidemiological mental health data can be both informative and misleading. These data too need to be contextualized, not only in relation to their adoption of universalist categories such as depression or PTSD, or of standardized questionnaires and indices that are often translated from American or European ones, but also by attending to cultural meanings and references that shape people's experience and interpretations of epidemiological data. When reading a medical article based on epidemiological studies, for example, we ought to ask what it means, experientially, for the results to be *consistent with those elsewhere* (often meaning Western, developed countries), a common note in the conclusion section of many articles published in medical journals. Or when, for example, referring to "full" and "partial" PTSD or measuring quality of life (often evaluated by using a standard "Quality of Life Index"), we need to consider the cultural domain in which one experiences this PTSD as full or partial and where that Quality of Life Index was designed and created. Such results need to be complemented with asking what it means, for example, for patients to respond to questionnaires and interviews that were themselves constructed in a completely different cultural setting. In other words, what are the implications of importing and adopting frameworks?[6] Of course, these questionnaires are usually adjusted when translated, but their underlying assumptions often remain untouched.[7] These questions are not merely a matter of historicizing such diagnostic or evaluative frameworks; rather, they have clinical implications for contextualized therapeutic interventions. To raise them is not to deny the merits of epidemiological studies. On the contrary, it is to underscore what statistics contribute to our perception of different forms of experience, and how they can be complemented with qualitative analysis of the lived experience of what underlies statistical figures. What discourses of care, one might ask, underlie the questionnaires and models that we translate, adjust, and use in clinical practice? Is it plausible that the Iranian *jānbāz* (disabled veteran) of the Iran-Iraq War *experiences* PTSD the same way as American veterans of the Vietnam or the Kuwait wars do? Significantly, how do historical conditions and new forms of legitimation shape the experience of psychiatric illnesses, interventions, and discourses? Is it possible today, for instance, to approach psychological well-being in Iraq without a discussion of memory and accountability for the illegal war ignited by the invasion of Iraq?

A pedagogical exploration starts with communication across disciplines (and methodologies) and a reexamination of universalist views. Often these interdisciplinary interactions are restricted as a result of hierarchies of expertise among disciplines and intellectual territories; but they are crucial for creating a new, culturally appropriate space for conceptual and practical innovations in mental health care. Cultural analysis in particular (and art, literature, and history in general) can help us better understand the actual social and medical experience and intricacies of mental health conditions. To undervalue the social life of illness compromises our understanding by overlooking its very building blocks.

Psychiatry, of course, is not the only site where viewing local practices through a universalist lens would be misleading. There are parallels in the virtual worlds of the Internet and its evolving forms. Most bloggers that I quote in this book have now moved on to other social media; but the short-lived Iranian blogging era still provides valuable lessons. Iranian blogs show how universal conceptualizations of the virtual self may overlook the affectivity and the situated forms of sociality that Iranian blogs (and social media) create. They provide sites for psychological working through, community building, the internalization of larger psycho-social discourses, and the constitution of social and emotional norms and networks.

Analyzing virtual space with a myopic focus on political frames and movements, as is common today in commentary on the Middle East, risks overlooking its psychologically and culturally generative capacities (and how they contribute to mental health discourses).

Last but not least, the psychopolitics of mental health in the region suggest not only possibilities for ethnography to write theory inside out, but also possibilities for contextualized bioethical frameworks. We teach medical students, especially in many clinical bioethics programs in the United States, that the self is to be empowered and recovered—as though there were such a thing as a coherent, essential self. Subjectivity is a curious ground for cultural work and historical witnessing. Its boundaries are porous. It contradicts itself in the multiplicity of its urges. Sometimes it deceives, at other times it denies. Sometimes it lags, and sometimes it catches up in bits and pieces of recollections. Whatever it does at any given time, it is not to be captured in its entirety, nor is it to be liberated, cured, or interpreted by clinical listening alone. I, therefore, use terms such as *choice* with hesitation. Patients assign meaning to what they perceive as *depreshen*, sometimes by medicalizing and medicating it, in the same breath that they historicize and situate it in distant pasts or in what is beyond their control. They destabilize the notion of individual choice, not by alternating it with passive compliance and/or victimhood, but by pointing to situational contingencies, uncertainties, ambivalences, fragmentations, and complexities of their choices. They nudge our attention toward the conditional falsehood of what we have come to assume as individual choice in the first place. Understanding clinical decisions, in other words, requires understanding the historical and cultural contexts in which they are made possible, meaningful, or instrumental. Several important beginnings by anthropologists and historians of the Turkish and Arab worlds have already opened up a space for situated analyses of individual psychological experiences and for exploring academic interaction with Western psy disciplines.[8] We need to build on and expand those spaces.

A Psychiatric Way of Life

The rise of a psychiatric self and language is relatively new to Persian modes of expression, but it is culturally generative and significant because it tells the story of changing cultural forms and interpretations. I have tried to piece together a mosaic through the lens of a psychiatric discourse that is both an outcome of, and a force behind, people's medicalizing desires. In this story, not unlike in many other societies, adults may or may not be on antidepressants, children may or may not be on Ritalin, doctors may or may not be on meds while prescribing them to their patients. Media may encourage psychiatric education while simultaneously negating it. Mothers may or may not feel morally obligated to be a "modern" woman who is educated enough to medicate her ADHD child. Children may no longer grow up under Iraqi bombs, but are raised by parents who were. Psychiatrists may know all about the contextual conditions their patients live in, but may still choose to sooth the *final common pathway* in their brains with medication. Medication may work for some and not for others. Psychiatry may or may not be practiced the same way by everyone, but it certainly enjoys a higher social and academic status now compared to thirty years ago.

In this Iranian story, people make great advances and calculated choices. Numerous innovations and cultural productions surface every day while Iranians remain conscious of what they have endured as a result of the Iran-Iraq War and the international sanctions that continually affected their lives in direct and indirect ways. Today, Iranians continue to commemorate those who sacrificed their lives during the Iran-Iraq War. Most recently, painful memories were stirred when the bodies of 175 divers who had been buried alive with their hands tied were returned to Iran.[9] As Iranians keep alive the memory of their fallen heroes and work through their losses, new generations mobilize their growing awareness about mental health toward a future in which no war is welcome. Their resolve to overcome and rise above renders Iranian society a dynamic and thriving one. In the meantime, policymakers' concerns about the psychological health of citizens grow and take different forms, but it is important, they caution, to situate hasty clinical interpretations in their cultural contexts.

In this Iranian story, psychiatry has become more than a medical discipline. It has entered popular common sense and become a way of life, an instrument for interpreting emotions and moods, and a language for making generational memories and affective introspections meaningful. Stripping specific mental illnesses of stigma, it has played savior by providing care when and where it is needed. In doing so, it has desocialized illness at times and has created new socialities at others.

Meanwhile, Iranian society continues to develop new cultural forms and frames. Many of the scenes or materials described in this book have now moved on, as has society itself, and evolved into other ever-evolving forms. So much has changed since these stories were told; new generational forms have emerged and new cultural frames of reference continue to create their own affective structures.[10] It is my hope that in a not too far away future, narratives of *Prozāk* will be but a distant memory as new forms of subjectivity will emerge. For now, hope is *daheh-ye shasti-hā*'s compass.

Several years after our interviews, Samāneh no longer takes medication, though she still has occasional "bombing" dreams. She gradually stopped blogging after graduate school.

Rāmin left Iran in 2010. He is still severely depressed and takes a combination of antidepressants.

Dina divides her time between NGO work and her engineering job in Northern California.

Sara is a designer in Tehran and uses "bright colors; canary, turquoise, red" in the manteaux she makes. She lost a cousin in 2009 and was briefly back on medication during 2010, but not since.

Omid, the actor who played Little Ali in the 1980s, now a father himself, lives in Tehran and has been interviewed on national TV as a cultural icon; he continues to live on in the fond memory of his generation.

Nell, it turned out in the original anime, was meant to be the Little Nell of Charles Dickens's *The Old Curiosity Shop*, on the run with her gambling grandfather. *Daheh-ye shasti-hā* watched a different story in the dubbed version, and remember Nell as the girl searching for *Pārādāis* where her mother allegedly lived.

Ruzbeh's Psychodynamic Psychotherapy program is successfully underway. Ruzbeh continues to nurture cutting-edge research, best practice psychiatric care, and talented medical students, interns, residents, and child psychiatry fellows.

And Freud, no longer the Golden Calf, appears in various psychoanalytical circles and enjoys a mixed reception.

Reference Matter

Acknowledgments

I wish to thank, first, those whose influence on this book predates it: My teachers, Mrs. Sharifi, for walking with three naïve fourteen-year-olds into that leprosy clinic and believing there was nothing trivial about collecting stories of illness; Mr. Jafari, who believed a life lived in fear was an unlived one; Mr. Mohammadi-Rad, the chemist whose devotion could turn dust into gold; Mrs. Haerizadeh, for making a different world possible; and a long list of Tehran University professors who developed my understanding of life and its fragility. I owe my questions to patients who, a lifetime ago, welcomed me into their experiences and became part of mine: Hamideh, who showed me, in her surrender to leukemia and to love, the power of endurance and the inevitability of ruptures in life; the ever four-year-old Mohammadreza, who made me see that sometimes sitting by his bed and blowing up red balloons could do much more than daily chemo injections did; the twelve-year-old Esma'il, who long endured an excruciating pain that medicine fell short to explain even as his bare organs were passed around on a metal tray in a morning report at the Children's Hospital; and Abdi, for whom the reality of schizophrenia was the only line between the real and the unreal.

Over the years since, several others left an imprint on this book. I am fortunate to have been at the receiving end of the most generous guidance and encouragement throughout the years, from those you can never thank enough, those who make nurturing others a priority. As a disciple of anthropology, I was taught, with unreserved generosity, by extraordinary individuals whose own scholarly work became my compass in writing this book. I owe a great debt of gratitude to Michael Fischer, who has nurtured this project with his intellect and empathy every step of the way, thought with me and patiently read and reread drafts, helped me see the forest from my perch in the trees, and believed in me when I hardly did; beyond all that, I am grateful for ten remarkable years of his invaluable friendship. Sherry Turkle has mentored, listened, and shared her magical insight and writerly intuition, but I am most grateful for all those years ago when she challenged me, in the deepest mark of friendship, to break through the blocks and put down words that became the seeds of this book. Vinh-Kim Nguyen trusted in my thinking before I did, gave me an academic home in Montreal, became my guide in my early walks back and forth between medicine and anthropology—and in many other walks over the years—and taught me generosity and ethnographic empathy by living it, in academia and beyond.

The ideas of this book have been challenged, nurtured, and discussed in countless conversations within and outside anthropology and academia. I have no words to express the depth of my gratitude: Byron Good and Mary-Jo Good set the bar high, decades ago, and inspired me with their legacy of tuning anthropology into the nuances of psychological distress in Iran; I am utterly grateful to Byron Good for his kindness and guidance over the years. I am equally grateful for the privilege of an ongoing conversation with Veena Das, her profound commitment to understanding the world of human suffering, and her thoughtful readings of earlier drafts of the manuscript. I have learned much from academic conversations with Nikolas Rose, particularly from his scholarship on psychiatry and selfhood that has informed this project greatly. Afsaneh Najmabadi has inspired me by her own meticulous scholarship on Iran and obliged me by sharing her astute reading and thoughts on the final manuscript. Dina Khoury's insight and friendship has been a gift I will cherish forever. James Faubion humbled me by welcoming me at Rice University and in his home and supporting me in ways too countless to recount. John Tirman's unwavering support and encouragement made impossibles possible; I owe him much and stand inspired by his commitment to making the world a better place. This project owes its life to invaluable conversations with several scholars and colleagues who patiently read, commented, talked things over, brainstormed, and helped me see gaps and openings; I owe an incredible debt to those conversations with Ali Banuazizi, Mehrzad Boroujerdi, Dominic Brookshaw, Houchang Chehabi, Omar Dewachi, Sue Estroff, Rita Giacaman, Stefan Helmreich, David Jones, David Kaiser, Pamela Karimi, Laleh Khalili, Mehdi Khorrami, Charles Kurzman, Bruce Lawrence, Jennifer Leaning, Julie Livingston, Mohsen Milani, Ali Mirsepassi, Siamak Movahedi, Zuzanna Olszewska, Barry Saunders, Reza Sheikholeslami, Allan Young, and my cohort of fellows in the 2008 Proposal Development Fellowship and 2009 International Dissertation Research Fellowship at the Social Science Research Council, as well as students whose enthusiasm and fresh outlook continue to inspire me every day.

Writing is a solitary endeavor, but it is never the work of a solitary person. My better ideas have always been born in conversation. Wonderful friends, whose own scholarship has been an unending source of inspiration, have contributed to this book with their insightful readings and suggestions. I am particularly and endlessly grateful to Pamela Karimi for her critical readings, for sharing her valuable time and experience, for seeing what was invisible to me, and for relating to the text and the experience of writing it with impeccable tact. I thank Zuzanna Olszewska for her astute suggestions and for a decade of stimulating conversations and friendship. Julie Kleinman enhanced my understanding of anthropology and gave me a gift of friendship I will always treasure. Naor Ben-Yehoyada and Omar Dewachi have, each in their own way, enriched my ethnographic thinking and broadened my world. Sarah Parkinson has been my American sister; with her I have shared a language we crafted, journeys we discovered, writing camps and conversations about ethnography and theory, and an equally priceless bond over all things unacademic.

A world of inspiring friendships is the best souvenir of the HASTS program at MIT. Thank you, especially, to Laurel Braitman, Nicholas Buchanan, Candis Callison, Xaq Frohlich, Karen Gardner, Chihyung Jeon, Kris Kipp, Shekhar Krishnan, Debbie Meinbresse, Lisa Messeri, Canay Özden, Esra Ozkan, Anne Pollock, Sophia Roosth, Michael Rossi, Aslihan Sanal, Tom Schilling, Ryan Shapiro, David Singeman, Ellan Spero, Judy Spitzer, Alma Steingart, Michaela Thompson, Emily Wanderer, Livia Wick,

Rebecca Woods, and Sara Wylie. I have been privileged to have the friendship of wonderful colleagues since. I wish to thank in particular Jerome Crowder and Jason Glenn at the Institute of Medical Humanities at UTMB; Lucy Brown, Laurie Corna, Sabrina Fernandez, Alysia Montrose, Barbara Prainsack, and Debbie Price at the Department of Social Science, Health and Medicine at King's College London; and the members of the Culture, Medicine, and Power Research Group, especially Carlo Caduff, Hanna Kienzler, Scott Vrecko, and our wonderful PhD students.

Fieldwork brought extraordinary individuals into my life, not all of whom could be named here. I wish to thank Iman Tavassoly for his ethnographic assistance; Dorna Bandari and Farzan Parsinejad and several others for hosting me during my fieldwork in California; Ali Nayeri for introducing me to several psychotherapy circles in southern California, and Foojan Zein for facilitating fieldwork and for participating, along with her colleagues, in interviews. I would also like to thank artists Amirali Ghasemi, Kousha Ghorbani, Shohreh Mehran, and Golrokh Nafisi, for permitting me to feature their work. I also wish to acknowledge the East 15 Drama School and the talented director Mehrdad Seyf who took two stories I had written based on this research to the stage in the UK. Several physicians and psychiatrists have shared with me their reflections and allowed me into their clinical and nonclinical experiences. I remain indebted and grateful to them, particularly to Javad Alāghband-Rād, Mahdieh Moin, and Mohammad Sanati for the long interviews and thoughtful comments that greatly informed this project. My fondest gratitude goes to psychiatrists, bloggers, and individuals who cannot be named, but whose willingness to share, host, debate, and invite me into their life experiences is the only reason this book has come to life. I am obliged to them for trusting me with their stories and allowing me to revisit my own.

I also wish to thank the following grants, awards, and fellowships that generously supported and made possible the research and writing of this book: the American Council of Learned Societies (ACLS) Fellowship; the 2011 Malcolm H. Kerr Award from the Middle East Studies Association (MESA); the Dissertation Fieldwork Grant from the Wenner-Gren Foundation for Anthropological Research; the International Dissertation Research Fellowship (DPDF) and the Proposal Development Fellowship (PDF) from the Social Science Research Council; the Diebel Monograph Award from the Institute for Medical Humanities at the University of Texas Medical Branch; the European Neuroscience and Society Network (ENSN) Award from the European Science Foundation and the former BIOS Center at the London School of Economics; the Iranian Association of Boston Award; and, at MIT, the Neekayinfar Award, the Ida M. Green Fellowship, and the program in History and Anthropology of Science, Technology and Society (HASTS).

Various parts of this project have been presented, discussed, and improved in seminars, workshops, and conferences. I wish to sincerely thank those who invited me and engaged with my work: George Washington University's Institute for Middle Eastern Studies; the School of Interdisciplinary Area Studies, St John's College, and St Antony's College at Oxford University; several departments at King's College London; Université Paris Diderot (Le programme interdisciplinaire Sorbonne Paris Cité); New York University's Hagop Kevorkian Center for Near Eastern Studies; University of Amsterdam;

University of California Irvine's Center for Persian Studies and Culture; University of California Los Angeles; Harvard University's Medical Anthropology Seminars; and the Association for Social Anthropologists of the UK and Commonwealth.

The realization of this book owes to the incredible support of the production team at Stanford University Press and the incredibly valuable comments I received from their chosen anonymous reviewers. I could not have asked for a more gifted editor-in-chief than Kate Wahl, without whose dedication and encouragement this book wouldn't have materialized. I am incredibly grateful to Nora Spiegel and Mariana Raykov at Stanford University Press for their patience and dedication to this project. The final version of the manuscript benefited immensely from the copy-editing mastery of Richard Gunde, Sue Hough, and Hope Steele, as did the earlier versions from Laura Helper-Farris's input and Letta Page's editorial artistry and eye for detail.

The long gestation of a monograph intersects with one's life in unimaginable ways. In the process of researching and writing this book, I lost three extraordinary women who, each in their unique ways, filled my youth with the desire and will to write. This book is an overdue debt to my grandmother Khadidjeh Haj Fath-Ali, my mentor Mokhadereh Amouzgar, and the irreplaceable poet Simin Banu Behbahani. Over the years, and away from my childhood home, I have made home in the kindness of loving others. Thank you to Shahrzad and Reza Sheikholeslami for being there, unconditionally, for making Iffley House my home, and for letting *dokhtar* become part of the family. To Susann Wilkinson, thank you for being my friend and my confidante, for sharing the warmth of your home and your heart during my incredible years in Boston and beyond. Kamran Safamensh, you taught me faith in roads untaken; thank you for sharing with me the world of magical thinking. And to Jean Goodwin, I will never have the right words to thank you for your incredible presence in this journey.

The best friends in the world have not only supported me through this project, but have hosted me, cooked for and fed me, rescued me from technical mishaps and crashed hard drives, shared joys and sorrows, attended to my qualms, and poured love and laughter into my life during the years this project was underway. I owe a most heartfelt and accented thank you to Tina Mazhari for a lifetime of knowing me too well and being there no matter what. In Oxford, Shiva Amiri brightened my world and stood by my side. Dominic Brookhaw, Adeel Malik, Zuzanna Olszewska, and Natalia Rodriguez welcomed me into their worlds and made mine a better place. Rana Amirtahmasebi made MIT a magical home of wonders and sisterhood through thick and thin. Life became unimaginable without having known Arash Afraz, Ali Boroumand, Kian Eisazadeh, Mohammad Hafezi, Farzan Parsinejad, Payam Parsinejad, Maryam Vaziri Pashkam, Hazhir Rahmandad, Sara Sarkhili, and Salome Siavoshi; thank you for all we shared, all we made, all we lived together in Boston and beyond. And thank you to Lily Burns, Bita Fakhri, Niall Henderson, Hector Hernandez, Arash Nekoei, Rossella Nicolini, Sara Passone, Giovanbattista Patalano, and Clara Zverina for your steady love and presence all these years. Finishing this book would have been impossible without friends who made my home in London one to cherish. Thank you, Payman Kassaei, for being my ally, and for the unwavering compassion, wisdom, and clarity with which you see everything; to Shirin

Biria, Ania Assadi-Sabet, and Kaveh Goudarzi for your invaluable friendship and kindness; to Najieh Gholami, for inspiring me with the person you are and the beauty you see in life; and to Samin Sahabi and Christopher Cooke for welcoming me into your beautiful life and for putting up with me during manuscript revisions. Last but certainly not least, to my lifelong friends, my sisters Sepideh and Padideh and my brother Alireza, I owe a great debt of gratitude: thank you for sharing with me an unending journey of love and discovery.

.   .   .

My parents retain pride of place. Words fall short. To my father: your grand vision brought near distant possibilities; thank you for all you braved and dreamed. To my mother: you open paths wherever you look and hearts wherever you go; your selfless spirit is the reason I believe in love. The light in the eyes of you two has sustained me through the years. This book, and any other endeavor worth anything, is dedicated to you.

Notes

INTRODUCTION

1. Two chapters in the book draw on previously published works: "Medicalization as a Way of Life," in "Beyond 'Trauma': Notes on Mental Health in the Middle East," ed. O. Behrouzan, *Medicine Anthropology Theory* 2 (3) (2015); "Writing *Prozāk* Diaries in Tehran: Generational Anomie and Psychiatric Subjectivities" *Culture, Medicine, and Psychiatry* 39 (3) (2015); and "'Behaves Like a Rooster and Cries Like a [Four Eyed] Canine': The Politics and Poetics of Depression and Psychiatry in Iran," with Michael M. J. Fischer, in *Genocide and Mass Violence Memory, Symptom, and Recovery*, ed. Devon E. Hinton and Alexander L. Hinton (Cambridge University Press, 2014).

2. Iranian newspapers commonly cite epidemiological data from Iranian medical publications; for instance, reports on anxiety disorders (8.35 percent) and depressive mood disorders (4.29 percent) as Iran's most common psychiatric conditions (Mohammadi et al. 2005) or on suicide, e.g., of 14 percent for lifetime suicide ideation and 4.1 percent for suicide attempts (Shooshtary et al. 2008). In "Disorders Without Borders," Nikolas Rose examined the expanding scope of psychiatric practices in terms of increasing diagnosis rates and medication for depression, ADHD, and personality disorders, by suggesting an exploration of incentives behind submission to psychiatric identification (Rose 2006b). I intend to extend this call by situating it in a non-Western context.

3. In this area of inquiry, epidemiological data are sparse and unreliable, even more than in the developed world. Even in the international arena of the World Health Organization (WHO), mental health categories are contested, having only been standardized in the *DSM* (*Diagnostic and Statistical Manual of Mental Disorders*) in the past few decades, and having undergone much contested revision in its fifth edition (*DSM-V*). Only recently has mental health been recognized as a major global priority for economic development and growth (Desjarlais et al. 1996). WHO's World Mental Health Survey has introduced diagnostic methods such as the Diagnostic Interview Schedule (DIS) and Composite International Diagnostic Interview (CIDI) to attempt to standardize the collection and reporting of these data. The surveys have been undertaken in fourteen countries so far, among which Lebanon is the closest to Iran in terms of sociopolitical circumstances (Mohit 2006). The reports of such surveys, however, should not be interpreted uncritically, since in-depth understanding and analysis of diverse cultural grounds are not thoroughly provided in the protocols. Nevertheless, this is a shift from WHO's previous exclusive focus on infectious diseases, childhood diseases,

or maternity issues, which are, in principle, more easily solved by sanitation and other public health measures. On concerns with cross-cultural applications of the *DSM*, see Chapters 1 and 7.

4. This corresponds to anthropological critiques of the moral economy of knowledge and of hierarchies of evidence that privilege evidence-based medicine—EBM—and trivialize "anecdotal" evidence. While evidence-based medicine and epidemiology are partially useful, they can reduce people to numbers if used in the absence of proper conceptual or theoretical frameworks. See the edited volume *When People Come First: Critical Studies in Global Health* (Biehl and Petryna 2013) and, in that volume, Adams 2013, and Fischer 2013. See also Das 2015 and Fischer 2009.

5. Das 2015: 2.

6. Affect can mean different things in different disciplines. In psychiatry, affect refers to the observed and expressed emotional responses and manifestations of one's emotions, whereas mood is a broader state, less specific and more diffused, sustained, longer term, thereby informing one's perception of oneself and the world and one's actions and thoughts. In the social sciences and humanities on the other hand, much of the so-called affective turn has focused on differentiating between affect and emotion by rendering the latter pre-social and defining the former as the all-encompassing outcome of all emotional possibilities and their social encounters (Massumi 2002; Gregg and Seigworth 2010). According to Massumi in the foreword to *A Thousand Plateaus*, their usage of affect refers to "an ability to affect and be affected. It is a prepersonal intensity corresponding to the passage from one experiential state of the body to another and implying an augmentation or diminution in that body's capacity to act" (Deleuze and Guattari 2001: xvi). Elsewhere, Massumi calls for reserving "the term 'emotion' for the personalized content, and affect for the continuation. Emotion is contextual. Affect is situational: eventfully ingressive to context. Serially so: affect is trans-situational. As processual as it is precessual, affect inhabits the passage. It is pre- and postcontextual, pre- and postpersonal, an excess of continuity invested only in the ongoing: its own" (Massumi 2002: 217). Massumi thus renders affect a virtual presence of all potential emotions. In much of the debates over affect theory, what is at risk of being perpetuated is a biological-social dichotomy by rendering emotion pre-social. I find the affect-emotion binary of little use, for a static rendition of emotion regards what is felt as given (see Csordas 2013, 1990; Martin 2013). Medical anthropology, on the other hand, regards bodies as both biologically and culturally affected and informed (if not performed). Bodies thus become sites of political contestation, of cultural construction of illness and health, and, more relevant here, of encounters with hegemonic systems of knowledge such as psychiatry, where illness becomes both medically and socially constructed (see Lock 1993; Lock and Nguyen 2011). For more on the affective turn, see Halley and Clough 2007, Gregg and Seigworth 2010, and Seyfert's work on a social theory of affect (Seyfert 2012).

7. See Akhavan 2013. A more comprehensive discussion of the Weblogestān will follow in Chapter 5.

8. See Turkle 1995; Fischer 1999 and 2003.

9. For a detailed discussion, see Chapter 5.

10. On experimental ethnography and cultural critique, see Clifford and Marcus 1986; Marcus and Fischer 1999; Marcus 1998, 2012. On "third spaces," see Fischer 2003 and 2009.

11. Fortun 2012.

12. Of course, the contours of the ethnographic field have long, perhaps always, been debated, especially in the last twenty-five years when such multi-locale or multisited ethnographies as Fischer and Abedi (1990) and Fortun (2001) have bowled over any possibility of explaining events in particular localities without equal ethnographic attention to other distributed localities within political economies or cultural and psychodynamic processes. For more on integrated digital ethnography, see Murthy 2011; for a more detailed discussion of cultural blogging and ethnographic blogging, see Markin 2010; and for more on ethnography in the digital space, see Wali 2010.

13. Marcus 1998.

14. Olszewska, for example, has raised issue with English-speaking scholarship's preoccupation with rebellious representations of middle-class youth (Olszewska 2015a: 9). For a thorough critique of such ethnographies of rebellion and resistance, see Olszewska 2013, and Adelkhah 1999.

15. Note, for example, the seamless usage of psy talk in a poem written by a young Afghan refugee woman in Iran, in Olszewska (2015a: 206): "Tayyebah's unwell again, make a phone call, take a day off from the office. . . . In her haphazard way, whatever she sees, be patient: take the moon or a star out of her sleeve. . . . If the psychiatrist has no time once again, take two small, suspicious pills again." Bayat's formulation of the "poor middle classes" comes to mind, although he is primarily concerned with political agency (Bayat 1997). In *Street Politics*, he relocates political agency in the ordinary daily lives of the "disenfranchised urban poor," tracing their position in mid-twentieth-century rural-urban migrations and problematizing poor urban citizens' situations following the revolution and the Iran-Iraq War. A rigid analysis of class also fails to capture several nuances of Iranian youth culture (e.g., unemployed holders of masters or doctorate degrees, or the nouveaux riche described in Khosravi 2008). For more, see Olszewska 2013 for an analysis of "status incongruence" (Dogan 2004) among youth whose status or rank in one domain is inconsistent with how they are perceived in another.

16. I find it useful to approach class in terms of Max Weber's or Pierre Bourdieu's classic formulations of forms of cultural capital: *embodied*, as integral to one's selfhood and shaping a habitus; *objectified*, in cultural productions; and *institutionalized*, as in academic qualifications (Bourdieu 1991, 1986). To these forms of capital, Bourdieu adds *social capital*, as the "aggregate of the actual or potential resources which are linked to the possession of a durable network of more or less institutionalized relationships of mutual acquaintances and recognition, or in other words, to membership in a group" (Bourdieu 1986: 51). In *Language and Symbolic Power* (1991), he argues for the interchangeability of these different forms of capital.

17. See Berlant 2007. I remain conscious of what Berlant cautions against and of the politics of sentimental reading practices and the risk of obscuring the material conditions beneath the production of illness.

18. For reflections on native ethnographic distance and proximity, see Mir-Hosseini 2009.

19. For more on divination, see the 1999 *Encyclopaedia Iranica* entry on fāl: http://www.iranicaonline.org/articles/fal; also in the print edition of the *Encyclopaedia Iranica*, vol. 7, fasc. 4, pp. 440–43 (New York: Encyclopaedia Iranica Foundation).

20. Taussig 1992: 7. Fischer likens these storied incidents and micro forms of life to ethnographic pebbles in the way of theory: "these minor loci and forms can irritate hegemonic narratives, like a loose pebble causing the foot to wobble" (Fischer 2009: 235).

THE POET-SATIRIST

1. Publication date: 4/10/1389 AP—25/12/2010.

CHAPTER 1

1. This new vernacular is indeed situated in a rich vocabulary of affect in Persian literature. Such renditions can also be traced in medical scripture such as the *Canon of Medicine*, the chef d'oeuvre of the eleventh-century Persian physician and philosopher Avicenna. In the third volume, under the section "Ailments of the Mind and Spirit," he devotes a chapter to love melancholy, diagnosed by detecting an increase in the patient's pulse when the name of the beloved is mentioned. In his diagnostic criteria, sorrow (*maluli*) is not a pathological symptom, but an inevitable state of infatuation (Avicenna 1989). Robert Burton, in his famous text *The Anatomy of Melancholy* (circa 1600), refers to Avicenna's love melancholy frequently under the category "head melancholies" (Burton 1927).

2. For more on anthropological investigations of Iranian affective structures, see Behzadi 1994; Beeman 1988, 1985, and 2001.

3. As was the case in other revolutions globally, including the rise of Bolshevism in Russia. On the uneven global distribution of psychiatry, see Derrida 1998.

4. See S. M. Razavi et al. 2014; Ebadi et al. 2009; Ebadi et al. 2014; Roshan et al. 2013; Khateri et al. 2003; Falahati et al. 2010; Khateri and Bajoghli 2015; Ghanei et al. 2005; Hashemian et al. 2006; Birch et al. 2014; and Karami et al. 2013. With the exception of a few studies that evaluated children (for example, S. H. Razavi et al. 2012; Taghva et al. 2014; and Yousefi and Sharif 2010), most epidemiological studies of PTSD and other psychiatric conditions in the aftermath of the Iran-Iraq War have primarily focused on adults. Among qualitative studies of the psychological impact of city bombardments on children, see Rahimi 2010 in *Negin-e Iran: The Journal of Research on the Sacred Defense*. For a detailed report on the health-related consequences of the Iran-Iraq War, see the Health Impact Assessment Report compiled by Medact (2014): http://www.medact.org/wp-content/uploads/2014/06/Health-Impact-Assessment-Word-Website-+-MB.pdf.

5. Note that practitioners frequently warn of growing self-prescription. For example, see "Self-medicated and Depressed" in the weekly newspaper *Sepid* (15/11/1393—4/02/2015): http://www.salamatiran.com/NSite/FullStory/?Id=76308&type=3.

6. See Kleinman 1989. Kleinman urged psychiatry to tune into cultural forms and narrative. Meanwhile, anthropology has come a long way in terms of correcting earlier biases, most importantly, the risk of narrative essentialization by both doctors and an-

thropologists. For a discussion of nuanced anthropological insight into social and clinical narratives, see "Anthropology: The Native's Point of View," in chapter 6 of Taussig's *Nervous System* (Taussig 1992).

7. For example, Allan Young has underscored the social and ideological relations that produce psychiatric diagnoses such as PTSD (Young 1997). Social critics commonly believe that biomedicine—itself social and one of the many systems of medical knowledge—is dismissive of the social conditions of knowledge production (Young 1997). See also Fassin 2007; and Farmer 2001.

8. This approach is informed by a tradition of cultural analysis, traced back to Geertz's interpretations of culture (1973), Fischer's cultural analysis of emergent forms of life (2003), Foucault's discourse analysis locating ruptures where particular ways of interpreting the world become normalized (1991 [1978], 1994a, 1994b, 1980), and Lacan's language-centered probing into the subject (1977). Key to this approach is the symbolic and cultural formation of languages, institutions, and interpretations. "Culture is not a variable," Fischer wrote. "Culture is relational, it is elsewhere, it is in passage, it is where meaning is woven and renewed often through gaps and silences, and forces beyond the conscious control of individuals, and yet the space where individual and institutional social responsibility and ethical struggle take place" (Fischer 2003: 7). In interpretive anthropology, Byron Good warned against the treatment of culture and belief as non-science and non-progressive and proposed understanding medicine as a symbolic form and mental illness as a process shaped and expressed in semantic networks (Good 1994: 1–24; and Good 1977).

9. Mattingly 1998; Lewis 2011; Kleinman 1989; Charon 2006.

10. Das 2015: 28.

11. Good et al. 1986; Good and Good, 1998.

12. Good 1977, 1994; Good and Good 1998.

13. Fischer 1973 and 1980.

14. Fischer and Abedi 1990.

15. Lotfalian 1996.

16. Throughout the book, I use *DSM* and *DSM-IV* to refer to the fourth edition of the *Diagnostic and Statistical Manual of Mental Disorders* (American Psychiatric Association 1994). The main diagnostic model in Iran is the *DSM-IV-TR*, translated into Persian. The *International Classification of Diseases* (*ICD*), published by WHO, is occasionally used in practice. For more on the differences between *ICD-10* (1992) and *DSM-IV* (1994), see Andrews et al. 1999.

17. For a discussion of the controversies and debates around the construction of the *DSM* and its various revisions, see Chapter 7.

18. Bateson et al. 1956.

19. *Double bind* describes conditions in which one develops a sense of loss in the face of ongoing experiences of defeat and contradictory instructions. In the double bind, one is faced with mutually exclusive messages. Based on communication theory, specifically "logical types," the double bind begins in parent-child relations and can be extended to other authority figures and institutional settings (such as schools, media, and the state) (Bateson et al. 1956).

20. Beeman 2001; Bateson et al. 1977. Scholars have noted that such double-bind conditions were a kind of reinscribing, albeit a perversion, of the age-old split between inner and outer, private and public Iranian lives (see Bateson et al. 1977) and Iranian deployments of psychological dissociation between internal purity and external requirements of living in a corrupt world. Traditionally, this public-private split was seen as a spiritual one; though its essentialization as an inherent "Iranian" trait has been anthropologically challenged (see Manoukian 2012; and Olszewska 2015a: 187–91).

21. Durkheim described *anomie* as a condition of rupture in social norms and order (1947 [1893]). He elaborated on the concept in his seminal work *Suicide* (1951 [1897]), wherein he argued that anomic conditions led to disaffection and hopelessness and eventually higher suicide rates. In these conditions, people feel lost and do not know what to expect. For Durkheim, the maintenance of stability and norms was contingent upon solidarity and coherence, themselves the outcome of moral regulation and regulatory constraints in organic and complex societies. Religion, he argued, was among the dynamic expressions of, and guarantors for, such order. Victor Turner's work on ritual processes further explored how social pressures of varying social structures create visceral-emotional states that are fused with cultural, cognitive, and moral symbols through the liminal phases of ritual work (Turner 1995). Religion, in his Freudian-Durkheimian synthesis, operates as glue, fusing together the corporeal-emotional and the cognitive-moral poles of meaning.

22. Durkheim 1951 [1897].

23. Indeed, both interpretive and critical anthropology have problematized the assumption of the universality of illness, by underscoring how illness is socially constructed and yet often reduced to biomedical and bodily interpretations, masking the social life of illness. More specifically regarding modern psychiatry, a large body of work has emphasized the role of pharmaceutical markets in creating what David Healy (1997) has famously called the "antidepressant era." See Chapter 7.

24. Despite the limitations of Freud's work on mourning (Clewell 2004; Ramazani 1994), it holds that *without* mourning, defined in Freud's earlier work (Freud 1957c [1917]) as a kind of hyper-remembering, melancholia follows. In his other works "On Transience" and "Thoughts for the Times on War and Death" (Freud 1957a [1915], 1957b [1915]), mourning is a means of healing, to "build up again all that war has destroyed, and perhaps on firmer ground and more lastingly than before" (Freud 1957a [1915]: 307).

25. Hierarchies of death and the creation of legitimized categories of death can create arrested psychological conditions such as those discussed by Judith Butler. In *Precarious Life: The Power of Mourning and Violence* (2006), Butler examines the violence that both prohibits a mourning discourse and dehumanizes death. Although her analysis focuses on mourning the "unfamiliar," it can also apply to prohibited mourning which un-familiarizes the familiar, by blocking its recognition, as was the case for many Iranians whose losses during the 1980s were not recognized as legitimate.

26. Das 1996a.

27. In Chapter 5, I elaborate on the concept of rupture and the Persian term *toromā*, which do not easily translate to the term *trauma* and its disciplinary assumptions in

psychoanalytical and psychiatric theories (e.g., childhood trauma in psychoanalysis) or in humanitarian discourses of trauma caused by natural disasters and mass violence.

28. Subjectivity work, memory-work, everyday life, and illness forms provide sites for cultural negotiation, contestation of claims, and the discursive formation of critical events. To turn to these sites, to shift the ethnographic angle and voice, is one way of accessing alternative visions, roles, and interpretations of events and their afterlife. In crossing several institutions (family, state, etc.), narratives of critical events (Das 1996a) become assimilated and inscribed into their ordinary afterlives. Abstract rationalities fail to capture the depth of these events, as does institutionalization of memory and the legitimation of certain ways of remembering at the cost of others (Das 1996a). In following the afterlife of past ruptures and how it ruptures the present, my concerns correspond with Das's on the fragility of the ordinary (2007) and the potential of the ordinary to morph into the catastrophic (2015). I, too, take issue with scholars such as Povinelli (2011) for giving the state apparatus the privilege of turning a quasi-event into an event, for instance, by locating in it the authority of an ethical and political response to the event; neither the authoritative apparatus nor the event resides outside of the everyday (Das 2015: 12–13).

29. Mannheim defined generations as based on sharing the consciousness of belonging to a cohort that have experienced in their youth a particular historical event and generational location, rather than belonging to a specific time frame, thereby assigning generations a clique quality that is not necessarily conveyed in the concept of a concrete generation unit (Mannheim 1952 [1927]). Later, sociologists Edmunds and Turner explored how generations created political and cultural impact. They extended Mannheim's legacy in their formulation of "global generations," which they defined by interactivity as a result of the "growth of electronic forms of global communication technology" that facilitated various mediations and interpretations of collective generational memories of certain events (Edmunds and Turner 2005: 573). In my analysis of generational experiences, I draw on their work and their call for a new agenda in studying generations in their relation with new media and their role in the formation of generational movements (Edmunds and Turner 2005). For more, see Chapter 4.

30. See Khosrokhavar 2002, 2004 on the rise of different social actors in the aftermath of the Iran-Iraq War, and the construction of new generations of post-Islamist youth. I hope to add a psychologically attuned approach to these constructions by engaging with the cultural aspects of memory.

31. Ian Hacking, in his *Mad Travelers*, writes about "transient mental illnesses," those that seem to be confined to a particular ecological niche that permits and even nourishes them (Hacking 1998). Although his is an exploration of the interaction between "expert knowledge and behavior of troubled people" (p. 30), the *ecological niche* is useful as a conceptual tool for exploring postwar contextual complexities in Iran; e.g., of brewing expectations and frustrations due to unreciprocated sacrifices and gifts of life (in a Maussian framework [Mauss 1954]).

32. I use *transference* in the psychoanalytical sense of unconsciously reproducing or redirecting the repressed feelings of a past experience onto a new situation. For more, see Chapter 6.

33. I use the terms *medicalization* and *biomedicalization* to refer to conditions where matters of life are brought into the purview of medicine and become subject to medical intervention (Conrad 2007). Foucault's (1991 [1978], 1994a, 1994b, and 1980) work on biopower, subjectification, and governmentality had a profound influence on twentieth-century scholarship on the relationship between subjectivity and medical technology and intervention. This scholarship was primarily concerned with agency and power relations (and in the case of psychiatry, often with pharmaceutical persuasions) and how individuals experience themselves and the world around them through biomedical intervention (Rabinow 1999; Rose 2006a; Dumit 2004, 2012; Petryna 2002; Biehl 2005; Rapp 1999; Turkle 2008). Equally important is scholarship on cultural analysis and interpretations of medicalization (Lock 2002; Cohen 2000; Sanal 2011) and of new technologies (Fischer 2009, and 2003).

34. An example is the medicalization of HIV/AIDS in Iran, where physicians and policymakers began to fight the stigma of the condition by focusing on a purely biomedical formulation of drug abuse. See Behrouzan 2010.

35. For example, several pilot studies in the 1990s showed an increased knowledge of mental health among health workers, as well as a significant increase in the number of rural and urban mental health care centers, with only 37 percent of the rural areas of the country not yet served (Yasamy et al. 2001).

36. This internalization of a new mode of thinking relies on what Foucault described as "health as salvation" and health as governmentality, and is traced in the work of technologies of self as well as surveillance that makes subjects internalize certain disciplines; he thus underscored decisive "ruptures" when new modes of perception were naturalized (Foucault 1980, 1994b, 1994a). On the other hand, a rational psychiatric discourse fit with many other policy changes in Iran, such as strikingly advanced initiatives in biotechnology and stem cell research, the success of the national plan to fight HIV/AIDS, and the recognition of many biomedical research centers as centers of excellence in the region. Also see Adelkhah 1999 for more on the rational mindsets behind public health policy in Iran.

37. Nguyen's work on therapeutic citizenship illustrates how medical interventions such as HIV treatment regimes in Africa shape new life forms around illness and transform social relations and individuals' vulnerabilities (Nguyen 2010). He specifically highlights the ways people express a need for moral platforms that give meaning to life; I compare this to the working of the *DSM* in modern Iranian psychiatry.

38. Rather than a top-down approach to medicalization, I am interested in the processes of internalization of biomedical discourses, how they collaborate with politics (Turkle 1978), and how they reflect power relations within professional cultures (Lakoff 2005; Sanal 2011). The naturalization of biomedical hegemony and discourses is indeed a work of culture, relying on a biomedical language that facilitates the reification of consciousness and social relations, and shapes new conceptualizations of not only illness and its meanings, but also its causes.

39. For elaborations on such modes of governmentality, see Foucault 1991 [1978], 1980; Rose 1990, 1996.

40. Biomedical psychiatry has too frequently been examined only through the lens of

governmentality and biopower, or, in non-Western contexts, of colonialism, all of which regard psychiatry as a domain of power struggle in which the patient's agency is medicalized away (Conrad 1992; Conrad and Potter 2000; Szasz 1997; Keller 2007). While anthropologists have, rightly, criticized medicalization for desocializing and depoliticizing lived experiences of illness (Conrad 2007, 1992; Illich 1975; Young 1997), my ethnographic findings underscore medicalizing *desires* among individuals for whom diagnosis allows specific types of discursive truth. In this, my work corresponds with anthropological studies that regard medicalization as a generative and negotiative process of (political) meaning making (Kleinman 1986; Kleinman et al. 1997; Das et al. 2000; Scheper-Hughes 1992; Martin 2007; Lock 1986; Kitanaka 2012).

41. One of the most recognized policy adjustments for instance is Iran's successful family control program, via a countrywide public health and educational campaign in the 1980s (recognized as distinctive by WHO). According to the Iranian Statistical Center's yearbook (March 2000–March 2001), after the baby boom of 1979 to the early 1980s, it shifted population growth from wartime, pronatalist rates of 3.9 percent in 1986 to an annual rate of 2 percent since 1996.

42. Obeyesekere 1990 and 1984.

43. This has been an ongoing project in anthropology since the 1930s (Obeyesekere 1990, 1984). Obeyesekere created a dialogue between anthropology and psychoanalysis that is illuminating for thinking about the dialectics between the inner work of symbols (unconscious as per Freud) and the formation of symbolics and cultural forms over time and at the social level. "Personal symbol," he wrote, "is generated primarily out of the unconscious; once generated, it exists on the public level as a cultural symbol" (Obeyesekere 1984: 37). In grief, for instance, people use symbols that are intelligible to others (Obeyesekere 1990, 1984).

FREUD

1. Both words, *sexualism* and *Freudism*, were used as spelled but with a French pronunciation.

2. See Shari'ati 2011, the twenty-first volume of his *Collected Works* (in Persan) that includes *Fatima Is Fatima, Women,* and *Expectations of the Muslim Woman.*

3. See the debate between Mohammad Sanati and Susan Shari'ati (in Persian), titled "Ravānkāvi-ye Doctor" (Psychoanalysis of the Doctor: Susan Shari'ati and Mohammad Sanati's Debate on Ali Shari'ati and His Views on Freud and Psychoanalysis), in *Mehrnameh* 1 (3) (June 10, 2010): 48–55.

CHAPTER 2

1. Schayegh 2009.

2. With the growing popularity of therapy and self-help culture in both Iran and its diasporic community in Southern California (where over twenty-eight Iranian TV channels are based and attract audiences inside Iran), another kind of psy talk entered the Persian lexicon, moving away from traditional views toward one that focused on displacements, traumatic or exilic pasts, relationship issues, and stress and anxiety. Self-help

psychologies are incredibly popular among Iranians, and most Persian-language self-help books are translations of American ones. But this should not obscure the prior history of self-help movements in Iran. One of the more important of such movements is the school of thought of PANA, or *Maktab-e PANA* (*Parvaresh-e Niruhā-ye Ensāni* or "Developing Human Skills"), founded by Belgian-educated lawyer and author Ebrāhim Khājehnouri and continuing in Tehran today. PANA's students have created a training curriculum for group leaders or teachers (*ostād*), with two-hour sessions in private houses, rotating among members of a circle. Attendees are mainly women, but there are also sessions for men, for children, and for couples. PANA's vocabulary has been taken up by many, including Farhang Holākuyi in Los Angeles, whose talks draw audiences of a thousand or more, and who is but one of a generation of immigrants who have found new professional careers as psychological counselors. The history of both PANA and the emergence of self-psychology talk shows in the Iranian diasporic community of Southern California deserves attention beyond the scope of this chapter.

3. See Fischer 1973 and 1980.

4. The intertwined roots of melancholia in the Islamic and European worlds go back to the humeral theory (in Persian called *yunāni* [Greek] medicine) of balancing the four humors, and of melancholia as the overabundance of the black (*melas*) bile (*kholes*), hence *melancholia*. But Persian and Sufi literature offer more descriptions of depressive portraits of the mad (pouring soil on his head, abandoning the material world, etc.) than of maniac pictures (often, as in Avicenna, described as aggressive). Among explanatory models for madness, possession does not seem dominant in Sufi literature, and there is anecdotal evidence for tolerance of the mad in hadith (Javanbakht and Sanati 2006). In Sufism, madness is intertwined with love and represents various stages of *soluk* (upward journey, ascendance toward union with the beloved). The madman has also been described as the wise in disguise, or the Wise of the Mad (*Oghalā-ol-majānin*), manifest in the character of Bohlul in Persian mythology, or as the one abandoning the material world in pursuit of transcendence and union with the almighty beloved, manifest in several accounts of *divāneh* (the madman) and *āghel* (the rational man). The lover—*majnun* (lovesick), *āshegh* (lover), *sālek* (pilgrim), *malul* (melancholic)—all aspire to evanesce as a path to illumination.

5. Good et al. 1986: 404. See also Fischer 1980. For more anthropological analyses of Iranian affective structures, see Beeman 1985 and 1988; Behzadi 1994. This affective structure is greatly influenced by Persian poetry and poetic heritages. On the significant role of poetry and poetics in the Iranian culture as an "articulation of the self" (Manoukian 2004: 41), see Manoukian 2012. For more anthropological insight into the relationship between melancholy, creativity, and poetry in contemporary Iran, see Olszewska 2015a and 2015b.

6. This, of course, is not unique to Iran. Europe, too, in the Baroque period saw melancholy as a sign of gravitas and realism. Both Walter Benjamin in the twentieth century and Robert Burton in the sixteenth century analyzed the social institutions shaping and regulating melancholia: Benjamin drew on German Lutheran and Spanish theater; Burton on attention to music and dance as counterbalances to melancholia, drawing explicitly on Avicenna's account in his *Canon* of depression from "love melancholies."

7. See Aghaie 2004; Fischer 1993 and 1980.

8. Most notable among pre-Islamic symbolics of martyrdom is the *Book of Kings* (*Shāhnāmeh*), the Iranian national epic and the world's longest poem (over 60,000 verses). Penned by Hakim Abolghāsem Ferdowsi (935–1025 AD), *Shāhnāmeh* is a mythical rendering of parts of the history of the Persian Empire. Notable among young martyrs in *Shāhnāmeh* are Sohrāb and Siāvush, both innocent martyrs. In the tragedy of father and son, Rostam and Sohrab, Sohrab was killed by his father in a duel and Rostam only found out who he was when Sohrab was dying. Siāvush, the young prince, rejected his seducing and manipulative stepmother. But his father, the king of Iran, refused to believe him. For more on this mythology, see Daryaee and Malekzadeh 2014; Meskoob 1971; Fischer 2004.

9. Along with seventy-two family members and followers, the third Imam refused to pledge allegiance to the caliph and chose to defend the legacy of the Prophet Mohammad. His death symbolizes, for Shi'ites, a call for sacrifice for justice. The mourning rituals and performances involved in the commemoration of the Battle of Karbala include performances such as *ta'ziah* (passion plays) (see Fischer 1980 and 2010).

10. The Iran-Iraq War additionally morphed the politics of martyrdom on both sides. In her *Iraq in Wartime: Soldiering, Martyrdom, and Remembrance* (Khoury 2013) historian Dina Khoury illustrates how martyrdom became, for Iraqis, a category of experience through which individuals could claim social and political rights.

11. Dāvidiān 2008; Chehrāzi 2003; Reza'i 2004; Mirsepāssi 1951. These autobiographical voices reveal tensions within and between identities and aspirations. Science studies has provided us with a legacy of tuning into the ways scientists formally narrate their lives and think about their science (Traweek 1992, 1982; Rabinow 1996; Fischer 2003). Certain forms of performativity are indeed integral to processes of knowledge formation (Fischer 1986, 2001). As such, these memoirs reveal how Iranian psychiatrists perform in fractured spaces and various bricolages of knowledge and practice.

12. My account of psychiatry's development in the 1980s is based on the small body of available literature and reports as well as extended interviews with psychiatrists, particularly those involved in the NMHP planning. Among them, I cite psychiatrist Mohammad Sanati and Javad Alāghband-Rād and keep others anonymous. In Chapter 7, I elaborate on the division between the two major orientations in psychiatry in Iran and globally: biomedical (understanding behavior in terms of brain physiology and neuroscience) and psychodynamic (understanding behavior in psychoanalytical terms).

13. This was also the period in which a small group of Iranian and American sociocultural anthropologists began to explore the interfaces between mental health, cultural models, and health care; suicide attempt rates were explored as indices of social pressures of urbanization on small towns and cities such as Shiraz, Isfahan, and Maragheh. Examples include the work of Byron Good and Mary-Jo DelVecchio Good and their colleagues on health care in Maragheh (1986 and 1998); the article of Mary Catherine Bateson et al. (1977) on Iranian deployments of psychological dissociation between internal purity and external requirements of living in a corrupt world; and Michael M. J. Fischer's exploration of short stories, film, epic, and the Karbala religious paradigms for Iranian "models of and models for" negotiation of affect and emotion (1980, 1982, 2004).

14. Shadpour 2000, 1994.

15. Jamalzadeh 1941.

16. See Katouzian 2003.

17. See Foucault's *Madness and Civilization* (1988), which lays out a genealogy of knowledge forms and explores how madness has been constructed historically and epistemologically in Europe. Cf. Sanal's examples of how madmen are linguistically characterized in Turkey (Sanal 2011).

18. In Persian literature, asylums are described extensively, often as marginal, harmless, and yet somehow mystical. Other terms for asylum include *divānestān* (as used by Persian Sufi poet Attar), *timārestān*, and *mārestān*. This literature includes a wide range of treatment options. In treating the mad, Avicenna advises empathy and lays out, according to Mohammad Sanati's analysis, what can be seen as early seeds of psychoanalysis and talk therapy in Islamic medicine (interviews with Sanati, 2009). Interestingly, Avicenna does not advise the physical restriction of madmen, unless they are harmful to themselves. In old texts, there is evidence of various ritualistic acts (such as burning *espand* or carrying the devil's eye), as well as sacrificing animals, tying a knot (*dakhil bastan*) on sacred shrines, and pulling out the wisdom teeth (often by *salmāni* [barbers]). In the 441st story of *One Thousand and One Nights*, a woman takes her son to the barber and tells him secretly the *tabib* (physician) has recommended that her mad son's two wisdom teeth be extracted (thus showing that madness was seen as a disease, since they had already seen the doctor; this is corroborated by the treatment of Majnun's love-spurred madness in *Oghalā-ol-majānin*, or *The Wise of the Mad*).

19. Reza'i 2004.

20. The college Dārolfonun was founded by Amir Kabir under the Qajar king Naser-e-din Shah in 1851; its medical teaching was supervised initially by Austrian teachers and returnee translators from France (Karamati 2004). The *Dāneshkadeh-ye Pezeshki* (Faculty of Medicine), the pioneering academic institution of modern medicine in Iran and one of the six main faculties of the new University of Tehran in 1934, succeeded the Dārolfonun Department of Medicine, which had become the School of Medicine (*Madreseh-ye Tebb*) in 1919.

21. Comparatively speaking, this was over a century after the inception of lunatic asylums in France, the introduction of "moral therapy" by Philippe Pinel (1745–1826) in Paris, and the formation of the York Retreat by William Tuke (1732–1819) in the UK. For more on the history of these asylums, see Scull 2005 and Porter 1990.

22. Dāvidiān 2008: 29–30. The first resident to be trained at Ruzbeh, in 1950, Dāvidiān finished high school at the Alborz American College and studied medicine at the University of Tehran and in London. As resident, he joined forces with the two founding fathers of Ruzbeh, now his mentors. An avid painter and a reader of literature and history, Dāvidiān taught at Tehran University and served two terms as the head of the Department of Psychiatry and Ruzbeh Hospital, while mediating collaborations with international organizations such as WHO (Dāvidiān 2008).

23. This also reflected the influence of Pinel's moralist intervention in the care of the mentally ill. For more on Pinel's legacy, see Porter 1990.

24. Dāvidiān 2008: 31.

25. He also founded the private psychiatric hospital Maymanat, which was later run by his son, Gholamreza Mirsepāssi, who returned from the UK and was among the leading attendings at Ruzbeh until his retirement in 2003.

26. Dāvidiān 2008: 135.

27. Schayegh 2009.

28. Ibid.

29. Ibid. See also Fischer 1990 for similar arguments regarding penal reform and Fischer 1984 regarding modernist writers and film auteurs in the 1960s and 1970s.

30. Mortazavi 2007: 19.

31. The distinction between diseases of the brain and diseases of the soul is rooted in Avicenna's *Canon of Medicine* (comp. 1025 AD), used also in Europe until the early modern era and still interesting for its phenomenology and classification of brain diseases in humoral and organic terms and its presentation of suggested treatments. Galenic (humoral) categories are still widely referred to in popular discourse across the Middle East including Iran, and doctors must be aware of these discourses to communicate (see Fischer 1973). In the *Canon*, Avicenna describes *demāghi* diseases and their treatments in humoral and organic terms (Avicenna 1989 [1025]). Rhazes (865–925 AD) also wrote on melancholia, mania, and delirium states in terms of organic models; both physicians emphasized the effects of emotions on cardiovascular systems (Moharrery 1994).

32. For more comprehensive accounts of the curricular formation of medical schools, see Shahri 2004; Koyagi 2009; Mahbubi-Ardakani 1975; Yar-Shater 2004; Karamati 2004.

33. Other returnees from France founded modern institutions and medical specialties such as ophthalmology (Mohammad-Gholi Shams) and pediatrics (Mohammad Gharib).

34. Milani 2008: 1063.

35. Chehrāzi 2003: 67–74.

36. The history of psychology is instrumental here, but beyond the scope of this book. When psychology, as a formal discipline, was established in Iran in 1926, significant effort had already gone into translating psychological concepts into Persian, notably *ravān* for "psyche" and *ravān-shenasi* for "psychology" (Najmabadi 2014: 188). Decades later, these efforts were partially undone with the interchangeable use of the terms *bimāri-ye ruhi* and *ravāni* for "psychiatric illness." Psychology became a major academic field by the mid-1960s. For more on parallel curricula formation for psychology and its training, see Alipour 2006. More recently, the government has granted equal status to "medical and psychological counseling services" and such services have become much more widespread. Despite the existence of numerous psychological associations, they enjoy little participation in the preparation and administration of their curriculum (Alipour 2006; see also Schayegh 2009).

37. A comprehensive historiography of psychoanalysis (or psychology) in Iran is yet to materialize. In this book, I only trace its points of rupture or affinity in its relation to *academic* psychiatry. For an overview of the history of psychoanalysis in Iran, see Barzin 2010.

38. In the 1950s, at least two popular radio shows discussed Freud and specifically the unconscious. *At the Crossroads* (*Bar Sar-e Do Rāhi*) was hosted by Ebrāhim Khājehnouri (the

founder of PANA; see note 2), who inserted psychoanalytical concepts such as the unconscious, along with some Sufi concepts, into his show. The other radio show, titled *They Don't
Know Why* (*Va Nemidānand Cherā*), was hosted by Nāsereddin Sāhebzamāni (b. 1930), a
German-trained psychologist and member of the faculty of theology at Tehran University,
also the author of many literary works including *The Third Script* (*Khat-e Sevvom*), who
returned to Iran in 1951. At this point, a number of translations of some of Freud's work had
also appeared in Iran (see Barzin 2010). The 1990s and 2000s later saw a new wave of translations of psychoanalytic books, with a special attention to Lacan (see Sanati 2014).

   39. Sanati 2014.

   40. On *Shāhnāmeh*, see note 8. The concept is obviously overly schematic and broad,
but it is a useful heuristic that Iranians often employ to explain failings in individual autonomy. The notion was later taken up by mythologists such as Shahrokh Meskoob and
Mostafa Rahimi, who interpreted it also in the context of patriarchy and the battle between the old and the new (thus the dilemma of modernity and tradition). See Fischer
2004 for analysis of three generational repeating units in the *Shāhnāmeh* in which there
is conflict between fathers and sons but alliances between grandfathers and grandsons. In
1977, writer Reza Barāheni would revive the idea in a tract called *Crowned Cannibals*, in
which he argued that the shah of Iran could not allow gradual democratization because
fathers cannibalize the autonomy and confidence of sons. See Fischer 2004: 84.

   41. For instance in the novels of F. M. Esfandiari set in the time of the overthrow of
Prime Minister Mosaddegh and the CIA-led coup of 1953, in which the adolescent protagonist participates more out of youthful rebellion than any political commitments. For
a thorough analysis, see Fischer 1984: 171–241.

   42. Jean Piaget, Eric Fromm, and Karen Horney were also widely translated and
taught in psychology departments, but Jung entered a more important debate on identity politics. Henri Corbin, the French translator of Heidegger, opened these ideas to
Iran in the 1940s and expanded them through his studies of the Iranian tradition of neo-
Platonist "Illuminationist Philosophy" (represented by such philosophers as Suhravardi,
Mir Dāmād, and Qutb al-Din Shirāzi). He identified the sources of Jung's archetypes with
the *ālam-e methal*, the zone between the physical world and the immaterial world of the
mind. Sanati credits Corbin with the rediscovery by Iranians of their own *āref*s, or mys-
tics, arguing that in Iran people understand Jung in terms of mysticism (interview with
author, London, 2009). While this is not literally true, it is probably the case that Corbin
sparked active thinking with these sources, rather than just learning them in a dry scho-
lastic fashion. His followers asserted that esoteric psychology was the alternative to socialism and other Western doctrines such as Marxism. See Sanati 2014; Fischer and Abedi
1990; Fischer 2014, 2010.

   43. Sanati 2014.

   44. This is part of the 1960s identity politics of returning to an authentic self, influenced
by postcolonialism. The term *gharbzadegi* (translated as Westoxification or Occidentosis)
was coined by controversial philosopher Ahmad Fardid (b. 1909) and was popularized by
Jalal Al-Ahmad (1923–1969) in an eponymously titled book. Ali Mirsepassi explains: "In
Fardid's re-rendering of the Orient-West binary and Heideggerian historicism, the Orient

represents the essence of the holy book and revelation, which has been concealed under a succession of Western mantles" (Mirsepassi 2010: 119). See also Boroujerdi 1996; and Matin-Asgari 2005.

45. See the interlude "Freud" on pages 37–38.

46. Abrahamian 1982b.

47. Interviews with Mohammad Sanati, London, 2009. In his lecture "On Ethics and Psychoanalysis," presented (in Persian) at Tehran's Annual Meeting of Iranian Psychiatrists in 2008, Sanati argued that the impact of both leftist propaganda and mysticism in the political epistemology of Iranians in the 1960s made it hard to reconcile psychoanalysis (a science of disclosure, demystifying, and unveiling) with the symbolism of hidden truths, mysteries, and ambiguities in mysticism. Moreover, psychiatrists too welcomed mystical thought more than they welcomed psychoanalysis; note that leading psychiatrists of the prerevolutionary era included the master of a well-known Sufi sect, Javad Noorbakhsh (1926–2008), who had served as the president of the Iranian Psychiatric Association and head of the Academic Departmental of Psychiatry at Tehran University. Thus, it is not surprising that, even before the revolution, psychiatrists did not find mainstream psychoanalysis and its demystifying imperative desirable.

48. See "Ravānkāvi-ye Doctor" (Psychoanalysis of the Doctor: Susan Shari'ati and Mohammad Sanati's Debate on Ali Shari'ati and His Views on Freud and Psychoanalysis), in *Mehrnameh* 1 (3) (June 10, 2010): 48–55.

49. Interview with Mohammad Sanati. See also Javanbakht and Sanati 2006.

50. See, for example, Abrahamian 1982a; Fischer 1993, 1980; Afary and Anderson 2010; Chehabi 1990; Milani 1994.

51. A detailed discussion of the Cultural Revolution is not the focus of this chapter; but insofar as academia was concerned, academics (especially female academics) were also embedded within larger shifts in gender dynamics, codes of dress, and legal structures such as the hybridization of family and penal laws with older Islamic *fiqh*-based jurisprudence; see Osanloo 2009. For more on subsequent shifts in gender roles, see Afary 2009; Zahedi 2006; Osanloo 2009; Fischer 2010; Adelkhah 1999; Kashani-Sabet 2011; Najmabadi 2005, 2014; Kia et al. 2009; Shakhsari 2010, 2011.

52. See Ashraf Zahedi's work on the wives of the Iran-Iraq War martyrs, and women related to martyrs more generally, as well as their relationship with the invisible economy of expectations, rights, and compensations (Zahedi 2006). For more on postwar semantics, see also Ghamari-Tabrizi 2009; Zahedi 2006; Fischer 1984; Sohrabi 1995; Sick 1989.

53. More broadly, too, revolutionaries formed bodies of social policing such as the *komiteh* (people's committees) and the *basij* (volunteers recruited to serve first in the war with Iraq, then as urban community keepers of morals), whose purview also included university campuses. The *basij*, the young volunteer army mobilized during the Iran-Iraq War, went on to create a new class of youth in the following decades. For more on younger postwar generations' cultural dynamics, see Olszewska 2013; Khosravi 2008.

54. Note, for example, a 1980 *Kayhān* newspaper article (13/02/1359 AP—03/05/1980) where Sādegh Zibākalām, today a reformist political science professor at the University of Tehran, called for *bumi kardan* (tailoring, customizing) of the sciences in accordance with

the revolution. He used the example of engineering schools, and suggested a new curriculum that would exempt students from learning technicalities considered useful only in the West. He argued for practical apprenticeships in the field, sending engineering students to rural areas, and adjusting the curriculum to the needs of the underprivileged *Ummat* (Muslim community). In recent years, he has revisited some of his past views on the matter.

55. This was visible, for instance where, at a time when wearing a *cravat* (necktie) was seen as a symbol of Westernization and *cravati* men were harassed by revolutionaries, many doctors still sported neckties at work.

56. For more on the advances and development of Iran's postrevolution scientific community, particularly in basic sciences, see Khosrokhavar et al. 2004; Khosrokhavar and Ghaneirad 2006. On developments in public health, see Kashani-Sabet 2011.

57. The parallel evolution of "psy" television talk shows in Los Angeles–based expat media further elevated the role of mental health discourses inside Iran. However, these shows began airing in 2000 and after domestic radio and television shows were already underway. Unlike domestic shows, they remained largely psychologically, as opposed to psychiatrically, oriented. During my fieldwork in Southern California, I learned there is now one therapist for every five or six Iranians and that the number of young, second-generation, LA-based Iranians who choose to study psychology is soaring.

58. See Ghobari and Bolhari 2001; Bolhari et al. 2012; Marandi 1996. According to Azizi there were "rises in the number of educational institutions from 10 to 46; student admissions in programmes of medical sciences from 1387 to 18141; medical student admissions from 632 to 3630; teaching staff from 1573 to 7979; and teaching bed to student ratio from 1.05 to 2.08" (Azizi 1997: 159). Similarly, in 1997, the number of clinical and masters students had increased and several programs in clinical and Ph.D. tracks had been established. The establishment of a joint Ministry of Health and Medical Education in 1985, Azizi reports, contributed to "upgrading medical education" (Azizi 1997: 159).

59. Sharifi 2009: 10.

60. Javanbakht and Sanati 2006: 409. Also see Yasamy et al. 2001.

61. See Javanbakht and Sanati 2006; and Mohammadi et al. 2005. This move, recalls committee member Sanati, was initiated by WHO and led by Iranian physician Ahmad Mohit, then head of the Eastern Mediterranean Region (EMR) region at WHO. Sanati believes the NMHP plan had a huge impact in resocializing psychiatry and bringing it out of its isolation (interview with author, London, 2009). It has twice been recognized internationally as one of the most successful experiences in the integration of mental health in primary health care (PHC) (Yasamy et al. 2001). This has been followed by the active involvement of the IPA in international and regional cooperation, partly by hosting and attending international conferences, and partly by way of its pedagogical aspirations.

62. Many proponents of the move, including Sanati, then Head of the Psychiatric Group at Tehran University, compare it to the 1960s and 1970s community psychiatry movement and the dramatic reduction in the number of psychiatric hospital beds in the United States and the UK (interview with author, London, July 2009), although subsequent debate on the movement's failures there (Grob 1991, 1994; Estroff 1985) have not followed in Iran.

63. In collaboration with the Association for Clinical Psychologists and Counselors as well as NGOs like Narcotics Anonymous, a number of research centers have been established, including the Addiction Research Center, Tehran Psychiatric Institute, Cognitive Sciences Research Center, Center for Psychiatric and Psychological Research, and Center for Family Studies. Psychiatric treatment remains largely focused on biology. See Javanbakht and Sanati 2006: 407.

64. Over a dozen training departments and twenty-three hospitals in 2006 (Javanbakht and Sanati 2006: 407).

65. For example, see Shahmohammadi et al. 1998.

66. In thinking about the characteristics of this emerging psychiatric discourse, I have been inspired by Sherry Turkle's *Psychoanalytic Politics* (1978), a historically informed ethnography and discourse analysis of emerging psychoanalytic politics in 1970s France. Before, Turkle writes, the Left scorned psychoanalysis as a bourgeois enterprise. Afterward, the French Left created its own reading of psychoanalysis by "reinventing" Freud and bringing together social activism and individual politics. This French, and specifically Lacanian, psychoanalytic revolution reflected the post-1968 politics in which it evolved. The Lacanian psychoanalytic "Protestant reformation" responded to Marxist critiques of psychoanalysis by distancing itself from ego psychology. Turkle situated "Freud's French Revolution" in the context of both the 1968 events and longer-term social change. In doing so, she mapped cultural change in French society through the lens of psychoanalysis. As in 1970s France, late-1980s Iran experienced disillusionment. In the 1990s, widespread attention to mental health followed the politicization of everyday life. In Iran, however, this turn to psychological sciences was emphatically medicalized.

67. Note that many psychiatrists practiced psychodynamic models and continue to do so in their private practice. But my focus in this book is solely on "academic" psychiatry and its pedagogical trajectories.

68. Sanati (b. 1945) finished medical school at Tehran University (1963–1970), and left Iran for the UK in 1974 to pursue training in psychiatry. He obtained his MRCPsych in 1982 and FRCPsych in 1992 from the Royal College of Psychiatrists in London. Since 1985, he has practiced and taught in Tehran. Upon his arrival at Ruzbeh, he was advised by his senior colleagues to tamp down his psychoanalytical side (interviews with the author, September 2009; also see Sanati 2014). Sanati found a voice, however, in the 1980s on television and through literary criticism while teaching interested residents at his home. At the moment, Sanati is the head of the Department of Psychoanalytic Psychotherapy and Group Therapy, director of the Psychotherapy Fellowship Course at Ruzbeh Hospital, and head of the newly formed Psychotherapy Section in the Iranian Psychiatric Association.

69. Psychoanalysts have criticized the fact that no oral interviews are required for admission to psychiatry residency programs.

70. Persian translations usually preserve medical terms in their original form, which are typically used with English or French pronunciations. For a comprehensive overview of the residency program, see Chapter 7.

71. Critics point out that the program is primarily identified with and run by Sanati and his psychiatrist wife and colleague, Mahdieh Moin, who had made the initial proposal for

a fellowship program in 2006. While this was initially the case, it is also important to note that several other psychiatrists joined forces with Sanati in the creation of a pedagogical legacy. Among them was Abdolhossein Rafatian, who was trained in France, taught residents at Rāzi Hospital, and continues to collaborate with Ruzbeh. Sanati justifies the initial efforts by saying he knew at the outset that creating formal groups or a large association would hit the walls of prejudice and bureaucracy. He believes that in such circumstances, working from outside or on the margins of the academy might be more successful in conveying the message. These contestations are ethnographically significant in terms of their contribution to internal tensions and the development of the field. For more, see note 25 in Chapter 7.

72. Among prominent faces on these shows were pediatrician Behrouz Jalili and psychiatrist Mohammad Vali Sahāmi. Jalili advocated a biologically minded focus on medication and biomedical models, while Sahāmi focused on family dynamics. Children's mental health was also occasionally mentioned in shows run by psychologists such as Gholmali Afrouz and Simā Ferdowsi, as well as others who emphasized counseling, healthy families, child rearing, developmental issues, and how and when to seek help.

73. I can identify at least two unaccredited academic precursors to child psychiatry, as well as private yet influential practices such as Sahāmi's. One of the academic precursors was Tehran's Imam Hossein Hospital, one of the training hospitals of Shahid Beheshti University of Medical Sciences. This was an unaccredited pediatric psychiatry ward until 1998. Psychiatry residents of Ruzbeh Hospital in the 1980s used to be sent to Imam Hossein Hospital for their pediatric psychiatry rotation (interview with Javad Alāghband-Rād, Halifax, July 2008). The second precursor was psychiatrist Mehrdad Mohammadian's training program for residents and his small child psychiatry ward in Navvāb Safavi Hospital of the Iran University of Medical Sciences. The Iran University of Medical Sciences is, in a way, younger than the other two medical schools in Tehran. After the 1979 Revolution, it was created through the merging of a number of medical and research centers, including the Tehran Institute of Psychiatry.

74. Family psychotherapist Sahāmi (1944–2013) returned to Iran from the UK in 1991, starting a private practice and becoming a lecturer in Tehran's major medical schools. Like Sanati, he engaged in the informal training of residents in psychodynamic methods. Sahāmi's training in and focus on family systems with strategic, dynamic, and structural orientations was a new addition to existing approaches to children's mental health within the Iranian psychiatric community, and has played an important role in the training of child psychiatrists to this day.

75. Identifying himself as a member of nasl-e sukhteh, Alāghband-Rād came of age at the brink of the revolution and the Cultural Revolution. After finishing his residency and his mandatory military service in Kermanshah in western Iran, he received a government scholarship and pursued a fellowship in child and adolescent psychiatry at the National Institute for Mental Health. Upon his return, he became a faculty member at Ruzbeh Hospital, where he worked toward creating a subspecialty board in child and adolescent psychiatry (interview with author, Halifax, July 2008). He is the first president and a founding member of the Iranian National Board of Child and Adolescent Psychiatry Subspecialty

(1997), and the first president and co-founder of the Iranian Association for Child and Adolescent Psychiatry (2001).

76. Some of these hospitals, attendings believe, have the potential to become accredited for training fellows (interview with Javad Alāghband-Rād, Halifax, July 2008).

THE COUNSELOR

1. http://moshavere.org/taxonomy/term/168 and http://moshavere.org/node/983.

2. Beck et al. 1961.

CHAPTER 3

1. This section is not about the psychiatrist himself, but it is rather an exploration of rhetorical tools and emerging discourses. Dr. M is both a graduate and attending of one of the major medical schools in Tehran, specializing in psychodynamic therapy. In the late 1990s, he was a frequent guest and commentator on television talk shows, but was also well known for his work on marriage therapy, relationships, disabilities, and PTSD. Later, he worked on the relationship between religion and mental health.

2. Good 1977.

3. Psychodynamic psychotherapist Mohammad Sanati was among the first psychiatrists to join the media, starting with a six-minute-long morning radio show that grew popular within weeks. Then he moved on to television. Eventually, he believes, in either medium, his advocacy of certain psychodynamic models did not sit well with media protocols (interview with Mohammad Sanati, London, October 2009).

4. Both these headlines are taken from the weekly *Salāmat* published on November 24, 2007 (03/09/1386 AP).

5. See note 4 in Chapter 1 for epidemiological data on the health impact of the war. A number of qualitative studies too have explored the impact of war on civilians and combatants. These include the series on the history of the Iran-Iraq War published in Tehran by the Center for Documentation and Research on the Sacred Defense (http://hdrdc.ir/fa; see also Doroudian 2012; Darvishi 2011). There are numerous medical and epidemiological studies on war injuries (see Chapter 6), but more work is needed on the longer term afterlife of the war. For an analysis of the war in social terms, see Ehsani 2009, 2003, and 2006; Ghamari-Tabrizi 2009; Khosrokhavar 2004. On the physical and psychological health impact of the Iran-Iraq War, see the Health Impact Assessment report by Medact (http://www.medact.org/weapons-war/health-impact-assessment/); see also Birch et al. 2014; Ali 2001; Ebrahimzadeh et al. 2006; Khateri et al. 2003; as well as Amirani's documentary on the impact of chemical injuries on the lives of civilians in western Iran (Amirani 2005).

6. Interview with Mohammad Sanati, London, September 2009.

7. Interview with Mohammad Sanati, London, October 2009.

8. Around the same time, an abundance of Persian language "psy" talk shows were reaching Iran's domestic population via satellite channels run by expats based in southern California. One stark distinction between the media landscapes in Iran and in the United States is the prominence of psychiatry, namely psychiatric illnesses and medication, in domestic discussions, as opposed to counseling and Americanized CBT in the expat discourse.

The first psy talk shows on the expat scene were broadcast in 2000, hosted by psychologists Foojan Zein and Ali Sadeghi, in Los Angeles, followed by the rapid growth of several others including one by the popular Farhang Holākuyi, who claims that the LA-based shows predated and triggered domestic ones (interview with author, Los Angeles, February 2009). While this is false, the role of the LA-based shows in destigmatizing counseling and attracting young Iranians inside Iran and in the diaspora is undeniable. The LA scene, however, seems at times to be oblivious to the dynamic and evolving nature of the domestic scene and discourse, in part dismissing anything broadcast inside Iran as propaganda.

9. Interview with the daily newspaper *Hamshahri* (14/12/1384 AP—05/03/2006).

10. *Āftāb-e Yazd* newspaper; May 5, 2010 (15/02/1389 AP).

11. Sources are Mehr News Agency (http://www.mehrnews.com/fa/newsdetail .aspx?NewsID=1646557) and Pezeshkan (http://www.pezeshkan.org/?p=20375), respectively.

12. Such biologizing and individualizing (depoliticizing historical and cultural categories) can mask important parts of the course of an illness. For instance, when rituals, traditional wisdom, and embodied cultural identities are perceived by Western biomedicine as risk factors, they tend to undermine the compelling reasons that drive individuals to resort to such practices (Frankenberg 1993). Moreover, associations between such variants are often interpreted as causation.

13. Fischer 2007a. For anthropological critiques of the moral and political economy of knowledge and hierarchies of evidence (privileging evidence-based medicine—EBM— and trivializing "anecdotal" evidence), see the edited volume *When People Come First: Critical Studies in Global Health* (Biehl and Petryna 2013) and, in that volume, Adams 2013, and Fischer 2013. See also Das 2015; and Fischer 2009. While evidence-based medicine and epidemiology are partially useful, they can reduce people to numbers if used in the absence of proper conceptual or theoretical frameworks.

14. See Bourgois 2003; Hammonds 1999; Latour 1988; Rosenberg 1992.

15. Bourgois 2002: 259. Also see Bourgois and Bruneau 2000.

16. Rumors influence the way data are collected or reported. I was advised by several colleagues not to trust data collected in Iran. Medical students are often instructed in public health courses to take statistics as rough estimates. Such anecdotes are informative for their underlying assumptions that would indirectly influence the way statistics are collected.

17. Noorbala et al. 2004.

18. Ibid., p. 70. Epidemiological reports are abundant in Iranian medical publications; some state that anxiety disorders and depressive mood disorders are Iran's most common psychiatric conditions (8.35 percent and 4.29 percent, respectively) (Mohammadi et al. 2005). A study of 25,180 individuals countrywide (Mohammadi et al. 2005) reported a 10.81 percent mental illness rate, with anxiety disorders and mood disorders making up the most common diagnoses. They reported that, at the time, for every 100,000 Iranians, there were 1.9 psychiatrists, 0.5 psychiatric nurses, 2 psychologists, and 6 social workers. Other surveys include a 2008 study on Gilān province in northern Iran by Modabernia and colleagues that showed that, in a sample of 4,020 subjects, 9.5 percent (63 percent female and 37 percent male) were diagnosed with depressive disorders (Modabernia et

al. 2008). The prevalence of minor depressive disorders, dysthymia, and major depressive disorders was 5 percent, 2.5 percent, and 1 percent, respectively. Socioeconomic class was significantly associated with depressive symptoms based on the Beck Depression Inventory (BDI) score (p<0.001) and depressive disorders based on clinical interview (p<0.001).

19. ILNA News Agency, 19/07/1388 AP—11/10/2009.

20. Commonly, officials are interviewed or cited in discussions of mental health policy in newspaper reports; most confirm that depression is the most common psychological condition in Iran, though they quote varying statistical evidence. A feature article on depression in the weekly paper *Sepid* (14/02/1388 AP—04/05/2009) argues that statistics vary because different diagnostic questionnaires are used with different target groups, but insists there is still consistency about the higher prevalence of depression among young women. Other articles point to the lack of adequate budget allocated to mental health (less than 3 percent of the national health care budget) or to the sole focus of the Bureau of Mental Health on addiction, calling for an efficient *moʿāvenat-e salāmat-e ravān* (Directorate of Mental Health) (*Hamshahri*, 01/03/1387 AP—21/05/2008: http://hamshahrionline .ir/print/52625).

21. Rey and Walter 2001; Nejatisafa et al. 2006.

22. Child and adolescent psychiatric research publications have grown since 1993, with 883 of 3,113 (28 percent) Iranian mental health articles dedicated to child psychiatry. According to Nejatisafa et al. (2006: 95), "eighty-one (9 percent) of these articles appeared in international journals, and the remaining were published in domestic journals (no international indexing). Among the first authors, 65 percent were male and 50 percent had a doctoral degree." Raising awareness is a running theme in these publications. In a pilot study on school mental health programs conducted in Damavand, a city of 250,000 inhabitants about 100 km north of Teheran, according to Yasamy and colleagues (Yasamy et al. 2001), the intervention significantly improved students' and parents' knowledge and attitudes toward mental health, increased students' self-esteem, relieved their problems with parents and teachers, and reduced fear of examinations. Similarly, the Bureau of Mental Health has initiated a program to prevent child abuse and violence against women in collaboration with the United Nations Children's Fund and WHO.

23. In this context, the pressure around getting into universities has not slackened, nor has the supply of appropriate jobs upon graduation increased. The ensuing resentments and culture war are often analyzed as class war, but the reality on the ground is more nuanced and complicated (see Olszewska 2013; Khosravi 2008).

24. Iranian neuroscience as a discipline is as old as Tehran University. Before the field was called such, experimental neuroscience was a field of inquiry in departments of physiology, pharmacology, and biophysics. But the trajectory of what is now prominent as cognitive and systems neuroscience, with its experimental and conceptual focus on the brain, should be traced to the foundation of the School of Cognitive Sciences (formerly School of Intelligent Systems) in the Iranian Institute for Theoretical Physics and Mathematics (IPM), where the first Ph.D. program in cognitive neuroscience was established in the 1990s under the leadership of Hossein Estaki. On par with leading international research labs, and with a dossier of high-ranked publications in scientific journals includ-

ing no less than *Nature*, the IPM (founded in 1989) remains one of the major sites for government-supported scientific investment.

25. In *Being Modern in Iran*, Adelkhah illustrates how the Iranian state has over time become increasingly professionalized and technocratic, employing modern biopolitics in the management of population, self, and health (Adelkhah 1999). One area that offers examples of such a leading role is that of health and biotechnologies, focusing on health policies, from family planning to Iran's successful reach to neighboring countries with its HIV/AIDS model (Kashani-Sabet 2011; Behrouzan 2010). While "the region" in the case of the HIV/AIDS program was limited to the Persian-speaking countries of Afghanistan and Tajikistan, often the greater Middle East or the Eastern Mediterranean Region (EMR in WHO's classifications) are implied in official rhetoric. See also Najmabadi 2014 for a situated analysis of the trajectory of government policies with regard to progressive and medical interpretations of the transgender condition.

26. Madarshahi 2012: 619. Madarshahi maps out the increase in scientific publications over the past fifteen years and outlines the gaps that need to be filled. Indeed, Iran's standing in terms of the quantity of publications has risen, with an annual growth rate of 236 percent. But the quality (such as citations per paper or number of patents) has not followed the same trend; Iran's global standing only improved from 135 in 2006 to 133 in 2010 (Madarshahi 2012: 631). One explanation, according to Madarshahi's analysis, is that the government remains the main entrepreneur and funder of research activities (more than 73 percent), with increasing investment in university research. Indeed, the role of economic sanctions imposed on Iran should not be overlooked.

27. November 26, 2008 (06/09/1387 AP).

28. May 23, 2009 (02/03/1388 AP).

29. The "agitation of public opinion" is a key term and is ethnographically significant; it influences the social life of data and the tension underlying interdisciplinary relationships between medicine and social studies, resulting in many medical professionals' reluctance to collaborate with social science projects.

30. WHO assesses the overall burden of disease using the disability-adjusted life year (DALY), a time-based measure that combines years of life lost due to premature mortality and years of life lost due to time lived in states of less than full health. DALY reports are incorporated into policy measures, albeit in varying forms. In 2008, for example, the Ministry of Health published a WHO disability-adjusted life years (DALY) report that indicated mental illnesses, led by depression, had resulted in the loss of 570,000 years of lifetime in the age range of 33–44; depression had the second highest DALY after death by accidents. The report was circulated in newspapers with little discussion of what DALY implied or what needed to be done.

31. Also see Najmabadi's discussion of the medical discourses that have contributed the formation of transsexual selves in Iran. State formation, she maintains, is an "ongoing, fractious, and volatile process," which "continues to shape and reshape, fracture and refracture, order and reorder what we name 'the state'" (Najmabadi 2014: 6).

32. For example, see the Mehr News Agency (30/02/1394 AP—20/05/2015) reports on educational campaigns to deal with suicide among university students. The emphasis there

is on depression and seasonal affective disorders. Also see http://www.parsine.com/fa/
tag/1/%D8%A2%D9%85%D8%A7%D8%B1%20%D8%AE%D9%88%D8%AF%DA%A9%D
8%B4%DB%8C%20%D8%AF%D8%B1%20%D8%A7%DB%8C%D8%B1%D8%A7%D9%86
for more official reports on suicide in news media.

33. These reports often cite epidemiological surveys: in one, lifetime prevalence rates
of 14 percent, 6.6 percent, and 4.1 percent have been reported for suicidal ideation, planning, and attempts, respectively (Shooshtary et al. 2008). Similarly, a survey of 89 admitted self-burning suicidal patients in Isfahan (Lari et al. 2007) reports higher rates in
twenty- to twenty-nine-year-olds and married women. The most frequently reported trig-
ger for suicidal behavior was conflict with family (61.8 percent). In another survey on
self-inflicted burn suicide (Maghsoudi et al. 2004), of 412 cases (from 1998 to 2002) in Tabriz, 99 percent were women, mostly housewives, with an average age of 25.5. Depression
was the most common psychiatric diagnosis among them. Ghazinour and his colleagues
too studied suicide-admitted patients in the large intoxication referral hospital in Tehran,
Loghmān Hospital, from 2000 to 2004 (Ghazinour et al. 2009); they found that the most
frequently used method was drugs (women 90 percent and men 83 percent), followed by
pesticides and agricultural chemicals (women 2.7 percent and men 9 percent).

34. *Aftab News* (04/12/1388 AP—23/02/2010: http://aftabnews.ir/vdcdnxon.ytokn6a22y
.html). In the article, an academic psychiatrist and a sociologist discussed social elements
such as poverty and warned of a potential "Durkheimian" condition.

35. *Hamshahri Newspaper*, citing the ISNA News Agency, 24/05/1390 AP—15/08/2011.

36. See, for an example among many newspaper articles, the one in *Shargh Daily*
(30/06/1391 AP—20/09/2012: page 11). According to the article, the Ministry of Health reported an average rate of thirteen suicides per day in 2009. The report indicates that Iran
has a lower rate of suicide compared to Western countries (ranking Iran 48 in the world),
but cautions that suicide is growing among young people (average age of suicide being
29) with regional variations across provinces: http://www.magiran.com/ppdf/nppdf/2387/
p0238716310111.pdf.

37. The name is taken from the game of seven stones, where the goal is for one team
to throw a ball and knock down a pile of seven stones set up by the opposing team. The
e-zine is independent, with contributors from around the world.

38. Over the past couple of decades, media representations of the drug user have
transformed from the poorly dressed and old opium addict TV character of the 1980s
Agha Taghi to the twenty-something heroin addict artist Ali in Mehrjouyi's 2007 feature
film *Santouri*. This shift reflects the privatization of drug use, changing modes of use,
changing gender patterns of addiction, and the spread of drugs in high schools and col-
leges. For more on shifting addiction patterns, see Behrouzan 2010.

39. Commonly, many Iranian sociologists and psychologists allude to a Durkheimian analysis of suicide in their commentaries in Iranian media (for example, see *Shargh
Daily* 30/06/1391 AP—20/09/2012: page 11). In *Le Suicide* (1897), Durkheim introduced the
breakdown of norms and moral order as a defining factor in suicide. Based on degrees of
moral regulation and social integration, he described four types of suicide: egoistic, al-
truistic, anomic, and fatalistic. These commentators argue that both anomic and fatalistic

conditions are useful in thinking about suicide in Iranian society. As mentioned earlier, however, this formulation needs to be culturally contextualized as it often assumes universal responses to social stressors.

40. Salamati 2013; also see Tavallaii et al. 2006 in the *Iranian Journal of Military Medicine*.

41. Suicide among veterans can be understood as anomic (caused by lack of social integration), and thus is more common in times of peace than in war; although there is no evidence yet that suicides are significantly common among Iranian veterans. There are comparative examples in studies of suicide in postsocialist countries such as Hungary and Belarus. For example, using Weber's theory of authority combined with Bateson's theory of the double bind, Smith situates socialism as a lived experience of "absurd propositions, impossible situations, and paradoxical political and economic relations," resulting in several strategies of dissimulation and disengagement, and rituals of resistance including suicide (Smith 2002).

42. In order to compensate veterans and their families, the Veterans Organization has used a scaling system based on the percentage of the body that is harmed. The quantification of *darsad-e jānbāzi* (infliction or disability percentage) has created bureaucratic protocols for veterans' welfare.

43. *Asr-e Iran News*, 30/11/1387 AP—18/02/2009, http://www.asriran.com/fa/news/65505/خودسوزي-يك-جانباز-در-مقابل-بنياد-شهيد-و-امور-ايثارگران. Within a short time frame, newspapers reported, a couple of other disabled veterans had followed suit in the cities of Khorramabad, Tehran (in front of the Iranian parliament), and Qom (*Tabnak News*, 26/11/1387 AP—14/02/2009, http://www.tabnak.ir/pages/?cid=36863, and Shomal News, 29/11/1387 AP—17/02/2009, http://www.shomalnews.com/view/10639/خودسوزي20%در20%مقابل20%مجلس،20%صحن20%را20%متاثر20%كرد8C20%E2%80%شعله 20%هاي/). Media and medical discussion followed, underscoring the long-term sacrifices of the veteran community and society's responsibility toward their welfare. More media attention followed the reaction of an official who asserted, almost immediately after the incidence in Tehran, that the suicidal person was not a *jānbāz* but a "mentally ill junkie," which evoked reactions from both the veteran and the medical communities debating the medical legitimacy of such claims (*Mehr News Agency*, www.mehrnews.com/fa/newsdetail.aspx?NewsID=834642; and *Aftab News*, http://aftabnews.ir/vdcd590j.yt0on6a22y.html). For an overview of veterans' suicide cases in the media, see http://www.dw-world.de/dw/article/0,,4053511,00.html, 27/11/1387 AP—15/02/2009).

44. Kitanaka 2012: 107. For more on self-burning as a mode of protest, see Crosby et al. 1977; Maghsoudi et al. 2004; Ahmadi 2007. India, Sri Lanka, and Ireland are among countries with high rates and various patterns of self-burning. So are the western provinces of Iran, including Kurdistan (one study suggests a 40 percent rate of suicides in the city of Kermanshah).

45. For example, on one such iniative, see http://basijpress.ir/fa/news-details/41691/ (17/10/1393 AP—07/01/2015).

46. The articles presented at the symposium reported growing rates of suicide in northern provinces such as Gilan, as well as increasing rates of hanging among men and self-immolation among women.

47. In December 2009, another national symposium on suicide was held in the war-inflicted city of Ilām in western Iran, the source of one of the country's highest rates of suicide and of self-immolation among women. Public health experts occasionally discuss the social aspects of mental illness and suicide in the media, for example, in a 2011 parliamentary report that linked Ilām's suicide crisis to unemployment, or in the comments of an attending at the Tehran Institute of Psychiatry emphasizing the role of a "sense of security" in society (as opposed to focusing solely on the individual). Elsewhere, these themes have given rise to official debates; the head of the State Welfare Organization, for example, has called on the Bureau of Mental Health in an interview with the newspaper *Resālat* (13/06/1385 AP—04/09/2006) for the shortcomings of psychiatric treatment and rehabilitation in urban settings. These debates remain sporadic yet ongoing.

48. There is a century-long history behind the conceptualizations of medicine and medication in Iran. In early twentieth-century Iran, access to medicine and medical technologies (medication included) was a crucial element of the modernization processes. In this medical modernization, drugs symbolized scarce Western technologies that reflected progress.

49. The *āmārnāmeh* is publicly available; however, some statistical data, even when systematically collected and available to the public, may still be difficult to access for technical or bureaucratic reasons.

50. These unit-based figures are not reliable on their own, since the forms of prescriptions of any given drug may vary across categories and also at different points within each category (e.g., pills versus syrups). I had to sort the tables manually and draw graphs to search for patterns and investigate how the tables of each year and each drug family corresponded to each other.

51. For example, the SSRI antidepressant Reboxetin, commonly prescribed at different points during this period and even used in clinical trials on ADHD children at Shahid Beheshti University (Arabgol et al. 2009), does not appear in the reports. This can be partly explained by noting that in Iran some imported drugs are sold by private representative companies. They are prescribed and purchased under the title *tak noskheh-i*, or single prescription, and are more expensive than Iranian-manufactured brands. Over the past few years, with the approval of private and individual drug company representatives in Iran, several such drugs have been sold and prescribed without being bound by ministry protocols.

52. For example, the most precise measurement of the burden of disease for depression was from 2003: it ranked Iran fourth for both genders, second for females, and ninth for males; the DALY for depression was one to three times more in women than in men. The DALY for depression in Iran was lower than what was reported in the EMR, but the report warned that, unlike the EMR, in Iran depression is more persistent and extends well into old age. The highest DALY was reported among thirty- to forty-four-year-olds. This detailed study was not repeated after 2004.

53. Most psychiatric medication is available in Iran, as are Iranian-manufactured brands. Imported brands are more expensive and are not covered by insurance if an Iranian-manufactured version exists.

54. Note that various media reports have acknowledged a crisis of the recreational use of Ritalin among young people, university students, and soldiers, as well as major exam candidates such as doctors sitting for residency exams.

55. For a comparative perspective on the calculated use in the United States of anti-depressants and other mood drugs to remain "high-functioning," see Kramer 1993, and Greenslit 2007. More generally on "dependent-normal" patients, see Dumit 2012.

56. The closest ethnographic study among non-European and non-American societies is that on the rise of psy discourses in Japan (Kitanaka 2012). Both Japan and Iran witnessed a comeback in psychiatric medicalization in the 1990s; in Japan, the main catalyst was the burst of the bubble economy and the unemployment crisis and subsequent anxieties. With rising rates of suicide among burned-out working men, explanatory models based on "so-cially caused pathologies" were sought. While in Japan the biomedical persuasion gen-dered depression, in Iran it contributed to the formation of generational categories.

57. Matza 2009 analyzes a particular radio show hosted by a psychotherapist to illus-trate how confessional modes were normalized through what Mickiewicz has called the "American effect" (Mickiewicz 1999: 21). The emphasis of the Russian psy shows on psy-chotherapy, Matza argues, was reflective of larger stories of "refashioning of subjectivities from the remnants of Soviet experience . . . unfolding at the intersection of market forces, state governance, and new forms of expertise" (Matza 2009: 492).

58. Matza 2009: 492.

THE STUDENT

1. Despite nostalgic reconstructions of Café Nāderi in the minds of young Iranians and in contemporary cinema and literature, Nāderi was only one among many cafés that, following European trends and particularly after the 1953 coup, became a hub for literary and intellectual debates of the 1960s. Culturally, Café Nāderi has become a shorthand for several of such gathering venues including Café Firuz, Café Ferdowsi, and Café Lāleh-zār.

2. In the absence of diplomatic relations, obtaining an entry visa to the United States has become difficult since the 1980s. Since 9/11, in the period when Samāneh applied for a visa, further clearance measures and restrictions had been put in place for Iranians, including making their student visas single-entry.

CHAPTER 4

1. Das 1996b.

2. http://parkingallery.org/projects/deep-depression/.

3. URLs of the blog posts remain on file with the author. This one was last accessed on January 8, 2015.

4. A recording of the "red siren" can be accessed on YouTube: www.youtube.com/watch?v=y4z4wmzMZVA.

5. During the Iran-Iraq War there were five intense episodes of attacks on Iranian civil-ians in non-border cities. During what became known as the War of Cities, particularly in 1984 and 1987, major cities became the target of air raids that killed tens of thousands of civilians. This was alongside chemical attacks on Iranian civilians and the use of mustard

gas and nerve agents by Iraq. Several studies, including those conducted by the Veterans Organization's Research Center, have investigated the psychological impact of city bombardments on children. See Rahimi 2010, in *Negin-e Iran: Journal of Research on Sacred Defense*.

6. Feeling stuck and placeless (*āvāreh*) was the fate of exiled intellectual figures like Sā'edi, but also of many ordinary émigrés. See Fischer and Abedi 1990, and Sā'edi's *Transformation and Liberation of the Āvāreh* (in Persian) in Mortazavi 2007.

7. The group podcast six programs, from Tehran, between November 2008 and May 2009: http://stillnessradio.blogspot.com/.

8. Young Iranians have incorporated new media platforms as a generational plateau. On the use of "plateaus" (and "third spaces") as temporary stabilizations of multiple complex emotional flows and technological decision-making constraints, see Fischer 2003 and 2009. Fischer adapts the term '*plateau*' from Gregory Bateson's studies of emotional plateaus in Bali and Gilles Deleuze and Félix Guattari's *A Thousand Plateaus* (Deleuze and Guattari 2001). He suggests a parallel term in Persian might be *hāl*, an achieved state of temporary fusion (personal communication with author; see also Fischer 1980, 2004).

9. The policies of the Cultural Revolution included the implementation of Shi'ite ethos in educational platforms. For a periodized map and analysis of policy priorities, the shifts and inconsistencies in the processes of reformation in postrevolutionary school textbooks, and the formation of New Islamic Citizens, see Malekzadeh 2012. Also see Shorish 1988, Paivandi 2005, and Moghadam 1999, on the reformulation of gender roles in school teachings after the revolution; Afary 2009, on ensuing sexual politics in contemporary Iran; and Siavoshi 1997, on state policies regarding publishing houses and the cinema after the formation of the Council for Cultural Revolution in 1980. In "Socialization of School Children in the Islamic Republic of Iran" (1989), Mehran describes the "new persona" reflected in textbooks as revolutionary, and religiously and politically savvy.

10. Turkle 2007: 311.

11. Fluoxetine is manufactured in Iran as a generic; Prozac is the Eli Lilly brand name; *Prozāk* is used colloquially in Iran for both, and frequently too for other antidepressants.

12. See the Introduction (pages 13–14) for more on divination by poetry and for the significance of poetic sensibilities in everyday Iranian life.

13. Mannheim 1952 [1927]; see note 29 in Chapter 1.

14. Edmunds and Turner 2005: 573; see note 29 in Chapter 1.

15. Sharifi 2008. At the time of the interview, I couldn't find access to the film. I only refer to Rāmin's reflections on it, which, regardless, remain ethnographically valuable.

16. For similar observations about Sharifi's film (2008), see Alireza Mir-Alinaghi's review "Negahi be mostanad-e Chehreh-ye Ghamgin-e Man" (A Look at the Documentary My Sad Face), in *Ensan va Farhang* (Anthropology and Culture) (26/07/1393 AP—18/10/2014), http://anthropology.ir/article/3323; and Ahmad Mir Ehsan's review (17/10/1388 AP—07/01/2010) "Afsordegi be ravayat-e shakhs-e avval" (Depression Narrated in the First Person), in Rybon Center for Documentary Cinema, http://www.rybon doc.com/global/index/section/guest/module/writings/lang/fa/catid/2/id/88/page/34.

17. For a discussion of critiques of individualistic biopolitics and neoliberal discourses of responsibilization in psy disciplines, see Chapter 7 (note 31).

18. I take a cue from Freud and from Benjamin's *dialectical images* (Buck-Morss 1991) and assign to the spectacle of psychiatry (its biomedical images, language, concepts, and other representations of knowledge and hope) the dialectical quality and power of awakening a utopian dream or phantasy of health. The term *spectacle* is derived originally from forms of entertainment and art in Roman times. The idea of spectacle in the context of modern society was furthered in Walter Benjamin's *Arcades Project* (see Buck-Morss 1991), in which he drew on Marx's concept of *phantasmagoria* (a magic lantern show of optical illusions). Marx had recycled the notion in its relation to commodification and fetish. For Marx, the phantasmagoria was primarily about the ideological transposition of new technological creations and their materiality; this, he believed, was represented in false desires. For Benjamin, phantasmagoria and spectacle functioned by working upon the unconscious. One's capacity to be critical is lost in a world saturated with the phantasmagorical. The spectacle, however, is not always necessarily oppressive and false (Debord 1990), though it always relies on an illusionary effect: "In all of its particular manifestations—news, propaganda, advertising, entertainment—the spectacle is the *model* of the prevailing way of life" (Debord 2004: 8). One can contend that the spectacular authority of Big Pharma or of biomedicine works because, in the absence of a utopia, all that remains is the truth constructed by the spectacle.

19. There is a vast literature on fantasy (phantasy) in psychoanalysis. Freud saw fantasy as a product of imagination in service of wish fulfillment; Melanie Klein regarded the unconscious as the locus of phantasies and early relations with internalized objects (object-relations); and Lacan saw phantasy as a defense against anxiety-evoking elements within the symbolic structure of one's life-worlds. For more, see Freud's "Screen Memories" (1962 [1899]), *The Interpretation of Dreams* (1953 [1900]), "Hysterical Phantasies and Their Relation to Bisexuality" (1959 [1908]), *Totem and Taboo* (1955a [1913]), and "A Child Is Being Beaten" (1955b [1919]). Other scholars have used the term *phantastic object* as "a mental representation of something (or someone) which in an imagined scene fulfils the protagonist's deepest desires to have exactly what she wants exactly when she wants it" (Tuckett and Taffler 2008: 395). This is a Freudian prospective and "wishful thinking" take on fantasies. When I use *phantastic*, I am referring to psychoanalytical phantasy as both *prospective* (as in Freud) and *retrospective* (as in Lacan's reference to the symbolic structure within which phantasy arises). For Iranians, this could mean the possibility of working through ruptured pasts and approaching uncertain futures.

20. Most contemporary thought on spectacle has focused on media, visual technologies, and occasionally early science (Darley 2000; Buck-Morss 1991). Attention needs to be paid to "performances, their performers, and the material and social resources that were deployed in their staging" (Morus 2006: 101). See, for example, Hewitt's study of the spectacle of popular science as a work of culture in the nineteenth century (Hewitt 1988).

21. For more on youth culture, gender, and public life in Iran, see Bahramitash and Esfahani 2011; Olszewska 2013, 2015a; Bayat 2010.

22. I intentionally depart from studies of youth culture that analyze youth through the lens of resistance and rebellion. Within these studies, however, I look for useful entry points into the subjective experience of and the inner struggles created by various modes

of regulation. For example, in a young girl's poetic reflections, "they liken my joy to sin. They close my eyes to happiness," Bayat (2010) points to the "gradual erosion of her youth," which, he argues, was translated in the official narrative in the postwar years to the growth of "degenerate behavior" among youth and the pathologization of their conduct (Bayat 2010: 113). Also see the section Social Nonmovements in Bayat 2010, where he discusses the inner struggles of youth as the result of such regulations.

23. See Turkle 2007, and in it Wight 2007; Dumit 2004; Greenslit 2007.

24. See Sanal 2011 for reflections on experiences of patients after kidney transplant in Turkey as a case of internalized objects and relations (with the organ, as well as with the Western epistemologies that the biomedical intervention is borrowed from). The displacement of these relationships following biomedical interventions results in what she has called a "truth explosion," mimicking the conditions of psychosis. In a similar and yet distinct way, the appropriation of psychiatric and neuroscientific epistemologies among Iranian doctors and laypeople is made possible through rites and rituals of meaning making. In *Prozāk*, however, this medical introjection comes *after* such truth explosion is already underway.

25. In Iran it is customary to hold wakes on the third, seventh, and the fortieth night after a death. At each, the extended family gathers for a ceremony, often following a visit to the grave, stays on for dinner, and generally makes sure that the immediate family of the deceased is not left alone. Depending on how close one is to the deceased, one wears black for seven days, forty days, or a year. The extended family gathers to mark the end of this mourning period, sometimes by bringing the mourner gifts of colorful clothes.

26. *Evocative objects* are objects we think with, feel (at one) with, relate to, and experience emotion and intellect through, as explained beautifully in Turkle's introduction in her *Evocative Objects* (2007). Also see Wight's essay "Blue Cheer" in Turkle 2007 for an intimate account of one's relationship with medication. In the cyborg existence, biological forms of being (both being diagnosed with illness and being medicated or intervened upon by biomedical technologies), precede intuitive, collective ones. Taking the pill in invites a liminal dream state. For more reflections on the cyborg state vis-à-vis medical technologies, see Turkle 2007, 2008; Wight 2007; Davis-Floyd and Dumit 2013.

27. Debates on the medicalization of sadness have often criticized its blind spot for stressful social conditions. Horwitz and Wakefield, in *The Loss of Sadness* (2007), traced the moment of such reconfiguration to the third revision of the diagnostic manual in the United States, the *DSM-III*, and the changes in diagnostic criteria that formed a new "symptom-based definition" of depression. They argued that, as opposed to "normal" sadness, which was context-based, a symptom-focused approach would lead to a pseudo-epidemic of depression. A series of responses and critiques followed, including, but not limited to, Arthur Kleinman's response in *Lancet*, questioning the authors' privileging of "normal" sadness without defining it (Kleinman 2007; see also Ehrenberg 2009, on a history of diagnosing depression; and Kleinman 2012, on bereavement). The psychiatrization of life in Iran raises further questions, in addition to the already raised issue of universalization of normal sadness in these responses. First, the boundaries of situational and clinical depression are—as any practicing psychiatrist would testify—not very clear. Second, might prolonged and sustained states of loss, situational depression, leave a mark

on the brain, as neuroscientists have suggested? Third, how can we measure the "proper" reaction to an ecology of distress or loss? Fourth, as many Iranian psychiatrists argue, by the time people seek help, it is the very "symptoms" of depression that they want to get rid of; practitioners further argue that suffering should not be normalized and left untreated. Here though, I aim to focus on a culturally specific critique of the *DSM* to go beyond binaries of local and universal, to investigate the hermeneutics of mental illness, and to offer an ethnographic opening into the experience of *depreshen* from *within*.

28. Underneath each individual loss lingers the ghost of several other collective losses; much has been lost to the war, to generational and ideological divides, to economic crises. For many, loss has endured for years, without due processes of mourning.

29. See Turkle 2008 for intimate ethnographies of the relationship between the self and objects. Medical technologies and interventions, in particular, offer possibilities for new modes of being and imagining, as well as for manifestations of the subjective experience of historical conditions (Petryna 2002; Lakoff 2005; Fortun 2001).

30. On pharmaceutical hegemonies, see Healy 1997; Dumit 2012; Lakoff 2005.

31. See Kleinman et al. 1997; Young 1997; Biehl 2005; Biehl and Locke 2010.

32. See Das 1996a, 2000, 2007.

33. I examine subjectivity in its most fluid and fragmented sense, shaped and reshaped by social, cultural, political, and medical webs of meaning and power that penetrate into the inner worlds of individuals. For anthropology, subjectivity has become the grounds on which a spectrum of historical and social changes intersect and emerge, leading to the ways in which people organize their selfhood and manage their public and private existence (see Biehl et al. 2007). It is more specifically the public and private domains of subjectivity that have shaped recent debates, bringing the private aspects of subjectivity, previously left to psychology and psychoanalysis, into anthropological inquiry. Different anthropological approaches to the study of the self have regarded subjectivity as an analytical category, as a site for historical inscription, as strategies for being in the world, and as platforms for the realization of what's at stake (Biehl et al. 2007). I simultaneously regard subjectivity as an unquiet site of political contestation (Fanon 1963) and ongoing recollection (Caruth 1996), historical inscription, strategies for "being" in the world, grounds for emerging historical and social change, and managing public and private existence (Obeyesekere 1984; Biehl et al. 2007; Byron J. Good et al. 2008). If subjectivity is dynamically formed, contested, and communicated, then its corresponding and emerging value systems need to be examined in a similar fashion to culture (see Fischer 2003; Das 1996a, 2000). Yet, in exploring subjective worlds, I remain focused on subjectivity-*work*, acknowledging that such efforts are, by definition, open-ended and incomplete (see Das 2015; and Mary-Jo DelVecchio Good et al. 2008).

34. My formulation of psychiatric subjectivity materialized in conversation with seminal works on medical and scientific forms of subjectivity and the ways in which biomedicine, political economy, and historical change can shape the inner states and senses of the self, including Fischer 1999, 2003; Turkle 1995, 2007; Rabinow 1999; Nguyen 2010; Petryna 2002; Biehl 2005; Comaroff 1978; Comaroff and Comaroff 2001, 2008; Kleinman 1986, 1988, 1989; Kleinman et al. 1997; Good et al. 1986; Scheper-Hughes and Lock 1987; Lock 1993, 2002; Cohen 2000; Martin 1994, 2007; Rapp 1999; Luhrmann 2001; Scheper-Hughes 1992; Young

1997; and Rose 1996, 2003, 2006a. Particularly informative has been work on the reconfigurations of the self vis-à-vis medical technologies and how people deploy technology to reconfigure possibilities of life and their values in Cohen 1999; Biehl and Eskerod 2007; Biehl 2005; Petryna 2002; Fischer 2003, 2009; Turkle 2007, 2008; Lakoff 2005; Fortun 2001; Sanal 2011; Hamdy 2012; and Rapp 1999. Psychiatric subjectivity can be seen as an extension of the notion of somatic individuality—in Nikolas Rose's words, "the tendency to define key aspects of one's individuality in bodily terms, that is to say to think of oneself as 'embodied', and to understand that body in the language of contemporary biomedicine. To be a 'somatic' individual, in this sense, is to code one's hopes and fears in terms of this biomedical body, and to try to reform, cure or improve oneself by acting on that body" (Rose 2003: 54). By situating the self in its historical context, psychiatric subjectivity additionally regards selfhood as an embodied site for historical negotiation and turns it into the vessel through which the descent of history into the realm of everyday life becomes possible (Das 1996b, 2000, 2007).

35. This performativity corresponds with Afsaneh Najmabadi's illuminating discussion of self as "contingent conduct." See her discussion of self and conduct in Najmabadi 2014: 297–301.

36. Deleuze's reflections on the clinical and symptomatological have been extremely helpful to me as I listen to my interlocutors and their "alternative universe of reference" (Deleuze 1997), as has Fischer's invocation of traumatized subjects "returning," linguistically and culturally, in speech acts, "active listening, participation, dialogues, and coproduction" (Fischer 2007b: 438). Biehl and Locke elaborate on Deleuze's point regarding how "diagnosis" can silence individual life accounts by stripping them of "the specificity of the complaints and frustrations of its inhabitants by calling them indicators of a universal psychiatric disorder" (2010: 332). For the narrators of this chapter, however, diagnosis is actively performed, while other forms of silencing have preempted diagnostic silencing.

37. Das 2007.

38. See Behrouzan 2015c.

CHAPTER 5

1. On the paradigm of PTSD in psychiatry, see Rechtman 2004. See also Young's historical analysis of the political economy and ideological contexts within which PTSD was constructed in the aftermath of World War II and the Vietnam War (Young 1997). Originally only used to describe physical wounds (thus a technical term among surgeons), *trauma* extended, in the twentieth century, first to head injuries, later to horrid experiences causing psychological symptoms, and finally, to repressed memories of those experiences. It was World War I that solidified traumatic neurosis as a diagnostic category and globalized trauma. During the 1970s, the American Psychiatric Association revised PTSD into a descriptive classification, thereby homogenizing its heterogeneous symptoms. PTSD replaced "traumatic neurosis" in the *DSM-III*, published in 1980. The medical and political term *trauma* has been similarly historicized by Fassin and Rechtman (2009) as being received with suspicion, as an unassessable mode of presenting pain at the time of World War I (when people thought it was an excuse not to fight), and again in the early twenty-first century among asylum seekers in Europe suspected of "gaming" immigration rules.

2. When new languages of description and categories of personhood become available and normalized, new experiences and "human kinds," to borrow from philosopher Ian Hacking, become possible (Hacking 1995); this "looping effect," in Hacking's terms, is useful in thinking about the trajectory of the concepts of trauma and PTSD within Euro-American psychiatry. Also see Hacking 2006.

3. On hyper-remembering, see Clewell 2004.

4. Deborah Durham's conceptualization of youth as "a social shifter, a kind of indexical term" (2004), as well as Katherine Ewing's work on narratives of victimization among young Turkish immigrants in Germany (2012, 2008), have informed the basis of my approach to the different domains in which youth cultures interact. For an engaged conversation on the anthropology of youth culture, see the special issue of *Cultural Anthropology on Youth*: http://culanth.org/?q=node/398.

5. Das 2000: 210.

6. My thinking about the psychopolitics of remembering is informed by and in conversation with scholarship on identity politics and memory-work, particularly work on the politics of remembering and forgetting (Ricoeur 2004). Interesting parallels are also found in scholarship on memory studies of Europe; however, most of this scholarship analyzes politics of memory often in terms of the (outer) political conditions that constitute the possibility of remembering and forgetting (Kõresaar et al. 2009) or the ways narratives act as cultural tools in service of normative views. Memory studies, particularly in Eastern Europe, have also often focused on the textuality of memory (as per Hayden White), using historical narratives as representational structures influenced by the conditions in which they are told (Portelli 1991); they are thus preoccupied with the traumatic event and "working through the past" in ways that are institutionally motivated. In the Middle East, too, collective memory has often been studied vis-à-vis institutional structures. Among exceptions, Laleh Khalili's rich ethnographic analysis of Palestinians' everyday, rather than institutionally organized, acts of remembering has helped me think about memory and the quotidian (Khalili 2009).

7. *Sāzemān-e Ettelāʿāt va Amniyat-e Keshvar* (State Intelligence and Security Organization), the secret police under the shah.

8. Blog posts and their URLs remain on file with author. Occasionally, minor details have been changed to protect anonymity.

9. See, for example, Rahimi 2010 in *Negin-e Iran: the Journal of Research on Sacred Defense*, for a study of the impact of city bombardments on children.

10. See Karimi 2008 on the urban distribution of murals, slogans, and sounds; and Karimi 2013 on the cultural and historical context in which these visuals were installed. See also the special issue of *Visual Anthropology*, "Unburied Memories: The Politics of Bodies, and the Material Culture of Sacred Defense Martyrs in Iran" (vol. 25, nos. 1–2, January–April 2012). In it, Christiane Gruber analyzes the institutionalization and aestheticization of war in postrevolutionary Iran (Gruber 2012; see also Gruber 2008, and Fromanger 2012). Also see Fischer and Abedi 1989, for an anthropological analysis of revolutionary posters and cultural signs.

11. *Zhiān* is the Persian name of the Citroën 2CV, or *deux chevaux*.

12. The Smiling Seyyed is a reference to the reformist president Mohammad Khātami (in office 1997–2005).

13. *Rend* (Libertine) is an important character in Persian poetic traditions who flouts moralistic taboos and celebrates life (Bateson 1979; Bateson et al. 1977).

14. This is a loose translation of the lyrics of the song "Jang," by 127. An underground band founded in 2001 by a group of Tehrani art students, 127 identified itself as located "at the center of progressive cultural change in Iran." Their music melds Iranian melodies and jazz with an alternative sound, while their lyrics tell of the "frustrations and joys of life." Now residing and performing outside of Iran, they have attracted an international audience and were featured in a 2005 UK Channel 4 documentary, titled *127, An Iranian Band*.

15. The term "weblog" is commonly used in Persian for "blog"; hence "Weblogestān" for the blogosphere.

16. For an overview of the social life of the Internet in Iran, see Akhavan 2013. Also for an example of dominant politicizing trends in the studies of Iranian blogs, see the report by Berkman Center for Internet and Society at Harvard University (Kelly and Etling 2008), which "analyzes the composition of the Iranian Blogosphere and its possible impact on political and democratic processes" by, among other models, creating and using a visual map of the Persian blogosphere (http://cyber.law.harvard.edu/publications/2008/Mapping_Irans_Online_Public). Various other similarly myopic initiatives grew in the 2000s under a US agenda of "understanding" and "decoding" Iranian youth. Such attempts were often out of context and misinformed, leaving the general impression that Iranian blogs were merely a mobilizing tool.

17. Reading blogs through the lens of political activism and movements obscures the cultural and psychosocial working of media. Even though several scholars of the Middle East have criticized overly politicized and developmentalist readings of the Internet that promote "the myths of 'technologies of freedom'" (Khiabany 2015: 350; also see Sreberny and Khiabany 2010), they have for the most part remained focused on the political implications of these media. See the roundtable series "The Digital Age in the Middle East" in the *International Journal of Middle East Studies* (vol. 27, no. 2, April 2015), where authors underscore the broader social context underlying the use of such technologies and warn of the impact of developmentalist views on foreign policy. An exception is Babak Rahimi, who, in the same series, draws attention to historical and cultural processes, and to contextualizing the implications of media in the fields of users' "human desire, fantasies, illusions or even delusions" (Rahimi 2015: 363). These debates of course predate Twitter and Facebook and the Arab Spring, and can be traced back to the time when Iranian blogs were celebrated, pundited, and closely read by Washington and scholars alike (Sreberny and Khiabany 2010). For alternative examples of contextualized and culturally attuned analyses of the Iranian blogosphere, see Shakhsari 2011, and Doostdar 2004.

18. See, for example, Doostdar 2004 for a discourse analysis of blogosphere debates on the vulgarity of blogging languages, and Shakhsari 2011 for a situated analysis of the representational practices of bloggers in the diaspora.

19. Anderson 1991. "Imagined communities" was Anderson's description of the way communities and nations were constructed based on how members perceived and imag-

ined themselves as belonging to them: "It is *imagined* because the members of even the smallest nation will never know most of their fellow-members, meet them, or even hear of them, yet in the minds of each lives the image of their communion" (Anderson 1991: 6). Howard Rheingold extended Anderson's concept of community to define a virtual community as groups of people who may or may not meet in person, but form a bond and exchange ideas through the virtual space (1993). Rheingold's virtual community has been criticized, however, for removing the virtual identity from its political and historical context. As Tara Brabazon has argued (http://motspluriels.arts.uwa.edu.au/MP1801tb2 .html), "he too often sees virtual communities as new and innovative ideological formations, rather than as part of an ongoing semiotic stitching of self, identity and community. Cyberspace is not a 'social petri dish' . . . but merely the continuation of an experiment." For more on early debates regarding virtual identity, see Turkle 1995 and 2005 [1984].

20. In making intelligible different categories of experience, individuals draw on what is culturally and linguistically available to them. A compelling example is discussed in Najmabadi's ethnographic study of transsexual selfhood in Iran (Najmabadi 2014). Going beyond the face value of numbers and categories, she investigates the way selves are in ongoing formation and the extent to which they draw on various religious, legal, and medical discourses to legitimize their practices; i.e., how transsexual as a "religio-state-sanctioned" category was made possible and meaningful in part because various "religious-legal-medical" discourses sanctioned it while denying the recognition of same-sex desires. She examines, for instance, what different discourses psychology made available to people's processes of self-production to navigate between what was or was not acceptable.

21. My argument is largely informed by seminal work in science and technology studies (STS), particularly Turkle's 1984 classic *Second Self*, wherein she introduced computers as psychological machines and objects to think "with" about self and society, in transparent and even utopian terms: "Relationships with a computer became the depository of longings for a better, simpler, and more coherent life" (2005 [1984]: 173–44). In describing the projected self among video gamers, she showed how the individual was able to project identities on the screen, perform self-insertion and role-playing while enabling a "world apart" for building a new self-image. These longings and desires were also anxious, Turkle argued, as the anxiety behind this preoccupation with the self is often overlooked in utopian narratives of virtual life. Later, in *Life on the Screen* (1995), Turkle approached the self as fragmented in the cultural and discursive forms of the virtual. In this ethnographic psychoanalysis of the self, life on the screen renders the self a realm of discourse rather than a real or permanent thing, illustrating the construction of new identities as a work of culture and showing how the multiplicity of this self challenges modern Western thought. Virtual communities become evocative because of their liminal place betwixt and between the real and unreal. See Turkle 1995.

22. The laboratory of experimentation is the term Turkle uses for the Internet as a space of constructing the self: "The internet has become a significant social laboratory for experimenting with the constructions and reconstructions of self that characterize postmodern life" (Turkle 1995: 180)

23. See the Introduction (pp. 8–9) for what I mean by affective.

24. These kinds of reminiscences are not exclusive to Iran, and particularly when it comes to the 1980s, many other youth groups have made them the subject of new art forms and creative expression, although for different reasons. In Portugal, for instance, the *Caderneta de Cromos*, a spin-off website from a blog written by TV host and comedian Nuno Markl, has created a depository of material and cultural products of the 1980s. In the Caderneta, too, which portrays the 1980s as kitsch, austerity is a shared theme. What differentiates the Iranian *daheh-ye shasti-hā*, however, is how these cultural pasts are perceived as ideologized and ruptured, at times rendered medicalized, and mobilized for historical claims.

25. Turkle 2007: 8.

26. *Hamshahri-ye Javān*, issue 97 (18/09/1385 AP—09/12/2006); issue 183 (13/07/1387 AP—04/10/2008); and issue 300 (03/11/1389 AP—23/01/2011).

27. One blog post's title summed it up: "To those who are not survived by their wills but by their Facebook pages." "Will" refers to the Iran-Iraq War martyrs' tradition of writing battlefield letters, often heartfelt last wishes, advising their families not to mourn but to be grateful for the gift of martyrdom. The post's claim to distinction, however, reflects the complex nature of remembering: the very semantics of loss and grief that the younger generations distance themselves from, actually, run deep in the ways they instrumentalize the semantics of the 1980s and construct their identities.

28. Turkle 1995: 263.

29. Margalit 2002.

30. See Marcus and Myers 1995 for reflections on visual art as ethnographic object and as context of art writing. For a critical overview of the place of the visual in anthropology, see MacDougall 2006. In *An Anthropology of Images*, art historian Hans Belting proposes an embodied anthropological theory for interpreting human picture making and pictures as embodied in various media such as painting, sculpture, or photography. Refusing to reduce images to their material embodiment yet acknowledging the importance of the historical media in which images are manifested, he sees the body as a "living medium" that produces, perceives, or remembers images that are different from those we encounter through handmade or technical pictures (Belting 2011). Also see Schneider and Wright 2010 for an exchange between ethnography and art.

31. Freud's argument that photography mirrors the work of memory because of its fragmentary and evocative nature can be extended to these visual cultural productions. For more, see Bergstein 2010. The Frankfurt School opened a range of debates on the emotional associations of images and memories, from Kracauer's early work on memory images (Kracauer 1993; Barnouw 1994) to Benjamin's reflections in his "Theses on the Concept of History" on material history as a memory process in the form of a montage: "The multiplicity of histories resembles the multiplicity of languages," wrote Benjamin, arguing for an alternative telling of history of the oppressed. "It is more difficult to honor the memory of the anonymous than it is to honor the memory of the famous, the celebrated" (Eiland and Jennings 2003: 406).

32. In reading these works of art, my lens is an anthropological one that specifically looks for cultural references in relation to generational memory-work. The works call for

more informed analyses of visual and artistic representations in Iran, which is beyond the scope of this book. For examples, see Balaghi and Gumpert 2002, as well as Karimi 2006, 2013, and 2003.

33. See Haghighi's description and review of Mehran's work in the Persian language magazine *Tandis* (Haghighi 2012). In a catalogue note for work displayed at Christie's (www.christies.com/lotfinder/paintings/shohreh-mehran-untitled-5486805-details.aspx) he writes that the girls' "identity is lost but instead of reducing them to a repetitive sameness, the uniform individualizes the girls. It sets them in relief against the drab and minimal urban setting in which they are moving. Although their facial expression cannot be seen, these women clearly own the city, they appear joyful and they wield their pens like daggers to prove it."

34. This resonates with Rosalind Shaw's work on the processes of self-creation for war-displaced young Pentecostals and the ways they create new spaces for negotiating the future. For youth, she argues, what's at stake is reconstructing a workable past that can be extended into an imaginable future (Shaw 2007).

35. Taussig 1992: 27.

36. The *mute dreamer* also struggles with narrating prophetic visions, images, or divine language that one feels cannot really be translated for ordinary people (Fischer 2004).

37. On the psychoanalytical interpretation of dreams, see Fromm 1951 and Freud 1953 [1900].

38. Adorno 1977. Alternatively, psychoanalysis locates trauma not in events alone, but in a structure of affect and perception extending back through a person's life course, even the birth trauma that sets up the body's mechanisms of responding to complex stresses.

39. Often, these acts are read through a primarily politicizing lens. Asef Bayat has described "subversive accommodation" as a condition where young people adopt, for example, the Ashura and Karbala vocabularies and Shi'ite allegories in rap music, thereby subverting the symbolics of the state into a form of rebellion (Bayat 2010: 116). For *daheh-ye shasti-hā*, I argue, this accommodation is not always necessarily meant as rebellion, but also a psychological, at times unconscious, attempt at working through the past. See note 30 in Chapter 6 for examples of such revival of wartime sounds.

40. I intentionally refrain from debates on collective memory (Halbwachs 1992) formulated as reliant on a group's normative views, cultural practices, rituals, and symbolics, as well as paradigms such as *cultural trauma* caused by revolutions and wars (Alexander et al. 2004) that imply a violent clash of "before and after" value systems. Primarily based in Holocaust studies, these formulations are partially useful insofar as they are concerned with *events* and *losses*, but these are assumed to be *total* and *singular*. They also reproduce the binaries of individual and social in a way that renders psychoanalytical and sociological investigations into trauma mutually exclusive. I find such binaries unhelpful as they overlook embodied, individual, and psychological experiences that, as evident in the stories of this book, flow across time and are fluid, multiple, and dynamic, different for different generations. Moreover, cultural trauma is constructed as disorder and focuses on victimhood, thereby implying a normative evaluation.

41. Summerfield 1999: 1449. Such trauma expertise, often functioning from a distance,

he argued, solidifies the terms of defining and diagnosing the problem in the absence of evidence for the efficacy of their intervention (Summerfield 1999).

42. Both physicians and anthropologists, Fassin and Rechtman map the ways trauma and its victims came to be "denaturalized" and "repoliticized," respectively. Problematizing the "new language of the event," their social constructionalist approach sets out to question the institutionalized and professionalized inscriptions of a rather new "moral economy," facilitated by (Western) mental health professionals (Fassin and Rechtman 2009).

43. It is important here to draw a distinction between different trauma theories. See note 49.

44. See Caruth's introduction "The Wound and the Voice" in Caruth 1996: 3–4. Much of this theory relies on rereadings of Freud's two seminal pieces, *Moses and Monotheism* and *Beyond the Pleasure Principle*. The former embarks on a collective history of violence, and the latter engages with an individual theory of trauma. Recurrent traumatic dreams perplexed Freud insofar as they could not be accounted for by his tenet of wish fulfillment and their imposition on the unconscious could not be prevented. In his earlier work, he designated an externality to the traumatic event, but he later moved toward a theory of trauma as the very origin of consciousness and life. The Freudian perspective was later challenged by Lacanians, who pursued the subject in its relation to the witnessed trauma in an ethical bound. For Lacan, the dream went beyond recollection to the impossibility of responding to the destruction caused by it (Laplanche and Pontalis 1988).

45. See Caruth's "Introduction: The Wound and the Voice," in Caruth 1996.

46. Ibid., 4.

47. Ibid., 11.

48. See Crapanzano 1980 and 1981; Maranhão 1990; Fischer 1986, 2015.

49. American trauma theory is fundamentally informed by clinical experiences with the survivors of traumatic memories as well as by the establishment of PTSD as a diagnostic category in the third and fourth editions of the *DSM* (Radstone 2007). This theory has also developed a strong relationship with the neuroscience of memory (Radstone 2007; Van der Kolk 1994; Van der Kolk et al. 1996), and upholds a neuroscientific emphasis on intersubjectivity, hence the role of the listener and witness in the assimilation of previously incomprehensible traumatic memories. It would follow that the unexperienced, ungrasped event is the key riddle to be unraveled and reassimilated into the consciousness during the analytical process. To this, sections of the French (Laplanchian theories based on formulations of Laplanche and Pontalis) and British (object relations) schools of psychoanalysis have added a new angle: an emphasis on the significance of the unconscious processes of producing associations with traumatic memory. These processes can include an identification with the aggressor or the catastrophe, which is absent from Caruth's analytical framework (Radstone 2007). The same schools of thought also take issue with the emphasis on the "recovery" of traumatic memory and its dependence on the witness; this dependence is, in part, turned inside out and challenged in terms of both the arguable fascination with trauma and the power structure at work in the dialogic nature of witnessing (Radstone 2007). Instead, they attend to the unconscious, culturally shaped spaces of

representation and mediation between the subjectivities of the narrator and the witness. For more, see Radstone 2007 and Garland 1998.

50. In terms of convergence with anthropology, the first contribution is in line with Veena Das's seminal work on the inscription of the knowledge of the past in the present (Das 2000 and 2007). The second resonates with Arthur Kleinman's pioneering work on the cultural and historical slippages between Chinese diagnoses of neurasthenia and depression (Kleinman 1982, 1986, 1988).

51. See Shaw 2007 for a comparative angle on youth culture and memory-work.

52. Hedāyat 1971 [1937].

53. For an overview of Hedāyat's life (1903–1951) and work, see Katouzian 2000; for a psychoanalytical deconstruction of *The Blind Owl* and Hedāyat's other writings, see Sanati 2001 and Katouzian 2000. Anthropologist Michael Fischer has described the ways Hedāyat's text has informed Persian literature, film, and politics in its portrayal of society as "diseased, a drugged dream, a progressive decay which can and must be thrown off" (Fischer 2004: 181; also see Fischer 1984). Hedāyat's bitter irony and satire was meant as a call to unveil beauty, health, and care for a country bedridden by cultural decay. Fischer's analysis of *The Blind Owl* underscores the psychoanalytical layering of the story; for example, in the author's treatment of writing as therapy, or his use of psychoanalytical symbolics in the structure of his narrative (Fischer 2004). There are indications that Hedāyat was familiar with Freud's theories; significantly, he had reportedly published a satirical piece titled "The Case of Freudism" in 1934 (see Sanati 2014).

54. The term "poisonous knowledge," as an embodied knowledge of the past entering and informing one's present, is from Das 2000.

CHAPTER 6

1. See Chapter 3. Not unlike in the United States, despite the consensus that medication and therapy work best in combination, medication remains the primary mode of intervention. Furthermore, recreational use of Ritalin among university students has recently made headlines. But the rise in prescription-only use of Ritalin, doctors believe, is an index of increased awareness and proper detection of ADHD. Serious academic debates about overmedication or concerns about medical enhancement (Parens 1998) have so far been absent from Iranian academic discussions.

2. I have already discussed, in Chapter 3, the reliance on evidence in the promotion of psychiatric discourses and how such evidence is collected, constructed, and interpreted in the media and by practitioners. Iranian medical publications report the mean age of the ADHD children is around 8–9. In a survey of 4,591 seventeen- and eighteen-year-old high school students, girls showed more mental health problems than boys (34.1 percent versus 23.7 percent), and the risk increased with age (Emami et al. 2007). Others report a 3–6 percent prevalence of ADHD among elementary schoolers in Tehran (Khushabi et al. 2006); authors note this is similar to reported statistics in the developed world. Many journal articles employ American and British standardized tests and questionnaires, raising questions about cross-cultural applicability, but they remain informative regardless, at the least for reflecting the underlying presumptions of professional discourses. There are more

nuanced works on the correlation between abuse and ADHD diagnoses (Alizadeh et al. 2007) and on child maltreatment in schools in Kurdistan Iran (Stephenson et al. 2006), though both gloss on sociocultural and biomedical parenting models. Publications from Ruzbeh Hospital have also focused on genetic studies (Ohadi et al. 2006), while other studies have examined symptom distribution (Ghanizadeh et al. 2008; Soltanifar et al. 2009).

3. I chose to exclude Shirin from any ADHD-related interviews, as I consider the grounds of consent and autonomy for children in relation to psychiatric diagnoses gray zones. All names are pseudonyms; I have altered and added details from other families to protect the identities of all involved.

4. The social science literature on medicalization is, in part, fueled by debates on ADHD. Conrad was among earlier critics of the medicalization of hyperkinesia and deviant behavior among children (Conrad 1975; Conrad and Potter 2000), pointing to depoliticizing and individualizing aspects of medical social control. As in Iran (albeit a decade earlier), ADHD was consolidated as a legitimate and popular diagnosis in the United States by the 1990s, relying on a medical-expert discourse led by clinicians whose readership extended from doctors to the public. Unlike Iran (thus far), debates around soaring rates of medication are loud there: a 500 percent increase in use of Ritalin over a five-year period was brought to public attention in Diller's article "The Run on Ritalin" (Diller 1996), and confirmed by DEA statistics that cite an eightfold increase in the use of methylphenidate between 1990 and 1998 (Breggin 2001: 13) and Department of Justice statistics reporting a 170 percent increase in the number of medicated children between five and fourteen years of age over the course of fifteen years ("Attention Deficit/Hyperactivity Disorder—Are We Overmedicating Our Children?" page 86, Hearing before the Committee on Government Reform, House of Representatives, 107th Congress Second Session, September 26, 2002: https://www.gpo.gov/fdsys/pkg/CHRG-107hhrg83516/pdf/CHRG-107hhrg83516.pdf). Peter Breggin, the author of Talking Back to Ritalin (2001), is among clinicians who have testified at anti-Ritalin hearings, and publicly argued that the drug "crushes a child's desire to socialize, to play, to escape, to be full of stuff like kids are" (Breggin, May 3, 2000, Interview with PBS, Frontline: http://www.pbs.org/wgbh/pages/frontline/shows/medicating/interviews/breggin.html).

5. Now the most commonly diagnosed mental disorder among American children (Mayes et al. 2008), ADHD is not a novelty. The earliest "modern" descriptions were proposed in 1902, largely framed in a language of moral control over behavior (Stubbe 2000). In the 1960s, the DSM and ICD suggested the title "hyperkinetic reaction of childhood" and indicated that "the behavior usually diminishes in adolescence" (American Psychiatric Association 1968: 50). Conceptualizations of the condition's etiologies, treatment options, and explanatory models have changed over time (Conrad and Potter 2000; Lakoff 2000). The most dire debates today are around the safety, efficacy, and developmental implications of medication for children (Neufeld and Foy 2006; Stubbe 2000; Timimi 2004). By the time of the DSM-IV, ADHD had gone from a "behavioral" to a "neurological" disorder (American Psychiatric Association 1994).

6. See American Psychiatric Association 1994 for the diagnostic criteria of ADHD, according to which Criterion C is met when "some impairment from the symptoms is

present in two or more settings (e.g., at school [or work] and at home)," and Criterion D indicates that for a diagnosis of ADHD, "there must be clear evidence of clinically significant impairment in social, academic or occupational functioning."

7. Child-rearing is a key theme in Iranian literary and epic traditions. One can mention *Kalileh va Demneh* (originally produced ca. 600 BC in India; followed by the Persian text by Abol Ma'ali Nasrollah Monshi in 1143 AD) as well as *Qabous Nameh* (ca. 1080 AD, by the Prince of Gurgan), literary works that have long been practical references for kings, princes, and politicians of ancient Iran and continue to shape the cultural imagination of contemporary literature. For an overview of the literary context of modern psychology in Iran, see Ayman 1992.

8. Despite clinical evidence that anxiety disorders are common, they are often considered secondary in medical publications; e.g., one study identifies anxiety disorders as the most common comorbid disorder with ADHD (Soltanifar et al. 2009).

9. American Academy of Pediatrics 1996: under "*DSM-PC*: Developmental Variation: Impulsive/Hyperactive Behaviors," see table 2. The creation of the *Diagnostic and Statistical Manual for Primary Care* (*DSM-PC*) was a response to practitioners' concern with the lack of "clear empirical data supporting the number of items required for the diagnosis" and the fact that "current criteria do not take into account gender differences or developmental variations in behavior. Furthermore, the behavioral characteristics specified in the *DSM-IV*, despite efforts to standardize them, remain subjective and may be interpreted differently by different observers" (American Academy of Pediatrics, Committee on Quality Improvement and Subcommittee on Attention-Deficit/Hyperactivity Disorder 2000: 1163). For further information on the *DSM-PC*, see American Academy of Pediatrics, Committee on Quality Improvement and Subcommittee on Attention-Deficit/ Hyperactivity Disorder 2000.

10. Parents' take on the creativity of ADHD children is ambivalent. Many parents like Leila embrace the creativity they recognize in their ADHD child though such tolerance is not equally present in classroom or family settings, in public, and in places where "behaving well" takes precedence over creativity.

11. See Rose 1990 and 1996 for a twentieth-century Foucauldian genealogy of human technologies resulting in a therapeutic culture of the self. Foucauldian critiques of modes of self-governance are partially useful in accounting for the Iranian psychiatric turn, but fail to fully explain historically and psychologically situated desires for psychiatric identification among the young.

12. In the United States, Rafalovich (2004) took up a Foucauldian textual analysis of the ideological representations of ADHD that targeted parents of ADHD children and illustrated that these knowledge-based texts legitimized particular ideologies for the formation of domestic discipline.

13. See Chapter 1, note 19 on *double binds*, and note 32 on *transference*.

14. Taraghi 1994: 115. Although hers is a description of the early 1980s experience of an upper-class family, Taraghi's description serves to capture the psychological sense of disjoint that many members of *nasl-e sukhteh* report when discussing their teens: "Like the end of an era; the closing of a door and the beginning of something new, something unfa-

miliar and unknown. We couldn't grasp the logic of events. Like a ravaging tribe, history was taking away our old habits and memories. We were perplexed; the pieces of the puzzle were all misplaced" (Taraghi 1994: 115).

15. See Das 2000.

16. This is a reference to an episode of the iconic television documentary series *Chronicles of Victory* (*Ravāyat-e Fath*), made for television by Morteza Avini (1947–1993) and screened during and after the Iran-Iraq War (1980–1988). Himself a renowned photographer, writer, filmmaker, and veteran of the Iran-Iraq War, Avini was killed on April 9, 1993, by an Iraqi-deployed landmine while filming a documentary about missing soldiers of the Iran-Iraq War. For more details, see Karimabadi 2011; also the forthcoming doctoral dissertation by Narges Bajoghli 2016, as well as Sohrabi 1995; Varzi 2006; and Naficy 2006 and 2009.

17. For a filmic ethnographic investigation into the lives of disabled veterans and their health conditions, see Bajoghli's documentary *The Skin That Burns* (Bajoghli 2012).

18. For examples on the long-term mental health effects of chemical injuries, see S. M. Razavi et al. 2014; Ebadi et al. 2009; Ebadi et al. 2014; and Roshan et al. 2013. On long-term health conditions, diminished quality of life, and chronic chemical injuries, see Khateri et al. 2003; Falahati et al. 2010; Khateri and Bajoghli 2015; Ebadi et al. 2009; Ghanei et al. 2005; Hashemian et al. 2006; Karami et al. 2013. For studies on the impact of veterans' experiences on their children and spouses, see S. H. Razavi et al. 2012; Taghva et al. 2014; and Yousefi and Sharif 2010. For the psychological impact of the War of Cities on children and adults, see Rahimi 2010. For a detailed report on the health-related consequences of the Iran-Iraq War, see the Health Impact Assessment Report compiled by Medact (2014): http://www.medact.org/wp-content/uploads/2014/06/Health-Impact-Assessment-Word-Website-+-MB.pdf.

19. See http://basijpress.ir/fa/news-details/41691/ (17/10/1393 AP—07/01/2015).

20. Bajoghli 2012.

21. Makhmalbaf 1989.

22. Iran-Iraq War veterans manifested many shell-shock symptoms similar to those of the traumatic neuroses of World War I that caused Freud and W. H. R. Rivers to focus on the survival mechanisms of the body, feeling states of helplessness in sleep, and screaming as a function of life-and-death matters.

23. The politicization of aesthetics, in Walter Benjamin's terms, calls for appreciation of the shock effect of new media, art, and visual productions and the ways they might reawaken us to past utopias. Like dialectical images, they revive our utopian dreams and create new sensations in the nervous system (Buck-Morss 1991). Michael Fischer extended this notion in his analysis of Iranian cinema, pointing to the ways film can engage new modes of perception, judgments, and ethics, thereby creating an element of self-reflexivity (2004). Iranian cinema, he argued, uses historical poesies and a prevailing philosophical sense of tragedy as platforms on which competing ideologies and rhetoric create and negotiate meaning. Fischer also underscored the intertextuality of this filmic discourse, as evident in *Marriage of the Blessed*, describing its style as post-traumatic realism, in which traces of master narratives (Shi'ism, epic literature, Sufism, poetry, etc.) are

at play. This cinema, he maintained, created a discourse about the role of cinema in the public sphere and ethical debates. The Sacred Defense genre of Iranian cinema builds on these discourses, while also underscoring the challenges of reintegration into society. The intricacies of incommunicability, for example, are beautifully explored in Ebrahim Hatamikia's *From Karkheh to the Rhine* (1992) and *The Glass Agency* (1998). For more detailed cultural analysis of Iranian cinema and of its genre of Sacred Defense, see Fischer 2004; Dabashi 2001, 2007; Mottahedeh 2008; Naficy 2012, 2006.

24. Among cinematic depictions of the experience of PTSD, Talebi's film *Empty Hands (Dast-hā-ye Khāli)* (Talebi 2006) best thematizes the psychological symptoms and alienation of the veteran who struggles to communicate with and be understood by others. Each time the POW/veteran protagonist hears the *daf* (a large tambourine-like instrument), a phone ringing, or fireworks, or even sees dying fish, he starts fighting, miming holding a machine gun, shouting for people to hit the ground. Talebi uses music as an entry point: the music in a taxi, in a store, any rhythm graduating into that of the battlefield, culminating in explosions. There is a very thin line between most of the music we hear in the movie and the music in the war scenes and on the battlefield. The film's catacoustics are not limited to wartime and reflect the complex layering of survival strategies and blocked communications in resonances of words, puns, silences, repressions, and paradoxes. This is also depicted in several other films such as Jafar Panahi's *Crimson Gold* (Panahi 2003).

25. "Film," wrote Fischer, "again, is not a direct mirror not only because the metaphor is inherently generative—at minimum, mirrors reverse left and right; at an angle, they create varied refractions and perspectives" (Fischer 2004: 368).

26. The liminal space(s) of life and experiences of directors such as Mohsen Makhmalbaf and Ebrahim Hatamikia, for example, reflect all these pieces.

27. Fasih 1987. Much like the author, who lived in the United States during the 1960s and 1970s, the secular protagonist of the novel returned to Iran and sought redemption in sacrificing himself for a collective cause. Also see Mohsen Makhmalbaf's *Glass Garden (Bāgh-e Bolur)* (Makhmalbaf 1986), which was among the earlier novels that threw a spotlight on the ordinary struggles of veterans and their families.

28. Mortezaeian-Abkenar 2006. The will to survive is the novel's central premise, reflecting a young man's naked desire to live, "to just live." For the protagonist, "life was a massive misunderstanding"; the scattered voice of the narrator confronts readers with the absurd. The author's stylistic choices, his stream of consciousness mixed with chaotic eventualities, reflects the ways in which the latter days of the war infused the chaotic exhaustion of the armed forces into soldiers'—and perhaps civilians'—minds. But style aside, the energy of the content is what conveys a sense of angst.

29. Among plots in which Iranian soldiers interact with Iraqi prisoners of war, eventually extracting the continuities and the breakages of kinship before and after the war, *Night Bus* (Poorahmad 2007) by Kiumars Poorahmad was the first film set on an Iranian bus carrying Iraqi POWs and a compelling juxtaposition of Iraqi and Iranian reflections on the war. Authors such as Ghobad Ayeen Azar, Mohammad Bokaei, and Ahmad Dehghan have followed similar threads in their novels of the 2000s. For a comparative analysis of

the Iran-Iraq War literature (on both sides), see Moosavi 2015. For more on contemporary fiction and its features, see Khorrami and Shirazi 2008; and Ghanoonparvar 2009.

30. One of the most famous voices of the war was that of vocalist Kuwaitipour, known for his charged recitations during the war and on nights when an *amaliyāt* (military strike) was to be launched. He famously sang "Chang-e del" ("The Heart's Harmonica"), which, opening with "my heart's harmonica is playing the song of flames; it is the song of love and it burns all," continues to circulate in the media today. The song captures poetry in the *masnavi* (rhyming couplets) form. Mystical in content and performed in the singing style of religious *nouheh* (slow, rhythmic mourning chant), it has now been revived and recycled online by *daheh-ye shasti-hā* as a nostalgic generational marker and token of appreciation for the sacrifices of those who fought in the war. For the older generation, the generation of veterans, from religious to secular, the emotional reaction is diverse but extremely visceral.

31. This manifests in a thematic of marginality in the thriving genre of women's literature, or *adabiyāt-e zanān* (Gheytanchi 2007). Also on the genre of women's literature, see Khorrami and Vatanabadi 2000.

32. Rahimieh has illustrated the creation of a new discursive domain and a new space by female authors and filmmakers that, contesting self-Orientalizing trends, underscores the centrality of women in Iranian filmic and literary productions (Rahimieh 2003).

33. The turn away from metanarratives and toward the micro-ordinary is also reflected in the popularity of similar works of translation in the 1990s and of authors such as novelist Alba de Céspedes (1911–1997), who exposed the secret desires of ordinary women in post–World War II Italy, in, e.g., *Forbidden Diary* (*Quaderno Proibito*, 1952) (De Céspedes 2000), translated into Persian by Bahman Farzaneh. This turn toward the ordinary also exists in Iranian cinematic depictions, particularly those explicitly focusing on fractured subjectivities and the spectrums of traditional-modern selfhood, and include, but are not limited to, Nikki Karimi's *One Night* (Karimi 2005), and Asghar Farhadi's *A Separation* (Farhadi 2011) and *About Elly* (Farhadi 2009).

34. Today's children are not completely distanced from memories of the Iran-Iraq War; not only do they inherit them from their parents, but the legacy of the war remains present in urban settings and commemorative practices, in images of martyrs in murals, streets named after martyrs, the recirculation of war images and music in the media, and new recirculation of wartime cultural work by younger generations and artists.

35. By definition, ADHD and its behavioral symptoms are culturally constructed. Singh (2004), for example, has juxtaposed the ethical implications of regimes of measurement in the United States that determine "good motherhood" against biomedical and local narratives of illness that locate agency in the brain, to show how these narratives displace the locus of responsibility. Moreover, she has argued, cultural formulations of success and a masculine model of the self-reliant American boy shaped the ways in which behavior was understood (Singh 2005).

36. See notes 4 and 5.

37. Lewis 2011; Halpern and Lewis 2013; Charon 2001, 2006. Also see Behrouzan 2015c for a conversation between anthropology and narrative psychiatry.

38. Lewis 2011.

39. Elsewhere, in a cultural critique of narrative psychiatry, I have provided the parallel example of a member of the 1980s generation who perceives her psychiatric diagnosis and her generational experience as related to the experience of her war-veteran father and her own childhood memories of the war. Like Leila, she mobilizes an illness narrative as a means to generational and historical differentiation, albeit with generational sensibilities that are distinct from Leila's (Behrouzan 2015c).

40. In other words, Leila legitimizes her assimilation of psychiatry's responsibilization discourse (Rose 1996, 2006a) or discourses of human agency (Garro 2010) by foregrounding her generational sensibilities and her perceptions of a ruptured selfhood.

CHAPTER 7

1. This situatedness of practice is conducive to a cultural critique, in the sense explained by Fischer in his *Emergent Forms of Life*: a critique of categories via interdisciplinary conversations across localities and temporalities. In emerging life worlds, he argues, the task of anthropology is to introduce new forms of ethnographic voice that not only acknowledge difference, but also realize that interactions of various cultures have become more complex with globalization. New ethical dilemmas and challenges would thus follow, necessitating new pedagogies and modes of legitimation (Fischer 2003).

2. See Chapter 2.

3. On the biomedical "coup" in the United States, see Kirk and Kutchins 1992. On the 1960s–1970s anti-psychiatry movement in the United States and UK, see Szasz 1961; and Laing 1965. On the anti-institutional movement in French psychiatry, see Deleuze and Guattari 2004; and Fanon 1963.

4. Mysticism, of course, can be world denying and isolating, but it can also provide us with worldly tools of autonomy and an ability to step outside immediate contexts to reflect critically upon them. Patterns such as a putative Rostam complex, for example, can be speculative tools to explore charged emotions of unexamined patriarchal worlds. See the discussion of such models in Chapter 2.

5. Fischer 2007a.

6. This chapter is deeply informed by extended interviews with psychiatrists of both biomedical and psychodynamic orientations, as well as discussions with interns and residents.

7. On psychopharmaceutical intervention, see Healy 1997. On the controversy surrounding overmedication of children, see Timimi 2004; Timimi et al. 2001; Healy 2006; and Healy and Le Noury 2007. On psychiatry's relationship with institutions, see Goffman 1961; Grob 1991; and Scull 1991. On critiques of psychiatrization, see note 27 in Chapter 4.

8. On the role of pharmaceutical companies in transforming psychiatric diagnoses and treatment, see Dumit 2012; Healy 1997; and Horwitz and Wakefield 2007. On the ideologies of self-fashioning through psychiatric medication, see Greenslit 2007; and Dumit 2003.

9. Now in its fifth edition, the *Diagnostic and Statistical Manual* is constructed around the two principles of specificity and reliability. While the first and second revisions of the *DSM* were largely influenced by Freudian psychoanalysis that was etiological and dynamic, *DSM-III* (1980) was inspired by the "descriptive" formulations of German psychia-

trist Emil Kraepelin (1856–1926). *DSM-III* became a milestone establishing biomedical psychiatry, via claims to scientific-ness, and not surprisingly, following the advent of psychopharmaceuticals in the 1950s. Kirk and Kutchins, in *The Selling of DSM* (1992), described this transformation of diagnosis from a conceptual and "practical" problem to a "technical" one as a coup and argued that the emphasis on "diagnostic reliability" was symbolic of psychiatry's self-doubt and marginality in medicine in the 1960s. Later, the debates following *DSM-IV* (1994) regarding medicalization of behavior, positivist claims over treatment, and strategic avoidance of etiology led to the publication of a revision of *DSM-IV*, called *DSM-IV-TR* (2000), which aimed to fill the gaps with empirical literature. The publication of *DSM-V* in 2013 created further heated debates around overmedicalization of life conditions and the influence of the pharmaceutical industry on *DSM* revisions. The NIMH even stated that it would design its own classification system. While in the United States the *DSM* serves the practical purpose of determining insurance coverage, in Iran it remains a rough diagnostic tool.

10. Healy 1997: 5. Extremists of the 1970s anti-psychiatry movement went as far as denying the reality of mental illness altogether (Szasz 1961, 1997).

11. Singh 2002, 2004; Rose 2006a, 1990, 1996.

12. There are few valuable ethnographies that have engaged with the experiences of psychiatry residents in wards and emergency rooms in the United States, including Luhrmann 2001 and Rhodes 1995.

13. The term "falsifiability," often uttered in English, circulates among many psychiatrists I talked to without serious engagement with philosopher Karl Popper, who defined the falsifiability of a hypothesis as a requirement for its being scientific. See Popper 2005 [1959].

14. Interview with child psychiatrist Javad Alāghband-Rād, Halifax NS, 2008.

15. Ibid.

16. The final common pathway model is a key hypothesis in biopsychiatry and neuropsychiatry, indicating that mental illnesses may be caused by flaws in brain synapses and the disruption of brain cells' functions, which can inhibit neuroplasticity and kill brain cells. Advocates and critics continue to debate the evidence for and the therapeutic promises of the hypothesis. For more on the neurobiology of the process, see Duman 2004. Also, on the growth of neuroscience in Iran see note 24 in Chapter 3.

17. Interview with child psychiatrist Javad Alāghband-Rād, Halifax NS, 2008.

18. Ibid.

19. Ibid.

20. Interview with Mohammad Sanati, London, September 2009.

21. Sanati 2001 and 2004. On *Shāhnāmeh*, see notes 8 and 40 in Chapter 2.

22. Interview with Mohammad Sanati, London, September 2009. On PANA, see note 2 in Chapter 2.

23. Ibid. Also see Good 1977.

24. Luhrmann 2001.

25. The dynamic psychotherapy program in Ruzbeh (underway since 1998 and added to the national curriculum's Requirements and Objectives in 2008) was primarily dependent on a few instructors, chief among them Mohammad Sanati and Mahdieh Moin.

However, the team has grown and the program also has benefitted from the teachings of non-Ruzbeh-affiliated psychiatrists as well. Although only a handful of attending psychiatrists are in charge of teaching dynamic therapy with an object-relation theoretical framework, training for CBT too has been consolidated. The challenge is that these training schemes are individual dependent, meaning that if one of them leaves, the scheme will struggle (as was the case with CBT training, where, during a hiatus between 2005 and 2009, residents reportedly sought training in private practices). Despite these struggles, between the two elective options, CBT is reported to have been more in demand, while dynamic psychotherapy enjoys a more detailed and advanced training that is followed by a three-month practicum. CBT is taught in the Department of Clinical Psychology at Ruzbeh, while dynamic psychotherapy is taught in Ruzbeh's Psychotherapy Unit. The latter program covers an inclusive overview of psychoanalysis, from Freud to Lacan to Melanie Klein and others, while more weight is given to an object-relation orientation. It includes a section of courses and practical training on child psychotherapy, where emphasis is on parenting, communication skills, and therapy for parents. See note 71 in Chapter 2.

26. The 1980s integration of mental health into the Primary Health Care plans (see Chapter 2) at the Ministry of Health resulted in a resounding success in rural areas, while primary mental health care struggled in cities. To tackle this problem, a community psychiatry track was designed by a committee of experts and led by the Tehran Institute of Psychiatry. The program is now required as a rotation during residency with proposed pilot studies for home visits, day centers, community health centers, and schools.

27. This context also differentiates them from other cases of ideological contestations such as those between Lacanian psychoanalysts and biological psychiatrists in Buenos Aires (e.g., in Lakoff's ethnography [(2005)]). Other non-Western settings too provide interesting parallels. In her *Depression in Japan*, for instance, Kitanaka (2012) illustrated Japanese psychiatry's unique features as both influenced by Western developments, and yet as institutionally, intellectually, and culturally reconfigured because the neurological trends of academic psychiatry remained unchallenged by American psychologism of the 1950s.

28. Larger debates are also ongoing outside of the medical establishment and often generate new openings. For example, discussion about the formation of customized Islamic renditions of psychotherapy are underway; and the usage of the term Islamic psychotherapy (*ravāndarmāni-ye eslāmi*) reflects reconciling attempts and possibilities for situated practice.

29. This is a reference to Kramer's *Listening to Prozac*, where he argued in favor of using antidepressants for their enhancement capacities and popularized the phrase "better than well" used by his patients to describe the effects of Prozac on them (Kramer 1993).

30. Lakoff 2005; Luhrmann 2001.

31. See Rose 1992, 1996, and 2006a; and Davis 2012. This scholarship maintains that psychiatry's neoliberal discourses have focused on individual responsibility for the self, which requires what Rose has called an active biological citizenship, where "an active citizenship is increasingly enacted, in which individuals themselves are taking a dynamic role in enhancing their own scientific, especially biomedical, literacy" (2006a: 141). This active

citizenship becomes possible through a discourse of responsibilization and "the instilling of a reflexive hermeneutics that will afford self-knowledge and self-mastery" (Rose 1992: 149). Comparatively speaking, Iranian psychiatry's normative tendencies share their rooting in the pedagogical ontologies of modern psychiatry's formulations in the West. But these characterizations are hardly uniform and each setting provides its own culturally defined grounds for negotiation. Elizabeth Davis has argued that in Greek psychiatry, for instance, these responsibility-centered discourses are situated in the placement of therapists in "a shaky ground between ethical guidance and coercion," leading to suspicions of deception, where "these suspicions mark a limit of collaborative responsibility in therapeutic relationships" between patients and practitioners (Davis 2012: 14 and 110). Unlike in Greece, in Iran the discourse of a responsible psychiatric practice is less influenced by suspicions of deception, perhaps reflecting the cultural significations of the doctor-patient relationship and its implications in larger societal terms.

32. Faubion 2011: 49, quoting Foucault.

33. See Faubion 2011; Davis 2012.

34. These entries belong to the years between 2009 and 2010, and were last accessed in 2012.

CONCLUSION

1. "Revisiting Iraq through the Eyes of an Exiled Poet: Interview with Dunya Mikhail," Special Series: Poetry, National Public Radio (NPR): http://www.npr.org/2013/03/21/17477 3962/revisiting-iraq-through-the-eyes-of-an-exiled-poet.

2. I have elaborated on the themes of this section elsewhere in the introduction to the special section "Beyond 'Trauma': Notes on Mental Health in the Middle East" in the journal *Medicine Anthropology Theory* (Behrouzan 2015b).

3. Morsy 1981.

4. Kirmayer has argued that "the future of cultural psychiatry lies in advancing a broad perspective that: (a) is inherently multidisciplinary . . . ; (b) attends to psychological processes but understands these as not exclusively located within the individual but as including discursive processes that are fundamentally social; and (c) critically examines the interaction of both local and global systems of knowledge and power" (Kirmayer 2006: 126).

5. Illness experiences are shaped by the local processes of moral and historical construction and by local biological processes. The concept of local biology, anthropologist Margaret Lock has written, explains how "the coproduction of biologies and cultures contributes to embodied experience, which, in turn, shapes discourse about the body" (Lock 2001: 478). Also see Lock 2002, 1993; and Cohen 2000.

6. The untranslatability of imported terminologies, concepts, categories, theoretical frameworks, and conceptual tools (e.g., *DSM*) is also reflected in other domains of subjectivity-work. In shifting the focus from epidemiologically surveying the given-ness of depression, I follow Najmabadi in asking "what borrowing, appropriation, and embracing means for the importers" (Najmabadi 2014: 9). Najmabadi has persuasively demonstrated the situatedness of imported Western conceptual and theoretical frameworks in her

ethnographic analysis of transsexual selfhood in Iran: while contributing to the formation of transsexual selves, these imported constructs remain untranslatable and situated in their own long historical trajectories.

7. See, for example, an epidemiological study of quality of life among PTSD patients (Kalafee and Adib 2000) in which "sixty-five outpatients with full PTSD, 93 with partial PTSD and 78 war veterans without PTSD" were interviewed using "Structured Clinical Interview for *DSM-IV* (SCID)" and a "standardized Quality of Life Index" taken from American models. While these studies have merit, I aim to draw attention to the construction of their language and to the direct and uncritical adoption of standardized models (that are designed and evaluated elsewhere) in local practice and research.

8. See Good 1977; Good et al. 1986; El Shakry 2014; Sanal 2011; Pandolfo 1998; Hamdy 2012; Dewachi et al. 2012, 2014; Dewachi 2013; Kienzler 2008; Atshan 2013; Giacaman et al. 2011; Giacaman and Zayt 2004; Giacaman et al. 2005; Wick 2008, 2011; Olszewska 2015a; Parkinson and Behrouzan 2015; as well as the Dewachi 2015; Olszewska 2015b; Kienzler and Amro 2015, in the special section "Beyond 'Trauma': Notes on Mental Health in the Middle East" in the journal *Medicine Anthropology Theory* (2015).

9. Karami 2015.

10. As this book goes to press, steps are being taken toward the lifting of international sanctions (with the implementation of the first stages of a Joint Comprehensive Plan of Action, known in the West as the Iran Deal); the psychological impact is already palpable as young Iranians find hope in the prospect of new beginnings, of a new moment of recognition, and of the possibility for psychological working through and reconciliation.

References

Abrahamian, Ervand. 1982a. *Iran Between Two Revolutions*. Princeton, NJ: Princeton University Press.

———. 1982b. "'Ali Shari'ati: Ideologue of the Iranian Revolution." *MERIP Reports*, no. 102 (January): 24–28. doi: 10.2307/3010795.

Adams, Vincanne. 2013. "Evidence-Based Global Public Health." In *When People Come First*, edited by João Biehl and Adriana Petryna, 54–90. Princeton, NJ: Princeton University Press.

Adelkhah, Fariba. 1999. *Being Modern in Iran*. London: Hurst & Company.

Adorno, Theodor. 1977. "The Actuality of Philosophy." *Telos* 31: 120–33. doi: 10.3817/0377 031120.

Afary, Janet. 2009. *Sexual Politics in Modern Iran*. Cambridge: Cambridge University Press.

Afary, Janet, and Kevin B. Anderson. 2010. *Foucault and the Iranian Revolution: Gender and the Seductions of Islamism*. Chicago: University of Chicago Press.

Aghaie, Kamran Scot. 2004. *The Martyrs of Karbala: Shi'i Symbols and Rituals in Modern Iran*. Seattle: University of Washington Press.

Ahmadi, Alireza. 2007. "Suicide by Self-Immolation: Comprehensive Overview, Experiences and Suggestions." *Journal of Burn Care & Research?: Official Publication of the American Burn Association* 28 (1): 30–41.

Akhavan, Niki. 2013. *Electronic Iran: The Cultural Politics of an Online Evolution*. New Brunswick, NJ: Rutgers University Press.

Alexander, Jeffrey C., Ron Eyerman, Bernard Giesen, Neil J. Smelser, and Piotr Sztompka. 2004. *Cultural Trauma and Collective Identity*. Berkeley: University of California Press.

Ali, Javed. 2001. "Chemical Weapons and the Iran-Iraq War: A Case Study in Noncompliance." *Nonproliferation Review* 8 (1): 43–58.

Alipour, Ahmad. 2006. "Teaching Undergraduate Psychology in the Islamic Republic of Iran." *International Journal of Psychology* 41 (1): 35–41. doi: 10.1080/00207590444000447.

Alizadeh, Hamid, Kimberly F. Applequist, and Frederick L. Coolidge. 2007. "Parental Self-Confidence, Parenting Styles, and Corporal Punishment in Families of ADHD Children in Iran." *Child Abuse & Neglect* 31 (5): 567–72. doi: 10.1016/j.chiabu.2006.12.005.

American Academy of Pediatrics. 1996. *The Classification of Child and Adolescent Mental Diagnoses in Primary Care: Diagnostic and Statistical Manual for Primary Care (DSM-PC) Child and Adolescent Version*. Elk Grove Village, IL: American Academy of Pediatrics.

American Academy of Pediatrics, Committee on Quality Improvement and Subcommittee on Attention-Deficit/Hyperactivity Disorder. 2000. "Clinical Practice Guideline: Diagnosis and Evaluation of the Child with Attention-Deficit/Hyperactivity Disorder." *Pediatrics* 105: 1158–70.

American Psychiatric Association. 1968. *Diagnostic and Statistical Manual of Mental Disorders*. DSM Library. American Psychiatric Association. doi: abs/10.1176/appi.books .9780890420355.dsm-ii.

———. 1994. *Diagnostic and Statistical Manual of Mental Disorders: DSM-IV*. 4th ed. Washington, D.C.: American Psychiatric Association.

Amirani, Amir, dir. "BBC Newsnight: *Zardeh*." 2005. https://vimeo.com/36969133.

Anderson, Benedict R. 1991. *Imagined Communities: Reflections on the Origin and Spread of Nationalism*. London: Verso.

Andrews, Gavin, Tim Slade, and Lorna Peters. 1999. "Classification in psychiatry: ICD-10 versus DSM-IV." *The British Journal of Psychiatry* 174: 3–5.

Arabgol, Fariba, Leily Panaghi, and Paria Hebrani. 2009. "Reboxetine versus Methylphenidate in Treatment of Children and Adolescents with Attention Deficit-Hyperactivity Disorder." *European Child & Adolescent Psychiatry* 18 (1): 53–59. doi: 10.1007/s00787-008-0705-9.

Atshan, Sa'ed Adel. 2013. "Prolonged Humanitarianism: The Social Life of Aid in the Palestinian Territories." Ph.D. dissertation, Harvard University. http://dash.harvard.edu/ handle/1/11169795.

Avicenna. 1989 [1025]. *Ghānun (Al-Qanun fi al-Tibb)* (Canon of Medicine). Vol. 3, part 3. (Original in Arabic.) Translated from Arabic into Persian by Abdul Rahman Sharafkandi. Tehran: Soroush.

Ayman, Iraj. 1992. "Iran." In *International Psychology: Views from Around the World*, edited by Virginia Staudt Sexton and John D. Hogan, 220–28. Lincoln: University of Nebraska Press.

Azizi, F. 1997. "The Reform of Medical Education in Iran." *Medical Education* 31 (3): 159–62.

Bahramitash, Roksana, and Hadi Salehi Esfahani. 2011. *Veiled Employment: Islamism and the Political Economy of Women's Employment in Iran*. Syracuse, NY: Syracuse University Press.

Bajoghli, Narges, dir. 2012. *The Skin That Burns*. Documentary film. New York: Film Media Group.

———. 2016. "Paramilitary Media: Revolution, War, and the Making of the Islamic Republic of Iran." Ph.D. dissertation, New York University.

Balaghi, Shiva, and Lynn Gumpert, eds. 2002. *Picturing Iran: Art, Society and Revolution*. London: I.B. Tauris.

Barnouw, Dagmar. 1994. *Critical Realism: History, Photography, and the Work of Siegfried Kracauer*. Baltimore: Johns Hopkins University Press.

Barzin, Nader. 2010. "La psychanalyse en Iran." *Topique* 1: 157–71.

Bateson, Gregory, Don D. Jackson, Jay Haley, and John Weakland. 1956. "Toward a Theory of Schizophrenia." *Behavioral Science* 1 (4): 251–64. doi: 10.1002/bs.3830010402.

Bateson, Mary Catherine. 1979. "'This Figure of Tinsel': A Study of Themes of Hypocrisy and Pessimism in Iranian Culture." *Daedalus* 108 (3): 125–34.

Bateson, Mary Catherine, J. W. Clinton, J. B. M. Kassarjian, H. Safavi, and M. Soraya. 1977. "Safā-Yi Bātin. A Study of the Interrelations of a Set of Iranian Ideal Character Types." In *Psychological Dimensions of Near Eastern Studies*, edited by L. Carl Brown and Norman Itzkowitz. Princeton, NJ: Darwin Press.

Bayat, Asef. 1997. *Street Politics: Poor People's Movements in Iran*. New York: Columbia University Press.

———. 2010. *Life as Politics: How Ordinary People Change the Middle East*. Stanford, CA: Stanford University Press.

Beck, A. T., C. H. Ward, M. Mendelson, J. Mock, and J. Erbaugh. 1961. "An Inventory for Measuring Depression." *Archives of General Psychiatry* 4 (6): 561–71. doi: 10.1001/archpsyc.1961.01710120031004.

Beeman, William O. 1985. "Dimensions of Dysphoria: The View from Linguistic Anthropology." In *Culture and Depression: Studies in the Anthropology and Cross-Cultural Psychiatry of Affect and Disorder*, edited by Arthur Kleinman and Byron J. Good, 216–43. Berkeley: University of California Press.

———. 1988. "Affectivity in Persian Language Use." *Culture, Medicine and Psychiatry* 12 (1): 9–30.

———. 2001. "Emotion and Sincerity in Persian Discourse: Accomplishing the Representation of Inner States." *International Journal of the Sociology of Language* 108: 31–58.

Behrouzan, Orkideh. 2010. "An Epidemic of Meanings: HIV and AIDS in Iran and the Significance of History, Language and Gender." In *The Fourth Wave: Violence, Gender, Culture & HIV in the 21st Century*, edited by Jennifer F. Klot and Vinh-Kim Nguyen, 319–45. Paris: UNESCO.

———. 2015a. "Writing *Prozāk* Diaries in Tehran: Generational Anomie and Psychiatric Subjectivities." *Culture, Medicine and Psychiatry* 39 (3): 399–426.

———. 2015b. "Beyond 'Trauma': Notes on Mental Health in the Middle East." Special Section: Beyond "Trauma." *Medicine Anthropology Theory* 2 (3): 1–6.

———. 2015c. "Medicalization as a Way of Life: The Iran-Iraq War and Considerations for Psychiatry and Anthropology." Special Section: Beyond "Trauma." *Medicine Anthropology Theory* 2 (3): 40–60.

Behzadi, K. G. 1994. "Interpersonal Conflict and Emotions in an Iranian Cultural Practice: Qahr and Ashti." *Culture, Medicine and Psychiatry* 18 (3): 321–59.

Belting, Hans. 2011. *An Anthropology of Images: Picture, Medium, Body*. Translated by Thomas Dunlap. Princeton, NJ: Princeton University Press.

Bergstein, Mary. 2010. *Mirrors of Memory: Freud, Photography, and the History of Art*. Ithaca, NY: Cornell University Press.

Berlant, Lauren. 2007. "Slow Death (Sovereignty, Obesity, Lateral Agency)." *Critical Inquiry* 33 (4): 754–80.

Biehl, João. 2005. *Vita: Life in a Zone of Social Abandonment*. Berkeley: University of California Press.

Biehl, João, and Torben Eskerod. 2007. *Will to Live: AIDS Therapies and the Politics of Survival*. Princeton, NJ: Princeton University Press.

Biehl, João, Byron Good, and Arthur Kleinman, eds. 2007. *Subjectivity: Ethnographic Investigations*. Berkeley: University of California Press.

Biehl, João, and Peter Locke. 2010. "Deleuze and the Anthropology of Becoming." *Current Anthropology* 51 (3): 317–51. doi: 10.1086/648541.

Biehl, João, and Adriana Petryna. 2013. *When People Come First: Critical Studies in Global Health*. Princeton, NJ: Princeton University Press.

Birch, Marion, Ben Cave, Fatima Elmi, and Bianca Karpf. 2014. "Predicting the Unthinkable: Health Impact Assessment and Violent Conflict." *Medicine, Conflict and Survival* 30 (2): 81–90. doi: 10.1080/13623699.2014.896174.

Bolhari, Jafar, et al. 2012. "Evaluation of Mental Health Program Integration into Primary Health Care Systems of Iran." *Iranian Journal of Psychiatry and Clinical Psychology* 17 (4): 271–78 (in Persian).

Boroujerdi, Mehrzad. 1996. *Iranian Intellectuals and the West: The Tormented Triumph of Nativism*. Syracuse, NY: Syracuse University Press.

Bourdieu, Pierre. 1986. "The Forms of Capital." In *Handbook of Theory and Research for the Sociology of Education*, edited by John Richardson, translated by Richard Nice, 241–58. New York: Greenwood.

———. 1991. *Language and Symbolic Power*. Cambridge: Polity Press.

Bourgois, Philippe I. 2002. "Anthropology and Epidemiology on Drugs: The Challenges of Cross-Methodological and Theoretical Dialogue." *International Journal of Drug Policy* 13: 259–69.

———. 2003. *In Search of Respect: Selling Crack in El Barrio*. Cambridge: Cambridge University Press.

Bourgois, Philippe, and Julie Bruneau. 2000. "Needle Exchange, HIV Infection, and the Politics of Science: Confronting Canada's Cocaine Injection Epidemic with Participant Observation." *Medical Anthropology* 18 (4): 325–50.

Breggin, Peter R. 2001. *Talking Back to Ritalin: What Doctors Aren't Telling You about Stimulants and ADHD*. Cambridge, MA: Da Capo Press.

Buck-Morss, Susan. 1991. *The Dialectics of Seeing: Walter Benjamin and the Arcades Project*. Cambridge, MA: MIT Press.

Burton, Robert. 1927. *The Anatomy of Melancholy*. Reprint; original 1621. New York: Farrar & Rinehart.

Butler, Judith. 2006. *Precarious Life: The Powers of Mourning and Violence*. London: Verso.

Caruth, Cathy, ed. 1995. *Trauma: Explorations in Memory*. Baltimore: Johns Hopkins University Press.

———. 1996. *Unclaimed Experience: Trauma, Narrative, and History*. Baltimore: Johns Hopkins University Press.

Charon, Rita. 2001. "Narrative Medicine: A Model for Empathy, Reflection, Profession, and Trust." *Journal of the American Medical Association* 286 (15): 1897–1902. http://dx.doi.org/10.1001/jama.286.15.1897.

———. 2006. *Narrative Medicine?: Honoring the Stories of Illness*. New York: Oxford University Press.

Chehabi, Houchang E. 1990. *Iranian Politics and Religious Modernism: The Liberation Movement of Iran under the Shah and Khomeini*. London: I.B. Tauris.

Chehrāzi, Ebrāhim. 2003. *Khāterāt va Zendegināmeh-ye Doctor Ebrāhim Chehrāzi* (Dr. Chehrāzi: An Autobiography). Tehran: Nashr-e Nogol.

Clewell, Tammy. 2004. "Mourning Beyond Melancholia: Freud's Psychoanalysis of Loss." *Journal of the American Psychoanalytic Association* 52 (1): 43–67. doi: 10.1177/000306 51040520010601.

Clifford, James, and George E. Marcus. 1986. *Writing Culture: The Poetics and Politics of Ethnography?: A School of American Research Advanced Seminar*. Berkeley: University of California Press.

Cohen, Lawrence. 1999. "Where It Hurts: Indian Material for an Ethics of Organ Transplantation." *Daedalus* 128 (4): 135–65.

———. 2000. *No Aging in India: Alzheimer's, the Bad Family, and Other Modern Things*. Berkeley: University of California Press.

Comaroff, Jean. 1978. "Medicine and Culture: Some Anthropological Perspectives." *Social Science & Medicine. Part B: Medical Anthropology* 12: 247–54.

Comaroff, Jean, and John L. Comaroff. 2008. *Law and Disorder in the Postcolony*. Chicago: University of Chicago Press.

Comaroff, John L., and Jean Comaroff. 2001. "On Personhood: An Anthropological Perspective from Africa." *Social Identities* 7 (2): 267–83.

Conrad, Peter. 1975. "The Discovery of Hyperkinesis: Notes on the Medicalization of Deviant Behavior." *Social Problems* 23 (1): 12–21. doi: 10.2307/799624.

———. 1992. "Medicalization and Social Control." *Annual Review of Sociology* 18 (January): 209–32. doi: 10.1146/annurev.so.18.080192.001233.

———. 2007. *The Medicalization of Society: On the Transformation of Human Conditions into Treatable Disorders*. Baltimore: Johns Hopkins University Press.

Conrad, Peter, and Deborah Potter. 2000. "From Hyperactive Children to ADHD Adults: Observations on the Expansion of Medical Categories." *Social Problems* 47 (4): 559–82. doi: 10.2307/3097135.

Crapanzano, Vincent. 1980. *Tuhami: Portrait of a Moroccan*. Chicago: University of Chicago Press.

———. 1981. "Rite of Return: Circumcision in Morocco." In *The Psychoanalytic Study of Society*, vol. 9, edited by Werner Muensterberger and L. Bryce Boyer, 15–36. New York: Psychohistory Press.

Crosby, Kevin, Joong-Oh Rhee, and Jimmie Holland. 1977. "Suicide by Fire: A Contemporary Method of Political Protest." *International Journal of Social Psychiatry* 23 (1): 60–69. doi: 10.1177/002076407702300111.

Csordas, Thomas J. 1990. "Embodiment as a Paradigm for Anthropology." *Ethos* 18 (1): 5–47. doi: 10.1525/eth.1990.18.1.02a00010.

———. 2013. "Somatic Modes of Attention." *Cultural Anthropology* 8 (2): 135–56. doi: 10.1525/can.1993.8.2.02a00010.

Dabashi, Hamid. 2001. *Close Up: Iranian Cinema, Past, Present, and Future*. London: Verso.

———. 2007. *Masters & Masterpieces of Iranian Cinema*. Washington, D.C.: Mage Publishers.

Darley, Andrew. 2000. *Visual Digital Culture: Surface Play and Spectacle in New Media Genres*. London: Routledge.

Darvishi, Farhad. 2011. *Porsesh-hā va Pāsokh-hā-ye Jang-e Iran va Erāgh* (The Iran-Iraq War: Questions and Answers). Tehran: Center for Documentation and Research on the Sacred Defense.

Daryaee, Touraj, and Soodabeh Malekzadeh. 2014. "The Performance of Pain and Remembrance in Late Antique Iran." *Silk Road* 12: 57–64.

Das, Veena. 1996a. *Critical Events: An Anthropological Perspective on Contemporary India*. Oxford: Oxford University Press.

———. 1996b. "Language and Body: Transactions in the Construction of Pain." *Daedalus* 125 (1): 67–91.

———. 2000. "The Act of Witnessing: Violence, Poisonous Knowledge, and Subjectivity." In *Violence and Subjectivity*, edited by Veena Das, Arthur Kleinman, Mamphela Ramphele, and Pamela Reynolds, 205–25. Berkeley: University of California Press.

———. 2007. *Life and Words: Violence and the Descent into the Ordinary*. Berkeley: University of California Press.

———. 2015. *Affliction: Health, Disease, Poverty*. New York: Fordham University Press.

Das, Veena, Arthur Kleinman, Mamphela Ramphele, and Pamela Reynolds, eds. 2000. *Violence and Subjectivity*. Berkeley: University of California Press.

Dāvidiān, Haratoun. 2008. *Tārikhcheh-ye Takvin-e Ravānpezeshki-ye Novin Dar Iran* (History of Modern Psychiatry in Iran). Tehran: Arjomand Publishing.

Davis, Elizabeth Anne. 2012. *Bad Souls: Madness and Responsibility in Modern Greece*. Durham, NC: Duke University Press.

Davis-Floyd, Robbie, and Joseph Dumit. 2013. *Cyborg Babies: From Techno-Sex to Techno-Tots*. London: Routledge.

Debord, Guy. 2004. *The Society of the Spectacle*. London: Rebel Press.

———. 1990. *Comments on the Society of the Spectacle*. Translated by Malcolm Imrie. London: Verso.

De Céspedes, Alba. 2000 [1952]. *Daftarcheh-ye Mamnu'* (Forbidden Diary). Translated into Persian by Bahman Farzaneh. Tehran: Badiheh Publishing.

Deleuze, Gilles. 1997. *Essays Critical and Clinical*. Minneapolis: University of Minnesota Press.

Deleuze, Gilles, and Félix Guattari. 2001. *A Thousand Plateaus: Capitalism and Schizophrenia*. Translated and with a foreword by Brian Massumi. London: Mansell.

———. 2004. *Anti-Oedipus: Capitalism and Schizophrenia*. London: A & C Black.

Derrida, Jacques. 1998. *Resistances of Psychoanalysis*. Stanford, CA: Stanford University Press.

Desjarlais, Robert, Leon Eisenberg, Byron Good, and Arthur Kleinman. 1996. *World Mental Health: Problems and Priorities in Low-Income Countries*. New York: Oxford University Press.

Dewachi, Omar. 2013. "Foreshadowing Iraq: The War on 'Life Itself.'" *P U L S E*. http://pulse media.org/2011/09/19/foreshadowing-iraq-the-war-on-"life-itself."

———. 2015. "When Wounds Travel." Special Section: Beyond "Trauma." *Medicine Anthropology Theory* 2 (3): 61–82.

Dewachi, Omar, Samer Jabbour, Nasser Yassin, Iman Nuwayhid, and Rita Giacaman. 2012. "Toward a Regional Perspective on Health and Human Security." In *Public Health in the Arab World*, edited by Samer Jabbour, Rita Giacaman, Marwan Khawaja, and Iman Nuwayhid, 467–76. Cambridge: Cambridge University Press.

Dewachi, Omar, Mac Skelton, Vinh-Kim Nguyen, Fouad M. Fouad, Ghassan Abu Sitta, Zeina Maasri, and Rita Giacaman. 2014. "Changing Therapeutic Geographies of the Iraqi and Syrian Wars." *Lancet* 383 (9915): 449–57. doi: 10.1016/S0140-6736(13)62299-0.

Diller, Lawrence H. 1996. "The Run on Ritalin: Attention Deficit Disorder and Stimulant Treatment in the 1990s." *Hastings Center Report* 26 (2): 12–18.

Dogan, Mattei. 2004. "From Social Class and Religious Identity to Status Incongruence in Post-Industrial Societies." *Comparative Sociology* 3 (2): 163–97. doi: 10.1163/1569133 041738054.

Doostdar, Alireza. 2004. "'The Vulgar Spirit of Blogging': On Language, Culture, and Power in Persian Weblogestan." *American Anthropologist*, New Series, 106 (4): 651–62. doi: 10.1525/aa.2004.106.4.651.

Doroudian, Mohammad. 2012. *Sayri dar Jang-e Iran va Erāgh: Āghāz tā Pāyān* (The Iran-Iraq War: From Beginning to End). Tehran: Center for Documentation and Research on the Iran-Iraq War.

Duman, Ronald S. 2004. "Role of Neurotrophic Factors in the Etiology and Treatment of Mood Disorders." *NeuroMolecular Medicine* 5 (1): 11–25. doi: 10.1385/NMM:5:1:011.

Dumit, Joseph. 2003. "Is It Me or My Brain? Depression and Neuroscientific Facts." *Journal of Medical Humanities* 24 (1–2): 35–47. doi: 10.1023/A:1021353631347.

———. 2004. *Picturing Personhood: Brain Scans and Biomedical Identity*. Princeton, NJ: Princeton University Press.

———. 2012. *Drugs for Life: How Pharmaceutical Companies Define Our Health*. Durham, NC: Duke University Press.

Durham, Deborah. 2004. "Disappearing Youth: Youth as a Social Shifter in Botswana." *American Ethnologist* 31 (4): 589–605. doi: 10.1525/ae.2004.31.4.589.

Durkheim, Émile. 1947 [1893]. *The Division of Labor in Society*. Translated by George Simpson. Glencoe, IL: Free Press.

———. 1951 [1897]. *Suicide: A Study in Sociology*. Edited by George Simpson. Translated by John A. Spaulding and George Simpson. Glencoe, IL: Free Press.

Ebadi, Abbas, Fazlollah Ahmadi, Mostafa Ghanei, and Anoshirvan Kazemnejad. 2009. "Spirituality: A Key Factor in Coping among Iranians Chronically Affected by Mustard Gas in the Disaster of War." *Nursing & Health Sciences* 11 (4): 344–50. doi: 10.1111 /j.1442-2018.2009.00498.x.

Ebadi, Abbas, Tayeb Moradian, Mohsen Mollahadi, Yaser Saeed, and Ali Akbar Refahi. 2014. "Quality of Life in Iranian Chemical Warfare Veterans." *Iran Red Crescent Medical Journal* 16 (5) (May). doi: 10.5812/ircmj.5323.

Ebrahimzadeh, Mohammad H., Asieh S. Fattahi, and Ali Birjandi Nejad. 2006. "Long-Term Follow-up of Iranian Veteran Upper Extremity Amputees from the Iran-Iraq War (1980–1988)." *Journal of Trauma and Acute Care Surgery* 61 (4): 886–88. doi: 10.1097/01.ta.0000236014.78230.77.

Edmunds, June, and Bryan S. Turner. 2005. "Global Generations: Social Change in the Twentieth Century." *British Journal of Sociology* 56 (4): 559–77. doi: 10.1111/j.1468-4446.2005.00083.x.

Ehrenberg, Alain. 2009. *Weariness of the Self: Diagnosing the History of Depression in the Contemporary Age*. Montreal: McGill-Queen's Press.

Ehsani, Kaveh. 2003. "Social Engineering and the Contradictions of Modernization in Khuzestan's Company Towns: A Look at Abadan and Masjed-Soleyman." *International Review of Social History* 48 (03): 361–99. doi: 10.1017/S0020859003001123.

———. 2006. "Rural Society and Agricultural Development in Post-Revolution Iran: The First Two Decades." *Critique: Critical Middle Eastern Studies* 15 (1): 79–96. doi: 10.1080/10669920500515143.

———. 2009. "The Urban Provincial Periphery in Iran: Revolution and War in Ramhormoz." In *Contemporary Iran: Economy, Society, Politics*, edited by Ali Gheissari, 38–76. Oxford: Oxford University Press.

Eiland, Howard, and Michael William Jennings, eds. 2003. *Walter Benjamin: Selected Writings: 1938–1940*. Cambridge, MA: Harvard University Press.

El Shakry, Omnia. 2014. "The Arabic Freud: The Unconscious and the Modern Subject." *Modern Intellectual History* 11 (01): 89–118. doi: 10.1017/S1479244313000346.

Emami, Habib, Mehdi Ghazinour, Hamed Rezaeishiraz, and Jörg Richter. 2007. "Mental Health of Adolescents in Tehran, Iran." *Journal of Adolescent Health* 41 (6): 571–76. doi: 10.1016/j.jadohealth.2007.06.005.

Estroff, Sue E. 1985. *Making It Crazy: An Ethnography of Psychiatric Clients in an American Community*. Berkeley: University of California Press.

Ewing, Katherine. 2008. *Stolen Honor: Stigmatizing Muslim Men in Berlin*. Stanford, CA: Stanford Law and Politics.

———. 2012. "Between Cinema and Social Work: Diasporic Turkish Women and the (Dis)Pleasures of Hybridity." *Cultural Anthropology* 21 (2): 265–94. doi: 10.1525/can.2006.21.2.265.

Falahati, Farahnaz, Khateri Shahriar, Soroush Mohammad Reza, and Amirali Salamat. 2010. "Late Psychological Impacts of Wartime Low Level Exposure to Sulfur Mustard on Civilian Population of Direh (17 Years after Exposure)." *Global Journal of Medical Research* 1 (1): 42–46.

Fanon, Frantz. 1963. *The Wretched of the Earth*. Translated by Constance Farrington. New York: Grove.

Farhadi, Asghar, dir. 2009. *Darbāreh-ye Elly* (About Elly). Feature film. Tehran: Dreamlab.

———, dir. 2011. *Jodāyi-ye Nader az Simin* (A Separation). Feature film. Tehran: Filmiran.

Farmer, Paul. 2001. *Infections and Inequalities: The Modern Plagues*. Berkeley: University of California Press.

Fasih, Esmā'il. 1987. *Zemestān-e 62* (Winter 1981). Tehran: Nashr-e Now.

Fassin, Didier. 2007. *When Bodies Remember: Experiences and Politics of AIDS in South Africa*. Berkeley: University of California Press.

Fassin, Didier, and Richard Rechtman. 2009. *The Empire of Trauma: An Inquiry into the Condition of Victimhood*. Translated by Rachel Gomme. Princeton, NJ: Princeton University Press.

Faubion, James D. 2011. *An Anthropology of Ethics*. Cambridge: Cambridge University Press.

Fischer, Michael M. J. 1973. "Zoroastrian Iran between Myth and Praxis." Ph.D. dissertation, University of Chicago.

———. 1980. *Iran: From Religious Dispute to Revolution*. Cambridge, MA: Harvard University Press.

———. 1982. "Islam and the Revolt of the Petit Bourgeoisie." *Daedalus* 111 (1): 101–25.

———. 1984. "Towards a Third World Poetics: Seeing Through Short Stories & Film in the Iranian Culture Area." *Knowledge & Society* 5: 171–241.

———. 1986. "Ethnicity and the Post-Modern Arts of Memory." In *Writing Culture: The Poetics and Politics of Ethnography*, edited by James Clifford and George Marcus, 194–233. Berkeley: University of California Press.

———. 1990. "Legal Postulates in Flux: Justice, Wit, and Hierarchy in Iran". In *Law and Islam in the Middle East*, edited by Daisy Hilse Dwyer, 115–42. New York: Bergen and Garvey.

———. 1993. "Five Frames for Understanding the Iranian Revolution." In *Critical Moments in Religious History*, edited by Kenneth Keulman, 173–97. Macon, GA: Mercer Press.

———. 1999. "Emergent Forms of Life: Anthropologies of Late or Postmodernities." *Annual Review of Anthropology* 28 (October): 455–78. doi: 10.1146/annurev.anthro.28.1.455.

———. 2001. "Ethnographic Critique and Technoscientific Narratives: The Old Mole, Ethical Plateaux, and the Governance of Emergent Biosocial Polities." *Culture, Medicine and Psychiatry* 25 (4): 355–93. doi: 10.1023/A:1013078230464.

———. 2003. *Emergent Forms of Life and the Anthropological Voice*. Durham, NC: Duke University Press.

———. 2004. *Mute Dreams, Blind Owls, and Dispersed Knowledges: Persian Poesis in the Transnational Circuitry*. Durham, NC: Duke University Press.

———. 2007a. "Culture and Cultural Analysis as Experimental Systems." *Cultural Anthropology* 22 (1): 1–65. doi: 10.1525/can.2007.22.1.1.

———. 2007b. "To Live with What Would Otherwise Be Unendurable: Return(s) to Subjectivities." In *Subjectivity: Ethnographic Investigations*, edited by João Biehl, Byron Good, and Arthur Kleinman, 423–46. Berkeley: University of California Press.

———. 2009. *Anthropological Futures*. Durham, NC: Duke University Press.

———. 2010. "The Rhythmic Beat of the Revolution in Iran." *Cultural Anthropology* 25 (3): 497–543. doi: 10.1111/j.1548-1360.2010.01068.x.

———. 2013. "The Peopling of Technologies." In *When People Come First: Critical Studies in Global Health*, edited by João Biehl and Adriana Petryna, 347–74. Princeton, NJ: Princeton University Press.

————. 2014. "The Lightness of Existence and the Origami of 'French' Anthropology: Latour, Descola, Viveiros de Castro, Meillassoux, and Their So-Called Ontological Turn." *HAU: Journal of Ethnographic Theory* 4 (1): 331–55. doi: 10.14318/hau4.1.018.

————. 2015. "Ethnography for Aging Societies: Dignity, Cultural Genres, and Singapore's Imagined Futures." *American Ethnologist* 42 (2): 207–29. doi: 10.1111/amet.12126.

Fischer, Michael, and Mehdi Abedi. 1989. "Revolutionary Posters and Cultural Signs." *Middle East Report*, 19 (159) (July): 29–32. doi: 10.2307/3012520.

————. 1990. *Debating Muslims: Cultural Dialogues in Postmodernity and Tradition*. Madison: University of Wisconsin Press.

Fortun, Kim. 2001. *Advocacy after Bhopal: Environmentalism, Disaster, New Global Orders*. Chicago: University of Chicago Press.

————. 2012. "Ethnography in Late Industrialism." *Cultural Anthropology* 27 (3): 446–64. doi: 10.1111/j.1548-1360.2012.01153.x.

Foucault, Michel. 1980. *The History of Sexuality*. Translated by Robert Hurley. New York: Vintage Books.

————. 1988. *Madness and Civilization: A History of Insanity in the Age of Reason*. Translated by Richard Howard. New York: Vintage Books.

————. 1991 [1978]. "Governmentality." In *The Foucault Effect: Studies in Governmentality*, edited by Graham Burchell, Colin Gordon, and Peter Miller, 87–104. Chicago: University of Chicago Press.

————. 1994a. *The Birth of the Clinic: An Archaeology of Medical Perception*. New York: Vintage Books.

————. 1994b. *The Order of Things: An Archaeology of the Human Sciences*. New York: Vintage.

Frankenberg, Ronald. 1993. "Risk: Anthropological and Epidemiological Narratives of Prevention." In *Knowledge, Power, and Practice: The Anthropology of Medicine and Everyday Life*, edited by Shirley Lindenbaum and Margaret M. Lock, 219–24. Berkeley: University of California Press.

Freud, Sigmund. 1953 [1900]. *The Interpretation of Dreams*. In *The Standard Edition of the Complete Psychological Works of Sigmund Freud*, edited by James Strachey and Anna Freud, vol. 4. London: Hogarth Press and the Institute of Psycho-Analysis.

————. 1955a [1913]. *Totem and Taboo and Other Works*. In *Standard Edition*, 13: 1–161.

————. 1955b [1919]. "A Child Is Being Beaten." In *Standard Edition*, 17: 179–204.

————. 1957a [1915]. "On Transience." In *Standard Edition*, 14: 305–7.

————. 1957b [1915]. "Thoughts for the Times on War and Death." In *Standard Edition*, 14: 273–300.

————. 1957c [1917]. "Mourning and Melancholia." In *Standard Edition*, 14: 237–58.

————. 1959 [1908]. "Hysterical Phantasies and Their Relation to Bisexuality." In *Standard Edition*, 9: 155–66.

————. 1962 [1899]. "Screen Memories." In *Standard Edition*, 3: 303–22.

Fromanger, Marine. 2012. "Variations in the Martyrs' Representations in South Tehran's Private and Public Spaces." *Visual Anthropology* 25 (1–2): 47–67. doi: 10.1080/08949468 .2012.629164.

Fromm, Erich. 1951. *The Forgotten Language: An Introduction to the Understanding of Dreams, Fairy Tales and Myths.* New York: Rinehart.

Garland, Caroline. 1998. *Understanding Trauma: A Psychoanalytical Approach.* New York: Routledge.

Garro, Linda. 2010. "By the Will of Others or By One's Own Actions?" In *Toward an Anthropology of the Will,* edited by Keith Murphy and C. Jason Throop, 69–101. Stanford, CA: Stanford University Press.

Geertz, Clifford. 1973. *The Interpretation of Cultures: Selected Essays.* New York: Basic Books.

Ghamari-Tabrizi, Behrooz. 2009. "Memory, Mourning, Memorializing on the Victims of Iran-Iraq War, 1980–Present." *Radical History Review* 2009 (105): 106–21. doi: 10.1215 /01636545-2009-007.

Ghanei, M., S. H. Assari, F. Alaeddini, and S. A. Tavallaie. 2005. "Pattern of Delayed Mortality in I.R.IRAN Veterans Exposed to Chemical Warfare Agents." *Journal of Military Medicine* 6 (4): 233–39.

Ghanizadeh, Ahmad, Mohammad Reza Mohammadi, and Rozita Moini. 2008. "Comorbidity of Psychiatric Disorders and Parental Psychiatric Disorders in a Sample of Iranian Children with ADHD." *Journal of Attention Disorders* 12 (2): 149–55. doi: 10 .1177/1087054708314601.

Ghanoonparvar, M. R. 2009. "Postrevolutionary Trends in Persian Fiction and Film." *Radical History Review* 2009 (105): 156–62. doi: 10.1215/01636545-2009-013.

Ghazinour, Mehdi, Habib Emami, Jorg Richter, Mohammad Abdollahi, and Abdolkarim Pazhumand. 2009. "Age and Gender Differences in the Use of Various Poisoning Methods for Deliberate Parasuicide Cases Admitted to Loghman Hospital in Tehran (2000–2004)." *Suicide & Life-Threatening Behavior* 39 (2): 231–39. doi: 10.1521/suli .2009.39.2.231.

Gheytanchi, Elham. 2007. "I Will Turn Off the Lights: The Allure of Marginality in Postrevolutionary Iran." *Comparative Studies of South Asia, Africa and the Middle East* 27 (1): 173–85. doi: 10.1215/1089201x-2006-05.

Ghobari, Bagher, and Jafar Bolhari. 2001. "The Current State of Medical Psychology in Iran." *Journal of Clinical Psychology in Medical Settings* 8 (1): 39–43. doi: 10.1023 /A:1011323822372.

Giacaman, Rita, and Jāmi'at Bīr Zayt. 2004. *Psycho-Social/mental Health Care in the Occupied Palestinian Territories: The Embryonic System.* Birzeit University, Institute of Community & Public Health.

Giacaman, Rita, Yoke Rabaia, Viet Nguyen-Gillham, Rajaie Batniji, Raija-Leena Punamäki, and Derek Summerfield. 2011. "Mental Health, Social Distress and Political Oppression: The Case of the Occupied Palestinian Territory." *Global Public Health* 6 (5): 547–59. doi: 10.1080/17441692.2010.528443.

Giacaman, Rita, Laura Wick, Hanan Abdul-Rahim, and Livia Wick. 2005. "The Politics of Childbirth in the Context of Conflict: Policies or de Facto Practices?" *Health Policy* 72 (2): 129–39.

Goffman, Erving. 1961. *Asylums: Essays on the Social Situation of Mental Patients and Other Inmates.* London: Penguin.

Good, Byron J. 1977. "The Heart of What's the Matter: The Semantics of Illness in Iran." *Culture, Medicine and Psychiatry* 1 (1): 25–58. doi: 10.1007/BF00114809.

———. 1994. *Medicine, Rationality, and Experience: An Anthropological Perspective*. Cambridge: Cambridge University Press.

Good, Byron J., Mary-Jo DelVecchio Good, Sandra Teresa Hyde, and Sarah Pinto. 2008. "Postcolonial Disorders: Reflections on Subjectivity in the Contemporary World." In *Postcolonial Disorders*, edited by Mary-Jo DelVecchio Good, Sandra Teresa Hyde, Sarah Pinto, and Byron J. Good, 1–42. Berkeley: University of California Press.

Good, Byron J., Mary-Jo DelVecchio Good, and Robert Moradi. 1986. "The Interpretation of Iranian Depressive Illness and Dysphoric Affect." In *Culture and Depression: Studies in the Anthropology and Cross-Cultural Psychiatry of Affect and Disorder*, edited by Arthur Kleinman and Byron J. Good, 369–428. Berkeley: University of California Press.

Good, Mary-Jo DelVecchio, and Byron J. Good. 1998. "Ritual, the State, and the Transformation of Emotional Discourse in Iranian Society." *Culture, Medicine and Psychiatry* 12 (1) (March): 43–63. doi: 10.1007/BF00047038.

Good, Mary-Jo DelVecchio, Sandra Teresa Hyde, Sarah Pinto, and Byron J. Good. 2008. *Postcolonial Disorders*. Berkeley: University of California Press.

Greenslit, Nathan P. 2007. "Pharmaceutical Relationships: Intersections of Illness, Fantasy, and Capital in the Age of Direct-to-Consumer Marketing." Ph.D. dissertation, Massachusetts Institute of Technology. http://search.proquest.com.ezproxy.cul.columbia.edu/docview/876604183?pq-origsite=summon.

Gregg, Melissa, and Gregory J. Seigworth. 2010. *The Affect Theory Reader*. Durham, NC: Duke University Press.

Grob, Gerald N. 1991. *From Asylum to Community: Mental Health Policy in Modern America*. Princeton, NJ: Princeton University Press.

———. 1994. *Mad Among Us*. New York: Simon and Schuster.

Gruber, C. J. 2008. "The Message Is on the Wall: Mural Arts in Post-Revolutionary Iran." *Persica* 22 (0): 15–46. doi: 10.2143/PERS.22.0.2034399.

Gruber, Christiane. 2012. "The Martyrs' Museum in Tehran: Visualizing Memory in Post-Revolutionary Iran." *Visual Anthropology* 25 (1–2): 68–97. doi: 10.1080/08949468.2012.629171.

Hacking, Ian. 1995. "The Looping Effects of Human Kinds." In *Causal Cognition: A Multidisciplinary Debate*, edited by Dan Sperber, David Premack, and Ann James Premack, 351–94. New York: Oxford University Press.

———. 1998. *Mad Travelers: Reflections on the Reality of Transient Mental Illnesses*. Charlottesville: University of Virginia Press.

———. 2006. "Making Up People." *London Review of Books* 28 (16): 23–26. http://www.lrb.co.uk/v28/n16/ian-hacking/making-up-people.

Haghighi, Mani. 2012. "Nāmomken Budan-e Foto-realism" (The Impossibility of Photo-realism). *Tandis* 234: 13.

Halbwachs, Maurice. 1992. *On Collective Memory*. Chicago: University of Chicago Press.

Halley, Patricia Ticineto, and Jean Clough, eds. 2007. *The Affective Turn: Theorizing the Social*. Durham, NC: Duke University Press.

Halpern, Jodi, and Bradley Lewis. 2013. "Introduction: Why Does Psychiatry Need the Humanities?" *Psychiatric Times*, March 12. http://www.psychiatrictimes.com/cultural -psychiatry/introduction-why-does-psychiatry-need-humanities.

Hamdy, Sherine. 2012. *Our Bodies Belong to God: Organ Transplants, Islam, and the Struggle for Human Dignity in Egypt*. Berkeley: University of California Press.

Hammonds, Evelynn Maxine. 1999. *Childhood's Deadly Scourge: The Campaign to Control Diphtheria in New York City, 1880–1930*. Baltimore: Johns Hopkins University Press.

Hashemian, Farnoosh, Kaveh Khoshnood, Mayur M. Desai, Farahnaz Falahati, Stanislav Kasl, and Steven Southwick. 2006. "Anxiety, Depression, and Posttraumatic Stress in Iranian Survivors of Chemical Warfare." *Journal of the American Medical Association* 296 (5): 560–66. http://jama.jamanetwork.com/article.aspx?articleid=917072.

Hatamikia, Ebrahim, dir. 1992. *Az Karkheh Ta Rhein* (From Karkheh to the Rhine). Feature film. Tehran: Sima Film.

———, dir. 1998. *Ājāns-e Shisheh-i* (The Glass Agency). Feature film. Tehran: Boshra Film.

Healy, David. 1997. *The Antidepressant Era*. Cambridge, MA: Harvard University Press.

———. 2006. "The Latest Mania: Selling Bipolar Disorder." *PLoS Medicine* 3 (4): e185. doi: http://dx.doi.org.ezproxy.cul.columbia.edu/10.1371/journal.pmed.0030185.

Healy, David, and Joanna Le Noury. 2007. "Pediatric Bipolar Disorder: An Object of Study in the Creation of an Illness." *International Journal of Risk and Safety in Medicine* 19 (4): 209–21.

Hedāyat, Sādegh. 1971 [1937]. *Buf-e Kur* (The Blind Owl). Tehran: Sepehr.

Hewitt, Martin. 1988. "Science as Spectacle: Popular Scientific Culture in Saint John, New Brunswick, 1830–1850." *Acadiensis* 18 (1): 91–119.

Horwitz, Allan V., and Jerome C. Wakefield. 2007. *The Loss of Sadness: How Psychiatry Transformed Normal Sorrow Into Depressive Disorder*. Oxford: Oxford University Press.

Illich, Ivan. 1975. *Limits to Medicine: Medical Nemesis, the Expropriation of Health*. London: Marion Boyers.

Jamalzadeh, Mohammad-Ali. 1941. *Dārolmajānin* (Lunatic Asylum). Tehran: Marefat.

Javanbakht, Arash, and Mohammad Sanati. 2006. "Psychiatry and Psychoanalysis in Iran." *Journal of the American Academy of Psychoanalysis and Dynamic Psychiatry* 34 (3): 405–14. doi: 10.1521/jaap.2006.34.3.405.

Kalafee, Y., and M. Adib. 2000. "Survey of Association between Combat Related Post-Traumatic Stress Disorder and Quality of Life among Iran-Iraq War Veterans." *Iranian Journal of Medical Sciences* 25 (4): 147–49.

Karamati, Yunos, and EIR. 2004. "Faculty of Medicine of the University of Tehran." In "The History of Medicine in Iran," edited by Ehsan Yar-Shater, 19–25. New York: Encyclopaedia Iranica Foundation. Originally published in *Encyclopaedia Iranica*, 1999. http://www.iranicaonline.org/articles/faculties-v.

Karami, Arash. 2015. "Return of 175 Iranian Bodies from Iraq Stirs Painful Memories." *Al-Monitor*, May 21. http://www.al-monitor.com/pulse/originals/2015/05/iran-175-mar tyrs-iran -iraq-war.html.

Karami, Gholam-Reza, Javad Ameli, Rahim Roeintan, Nematollah Jonaidi-Jafari, and

Amin Saburi. 2013. "Impacts of Mustard Gas Exposure on Veterans Mental Health: A Study on the Role of Education." *Industrial Psychiatry Journal* 22 (1): 22–25. http://dx.doi.org/10.4103/0972-6748.123604.

Karimabadi, Mehrzad. 2011. "Manifesto of Martyrdom: Similarities and Differences between Avini's *Ravaayat-E Fath* [Chronicles of Victory] and More Traditional Manifestoes." *Iranian Studies* 44 (3): 381–86.

Karimi, Niki, dir. 2005. *Yek Shab* (One Night). Feature film. Tehran: Sazeman Cinemai.

Karimi, Pamela. 2008. "Imagining Warfare, Imagining Welfare: Tehran's Post Iran-Iraq War Murals and Their Legacy." *Persica* 22 (0): 47–63. doi: 10.2143/PERS.22.0.2034400.

———. 2013. *Domesticity and Consumer Culture in Iran: Interior Revolutions of the Modern Era*. London: Routledge.

Karimi, Z. Pamela. 2003. "Women's Portable Habitats." *ISIM Newsletter* (1) 13: 14–15. https://openaccess.leidenuniv.nl/handle/1887/16921.

———. 2006. "Iranian Cinema: Texts and Contexts." *Art Journal* 65 (2): 136.

Kashani-Sabet, Firoozeh. 2011. *Conceiving Citizens: Women and the Politics of Motherhood in Iran*. Oxford: Oxford University Press.

Katouzian, Homa. 2000. *Sadeq Hedayat: The Life and Legend of an Iranian Writer*. London: I.B. Tauris.

———. 2003. *Darbāreh-ye Jamalzadeh va Jamalzadeh-shenāsi* (About Jamalzadeh). Tehran: Pajouheh.

Keller, Richard C. 2007. *Colonial Madness: Psychiatry in French North Africa*. Chicago: University of Chicago Press.

Kelly, John, and Bruche Etling. 2008. "Mapping Iran's Online Public: Politics and Culture in the Persian Blogosphere." Berkman Center Research Publication No. 2008-01. Berkman Center for Internet & Society, Harvard University. http://cyber.law.harvard.edu/publications/2008/Mapping_Irans_Online_Public.

Khalili, Laleh. 2009. *Heroes and Martyrs of Palestine: The Politics of National Commemoration*. Cambridge: Cambridge University Press.

Khateri, Shahriar, and Narges Bajoghli. 2015. "Blisters and Sanctions | Middle East Research and Information Project." *Middle East Research and Information Project* (*MERIP*). http://www.merip.org/blisters-sanctions (accessed November 26, 2015).

Khateri, Shahriar, Mostafa Ghanei, Saeed Keshavarz, Mohammad Soroush, and David Haines. 2003. "Incidence of Lung, Eye, and Skin Lesions as Late Complications in 34,000 Iranians with Wartime Exposure to Mustard Agent." *Journal of Occupational and Environmental Medicine* 45 (11): 1136–43. doi: 10.1097/01.jom.0000094993.20914.d1.

Khiabany, Gholam. 2015. "Technologies of Liberation and/or Otherwise." *International Journal of Middle East Studies* 47 (2): 348–53. doi: 10.1017/S0020743815000094.

Khorrami, Mohammad Mehdi, and Pari Shirazi. 2008. *Sohrab's Wars: Counter-Discourses of Contemporary Persian Fiction: A Collection of Short Stories and a Film Script*. Costa Mesa, CA: Mazda Publishers.

Khorrami, Mohammad Mehdi, and Shouleh Vatanabadi. 2000. *A Feast in the Mirror: Stories by Contemporary Iranian Women*. Boulder, CO: Lynne Rienner.

Khosravi, Shahram. 2008. *Young and Defiant in Tehran*. Philadelphia: University of Pennsylvania Press.

Khosrokhavar, Farhad. 2002. "Postrevolutionary Iran and the New Social Movements." In *Twenty Years of Islamic Revolution: Political and Social Transition in Iran Since 1979*, edited by Eric Hooglund, 3–18. Syracuse, NY: Syracuse University Press.

———. 2004. "The Islamic Revolution in Iran: Retrospect after a Quarter of a Century." *Thesis Eleven* 76 (1): 70–84. doi: 10.1177/0725513604040110.

Khosrokhavar, Farhad, Shapour Etemad, and Masoud Mehrabi. 2004. "Report on Science in Post-revolutionary Iran—Part I: Emergence of a Scientific Community?" *Critique: Critical Middle Eastern Studies* 13 (2): 209–24. doi: 10.1080/1066992042000244335.

Khosrokhavar, Farhad, and M. Amin Ghaneirad. 2006. "Iran's New Scientific Community." *Iranian Studies* 39 (2): 253–67. doi: 10.1080/00210860600628823.

Khoury, Dina Rizk. 2013. *Iraq in Wartime: Soldiering, Martyrdom, and Remembrance*. Cambridge: Cambridge University Press.

Khushabi, K., H. Pour-Etemad, N. Mohammadi, and P. Mohammadkhani. 2006. "The Prevalence of ADHD in Primary School Students in Tehran." *Medical Journal of the Islamic Republic of Iran* 20 (3): 147–50.

Kia, Mana, Afsaneh Najmabadi, and Sima Shakhsari. 2009. "Women, Gender, and Sexuality in Historiography of Modern Iran." *Iran in the 20th Century: Historiography and Political Culture*, edited by Touraj Atabaki, 177–97. London: I.B. Tauris.

Kienzler, H. 2008. "Debating War-Trauma and Post-Traumatic Stress Disorder (PTSD) in an Interdisciplinary Arena." *Social Science & Medicine* 67 (2): 218–27. doi: 10.1016/j.soc scimed.2008.03.030.

Kienzler, Hanna, and Zeina Amro. 2015. "'Unknowing' and Mental Health System Reform in Palestine." Special Section: Beyond "Trauma." *Medicine Anthropology Theory* 2 (3): 113–27.

Kirk, Stuart A., and Herb Kutchins. 1992. *The Selling of DSM: The Rhetoric of Science in Psychiatry*. New York: A. de Gruyter.

Kirmayer, Laurence J. 2006. "Beyond the 'New Cross-Cultural Psychiatry': Cultural Biology, Discursive Psychology and the Ironies of Globalization." *Transcultural Psychiatry* 43 (1): 126–44. doi: 10.1177/1363461506061761.

Kitanaka, Junko. 2012. *Depression in Japan: Psychiatric Cures for a Society in Distress*. Princeton, NJ: Princeton University Press.

Kleinman, Arthur. 1982. "Neurasthenia and Depression: A Study of Somatization and Culture in China." *Culture, Medicine and Psychiatry* 6 (2): 117–90.

———. 1986. *Social Origins of Distress and Disease: Depression, Neurasthenia, and Pain in Modern China*. New Haven, CT: Yale University Press.

———. 1988. *Rethinking Psychiatry: From Cultural Category to Personal Experience*. New York: Free Press.

———. 1989. *Illness Narratives: Suffering, Healing and the Human Condition*. Reprint ed. New York: Basic Books.

———. 2007. "Psychiatry without Context: Turning Sadness into Disease." *Lancet* 370 (9590): 819–20. doi: 10.1016/S0140-6736(07)61398-1.

————. 2012. "Culture, Bereavement, and Psychiatry." *Lancet* 379 (9816): 608–9. doi: 10.1016 /S0140-6736(12)60258-X.

Kleinman, Arthur, Veena Das, and Margaret Lock. 1997. *Social Suffering.* Berkeley: University of California Press.

Kõresaar, Ene, E. Lauk, and K. Kuutma, eds. 2009. *The Burden of Remembering?: Recollections & Representations of the 20th Century.* Helsinki: Finish Literature Society.

Koyagi, Mikiya. 2009. "Modern Education in Iran during the Qajar and Pahlavi Periods." *History Compass* 7 (1): 107–18. doi: 10.1111/j.1478-0542.2008.00561.x.

Kracauer, Siegfried. 1993. "Photography." Translated by Thomas Y. Levin. *Critical Inquiry* 19 (3): 421–36.

Kramer, Peter D. 1993. *Listening to Prozac: The Landmark Book about Antidepressants and the Remaking of the Self.* Revised ed. New York: Viking.

Lacan, Jacques. 1977. *The Four Fundamental Concepts of Psychoanalysis.* Edited by Jacques-Alain Miller, translated by Alan Sheridan. New York: W.W. Norton.

Laing, R. D. 1965. *The Divided Self: An Existential Study in Sanity and Madness.* Reprint. London: Penguin.

Lakoff, Andrew. 2000. "Adaptive Will: The Evolution of Attention Deficit Disorder." *Journal of the History of the Behavioral Sciences* 36 (2): 149–69. doi: 10.1002/ (SICI)1520-6696(200021)36:2<149::AID-JHBS3>3.0.CO;2-9.

————. 2005. *Pharmaceutical Reason: Knowledge and Value in Global Psychiatry.* Cambridge: Cambridge University Press.

Laplanche, Jean, and Jean-Bertrand Pontalis. 1988. *The Language of Psycho-Analysis.* London: Karnac Books.

Lari, Abdolaziz Rastegar, Mohammad Taghi Joghataei, Yasaman Rezaei Adli, and Yashar Aliabadi Zadeh. 2007. "Epidemiology of Suicide by Burns in the Province of Isfahan, Iran." *Journal of Burn Care & Research?: Official Publication of the American Burn Association* 28 (2): 307.

Latour, Bruno. 1988. *The Pasteurization of France.* Translated by Alan Sheridan and John Law. Cambridge, MA: Harvard University Press.

Lewis, Bradley. 2011. *Narrative Psychiatry: How Stories Can Shape Clinical Practice.* Baltimore: Johns Hopkins University Press.

Lock, Margaret. 1986. "Plea for Acceptance: School Refusal Syndrome in Japan." *Social Science & Medicine* 23 (2): 99–112. doi: 10.1016/0277-9536(86)90359-X.

————. 1993. *Encounters with Aging: Mythologies of Menopause in Japan and North America.* Berkeley: University of California Press.

————. 2001. "The Tempering of Medical Anthropology: Troubling Natural Categories." *Medical Anthropology Quarterly* 15 (4): 478–92. doi: 10.1525/maq.2001.15.4.478.

————. 2002. *Twice Dead: Organ Transplants and the Reinvention of Death.* Berkeley: University of California Press.

Lock, Margaret, and Vinh-Kim Nguyen. 2011. *An Anthropology of Biomedicine.* New York: John Wiley & Sons.

Lotfalian, Mazyar. 1996. "Working Through Psychological Understandings of the Diasporic Condition." *Ethos* 24 (1): 36–70. doi: 10.1525/eth.1996.24.1.02a00020.

Luhrmann, Tanya M. 2001. *Of Two Minds: The Growing Disorder in American Psychiatry.* New York: Alfred A. Knopf.

MacDougall, David. 2006. "The Visual in Anthropology." In *The Corporeal Image: Film, Ethnography, and the Senses,* by David MacDougall, 213–26. Princeton, NJ: Princeton University Press.

Madarshahi, Monir Sadat. 2012. "Iran's 'Twenty-Year Vision Document': An Outlook on Science and Technology." *Iranian Studies* 45 (5): 619–43. doi: 10.1080/00210862.2012 .703486.

Maghsoudi, Hemmat, Abasad Garadagi, Golam Ali Jafary, Gila Azarmir, Nahid Aali, Bahram Karimian, and Mahnaze Tabrizi. 2004. "Women Victims of Self-Inflicted Burns in Tabriz, Iran." *Burns* 30 (3): 217–20. doi: 10.1016/j.burns.2003.10.010.

Mahbubi-Ardakani, Hosayn. 1975. *Tārikh-e Mo'assesāt-e Tamaddoni-ye Jadid Dar Iran* (History of Modern Institutions in Iran). Tehran: Tehran University Press.

Makhmalbaf, Mohsen. 1986. *Bāgh-e Bolur* (Glass Garden). Tehran: Nashr-e Nay.

———, dir. 1989. *Arusi-ye Khubān* (Marriage of the Blessed). Feature film. Tehran: Open City Entertainment.

Malekzadeh, Shervin. 2012. "Children without Childhood, Adults without Adulthood: Changing Conceptions of the Iranian Child in Postrevolutionary Iranian Textbooks (1979–2008)." *Comparative Studies of South Asia, Africa and the Middle East* 32 (2): 339–60. doi: 10.1215/1089201X-1628971.

Mannheim, Karl. 1952 [1927]. "The Problem of Generations." In *Essays on the Sociology of Knowledge by Karl Mannheim,* edited by Paul Kecskemeti, 276–320. New York: Routledge & Kegan Paul.

Manoukian, Setrag. 2004. "Culture, Power and Poetry in Shiraz." ISIM Newsletter 14 (June): 40–41.

———. 2012. *City of Knowledge in Twentieth Century Iran: Shiraz, History and Poetry.* London: Routledge.

Marandi, A. 1996. "Integrating Medical Education and Health Services: The Iranian Experience." *Medical Education* 30: 4–8. doi: 10.1111/j.1365-2923.1996.tb00709.x.

Maranhão, Tullio, ed. 1990. *The Interpretation of Dialogue.* Chicago: University of Chicago Press.

Marcus, George E. 1998. *Ethnography Through Thick and Thin.* Princeton, NJ: Princeton University Press.

———. 2012. "The Legacies of Writing Culture and the Near Future of the Ethnographic Form: A Sketch." *Cultural Anthropology* 27 (3): 427–45. doi: 10.1111/j.1548-1360.2012 .01152.x.

Marcus, George E., and Michael M. J. Fischer. 1999 [1986]. *Anthropology as Cultural Critique: An Experimental Moment in the Human Sciences.* 2nd ed. Chicago: University of Chicago Press.

Marcus, George E., and Fred R. Myers. 1995. "The Traffic in Art and Culture: An Introduction." In *The Traffic in Culture: Refiguring Art and Anthropology,* edited by George E. Marcus and Fred R. Myers, 1–51. Berkeley: University of California Press.

Margalit, Avishai. 2002. *The Ethics of Memory.* Cambridge, MA: Harvard University Press.

Markin, Pablo. 2010. *Essays on Cultural Blogging, Everyday Ethnography and the Postmodern Self.* Munich: GRIN Verlag.

Martin, Emily. 1994. *Flexible Bodies.* Boston: Beacon Press.

———. 2007. *Bipolar Expeditions: Mania and Depression in American Culture.* Princeton, NJ: Princeton University Press.

———. 2013. "The Potentiality of Ethnography and the Limits of Affect Theory." *Current Anthropology* 54 (S7): S149–58. doi: 10.1086/670388.

Massumi, Brian. 2002. *Parables for the Virtual: Movement, Affect, Sensation.* Durham, NC: Duke University Press.

Matin-Asgari, Afshin. 2005. "The Rise of Modern Subjectivity in Iran." *Critique: Critical Middle Eastern Studies* 14 (3): 333–37. doi: 10.1080/10669920500280730.

Mattingly, Cheryl. 1998. *Healing Dramas and Clinical Plots: The Narrative Structure of Experience.* Cambridge: Cambridge University Press.

Matza, Tomas. 2009. "Moscow's Echo: Technologies of the Self, Publics, and Politics on the Russian Talk Show." *Cultural Anthropology* 24 (3): 489–522. doi: 10.1111/j.1548-1360.2009.01038.x.

Mauss, Marcel. 1954. *The Gift: Forms and Functions of Exchange in Archaic Societies.* London: Cohen & West.

Mayes, Rick, Catherine Bagwell, and Jennifer Erkulwater. 2008. "ADHD and the Rise in Stimulant Use among Children." *Harvard Review of Psychiatry* 16 (3): 151–66. doi: 10.1080/10673220802167782.

Mehran, Golnar. 1989. "Socialization of Schoolchildren in the Islamic Republic of Iran." *Iranian Studies* 22 (1): 35–50. doi: 10.1080/00210868908701724.

Meskoob, Shahrokh. 1971. *Sug-e Siāvush* (Mourning for Siāvush). Tehran: Kharazmi.

Mickiewicz, Ellen Propper. 1999. *Changing Channels: Television and the Struggle for Power in Russia.* Durham, NC: Duke University Press.

Milani, Abbas. 2008. *Eminent Persians.* Syracuse, NY: Syracuse University Press.

Milani, Mohsen M. 1994. *The Making of Iran's Islamic Revolution: From Monarchy to Islamic Republic.* Boulder, CO: Westview.

Mir-Hosseini, Ziba. 2009. "Being from There: Dilemmas of a Native Anthropologist." In *Conceptualizing Iranian Anthropology,* edited by Shahnaz Najmabadi, 180–91. New York: Berghahn.

Mirsepāssi, Abdolhossein. 1951. *Ravānpezeshki* (Psychiatry). Tehran: Tehran University Press.

Mirsepassi, Ali. 2010. *Political Islam, Iran, and the Enlightenment: Philosophies of Hope and Despair.* Cambridge: Cambridge University Press.

Modabernia, Mohamad Jafar, Hossein Shodjai Tehrani, Mahnaz Fallahi, and Maryam Shirazi. 2008. "Prevalence of Depressive Disorders in Rasht, Iran: A Community Based Study." *Clinical Practice and Epidemiology in Mental Health: CP & EMH* 4: 20. doi: 10.1186/1745-0179-4-20.

Moghadam, Valentine M. 1999. "Revolution, Religion, and Gender Politics: Iran and Afghanistan Compared." *Journal of Women's History* 10 (4): 172–95. doi: 10.1353/jowh.2010.0536.

Mohammadi, Mohammad-Reza, Haratoon Davidian, Ahmad Ali Noorbala, Hossein Malekafzali, Hamid Reza Naghavi, Hamid Reza Pouretemad, Seyed Abbas Bagheri Yazdi, et al. 2005. "An Epidemiological Survey of Psychiatric Disorders in Iran." *Clinical Practice and Epidemiology in Mental Health: CP & EMH* 1 (September): 16. doi: 10.1186/1745-0179-1-16.

Moharrery, Mohammad Reza. 1994. "Negāhi be Tārikh-e Ravānpezeshki dar Iran" (A Glance at the History of Psychiatry in Iran). *Andisheh va Raftar: Iranian Journal of Psychiatry and Clinical Psychology* 1 (2 and 3): 27–49.

Mohit, Ahmad. 2006. "Report of WHO's World Mental Health Survey." *Lancet* 367 (9515): 968–69. doi: 10.1016/S0140-6736(06)68405-5.

Moosavi, Amir. 2015. "How to Write Death: Resignifying Martyrdom in Two Novels of the Iran-Iraq War." *Alif: Journal of Comparative Poetics* 35 (January): 9–23.

Morsy, Soheir A. 1981. "Towards a Political Economy of Health: A Critical Note on the Medical Anthropology of the Middle East." *Social Science & Medicine. Part B: Medical Anthropology* 15 (2): 159–63. doi: 10.1016/0160-7987(81)90039-9.

Mortazavi, Bagher, ed. 2007. *Sāedi: Az U va Darbareh-ye U* (Sāed: From Him and About Him). Cologne: Forough Publishing.

Mortezaeian-Abkenar, Hossein. 2006. *Aghrab Rooye Pelleh-hā-ye Ghatār-e Andimeshk* (A Scorpion on the Steps of Andimeshk Railroad Station, or Blood's Dripping from This Train, Sir!). Tehran: Nashr-e Nay.

Morus, Iwan Rhys. 2006. "Seeing and Believing Science." *Isis* 97 (1): 101–10. doi: 10.1086 /501103.

Mottahedeh, Negar. 2008. *Displaced Allegories: Post-Revolutionary Iranian Cinema*. Durham, NC: Duke University Press.

Murthy, Dhiraj. 2011. "Emergent Digital Ethnographic Methods for Social Research." In *The Handbook of Emergent Technologies in Social Research*, edited by Sharlene Nagy Hesse-Biber, 158–79. New York: Oxford University Press.

Naficy, Hamid. 2006. "The Open Image: Poetic Realism and the New Iranian Cinema." In *Genre, Gender, Race, and World Cinema*, edited by Julie Codell, 322–44. Malden, MA: Wiley-Blackwell.

———. 2009. "From Accented Cinema to Multiplex Cinema." In *Convergence Media History*, edited by Janet Staiger and Sabine Hake, 3–13. New York: Routledge.

———. 2012. *A Social History of Iranian Cinema*, Volume 4: *The Globalizing Era, 1984–2010*. Durham, NC: Duke University Press.

Najmabadi, Afsaneh. 2005. *Women With Mustaches and Men Without Beards: Gender and Sexual Anxieties of Iranian Modernity*. Berkeley: University of California Press.

———. 2014. *Professing Selves: Transsexuality and Same-Sex Desire in Contemporary Iran*. Durham, NC: Duke University Press.

Nejatisafa, Ali-Akbar, Mohammad-Reza Mohammadi, Vandad Sharifi, Reza Rad Goodarzi, Elaheh Sahimi Izadian, Ali Farhoudian, Naghmeh Mansouri, and Afarin Rahimi-Movaghar. 2006. "Iran's Contribution to Child and Adolescent Mental Health Research (1973–2002): A Scientometric Analysis." *Iranian Journal of Psychiatry* 1 (3): 93–97.

Neufeld, Paul, and Michael Foy. 2006. "Historical Reflections on the Ascendancy of ADHD in North America, c. 1980–c. 2005." *British Journal of Educational Studies* 54 (4): 449–70. doi: 10.1111/j.1467-8527.2006.00354.x.

Nguyen, Vinh-Kim. 2010. *The Republic of Therapy: Triage and Sovereignty in West Africa's Time of AIDS.* Durham, NC: Duke University Press.

Noorbala, A. A., S. A. Bagheri Yazdi, M. T. Yasamy, and K. Mohammad. 2004. "Mental Health Survey of the Adult Population in Iran." *British Journal of Psychiatry* 184 (1): 70–73. doi: 10.1192/bjp.184.1.70.

Obeyesekere, Gananath. 1984. *Medusa's Hair: An Essay on Personal Symbols and Religious Experience.* Chicago: University of Chicago Press.

———. 1990. *The Work of Culture: Symbolic Transformation in Psychoanalysis and Anthropology.* Chicago: University of Chicago Press.

Ohadi, Mina, Elham Shirazi, Mehdi Tehranidoosti, Narges Moghimi, Mohammad R. Keikhaee, Sima Ehssani, Ali Aghajani, and Hossein Najmabadi. 2006. "Attention-Deficit/Hyperactivity Disorder (ADHD) Association with the DAT1 Core Promoter -67 T Allele." *Brain Research* 1101 (1): 1–4. doi: 10.1016/j.brainres.2006.05.024.

Olszewska, Zuzanna. 2013. "Classy Kids and Down-at-Heel Intellectuals: Status Aspiration and Blind Spots in the Contemporary Ethnography of Iran." *Iranian Studies* 46 (6): 841–62. doi: 10.1080/00210862.2013.810078.

———. 2015a. *The Pearl of Dari: Poetry and Personhood among Young Afghans in Iran.* Bloomington: Indiana University Press.

———. 2015b. "The Poet's Melancholy: Depression, Structures of Feeling, and Creativity among Afghan Refugees in Iran." Special Section: Beyond "Trauma." *Medicine Anthropology Theory* 2 (3): 40–60.

Osanloo, Arzoo. 2009. *The Politics of Women's Rights in Iran.* Princeton, NJ: Princeton University Press.

Paivandi, S. 2005. "L'éducation Populaire en Iran, Ruptures et Continuités." *Pratiques de Formation* 49: 153–65.

Panahi, Jafar, dir. 2003. *Talā-ye Sorkh* (Crimson Gold). Feature film. Tehran: Panahi Film Productions.

Pandolfo, Stefania. 1998. *Impasse of the Angels: Scenes from a Moroccan Space of Memory.* Chicago: University of Chicago Press.

Parens, Erik. 1998. "Is Better Always Good? The Enhancement Project." *Hastings Center Report* 28 (1): S1–17.

Parkinson, Sarah E., and Orkideh Behrouzan. 2015. "Negotiating Health and Life: Syrian Refugees and the Politics of Access in Lebanon." *Social Science and Medicine* 146: 324–31.

Petryna, Adriana. 2002. *Life Exposed: Biological Citizens after Chernobyl.* Princeton, NJ: Princeton University Press.

Poorahmad, Kiumars, dir. 2007. *Otobus-e Shab* (Night Bus). Feature film. Tehran: Cima Film Center.

Popper, Karl. 2005 [1959]. *The Logic of Scientific Discovery.* London: Routledge.

Portelli, Alessandro. 1991. *The Death of Luigi Trastulli and Other Stories: Form and Meaning in Oral History*. Albany, NY: SUNY Press.

Porter, Roy. 1990. *Mind-Forg'd Manacles: History of Madness in England from the Restoration to the Regency*. London: Penguin.

Povinelli, Elizabeth A. 2011. *Economies of Abandonment: Social Belonging and Endurance in Late Liberalism*. Durham, NC: Duke University Press.

Rabinow, Paul. 1996. *Making PCR: A Story of Biotechnology*. Chicago: University of Chicago Press.

———. 1999. "Artificiality and Enlightenment: From Sociobiology to Biosociality." In *The Science Studies Reader*, edited by Mario Biagioli, 407–16. New York: Routledge.

Radstone, Susannah. 2007. "Trauma Theory: Contexts, Politics, Ethics." *Paragraph* 30 (1): 9–29. doi: 10.3366/prg.2007.0015.

Rafalovich, Adam. 2004. *Framing ADHD Children: A Critical Examination of the History, Discourse, and Everyday Experience of Attention Deficit/Hyperactivity Disorder*. Lanham, MD: Lexington Books.

Rahimi, Babak. 2015. "Rethinking Digital Technologies in the Middle East." *International Journal of Middle East Studies* 47 (02): 362–65. doi: 10.1017/S0020743815000124.

Rahimi, Zahra. 2010. "The City Bombardment and Its Aftermaths in Iran." *Negin-e Iran: Faslnāmeh-ye Takhassosi-ye Motāle'āt-e Defā'e Moghaddas* (*Negin-e Iran: Journal of Research on the Sacred Defense*) 8 (31): 53–70.

Rahimieh, Nasrin. 2003. "Overcoming the Orientalist Legacy of Iranian Modernity: Women's Post-Revolutionary Film and Literary Production." *Thamyris/Intersecting: Place, Sex and Race* 10 (1): 147–63.

Ramazani, Jahan. 1994. *Poetry of Mourning: The Modern Elegy from Hardy to Heaney*. Chicago: University of Chicago Press.

Rapp, Rayna 1999. *Testing Women, Testing the Fetus: The Social Impact of Amniocentesis in America*. Vol. 1. New York: Psychology Press.

"Ravānkāvi-ye Doctor" (Psychoanalysis of the Doctor: Susan Shari'ati and Mohammad Sanati's Debate on Ali Shari'ati and His Views on Freud and Psychoanalysis). 2010. *Mehrnameh* 1 (3) (June 10): 48–55.

Razavi, Seyed Hossein, Seid Kazem Razavi-Ratki, Marzieh Molavi Nojomi, and Nasim Namiranian. 2012. "Depression and General Anxiety in the Prisoner of War's Children: A Cross Sectional Study." *Medical Journal of the Islamic Republic of Iran* 26 (4): 179.

Razavi, Seyed Mansour, Zahra Negahban, Mohsen Pirhosseinloo, Mahdiyeh Sadat Razavi, Gholamreza Hadjati, and Payman Salamati. 2014. "Sulfur Mustard Effects on Mental Health and Quality-of-Life: A Review." *Iranian Journal of Psychiatry and Behavioral Sciences* 8 (3): 11.

Rechtman, Richard. 2004. "The Rebirth of PTSD: The Rise of a New Paradigm in Psychiatry." *Social Psychiatry and Psychiatric Epidemiology* 39 (11): 913–15.

Rey, Joseph M., and Garry Walter. 2001. "Child and Adolescent Psychiatry Research Comes of Age." *Australian & New Zealand Journal of Psychiatry* 35 (3): 261–62. doi: 10.1046/j.1440-1614.2001.00898.x.

Reza'i, Hossein. 2004. *Sargozasht-e Yek Ravānpezeshk-e Irani* (The Life of an Iranian Psychiatrist). Tehran: Jahan-e Ejtema'ie.

Rhodes, Lorna A. 1995. *Emptying Beds: The Work of an Emergency Psychiatric Unit.* Berkeley: University of California Press.

Rheingold, Howard. 1993. *The Virtual Community: Homesteading on the Electronic Frontier.* Cambridge, MA: MIT Press.

Ricoeur, Paul. 2004. *Memory, History, Forgetting.* Chicago: University of Chicago Press.

Rose, Nikolas. 1990. *Governing the Soul: The Shaping of the Private Self.* Vol. 14. Florence, KY: Taylor & Frances/Routledge.

———. 1992. "Governing the Enterprising Self." In *The Values of the Enterprise Culture: The Moral Debate,* edited by Paul Hellas and Paul Morris, 141–64. London: Routledge.

———. 1996. *Inventing Our Selves: Psychology, Power, and Personhood.* Cambridge: Cambridge University Press.

———. 2003. "Neurochemical Selves." *Society* 41 (1): 46–59.

———. 2006a. *The Politics of Life Itself: Biomedicine, Power, and Subjectivity in the Twenty-First Century.* Princeton, NJ: Princeton University Press.

———. 2006b. "Disorders Without Borders? The Expanding Scope of Psychiatric Practice." *BioSocieties* 1 (4): 465–84. doi: 10.1017/S1745855206004078.

Rosenberg, Charles E. 1992. *Explaining Epidemics and Other Studies in the History of Medicine.* Cambridge: Cambridge University Press.

Roshan, Rasoul, Parvin Rahnama, Zeinab Ghazanfari, Ali Montazeri, Mohammad Reza Soroush, Mohammad Mehdi Naghizadeh, Mahdiyeh Melyani, Azadeh Tavoli, and Tooba Ghazanfari. 2013. "Long-Term Effects of Sulfur Mustard on Civilians' Mental Health 20 Years after Exposure (The Sardasht-Iran Cohort Study)." *Health and Quality of Life Outcomes* 11 (1): 1–7. http://dx.doi.org/10.1186/1477-7525-11-69.

Sacks, Jeffrey. 2015. *Iterations of Loss: Mutilation and Aesthetic Form, Al-Shidyaq to Darwish.* New York: Fordham University Press.

Salamati, Payman, Seyed Mansour Razavi, Farhad Shokraneh, Saman Mohazzab Torabi, Marjan Laal, Gholamreza Hadjati, et al. 2013. "Mortality and Injuries among Iranians in Iraq-Iran War: A Systematic Rview." *Archives of Iranian Medicine* 16 (9): 542–50.

Sanal, Aslihan. 2011. *New Organs Within Us: Transplants and the Moral Economy.* Durham NC: Duke University Press.

Sanati, Mohammad. 2001. *Sādegh Hedāyat va Harās az Marg* (Sādegh Hedāyat and the Fear of Death). Tehran: Nashr-e Markaz.

———. 2004. "Practicing Psychoanalysis in a Death-Conscious Society." Paper presented at the Second Asian International Congress for Psychotherapy. Tehran. September 2004.

———. 2014. "Psychoanalysis in Iran: Changing Sociocultural Context" Lecture delivered at the First Iranian Congress of Psychoanalysis and Dynamic Psychotherapy. Tehran. October 2014.

Schayegh, Cyrus. 2009. *Who Is Knowledgeable Is Strong: Science, Class, and the Formation of Modern Iranian Society, 1900–1950.* Berkeley: University of California Press.

Scheper-Hughes, Nancy. 1992. *Death Without Weeping: The Violence of Everyday Life in Brazil.* Berkeley: University of California Press.

Scheper-Hughes, Nancy, and Margaret M. Lock. 1987. "The Mindful Body: A Prolegomenon to Future Work in Medical Anthropology." *Medical Anthropology Quarterly* 1 (1): 6–41. doi: 10.1525/maq.1987.1.1.02a00020.

Schneider, Arnd, and Christopher Wright, eds. 2010. *Between Art and Anthropology: Contemporary Ethnographic Practice.* Oxford: Berg.

Scull, Andrew. 1991. "Psychiatry and Social Control in the Nineteenth and Twentieth Centuries." *History of Psychiatry* 2 (6): 149–69. doi: 10.1177/0957154X9100200603.

———. 2005. *The Most Solitary of Afflictions: Madness and Society in Britain, 1700–1900.* New Haven, CT: Yale University Press.

Seyfert, Robert. 2012. "Beyond Personal Feelings and Collective Emotions: Toward a Theory of Social Affect." *Theory, Culture & Society* 29 (6): 27–46. doi: 10.1177/02632764124 38591.

Shadpour, K. 1994. *The PHC Experience in Iran.* Tehran: Ministry of Health and Medical Education, and UNICEF.

———. 2000. "Primary Health Care Networks in the Islamic Republic of Iran." *Eastern Mediterranean Health Journal (La Revue de Santé de La Méditerranée Orientale)* 6 (4): 822.

Shahmohammadi, D., et al. 1998. "Barresi-ye Masir-e Morāje'eh-ye Bimārān-e Ravāni be Marākez-e Ravānpezeshki-ye Keshvar" (Pathways to Psychiatric Care in Iran). *Andisheh va Raftar: Iranian Journal of Psychiatry and Clinical Psychology* 3 (4): 4–14.

Shahri, Ja'far. 2004. *Tehran-E Qadim* (Old Tehran). Tehran: Amir Kabir.

Shakhsari, Sima. 2010. "Blogging, Belonging, and Becoming: Cybergovernmentality and the Production of Gendered and Sexed Diasporic Subjects in Weblogistan." Ph.D. dissertation, Stanford University.

———. 2011. "Weblogistan Goes to War: Representational Practices, Gendered Soldiers and Neoliberal Entrepreneurship in Diaspora." *Feminist Review* 99 (1): 6–24. doi: 10 .1057/fr.2011.35.

Shari'ati, Ali. 2011. *Mamju'eh Āsār 21: Zan* (Collected Works, Volume 21: Woman). Tehran: Ali Shari'ati Cultural Foundation.

Sharifi, Farahnaz, dir. 2008. *Chehreh-ye Ghamgin-e Man* (My Sad Face). Documentary. Tehran: Not distributed.

Sharifi, Vandad. 2009. "Urban Mental Health in Iran: Challenges and Future Directions." *Iranian Journal of Psychiatry and Behavioral Sciences* (IJPBS) 3 (1): 9–14.

Shaw, Rosalind. 2007. "Displacing Violence: Making Pentecostal Memory in Postwar Sierra Leone." *Cultural Anthropology* 22 (1): 66–93. doi: 10.1525/can.2007.22.1.66.

Shooshtary, Mitra Hakim, Seyed Kazem Malakouti, Jafar Bolhari, Marzieh Nojomi, Marjan Poshtmashhadi, Safieh Asgharzadeh Amin, José M. Bertolote, and Alexandra Fleischmann. 2008. "Community Study of Suicidal Behaviors and Risk Factors among Iranian Adults." *Archives of Suicide Research* 12 (2): 141–47. doi: 10.1080/1381111 0701857475.

Shorish, M. Mobin. 1988. "The Islamic Revolution and Education in Iran." *Comparative Education Review* 32 (1): 58–75. doi: 10.1086/446737.

Siavoshi, Sussan. 1997. "Cultural Policies and the Islamic Republic: Cinema and Book Publication." *International Journal of Middle East Studies* 29 (4): 509–30.

Sick, Gary. 1989. "Trial by Error: Reflections on the Iran-Iraq War." *Middle East Journal* 43 (2): 230–45. doi: 10.2307/4327921.

Singh, Ilina. 2002. "Biology in Context: Social and Cultural Perspectives on ADHD." *Children & Society* 16 (5): 360–67. doi: 10.1002/chi.746.

———. 2004. "Doing Their Jobs: Mothering with Ritalin in a Culture of Mother-Blame." *Social Science & Medicine* 59 (6): 1193–1205. doi: 10.1016/j.socscimed.2004.01.011.

———. 2005. "Will the 'Real Boy' Please Behave: Dosing Dilemmas for Parents of Boys with ADHD." *American Journal of Bioethics* 5 (3): 34–47. doi: 10.1080/15265160590945129.

Smith, Jeffrey Alyn. 2002. "Suicide in Post-Socialist Countries: Examples from Hungary and Belarus." *Anthropology of East Europe Review* 20 (1): 55–65.

Sohrabi, Nader. 1995. "Weapons of Propaganda, Weapons of War: Iranian Wartime Rhetoric, 1980–1988." Bachelor of Science thesis, Massachusetts Institute of Technology.

Soltanifar, Atefeh, Fatemeh Moharreri, and Azadeh Soltanifar. 2009. "Depressive and Anxiety Symptoms in Mothers of Children with ADHD Compared to the Control Group." *Iranian Journal of Psychiatry* 4 (3): 112–15.

Sreberny, Annabelle, and Gholam Khiabany. 2010. *Blogistan: The Internet and Politics in Iran.* London: I.B. Tauris.

Stephenson, Rob, Payam Sheikhattari, Nazilla Assasi, Hassan Eftekhar, Qasem Zamani, Bahram Maleki, and Hamid Kiabayan. 2006. "Child Maltreatment among School Children in the Kurdistan Province, Iran." *Child Abuse & Neglect* 30 (3): 231–45. doi: 10.1016/j.chiabu.2005.10.009.

Stubbe, D. 2000. "Attention-Deficit/Hyperactivity Disorder Overview. Historical Perspective, Current Controversies, and Future Directions." *Child and Adolescent Psychiatric Clinics of North America* 9 (3): 469–79.

Summerfield, Derek. 1999. "A Critique of Seven Assumptions behind Psychological Trauma Programmes in War-Affected Areas." *Social Science & Medicine* 48 (10): 1449–62. doi: 10.1016/S0277-9536(98)00450-X.

Szasz, Thomas S. 1961. *The Myth of Mental Illness: Foundations of a Theory of Personal Conduct.* St. Albans, Herts: Paladin.

———. 1997. *The Manufacture of Madness: A Comparative Study of the Inquisition and the Mental Health Movement.* Syracuse, NY: Syracuse University Press.

Taghva, Arsia, Parviz Dabbaghi, Susan Shafighi, Seyyed Mohammad Ali Mortazaviha, and Vahid Donyavi. 2014. "Mental Health in Spouses of Iraq-Iran War Veterans with PTSD." *Journal of Archives in Military Medicine* 2, (1): e17010. http://dx.doi.org/10.5812/jamm.17010.

Talebi, Abolghasem, dir. 2006. *Dast-hā-ye Khāli* (Empty Hands). Feature film. Tehran: THD Home Entertainment.

Taraghi, Goli. 1994. *Khātereh-hā-ye Parākandeh* (Scattered Memories). Tehran: Bagh-e Ayne.

Taussig, Michael. 1992. *The Nervous System.* London: Taylor & Francis.

Tavallaii, S. A., Ghanei M., Assari SH., Lorgarde Dezfuli Nezhad M., and Habibi M. 2006.

"Risk Factors Correlated to Suicide in Deceased Iranian Veterans." *Journal of Military Medicine* 8 (2): 143–48.

Timimi, Sami. 2004. "A Critique of the International Consensus Statement on ADHD." *Clinical Child and Family Psychology Review* 7 (1): 59–63. doi: 10.1023/B:CCFP.00000 20192.49298.7a.

Timimi, Sami, Maurizio Bonati, Piero Impicciatore, and Chiara Pandolfini. 2001. "Evidence and Belief in Attention Deficit Hyperactivity Disorder." *BMJ: British Medical Journal* 322 (7285): 555–56.

Traweek, Sharon. 1982. "Uptime, Downtime, Spacetime, and Power: An Ethnography of the Particle Physics Community in Japan and the United States." Ph.D. dissertation, University of California, Santa Cruz.

———. 1992. *Beamtimes and Lifetimes: The World of High Energy Physicists.* Cambridge, MA: Harvard University Press.

Tuckett, David, and Richard Taffler. 2008. "Phantastic Objects and the Financial Market's Sense of Reality: A Psychoanalytic Contribution to the Understanding of Stock Market Instability." *International Journal of Psychoanalysis* 89 (2): 389–412. doi: 10.1111 /j.1745-8315.2008.00040.x.

Turkle, Sherry. 1978. *Psychoanalytic Politics: Freud's French Revolution.* New York: Basic Books.

———. 1995. *Life on the Screen: Identity in the Age of the Internet.* New York: Simon & Schuster.

———. 2005 [1984]. *The Second Self: Computers and the Human Spirit.* Cambridge, MA: MIT Press.

———, ed. 2007. *Evocative Objects: Things We Think With.* Cambridge, MA: MIT Press.

———, ed. 2008. *The Inner History of Devices.* Cambridge, MA: MIT Press.

Turner, Victor. 1995. *The Ritual Process: Structure and Anti-Structure.* New Brunswick, NJ: Transaction Publishers.

Van der Kolk, Bessel A. 1994. "The Body Keeps the Score: Memory & the Evolving Psychobiology of Post Traumatic Stress." *Harvard Review of Psychiatry* 1 (5): 253–65. doi: 10.3109/10673229409017088.

Van der Kolk, Bessel A., Alexander C. McFarlane, and Lars Weisaeth, eds. 1996. *Traumatic Stress: The Effects of Overwhelming Experience on Mind, Body, and Society.* New York: Guilford Press.

Varzi, Roxanne. 2006. *Warring Souls: Youth, Media, and Martyrdom in Post-Revolution Iran.* Durham, NC: Duke University Press.

Wali, Alaka. 2010. "Ethnography for the Digital Age: http://www.YouTube/DigitalEthnog raphy (Michael Wesch)." *American Anthropologist* 112 (1): 147–48. doi: 10.1111/j.1548 -1433.2009.01204.x.

Wick, Livia. 2008. "Building the Infrastructure, Modeling the Nation: The Case of Birth in Palestine." *Culture, Medicine, and Psychiatry* 32 (3): 328–57. doi:10.1007/s11013 -008-9098-y.

———. 2011. "The Practice of Waiting under Closure in Palestine." *City & Society* 23 (s1): 24–44. doi:10.1111/j.1548-744X.2011.01054.x.

Wight, Gail. 2007. "Blue Cheer." In *Evocative Objects: Things We Think With*, edited by Sherry Turkle, 93–99. Cambridge, MA: MIT Press.

Yar-Shater, Ehsan, ed. 2004. *The History of Medicine in Iran*. New York: Bibliotheca Persica Foundation.

Yasamy, M. T., D. Shahmohammadi, S. A. Bagheri Yazdi, and H. Layeghi. 2001. "Mental Health in the Islamic Republic of Iran: Achievements and Areas of Need." *Eastern Mediterranean Health Journal (La Revue de Santé de La Méditerranée Orientale)* 7 (3): 381–91.

Young, Allan. 1997. *The Harmony of Illusions: Inventing Post-Traumatic Stress Disorder*. Princeton, NJ: Princeton University Press.

Yousefi, Alireza, and Nasim Sharif. 2010. "Stress and Personal Well-Being among a Sample of Iranian Disabled Veteran's Wives." *Iranian Journal of Psychiatry* 5 (2): 66–73.

Zahedi, Ashraf. 2006. "State Ideology and the Status of Iranian War Widows." *International Feminist Journal of Politics* 8 (2): 267–86. doi: 10.1080/14616740600612897.

Index

Page numbers in italics refer to illustrations.